SPORTS MARKETING AND THE PSYCHOLOGY OF MARKETING COMMUNICATION

Advertising and Consumer Psychology

A Series Sponsored by the Society for Consumer Psychology

SPORTS MARKETING AND THE PSYCHOLOGY OF MARKETING COMMUNICATION

Edited by

Lynn R. Kahle
Warsaw Sports Marketing Center
Lundquist College of Business
University of Oregon

Chris Riley
Founder, Studioriley
Portland, Oregon

LEA LAWRENCE ERLBAUM ASSOCIATES, PUBLISHERS
2004   Mahwah, New Jersey   London

This book was typeset in 11 / 13 pt. Dante, Bold, and Italic.
The heads were typeset in Franklin Gothic, Bold, and Bold Italic.

Cover design by Sean Trane Sciarrone

Lawrence Erlbaum Associates, Inc., Publishers
10 Industrial Avenue
Mahwah, New Jersey 07430
www.erlbaum.com

Library of Congress Cataloging-in-Publication Data

Sports marketing and the psychology of marketing communication / edited by
Lynn R. Kahle, Chris Riley.
p.   cm.—(Advertising and consumer psychology)
Includes bibliographical references and index.
ISBN 0-8058-4826-6
1. Sports—United States—Marketing.   2. Sports—United States—Psychological aspects.
3. Communication in marketing.   I. Kahle, Lynn R.   II. Riley, Chris, 1958–III. Series.
GV716.S649   2004
338.4'3—dc22   2003020653

Printed in the United States of America
10   9   8   7   6   5   4   3   2   1

To Dan Wieden, David Kennedy, and
Jim Warsaw, all stars in sports marketing

Contents

Foreword

Those of us who do sport marketing or who study sport marketing are often asked by other marketers, "What makes sport marketing special?" After all, it seems reasonable to expect that marketing sport should be like marketing any other service. For decades marketers have amassed an array of strategies, tactics, and principles that, it is claimed, can be applied as needed to any particular product or service. Surely, then, the challenge is to apply our knowledge about marketing to the task of marketing sport. There should be no need to claim any special status for sport marketing.

Yet events of the past two decades would seem to belie that assumption. Two journals have been founded that focus explicitly on sport marketing (*Sport Marketing Quarterly* and *International Journal of Sports Marketing and Sponsorship*). Graduate and undergraduate courses in sport marketing have appeared, as have texts on the subject. Half the contributions to the annual North American Society for Sport Management conference and to its journal (*Journal of Sport Management*) are about sport marketing. The American Marketing Association has a special interest group in sport marketing, and a new Sport Marketing Association was recently formed. Does all this interest and activity represent the mere application of marketing to sport, or have those who study sport marketing suddenly discovered that there is something special going on?

Actually, the phrase "sport marketing" refers to three very different marketing objectives. One is marketing intended to sell sport as an entertainment. Here the objective is to nurture a fan base and to create audiences for sport. The second marketing objective is concerned with building sport participation—motivating people to engage in sport activities, join a sport club, or take part as competitors in sport events. The third marketing objective has to do with using sport to sell non-sport products or services. Each of these three marketing objectives is represented in this book, and each needs to be considered separately.

Many reasons have been argued over the years for the claim that unique concerns need to be taken into account when marketing sport as an entertainment. The product life cycle curve for sports teams and mega sport events seems to be longer than that for most other products and services. In fact, for many teams and events, it is not clear that the curve is even diatonic, because the popularity of many seems to have grown unabated, with fanship and interest being transmitted from one generation to the next. Several arguments have been advanced to account for this phenomenon. It has been argued that athletes and teams engender a level of personal identification that is not found with other products or services. Nor, it is argued, do other products or services typically stand as iconographic representations of their community, as sport does. Many fans do seem to develop a deep emotional attachment to the athletes and teams of which they are fans, and teams and athletes are often symbols of their home communities or even the country from which they come. How this attachment occurs, the best means to foster it, and the tactics by which to capitalize on it are significant realms of inquiry in sport marketing. This, of course, begs the question of whether sport is somehow unique—a matter to which we shall return.

It has similarly been argued that marketing for sport participation requires that unique factors be considered when formulating marketing strategy. Most sports entail physical activity. Increasing physical activity has been a key objective of public health and anti-obesity campaigns. This is one reason that social marketing campaigns to increase sport participation are found throughout the world. However, as social settings, sports have their own subcultures. One of the consequent marketing challenges is to find means to socialize participants into the sport organization and into the beliefs and values associated with participation in a particular sport subculture. How to foster a social climate that encourages sport participation, and how to recruit and then build commitment among those who participate in sport are therefore vital realms of sport marketing inquiry. It is not clear, however, whether these aspects of marketing sport are in any way different from marketing to promote other leisure behaviors.

Marketing non-sport products through sport builds on the foundation established by marketing to promote audiences and participation. The attention and attachment that sport obtains from fans and participants makes sport an attractive medium for sponsorship. Although sponsorship has been a marketing tactic for more than a century, it has been most intensively studied in recent years and in the context of sport. This is reflected in the contents of this book, in which more than half the chapters are devoted to matters having to do with sponsorship. The largest section (comprised of five chapters) is devoted to the consequences of sponsorship; another section (three chapters) considers athlete endorsements; the section on marketing strategy includes two chapters on sponsorship-related topics—a review of licensing and an examination of ambush marketing.

The emphasis on sponsorship in the book's contents is certainly consistent with the emphasis on sponsorship in the academic study of sport marketing. Yet it is an aspect of sport marketing that is clearly not unique in character or content. Sponsorship has long been a core element of the entertainment industry, enjoying substantial prominence in print media, radio, and television throughout the 20th century. Nevertheless, sponsorship did not become a significant realm of academic study until sport marketing became a popular context for research.

It is somewhat surprising that sponsorship (including licensing and endorsements) has come to dominate academic work on sport marketing in the way that it has. Sponsorship first requires that an audience or a participation base has been obtained, thus it would seem that marketing to foster fanship or participation should be deemed more fundamental. Certainly, more work is needed that considers fan and participant development. More work is also needed that examines the trajectories of sport involvement so that the interactions among fanship, participation, and the choice to consume (or not to consume) sponsored, endorsed, or licensed products can be better understood.

Perhaps one reason that sponsorship has dominated sport marketing research to date is that it can be readily studied using familiar theories and methods from advertising and consumer behavior, fields that are congenial to most marketing researchers. One of the distinct challenges of research in sport marketing is that there has been a great deal of research into sport, but nearly all of that work has been undertaken by non-marketers. The bases for participation and fanship have been studied for several decades by sport sociologists and sport psychologists. Although that work has paid scant attention to its own marketing implications, it could just as easily have been called "sport consumer behavior" (in lieu of "sport sociology" or "sport psychology"). The requisite foundation for theoretically informed research into marketing aimed at fostering fanship or building participation exists in the sport sociology and sport psychology literatures, but it has yet to be married to marketing insight.

Explanations for the lack of cross-dialogue between sport studies and sport marketing can be found in the insularity of academic disciplines and disparities in their prestige. The study of sport has long been relegated to the undervalued academic departments that specialize in sport and exercise (variously called "kinesiology," "human performance," "physical education," and so on). These departments have historically enjoyed low prestige at our universities, which means that any effort by marketing researchers to mine their discourse has been looked down upon.

In fact, sport is commonly separated as a social category. It not only has separate (but unequal) academic departments but also has its own section of the newspaper, its own magazines, its own television network, its own radio network, and its own segment on the evening news show. These might seem to be signals of sport's importance, but what is relevant here is not the ubiquitous presence of sport but rather sport's overt separation. Consider, for example, that although there have been sport businesses for over a century, sport is rarely represented in the business section of our newspapers and business is rarely represented on the sports pages. Sport falls under the rubric of "play" in popular discourse, and play is associated with childishness and triviality. It is no wonder, then, that sport is treated as a separate realm, and that those who study it risk relegation to depressed academic status.

However, the separation of sport from other elements of the economy misrepresents the economic impact of sport, and thereby underestimates the challenges of sport marketing. Sport has become a significant driver of tourism and, consequently, a vital component in place marketing. Sport has become an essential concern when developing property as sport amenities play a significant role in determining (and maintaining) property values. Sport has catalyzed the development of new technologies, many of which are then marketed for non-sport use.

This takes us back to the concern with which we began. If sport links to other things that we market (e.g., places, homes, technologies), then how different can it be? If sport is not as separate as our treatment of it pretends, then how can marketing it require special theories or tactics?

In fact, the academic study of sport marketing represents a new direction for marketing research. Traditionally, we have studied marketing by seeking to identify core strategies and processes. The objective has been to create a body of knowledge with general application. In contrast, the study of sport marketing places its industry (sport) at the center of study and asks how strategies or processes need to be adapted (or even created) in order for it to be marketed well. Research begins by taking seriously the possibility that the industry does, indeed, make a difference when formulating the marketing strategies and tactics that would most effectively be used. Whether those strategies and tactics (or the processes of their formulation) are specific to sport or have potential application elsewhere is itself an empirical question. Appropriately devised, the study of sport marketing both informs and is informed by other work in marketing. The chapters in this book make a distinctive contribution to that endeavor.

Laurence Chalip
University of Texas at Austin

Preface

Sports marketing is one of the fastest growing areas of marketing communication. It provides a different type of vehicle for communicating with consumers that does not necessarily follow all of the rules of other types of marketing communication (Burnett & Menon, 1993; Jones, Bee, Burton, & Kahle, 2004). Sport has (1) unique combinations of characteristics that (2) lead to unique patterns of psychological responses that therefore (3) demand out of the ordinary attention to a variety of marketing tactics. As Chalip articulated so well in the Foreword, sports marketing means different things to different people. We touch on most of those definitions during the course of this book.

Consider the unique characteristics of sports. None of these characteristics exists only in sports, but the combination of all of the phenomena in one place give sports a special situation in society. Sports provide real-time drama, often connected to a place or institution, which emphasizes strategy and skill, beauty and talent, competition and teamwork, winners and losers. Most sports appeal to the most basic human understanding, making sports a popular subject for media coverage and fundamental social interaction (Kahle, Elton, & Kambara, 1997). Special consumption communities arise surrounding sport (Chapters 1 and 14; Shoham & Kahle, 1996; Shoham, Rose, Kropp, & Kahle, 1997).

Because of these unique aspects of sports, as well as because of other aspects, several psychological characteristics are connected with sport marketing. Examples include basking in reflected glory (Chapter 3; Cialdini, Borden, Thorne, Walker, Freeman, & Sloan, 1976), consumption communities (Chapter 1), fanaticism (Chapter 2), special target markets (Chapter 14), identification (Hirt, Zillman, Erickson, & Kennedy, 1992; Kahle, Kambara, & Rose, 1996), heroism (Chapters 5, 6, and 7; Kahle & Homer, 1985), patriotism, eroticism, fear, bonding, symbolism (Branscrombe & Wann, 1992), values (Kahle, Duncan, Dalakas, & Aiken, 2001; Sukhdial, Aiken, & Kahle, 2002), child rearing, and risk taking (Chapter 4; Shoham, Rose, & Kahle, 1998, 2000).

The marketer therefore approaches sports marketing differently than other types of marketing. Sponsorship is the giant in the arena (Dean, 1999), and several chapters explore it (Chapters 8, 9, 10, 11, and 12), but do not overlook unique approaches to segmentation (Chapter 14), licensing (Chapter 13), ambush marketing (Chapter 15), hospitality, and atmospherics (Kahle, Aiken, Dalakas, & Duncan, 2003). Media function differently in sport (Chapters 5, 15, and 19; Kahle, Madrigal, Melone, & Szymanski, 1999; Kahle & Meeske, 1999).

The purpose of this book is to advance the understanding of sports marketing. It presents chapters that deal with topics in sports marketing in a scholarly and comprehensive way. It covers most of the major topics of discussion in sports marketing and the psychology of communication. Several new, innovative topics are introduced (SportNEST, consumption communities). Many classic topics are brought up to date (sponsorship, ambush marketing, identification, endorsements, basking in reflected glory, licensing), and many of the topics that seem to center around sports show up as well, such as sneakers (Chapters 9 and 19), ethics (Chapters 16, 17, 18, and 19; Kahle, Boush, & Phelps, 2000), risky behavior (Chapter 4), and even investments (Chapter 11). We hope this book focuses attention on the state of knowledge in sports marketing. Carefully examined ideas are the ones most likely to improve dialectically, and this book should serve as a challenge for this field to advance. After reading this book, you should develop a new appreciation for what someone in Oregon means when he or she says, "Go Ducks."

Lynn R. Kahle
Chris Riley
Oregon, May 2003

REFERENCES

Branscrombe, N. R., & Wann, D. L. (1992). Role of identification with a group, arousal categorization processes, and self-esteem in sport spectator aggression. *Human Relations, 45,* 1013–1033.

Burnett, J., & Menon, A. (1993). Sports marketing: A new ball game with new rules. *Journal of Advertising Research, 33*(5), 21–36.

Cialdini, R. B., Borden, R. J., Thorne, R. J., Walker, M. R., Freeman, S., & Sloan, L. R. (1976). Basking in reflected glory: Three (football) field studies. *Journal of Personality and Social Psychology, 34*(3), 366–375.

Dean, D. H. (1999). Brand endorsement, popularity, and event sponsorship as advertising cues affecting consumer pre-purchase attitudes. *Journal of Advertising, 28*(3), 1–13.

Hirt, E. R., Zillman, D., Erickson, G. A., & Kennedy, C. (1992). Costs and benefits of allegiance: Changes in fans' self-ascribed competencies after team victory versus defeat. *Journal of Personality and Social Psychology, 63,* 724–738.

Jones, S., Bee, C., Burton, R., & Kahle, L. R. (2004). Marketing through sports entertainment: A functional approach. In L. J. Shrum (Ed.), *The Psychology of Entertainment Media.* Mahwah, NJ: Lawrence Erlbaum. (pp. 309–322).

Kahle, L. R., Aiken, D., Dalakas, V., & Duncan, M. (2003). Men's versus women's collegiate basketball customers: Attitudinal favorableness and the environment. *International Journal of Sports Marketing and Sponsorship, 5*(2), 145–159.

Kahle, L. R., Boush, D. M., & Phelps. M. (2000). Good morning, Vietnam: An ethical analysis of Nike activities in Southeast Asia. *Sport Marketing Quarterly, 9*(1), 43–52.

Kahle, L., Duncan, M., Dalakas, V., & Aiken, D. (2001). The social values of fans for men's versus women's university basketball. *Sport Marketing Quarterly, 10*(2), 156–162.

Kahle, L. R., Elton, M. P., & Kambara, K. M. (1997). Sports talk and the development of marketing relationships. *Sport Marketing Quarterly, 6*(2), 35–40.

Kahle, L. R., & Homer, P. M. (1985). Physical attractiveness of celebrity endorsers: A social adaptation perspective. *Journal of Consumer Research, 11,* 954–961.

Kahle, L R., Kambara, K. M., & Rose, G. M. (1996, December). A functional model of fan attendance motivations for college football. *Sport Marketing Quarterly, 5,* 51–60.

Kahle, L. R., Madrigal, R., Melone, N. P., & Szymanski, K. (1999). An audience survey from the first gridiron cybercast. In D. W. Schumann & E. Thorson (Eds.), *Advertising and the World Wide Web.* Mahwah, NJ: Lawrence Erlbaum Associates. (pp. 275–286).

Kahle, L. R., & Meeske, C. (1999). Sports marketing and the Internet: It's a whole new ball game. *Sport Marketing Quarterly, 8*(2), 9–12.

Shoham, A., & Kahle, L. R. (1996). Spectators, viewers, readers: Communication and consumption communities in sport marketing. *Sport Marketing Quarterly, 5,* 11–19.

Shoham, A., Rose, G. M., & Kahle, L. R. (1998, Fall). Marketing of risky sports: From intention to action. *Journal of the Academy of Marketing Science, 26,* 307–321.

Shoham, A., Rose, G. M., & Kahle, L. R. (2000). Practitioners of risky sports: A quantitative examination. *Journal of Business Research, 47,* 237–251.

Shoham, A., Rose, G. M., Kropp, F., & Kahle, L. R. (1997). Generation X women: A sport consumption community perspective. *Sport Marketing Quarterly, 6*(4), 23–34.

Sukhdial, A., Aiken, D., & Kahle, L. (2002, July / August). Are you old school? An investigation of the sports fans' attitudes and values. *Journal of Advertising Research, 42,* 71–81.

List of Contributors

Keri L. Anderson Campbell School of Business, Berry College, Mount Berry, Georgia.

David L. Andrews Department of Kinesiology, University of Maryland, College Park, Maryland.

Ainsworth A. Bailey College of Business Administration, University of Toledo, Toledo, Ohio.

Michael D. Basil Faculty of Management, University of Lethbridge, Lethbridge, Alberta, Canada.

Gregg Bell College of Business Administration, University of Alabama, Tuscaloosa, Alabama.

William J. Brown Department of Communication Studies, Regent University, Virginia Beach, Virginia.

Rick Burton National Basketball League (Australia and New Zealand), Sydney, New South Wales, Australia.

Laurence Chalip Sport Management Program, University of Texas, Austin, Texas.

Catherine A. Cole Department of Marketing, Henry B. Tippie College of Business, University of Iowa, Iowa City, Iowa.

Vassilis Dalakas Campbell School of Business, Berry College, Mount Berry, Georgia.

Timothy Dewhirst College of Commerce, University of Saskatchewan.

Thomas R. Donohue School of Mass Communication, Virginia Commonwealth University, Richmond, Virginia.

Katheryn Gettelman Market Probe, Milwaukee, Wisconsin.

Dianna P. Gray   School of Sport and Exercise Science, University of Northern Colorado, Greeley, Colorado.

John J. Jackson   Public Administration, University of Victoria, Victoria, British Columbia, Canada.

Steven J. Jackson   School of Physical Education, University of Otago, Dunedin, New Zealand.

Mick Jackowski   Department of Marketing, Metropolitan State College of Denver, Denver, Colorado.

Melinda J. Jones   Department of Marketing, Mendoza College of Business, The University of Notre Dame Notre Dame, Indiana.

Lynn R. Kahle   Warsaw Sports Marketing Center, Charles H. Lundquist College of Business, University of Oregon, Eugene, Oregon.

Scott W. Kelley   Gatton College of Business and Economics, University of Kentucky, Lexington, Kentucky.

Lance Kinney   Advertising and Public Relations, College of Communication and Information Sciences, University of Alabama, Tuscaloosa, Alabama.

Carla Lloyd   Newhouse School of Communication, Syracuse University, Syracuse, New York.

Robert Madrigal   Charles H. Lundquist College of Business, University of Oregon, Eugene, Oregon.

Stephen R. McDaniel   Department of Kinesiology, University of Maryland, College Park, Maryland.

Timothy P. Meyer   Department of Communication, University of Wisconsin—Green Bay, Green Bay, Wisconsin.

John W. Pracejus   Department of Marketing, Business Economics and Law, University of Alberta Edmonton, Alberta, Canada.

Chris Riley   Studioriley, Portland, Oregon.

Gregory M. Rose   Department of Management and Marketing, University of Washington, Tacoma, Washington.

David W. Schumann   Department of Marketing, Logistics and Transportation, The University of Tennessee, Knoxville, Tennessee.

Aviv Shoham   Graduate School of Business, The University of Haifa, Haifa, Israel.

Jan Slater   E. W. Scripps School of Journalism, Ohio University, Athens, Ohio.

Tao Sun   Department of Marketing Communication, Emerson College, Boston, Massachusetts.

Kelly Tian   Department of Marketing, New Mexico State University, Las Cruces, New Mexico.

William D. Wells   School of Journalism and Mass Communication, University of Minnesota, Minneapolis, Minnesota.

Seounmi Youn   School of Comminication, University of North Dakota, Grand Forks, North Dakota.

SPORTS MARKETING AND THE PSYCHOLOGY OF MARKETING COMMUNICATION

I

Consumer Behavior

Consumer behavior is the foundation of all marketing. Without understanding the consumer, success in marketing is unlikely. The chapters in this section illustrate how characteristics of consumers and their behavior interact with sports to produce some of the unique characteristics of sports marketing. Chapter 1 presents the original and important concept of the sports consumption community. Collections of people in lifestyle relationships characterize how sports are consumed, and Chapter 1 provides insight into this phenomenon. Chapter 2 details findings about fanatical consumption. From British soccer fans to U.S. Super Bowl celebrants, fans often display an intensity of involvement rarely seen in other aspects of life. Chapter 3 discusses one of the most important concepts of sports marketing—basking in reflected glory (BIRGing). Fans take credit when "their" team does well. This phenomenon has widespread implications for marketing. Finally, Chapter 4 deals more with sports participation than identities provided by sports marketers. The related findings about risk, nevertheless, illuminate the area of consumer behavior and sports marketing.

Exploration of Consumption and Communication Communities in Sports Marketing

Tao Sun
Emerson College

Seounmi Youn
Emerson College

William D. Wells
University of Minnesota

Much of the research on consumers' involvement in sports distinguishes between participation and spectatorship (for a review, see Burnett, Menon, & Smart, 1993). In a seminal segmentation study, Shoham and Kahle (1996) went one step further by subdividing and analyzing these two traditional categories. Within the two categories, they identified three "communication communities" and three "consumption communities." The first consumption community includes those who engage in competitive sports (either team or individual), the second includes those who participate in fitness sports (e.g., jogging), and the third includes those who participate in nature-related sports (e.g., fishing). Communication communities include those who attend live sport events (spectators), those who watch sports on television (viewers), and those who read sports magazines (readers). Through analysis of a consumer survey, Shoham and Kahle found that members of different consumption communities tend to belong to different communication communities.

Based on an independent data file, this chapter repeats and extends Shoham and Kahle's (1996) analysis. It then goes on to explore some relationships among sports communities and other variables not present in Shoham and Kahle's study. Replication is important because it adds confidence to findings. Extension is important because it broadens and deepens our under-standing of the relationships involved.

LITERATURE REVIEW

Sports and the mass media enjoy a symbiotic relationship (Eitzen & Sage, 1989). On one hand, the mass media, more than anything else, were respon-sible for turning organized sports from a relatively minor element of culture into a full-blown social institution. On the other hand, sports has been the vehicle for bringing dramatic attention to new mass media forms, which in turn have brought new sporting experiences to the public. This marriage of sports and the mass media has enabled each to flourish (Lever & Wheeler, 1993). Sports marketers are interested in the relationship between sports and the mass media and in how to use the media to target their messages at sports consumers. In a sense, sports marketing offers a form of narrow-casting, whereby a large group of consumers with common interests is brought together through sports events and programming (Fitch, 1986). The more specific the analysis of the sports-media relationship, the more targeted is the message, and the more effective and powerful is the sports marketing strategy.

However, one downside for sports marketing is that sports marketers have not yet clearly identified their consumers (Burnett et al., 1993) or their con-sumers' specific media usage. Like the larger society, sports are stratified (Eitzen & Sage, 1989). Previous research on sports consumers has gener-ally divided the consuming of sports into sports participation and sports spectatorship. For example, Kenyon and McPherson (1973) made a distinc-tion between primary sports roles (participants) and secondary sports roles (spectator, viewer, listener, and reader). Likewise, Burnett et al. (1993) con-cluded that existing evidence suggests two major forms of behavioral in-volvement in sports: (1) directly participating in various sports and physical activities; and (2) being a spectator or fan, as manifested in reading about and watching sports events in the arena or on television. Since the late 1960s, the two types of sports involvement have been studied separately and exten-sively from various perspectives (Burnett et al., 1993; Dickinson, 1976; Gaskell & Pearton, 1979; Harris, 1973; Kenyon, 1968; Lang, 1981; Luschen, 1980; Sofranko & Nolan, 1972; Spreitzer & Snyder, 1976; Taylor, 1972; Zillman, Bryant, and Sapolsky, 1979. For a review, see Burnett et al., 1993). In a sim-ilar vein, McPherson, Curtis, and Loy (1989) divided sport consumers into those who consume sports directly at a stadium, arena, or field; indirectly via television, radio, newspapers, and magazines; and indirectly by discussing sport topics in a variety of social situations.

For those sports marketers who are interested in fine and narrow segmentation, however, it is not enough to divide sports involvement into the two categories of spectator (indirect) and participant (direct). Each of the segments must be further classified and characterized. Shoham and Kahle (1996) did this in their pioneering segmentation studies. They subdivided sports participation into three categories: competitive sports, fitness sports, and nature-related sports; and they subdivided spectatorship into another three categories: attending sporting events, watching sports on TV, and reading sports magazines. Because the three kinds of participation suggest shared consumption of sport products and services, Shoham and Kahle termed them *consumption communities*. Three kinds of spectatorship were designated as *communication communities* because they suggest associated media habits of differing consumption communities.

Shoham and Kahle's (1996) categorization of sports involvement was derived from the perspective of values research, which is intertwined with the concepts of lifestyles and psychographics (Kahle & Chiagouris, 1997). For those consumer researchers who are interested in these concepts, it is very important to understand the social context in which values are enacted (Prensky & Wright-Isak, 1997). Communities provide this social context. A *community* is defined as a group of people who share a set of values and common understandings about how these shared values will be enacted in attitudes and behaviors (Prensky & Wright-Isak, 1997).

Over the past century, traditional residential and occupational communities have been replaced in part by consumption communities as a basis for expressing values (Boorstin, 1974). Boorstin first introduced the concept of "consumption community" as a reflection of the cultural changes induced by the rise of mass media advertising and the early mail order catalog businesses (Boorstin, 1974). Sports fans form their own consumption communities, in which sport as a social institution reflects and affirms many values as well as the apparent tensions among them (Trujillo & Ekdom, 1985). Residential and occupational communities feature face-to-face contacts, whereas consumption communities are "virtual"—that is, attitudinal and behavioral enactment of values is conveyed via modern media, both mass and individualized. Media exposure provides consumers information that they might use to learn about their consumption communities (Prensky & Wright-Isak, 1997). Inspired by these concepts of "communities" and "values," Shoham and Kahle (1996) identified the consumption and communication communities among sports fans, described earlier. What distinguishes Shoham and Kahle's segmentation from previous ones is that their studies further categorized sports involve-ment, and most importantly, this categorization exactly reflects sports-media relationships. Sports marketers are interested in this relationship because what concerns them is how to reach different segments of sports fans effectively via different media channels.

REPLICATION OF SHOHAM AND KAHLE'S FINDINGS

Based on the assumption that individuals from different consumption com-munities tend to belong to distinct communication communities, Shoham and Kahle (1996) conducted regression analysis, taking consumption communi-ties as independent variables and communication communities as dependent variables.

Shoham and Kahle's Data Source and This Study's Data Source

Shoham and Kahle's study was based on a national mail survey of 663 respon-dents conducted by a professional market research firm. With an effective response rate of 66.3%, the questionnaire used in their survey covered diverse questions about attitudes, activities, and interests.

We obtained the data for this chapter from the 1995 *DDB Needham Life Style Study*. This study is conducted annually through the Market Facts' consumer mail panel. In 1995, 5,000 questionnaires were sent to the U.S. households selected and balanced for geographic region, family size, age, income, and population density. Of the questionnaires sent, 3,613 were completed and returned, for an effective response rate of 72%. The questionnaire included questions about attitudes, interests, opinions, product usage and media prefer-ences. Only the responses related to the purpose of this study were used in the analysis.

Definition of Shoham and Kahle's Independent Variables and This Study's Definition

Shoham and Kahle's independent variables were derived from a factor anal-ysis of 12 sport activities. The 12 items captured three types of sport con-sumption communities: competitive sport, fitness sport, and nature-related sport. Their variable "competitive sport" was a summated scale composed of team competitive sport, individual competitive sport, golfing, and bowl-ing ($\alpha = 0.63$). "Fitness sport" was a summated scale of aerobics, jogging, bicycling, swimming, and walking for pleasure ($\alpha = 0.48$). The third variable, "nature-related sport," was a summated scale of camping, fishing, and hiking/backpacking ($\alpha = 0.52$).

The 1995 Life Style data included a question asking people the extent to which they engaged in different sports/exercise/outdoor activities in the past year. The question contains 17 items (bowling, bicycling, skiing, jogging, fishing, swimming, walking, hunting, playing tennis, playing golf, playing softball, playing volleyball, boating, camping, going to exercise class, going to a health club, and doing home exercise). These items are similar to those that Shoham and Kahle used in their data analysis. Factor analysis was performed and similar factors were extracted (Table 1.1).

TABLE 1.1
Factor Loading of Sports/Exercise/Outdoor Activities
(Rotated Component Matrix)

Activity	Factor 1: Competitive Sport	Factor 2: Fitness Sport	Factor 3: Nature-related Sport	Factor 4: Paid Fitness Sport	Factor 5
Played tennis	0.55				
Played softball	0.58				
Went skiing	0.59				
Played volleyball	0.67				
Rode a bicycle		0.44			
Jogged		0.46			
Walked over a mile 'for exercise		0.76			
Did exercise at home		0.78			
Went camping			0.58		
Went hunting			0.66		
Went boating			0.74		
Went fishing			0.82		
Went to a health club				0.84	
Went to an exercise class				0.86	
Played golf					0.50
Went bowling					0.83

Note: Extraction method: Principal Component Analysis. Rotation method: Varimax with Kaiser Normalization.

What is different from Shoham and Kahle's design is that the new factor analysis extracted five rotated components. Golfing and bowling did not fall under the same factor as team competitive sport (e.g., softball) and individual competitive sport (e.g., tennis), as Shoham and Kahle had found. As a result, "competitive sport" in this study included four items: volleyball, softball, skiing, and tennis ($\alpha = 0.50$). For "fitness sport," the summated scale was composed of bicycling, jogging, walking, and home exercising ($\alpha = 0.58$). Swimming was not included in the scale because it was not clear to which factor it belonged (it was split among several factors). "Nature-related sport" summated scores on four items: fishing, camping, boating, and hunting ($\alpha = 0.67$). All of the items used here were originally measured on seven-step scales (1 = none in past year, and 7 = 52 or more times).

Definition of Shoham and Kahle's Dependent Variables and This Study's Definition

In Shoham and Kahle's study, the variable "attending sport events" was measured by how often respondents had attended a sporting event in the past two months. It used a four-point scale (a = at least once a week, b = twice a month or so, c = once a month or so, and d = not at all in the last two months). Based on a seven-point scale (1 = like extremely well, 7 = do not like at all), the variable "watching sports on TV" was measured by asking respondents "how much you like or dislike . . . the weekend sport games/shows." The third variable "reading sport magazines" was measured by asking respondents how frequently they read "sport/hobby magazines (e.g., *Sports Illustrated, Field and Stream*)." Again, this question used a seven-point response scale (1 = read frequently, 7 = never read).

The Life Style data included a question specifically asking the extent to which respondents attended a sporting event in the past year. The response was measured by a seven-step scale (1 = none in past year, 7 = 52 or more times). "Watching a sporting event on TV" was measured on the same scale (1 = none in past year, 7 = 52 or more times). The third variable, reading sport magazines, was measured by the question asking the extent to which people read the weekly magazine *Sports Illustrated*. It was measured dichotomously (0 = don't read most or all, 1 = read most or all issues). Reading *Field and Stream*, also in the Life Style data, did not correlate highly enough with reading *Sports Illustrated* to be considered part of the same dimension.

Similarities and Differences Between Shoham and Kahle's Regression Analysis and This Study's Analysis

Designating three communication communities as dependent variables and three consumption communities as independent communities, Shoham and Kahle (1996) conducted a multiple regression analysis to see how the consumption communities were associated with the communication communities. They found that the three consumption communities all contributed significantly to predicting which respondents attended sporting events. The competitive sport scale was the only significant predictor of watching sports on television. Attending competitive sport and nature-related sport were significant predictors of sport magazine reading.

Using regression analysis of similar dependent and independent variables, the present investigation arrived at generally similar, although somewhat different, findings.

Attending Sport Events.   Like Shoham and Kahle, we found that competitive sport, fitness sport, and nature-related sport were all significant predictors of attending sporting events ($\rho = 0.01$).

Watching Sports on Television.   Shoham and Kahle found that only competitive sport contributed significantly to watching sports on TV. Our analysis showed that all three consumption communities contributed significantly to "watching sports on television" ($\rho = 0.01$).

Reading Sport Magazine.   Again, this study arrived at basically the same results as Shoham and Kahle's. Competitive sport and nature-related sport were both significant predictors of reading *Sports Illustrated* (at $\rho = 0.01$ and $\rho = 0.05$, respectively). See Table 1.2 for multiple regression coefficients.

Discussion and Implications.   As mentioned, this study is quite similar to Shoham and Kahle's conceptually. One difference lies in the measurement of "watching sports on TV." Shoham and Kahle asked about watching weekend sport games/shows, whereas this study measured frequency of watching sports on TV in general. Weekend sports are mostly competitive sports (e.g., football and tennis). Sports in general can cover all kinds of sports. This may explain why fitness sport and nature-related sport in Shoham and Kahle's study were not significant predictors of "watching sports on television" (mainly

TABLE 1.2
Multiple Regression Coefficients (Standardized Coefficient
and with P-Values < in Parenthesis): Replication of Shoham
and Kahle's Analysis

	Attending Sporting Events	Watching Sports on Television	Reading Sports Illustrated
Competitive sports	0.19 (.00)**	0.13 (.00)**	0.03 (.00)**
Fitness sports	0.04 (.00)**	0.04 (.00)**	0.00 (.58)
Nature-related sports	0.04 (.00)**	0.07 (.00)**	0.00 (.01)*

*Significant at .05.
**Significant at .01.

weekend sport games/shows) and why all the consumption communities in this study were significant predictors of "watching sports on television" (sports in general).

Another difference between Shoham and Kahle's study and the present study is that the variable "reading sports magazines" in Shoham and Kahle's study included *Sports Illustrated* and *Field and Stream*, whereas the variable in this study included only *Sports Illustrated*. Although directionally identical results were obtained from the two measurements, for this study, the nature-related sport scale was a significant predictor only at the 0.05 level.

In all, this study essentially replicated Shoham and Kahle's findings. This outcome is important because it enhances our confidence in the generalizability of both sets of findings. Members of different consumption communities differ in their media exposure, and this membership can help us segment consumers to reach each segment more efficiently and effectively (Shoham & Kahle, 1996). For example, because the fitness sports scale was not significantly associated with reading *Sports Illustrated* in both studies, advertisers might learn that it is not worthwhile to put ads about fitness-related sports products or services in this sports magazine. However, advertisers will not hesitate to promote products or services related to competitive sports and nature-related sports in *Sports Illustrated*. Because all the consumption communities were significantly associated with attending sporting events, marketing managers of products or services related to fitness sport, competitive sport, and nature-related sport will also benefit from outdoor or indoor promotions in sport arenas, through either advertising or sponsorship.

NEW FINDINGS

Paid Fitness Sport as Another Consumption Community

In the present study, the factor analysis of sports/exercise/outdoor activities extracted five factors (see Table 1.1). The fifth factor (composed of golf and bowling) was not included in the analysis because it had low reliability. The fourth factor, going to an exercise class and going to a health club, was not included in Shoham and Kahle's data. It can be designated as "paid fitness sport" to differentiate it from "fitness sport." The summated "paid fitness sport" scale has a reliability of $\alpha = 0.67$. When "paid fitness sport" was added to the consumption communities, it did not alter the original relationships between three consumption communities and three communication communities. For itself, it contributed significantly (negatively) to "watching sports on TV" (at $\rho = 0.02$), but not to "attending sport events" and "reading *Sports Illustrated*." See Table 1.3

    Discussion and Implications.   With the expanded list of the consumption communities, we have a clearer picture of how people from different consumption communities differ in their media preferences. All the consumption communities (negative for "paid fitness sport") were significantly associated with "watching sports on television." "Competitive sports" and "nature-related sports" were significant predictors of all the three communication communities. However, "fitness sports" and "paid fitness sports" differ in their media implications. Neither of them was significantly associated with "reading *Sports Illustrated*." "Paid fitness sports" was the only consumption community that did not contribute significantly to "attending sporting events."

    "Paid fitness sport" was not a significant predictor of "attending sporting events" or "reading *Sports Illustrated*," probably because more women than men participate in paid fitness sports and more men than women attend sporting events and read *Sports Illustrated*. "Paid fitness sport" was negatively associated with "watching sports on TV." This will discourage marketing managers from putting ads related to "paid fitness sport" on TV sports programs. On the other hand, in order to expand the market share of *Sports Illustrated*, the magazine might consider adjusting its marketing strategy by

TABLE 1.3

Multiple Regression Coefficient (Standardized Coefficient
and with P-Values < in Parenthesis): Adding One Variable
to Consumption Communities

	Attending Sporting Events	Watching Sports on Television	Reading Sports Illustrated
Competitive sports	0.27 (.00)**	0.13 (.00)**	0.18 (.00)**
Fitness sports	0.16 (.00)**	0.10 (.00)**	0.01 (.48)
Nature-related sports	0.08 (.00)**	0.10 (.00)**	0.05 (.01)*
Paid fitness sport	0.01 (.71)	−0.04 (.02)**	−0.01 (.46)

*Significant at .05.
**Significant at .01.

also trying to appeal to those who participate in fitness sports and paid fitness sports (Table 1.3).

Relationship Between Sports Communities and Other Variables

As Shoham and Kahle stated (1996), while consumption communities are composed of groups of people having common consumption interests, communication communities can be viewed as groups of people sharing some communication tendencies. Through their regression analysis, Shoham and Kahle (1996) found that different sport communication communities are associated with different social values, attitudes, and opinions. Their findings helped us formulate another research question: Do different communication communities and consumption communities have unique sets of shared values, interests, and buying behavior? If so, what are they?

With this research question in mind, we conducted an exploratory correlation analysis of relationships among membership in these sports communities and all the other variables in the Life Style data, including people's interests, attitudes, activities, and product/media usage. Although there are more men than women in the sport communities, we did not analyze female communities and male communities separately because these communities are open to both genders. However, we did find out that some communities were male- or female-dominated. This might help sports marketers find some ways to target one gender or the other.

Consumption Communities

We factor analyzed all the variables having correlation coefficients higher than .10 with one or more of the consumption communities. We chose items with loading of at least .45 to represent each of the 44 resulting factors, and we cross-tabulated these items with membership in the four consumption communities. Some of the results are represented in Tables 1.4 and 1.5. The analysis helped us find out some interesting characteristics of these consumption communities.

Attending Competitive Sports. Those who attend competitive sports events were more likely than people in the other consumption communities to play or buy video games and watch comedy shows (see Table 1.4). The video game relationship seems reasonable in that those who play video games compete by certain rules, sometimes in group settings. This relationship might also have something to do with having children at home. It turned out that over 63% of people in this community had at least one child living at home (versus 46% for those who did not attend competitive sports).

People who watch comedy shows, especially young males, enjoy putdowns and verbal (and sometimes physical) battling. The data showed that people watch fewer comedy shows as they age. We found that 72% of people in this community were younger than 45 years old (versus 42% for those who did not attend competitive sports) and that 55% of people from this community were male (versus 42% for those who did not attend competitive sports). We can conclude that this is a community dominated by young males.

Participating in Nature-Related Sports. As might be expected, those who participate in nature-related sports showed stronger interests in nature shows and programs on the Discovery Channel (see Table 1.4). They were less interested in their personal appearance (see Table 5) and less involved in community or civic activities (see Table 1.4). The results coincide with those of an earlier Life Style study, in which Wells and Reynolds (1979) pointed out that emphasis on nature is at some level related to the relative de-emphasis on mouthwash and deodorant. Men pay less attention to their appearance than women, and this community seems to be male-dominated: 53% of them were male (vs. 38% for those who did not attend nature-related sports). It is

TABLE 1.4
Characteristics of Consumption Communities

	Attended Competitive Sports Last Year (at Least Once for Each on Average) N = 1,059	Participating in Nature-Related Sports (at Least Once for Each on Average) N = 1,832	Participating in Fitness Sport (More than Once for Each on Average) N = 2,062	Participating in Paid Fitness Sport (at Least Once for Each on Average) N = 851	General Percentage
Video Game					
Played home video game (at least once last year) (.67)	58*	50	44**	46	41
Bought a home video game (at least once last year) (.72)	36*	34	29**	31	28
Purchased college sweats (at least once last year) (.47)	49*	40	38**	44	34
Comedy					
Seinfeld (.63)	39*	32	33	33	30
Home Improvement (.70)	53*	51	47	45	45
Nature Programs					
Discovery Channel (.79)	58	62*	56	54	39
Nature shows (.78)	41	47*	43	39	41

Active Participation					
Worked on a community project (at least once last year) (.75)	45	44	39	37**	32
Did volunteer work (at least once last year) (.76)	63	64	59	56**	50
Went to a club meeting (at least once last year) (.70)	52	58	51	48**	45
Environmental Consciousness					
Recycle newspaper (always) (.80)	47	50	53*	47	49
Recycle plastic bottles/containers (always) (.82)	39	42	44*	39	41
Make effort to recycle everything I can (.74)	64	68	70*	63	64
Diet Drinks					
Used diet cola (at least 1–2 servings each week) (.73)	35	42*	40*	35	34
Diet non-cola carbonated soft drinks (at least 1–2 servings each week) (.40)	21	25*	25*	21	21

*Highest numbers.
**Lowest numbers.

TABLE 1.5

Characteristics of Consumption Communities

	Attended Competitive Sports Last Year (at Least Once for Each on Average) N = 1,059	Participating in Nature-Related Sports (at Least Once for Each on Average) N = 1,832	Participating in Fitness Sport (More than Once for Each on Average) N = 2,062	Participating in Paid Fitness Sport (at Least Once for Each on Average) N = 851	General Percentage
Children's Entertainment					
Visited local theme park (at least once last year) (.68)	49	42	40**	48	35
Visited out-of-town theme park (at least once last year) (.58)	46	41	39**	45	35
Went to a zoo (at least once last year) (.40)	45	39	37**	46	32
Health Conscious (loading over .70 selected)					
Try to avoid high cholesterol (.73)	63	64	72*	73*	66
Nutrition information on label determines what to buy (.73)	48	45	57*	60*	49

Try to avoid fried food (.70)	67	66	78*	78*	55
Avoid food that is high in fat (.80)	53	52	63*	63*	69
Check ingredient labels when buying food (.71)	51	51	62*	64*	54
Appearance Consciousness					
Care about maintaining youthful appearance (.64)	60	60**	67	72*	60
Like to feel attractive (.54)	88	83**	84	88*	81
Have more stylish clothes than friends (.62)	31	27**	30	36*	27
Dress well is important (.74)	68	65**	79	73	67

*Highest numbers.
**Lowest numbers.

possible that those who are close to nature might be less interested in such artificialities as mouthwash and deodorant.

Participating in Fitness Sports.   As opposed to competitive sports, fitness sports (jogging, bicycling, walking exercise, and home exercise) are usually neighborhood or home activities. These people were more willing than people in the other communities to do recycling (see Table 1.4). It is possible that environmental consciousness is related to education. In fact, 66% of the people in this community attended college or received higher education (vs. 52% for those who did not participate in fitness sport). People from this community also engaged less in children's entertainment (see Table 1.5) and less in home video games playing (see Table 1.4). This might be due to the fact that only 50% of people in this community had at least one child living at home (vs. 52% for those who did not participate in fitness sport), a far cry from those who attended competitive sports (63% of them had at least one child living at home).

Participating in Paid Fitness Sports.   People go to health clubs to stay fit and, most importantly (for quite a few people), to meet attractive others. It is not surprising that these people were more concerned about their personal appearance, than even those who participated in a similar sport activity, fitness sports (see Table 1.5). This probably has to do with the fact that 62% of people in this community are female (vs. 52% for those who did not participate in paid fitness sports). In comparison, 56% of people who participated in fitness sports were female (vs. 52% for those who did not participate).

Participating in Fitness Sports and Paid Fitness Sports.   People in both communities indicated higher levels of diet drink consumption (see Table 1.4) and were more concerned about their nutrition intake than people in the other communities (see Table 1.5). People from the latter community indicated higher diet and nutrition consciousness. It makes sense that people who belong to the two communities try to keep fit by participating in these sports on the one hand and by controlling their food consumption on the other. For the sake of personal appearance, females tend to be heavier users of diet foods and beverages than males. As was indicated earlier, both communities are female-dominated.

Discussion and Implications.   To summarize, people in the four sports consumption communities indicated higher levels of certain activities and interests than the general population (see Tables 1.4 and 1.5). The exception is that people who attended competitive sports or nature-related sports were less environmentally conscious than the general population. Both communities were male-dominated. In comparison, participation in fitness sports and paid fitness sports was female-dominated. Therefore, we can roughly say that there exists a gender-based dimension in the sport consumption communities, one is male-dominated (e.g., "competitive sports" and "nature-related sports") and the other is female-dominated (e.g., "fitness sports" and "paid fitness sports"). This gender-based dimensional difference will be helpful for sports marketers to map out their strategies.

Since the U.S. Congress passed its Title IX of the Higher Education Act in 1972, and as a result of women's movement and civil rights legislation, the number of female participants at all levels of sports competition has increased. Sport and fitness activities have become more socially acceptable and available for women of all ages (McPherson et al., 1989). Statistics on sports participation in the United States (from 1984 to 1988) have shown a growing movement away from rigorous sports and team sports toward less intensive, individual sports, such as swimming, exercise walking, and bicycle riding (Burnett et al., 1993). Our data also indicate that female-dominated fitness sports and paid fitness sports have evolved to be important parts of sports participation. This increasing level of participation in fitness and paid fitness sports by women will spur sports marketers to be aware of this change and to adjust their traditional male-oriented strategies toward a wider range of market segments.

As we can tell from analysis of interests or buying behaviors, each community has its own unique characteristics. To pinpoint these characteristics will be of much help for sport marketers to target their products at certain community members. For example, because those who attend competitive sports also like video games and comedy shows, it will be a good strategy for marketers to consider putting ads for video games and comedy shows in sports arenas. Women are often the primary decision makers of such product categories as financial services, health care, insurance, and automobiles (Erickson, 1988); therefore, marketers may also promote these products along with perfume and fitness-related products.

Communication Communities

As we did in analyzing consumption communities, we factor analyzed all the variables having correlation coefficients higher than .10 with one or more of the communication communities. Items with loading of at least .45 were selected to represent each of the 33 factors. Then we cross-tabulated these items by all the three communication communities. In Tables 1.6 and 1.7, we present part of the results.

Attending Sporting Events. Those who attended sporting events indicated higher levels of active participation in community / civic work (see Table 1.6). Compared with people in the other communication communities, they were less interested in news and politics (see Table 1.7), and they had more liberal attitudes toward gender roles in society (see Table 1.6). Those who attend sporting events might tend to have equal concern and respect for all participants, be they male or female, and equal concern and respect are not in conflict with recognition of difference, as the latter does not necessarily require dominance or subordination (Simon, 1985). Yet, compared with the general population, people from this community were a bit more conservative about gender equality, people from the other communication communities were also more conservative than the general population. This conforms to previous findings that people connected with sports tend to be conservative in terms of gender roles. (Eitzen & Sage, 1989).

The relatively liberal attitude of those who frequently engage in group activities might also be due to the age category into which most of the people of this community fall. Our data showed that 55% of the people in this community were younger than 45 years old (vs. 45% for those who did not attend sporting events). Hocking (1982) found that those who attended a live sport event experienced certain degrees of arousal, excitement, and enjoyment. These so-called intra-audience effects constituted a major factor in making attendance of sporting events a very different experience from viewing the same event on television. Young people might like intra-audience experience more than old people. Young people also tend to have more energy to do things in communities, and they tend to be less conservative.

People who attend sporting events seem to enjoy group activities, which might explain why they like community work as well. Kahle, Kambara, and Rose (1996) found that fan attendance is motivated by a desire for camaraderie, that is, a desire for group affiliation, among other factors (e.g., self-expressive experience, internalization) (see also Gantz, 1981; Wann, 1995). People usually go to sporting events to support their local team, which is the representative of community interests (Hardy, 1997). It is this same communal or community logic that might lead those who attend sporting events to engage in community work.

Watching Sports on TV. People who watched TV sports were less likely than people in the other communities to purchase sports wear. They also

TABLE 1.6

Characteristics of Communication Communities

	Attended Sporting Events (at Least Once Last Year) N = 1,835	Watched Sports on Television (12 Times or More Last Year) N = 1,838	Read Sports Illustrated (Read Most or All Last Year) N = 265	General Percentage
Active Participation				
Worked on a community project (at least once last year) (.73)	42*	34**	40	32
Did volunteer work (at least once last year) (.80)	60*	52**	54	49
Went to a club meeting (at least once last year) (.68)	54*	47**	51	44
Sex Roles				
Men are smarter than women (.79)	17**	19	22	17
Men are better leaders than women (.82)	29**	32	37	28
Father should be boss of house (.73)	44**	46	51	43
Men are better at investing than women (.71)	38**	39	40	36
Sportswear				
Purchased athletic shoes (at least once last year) (.60)	69	63**	73*	59
Shopped at specialty athletic shoe stores (at least once last year) (.61)	52	45**	61*	40
Purchased sweats with college name on it (at least once last year) (.47)	45	40**	61*	34
Competitive/Leadership				
I like to be considered a leader (.58)	72	71	76*	67
I would do better than average in a fist fight (54)	45	46	66*	41
I am influential in neighborhood (.66)	38	36	40*	34

*Highest numbers.
**Lowest numbers.

TABLE 1.7
Characteristics of Communication Communities

	Attended Sporting Events (at Least Once Last Year) N = 1,835	Watched Sports on Television (12 Times or More Last Year) N = 1,838	Read Sports Illustrated (Read Most or All Last Year) N = 265	General Percentage
Convenience Store (Loading over .50 Selected)				
Shopped at gas station/Convenience store (at least once last year) (.68)	67	63	70*	61
Shopped at convenience store (5 times or more last year) (.74)	63	60	68*	55
Brought home food from fast food restaurants (9 times or more last year) (.58)	49	48	56*	42
Stimulus-Seeking/Impulsivity				
Like the feeling of speed (.62)	45	44	47*	40
Like sports car (.61)	68	66	78*	61
Would try anything once (.59)	59	57	75*	55
Greatest achievement ahead (.45)	69	65	80*	65
News/Politics				
Watched local news (.67)	72**	75	75	70
Watched CNN (.46)	49**	54	54	50
Need to get the news everyday (.62)	70**	73	83	67
I am interested in politics (.47)	51**	52	52	48
Read editorial section (.52)	50**	50	44	47
Watch evening network news (.69)	51**	55	55	51

*Highest numbers.
**Lowest numbers.

indicated lower levels of participation in community work as compared to those in the other communities, but still higher than the general population. It is possible that quite a few people in this community are so-called couch potatoes and less likely to attend sports events themselves. These relationships might be due to the fact that 52% of the people in this community were 45 or older (vs. 48% who did not watch sports on television). It is possible that older people are less likely to wear sport wear than young people be actively involved in.

Reading Sports Illustrated.   Those who read *Sports Illustrated* indicated a higher level of interest in sports wear and convenience store shopping. *Sports Illustrated* is usually sold in convenience stores. People in this community tend to be aspiring, ambitious, competitive, and stimulus-seeking. This replicates Shoham and Kahle's (1966) finding that having an aggressive and powerful personality is associated with sport magazine readership. Because *Sports Illustrated* features coverage of exciting sport events, people who value ambition and competition might like to find similar messages in that medium. This magazine mainly appeals to young males. Sixty-two percent of the people in this community were younger than 45 years old (vs. 47% for those who did not read *Sports Illustrated*), and 74% of them were male (vs. 42% for those who did not read this magazine).

Discussion and Implications.   The gender inequality among the readers of *Sports Illustrated* might be due to the traditional bias of sports magazine editors to cover mostly male sports. As women's active involvement in sports has increased, *Sports Illustrated* might expand its market share if it could continue to increase its coverage of women's sports.

Compared with the general population, people in these communication communities indicated higher levels of certain activities, interests, and personality traits (see Tables 1.6 and 1.7). As in the consumption communities, we can also roughly delineate another dimension (along the age continuum) for the communication communities. One is dominated by relatively young people (e.g., "attending sporting events" and "read *Sports Illustrated*") and the other is dominated by older people (e.g., "watching sports on television").

The unique interests and buying behaviors of each communication community also help define community membership. These traits serve as hints or guides for sports marketers when they set out to target their products or services to different segments. For instance, our findings justify marketers' efforts to put ads for sports wear in *Sports Illustrated*. Advertising executions emphasizing competition and ambition may also appeal to this group of people.

Summaries of New Findings

This chapter added "paid fitness sport" to the consumption communities. This addition furthered our understanding of the relationships between consumption communities and communication communities. Cross-tabulation analyses between specific sports communities and other variables showed that people from different sports communities were characterized by the nature of communities to which they belong. This characterization and the original regression analysis between consumption communities and communication communities are meaningful for sports marketers in their creative strategy formulation and media selection.

This chapter contributes to the segmentation studies of sports consumers by replicating Shoham and Kahle's seminal categorization and adding a new segmentation variable. As a result, campaigns built around sports enthusiasts should not merely distinguish between sports participants and sports spectators or between males and females (Burnett et al., 1993). Rather, media planners should plan different types of media strategies (e.g., advertising, licensing, promotional tie-ins, and sponsorships), to reach more specific segments of sports participants and spectators.

FINAL SUMMARY

The purpose of this chapter is to further test and expand the narrow segmentation of the sports fan market started by Shoham and Kahle (1996). Proceeding from the Shoham and Kahle study, we began by replicating many of most important findings with another data file, the 1995 Life Style data. This replication increases confidence in both sets of findings. We added "paid fitness sport" to Shoham and Kahle's list of consumption communities. We then conducted cross-tabulation analyses between communication communities and values, interests, and buying behaviors, among others. We did a parallel analysis of consumption communities. The relationships discovered will serve as a guide for sports marketers to address their targets more efficiently and effectively.

ACKNOWLEDGMENT

The authors would like to thank DDB Needham (Chicago) for providing its Life Style data.

REFERENCES

Boorstin, D. (1974). *The Americans: The Democratic Experience.* New York: Vintage Books.

Burnett, J., Menon, A., & Smart, D. T. (1993). Sports marketing: A new ball game with new rules. *Journal of Advertising Research, 33*(5), 21–35.

DDB Needham Worldwide, Inc. (1995). *The DDB Needham Life Style Study.* Unpublished data.

Dickinson, J. (1976). *A Behavioral Analysis of Sport.* London: Lepus Books.

Eitzen, D. S., & Sage, G. H. (1989). *Sociology of Northern American Sport* (4th ed.). Dubuque, Iowa: Brown.

Fitch, E. D. (1986, September 1). Methods of keeping score for advertisers. *Advertising Age.*

Gantz, W. (1981). An exploration of viewing motives and behaviors associated with television sports. *Journal of Broadcasting, 25*(3), 263–275.

Gaskell, G., & Pearton, R. (1979). Aggression and sport. In J. H. Goldstein (Ed.), *Sport, Games and Play: Social and Psychological Viewpoints.* Hillsdale, NJ: Lawrence Erlbaum Associates.

Hardy, S. H. (1997). Entrepreneurs, organizations, and the sports marketplace. In S. W. Pope (Ed.), *The New American Sport Industry: Recent Approaches and Perspectives.* Chicago: University of Illinois Press.

Harris, D. V. (1973). *Involvement in Sport — A Somatopsychic Rational.* Philadelphia: Lea-Febiger.

Hocking, J. E. (1982). Sports and spectators: Intra-audience effects. *Journal of Communication, 3*(1), 100–108.

Kahle, L. R., & Chiagouris, L. (1997). (Ed.), Values, Lifestyles, and Psychographics. Mahwah, NJ: Lawrence Erlbaum.

Kahle, L. R., Kambara, K. M., & Rose, G. M. (1996). A functional model of fan attendance motivations for college football. *Sport Marketing Quarterly, 5*(4), 51–60.

Kenyon, G. S. (1968). Six scales for assessing attitude toward physical activity. *Research Quarterly, 39,* 566–574.

Kenyon, G. S., & McPherson, B. D. (1973). Becoming involved in physical activity and sport: A process of socialization. In G. L. Rarick (Ed.), *Physical Activity: Human Growth and Development.* New York: Academic Press.

Lang, G. E. (1981). Riotous outbursts in sports events. In G. R. F. Luschen & G. H. Sage (Ed.), *Handbook of Social Sciences of Sport.* Champaign, IL: Stipes.

Lever, J., & Wheeler, S. (1993). Mass media and the experience of sport. *Communication Research, 20*(1), 125–143.

Luschen, G. (1980). Sociology of sport. *Annual Review of Sociology, 6,* 315–347.

McPherson, B. D., Curtis, J. E., & Loy, J. W. (1989). *The Social Significance of Sport: An Introduction to the Sociology of Sport.* Champaign, IL: Human Kinetics Books.

Prensky, D., & Wright-Isak, C. (1997). Advertising, values, and the consumption community. In L. R. Kahle & L. Chiagouris (Eds.), *Advertising and Consumer Psychology: Values, Lifestyles, and Psychographics.* Mahwah, NJ: Lawrence Erlbaum Associates.

Shoham, A., & Kahle, L. R. (1996). Spectators, viewers, readers: Communication and consumption communities in sport marketing. *Sport Marketing Quarterly, 5*(1), 11–19.

Simon, R. L. (1985). *Sports and Social Values.* Englewood Cliffs, NJ: Prentice-Hall.

Sofranko, A. T., & Nolan, M. F. (1972). Early life experiences and adult sport participation. *Journal of Leisure Research, 4*(6), 6–18.

Spreitzer, F. A., & Snyder, E. E. (1976). Socialization into sport: An exploratory path analysis. *Research Quarterly, 47,* 238–245.

Taylor, I. (1972). Football mad: A speculative sociology of football hooliganism. In E. Dunning (Ed.), *Sport: Readings from a Sociological Perspective*. Toronto: University of Toronto Press.

Trujillo, N., & Ekdom, L. R. (1985). Sportswriting and American cultural values: The 1984 Chicago Cubs. *Critical Studies in Mass Communication, 2*, 262–281.

Wann, D. L. (1995, November). Preliminary validation of the sport fan motivation scale. *Journal of Sport and Social Issues, 19*(4), 377–357.

Wells, W. D., & Reynolds, F. D. (1979). Psychological geography. *Research in Marketing, 2*, 345–357.

Zillman, D., Bryant, H., & Sapolsky, B. S. (1979). The enjoyment of watching sport contests. In J. H. Goldstein (Ed.), *Sport, Games and Play: Social and Psychological Viewpoints*. Hillsdale, NJ: Lawrence Erlbaum Associates.

2

Fanatical Consumption: An Investigation of the Behavior of Sports Fans Through Textual Data

Scott W. Kelley
University of Kentucky

Kelly Tian
New Mexico State University

To be a WILDCAT fan, you must have pride and respect for your team no matter what. One has loyalty and admiration for the team and the university in general. One has support for the team and its achievements as well as for the individual players themselves. You love the team unconditionally and want the best for them always. You stick with the team in good times and bad ones. One can almost compare it to a marriage and the vows one takes. The saying that I "bleed blue" is definitely true in my case, because I always want them to do the very best that they possibly can. So when they hurt, I hurt and vice versa. I love being a representative and graduate of UK and the traditions that go along with it.

—(#7—3 / 21)

fanatic—a person possessed by an excessive zeal for and uncritical attachment to a cause or position.

—*The American Heritage Dictionary* (1985)

Sports are pervasive throughout our society and culture. Most of our lives are touched daily in some respect by sports, whether we realize it or not. The entertainment we seek out, the media we are exposed to, and our interactions with others are often influenced by the world of sports. For some, the impact of sports on their lives is much more dramatic. Individuals whose lives are deeply impacted by sports are the fanatical supporters of "their" team. The exploits of fanatical supporters of athletic teams have taken on legendary proportions. The Chicago Cubs have the Bleacher Bums. The Cleveland Browns have the Dawg Pound. The Green Bay Packers have the Cheeseheads. In fact, many, if not most, professional and collegiate athletic teams have avid fans or fanatical supporters. Informal observation of fanatical supporters attending athletic events has become commonplace. These individuals are often covered by various forms of media. In addition, limited academic research has also investigated various forms of fan behavior (Cialdini et al., 1976; Fisher & Wakefield, 1998; Holt, 1995). However, very little research has investigated fanatical support within the context of an individual's life. This research investigates fanatical support of an athletic team and its impact on individuals. Investigating fanatical support and its impact on individuals' lives has merit because fanaticism implies the pursuit of a given interest to lengths that are considered inordinate and even irrational, often to the exclusion of virtually all other interests. This study examines fanaticism among University of Kentucky (UK) Wildcat basketball fans. The strong support of the UK basketball program is well documented and provides a context in which fanatical support is pervasive.

PURPOSE

The purpose of this chapter is to phenomenologically investigate the perceptions, attitudes, and behaviors of fanatical followers of an athletic team. Although previous researchers have considered the consumption activities associated with fans in attendance at an athletic event (Holt, 1995), our chapter takes a broader view of the consumption experience in that it is not restricted to the activities associated directly with attending the event. Rather, our chapter considers the consumption experiences of fanatics that extend beyond game attendance and thus, potentially have a greater impact on their lives.

This chapter utilizes qualitative research methods as a basis for providing rich and detailed description of phenomena associated with sports fanaticism. The data for this chapter were collected through written journals that enabled the researchers to consider life phenomena as they relate to fanatical consumption through relational themes that emerged during the data analysis process. Following a detailed description of this research method, we present the emergent themes, grounding these in comments from participants' journals (Spiggle, 1994). We then discuss insights for practitioners and researchers suggested by the findings.

RESEARCH METHODOLOGY

Overview

Collecting data via participants recruited to write about their experiences in daily journals is a rather novel method. The only comparable method in prior consumer research is Belk's (1992) collection of textual data taken from journals that had been preserved as historical records. We deemed the journal method as preferable to other qualitative methods such as personal depth interviews for two reasons. First, given the potential that some fans might fear being labeled by the researcher as a "fanatic," journals, in contrast to interviews, protected the participants' anonymity. Ensuring anonymity increased the opportunity for participants to candidly disclose their experiences. Second, because being a sports fan involves an extended period of intermittent activity, the journal method corresponded better with this experience. In other words, with the journal method, a continual log is kept that can reflect changes in feelings and activities linked to the ebbs and flows of fan and team activities and outcomes over time.

Structure and Content of Journal Entries

Participants were asked to complete a daily journal from March 4, 1998 through March 31, 1998. These dates corresponded to the beginning of the Southeastern Conference (SEC) Men's Basketball Tournament, which was held in Atlanta, and the NCAA Men's Basketball Tournament, which was held at various sites but culminated with the Final Four in San Antonio, Texas. The journal consisted of four parts (Table 2.1).

The first part of the journal focused on the SEC Tournament. In this part, participants were asked to complete the following tasks:

1. Fill out tournament pairing brackets before the first game of the tournament.
2. Provide thoughts about the upcoming SEC tournament.
3. List SEC tournament games that UK did not participate in that were watched and reactions to these games.
4. Provide information concerning pregame activities for UK games.
5. List people with whom they watched the UK games.
6. Provide personal reactions to the UK games.
7. Describe postgame experiences or activities.

This part of the journal was completed from March 4 through 8, 1998.

TABLE 2.1
Sequence of the Journal

Journal Section	Date(s) for Completion
Part 1. SEC Tournament	
SEC Tournament Bracket	March 4th
SEC Tournament Activities	March 5th through March 8th
and Reactions	
Part 2. NCAA Tournament	
NCAA Tournament Bracket	March 9th
NCAA Tournament Activities	Round 1: March 12th through March 15th
and Reactions	Round 2: March 19th through March 22nd
	The Final Four: March 28th
	NCAA Championship Game: March 30th
Part 3. Daily Log	Every day, March 4th through March 31st
Part 4. Demographic Information	March 31st

Note. NCAA, National Collegiate Athletic Association.
SEC, Southeastern Conference.

The second part of the journal focused on the NCAA Men's Basketball Tournament. In this section of the journal, participants were asked to provide the same seven pieces of information completed throughout the SEC Tournament with regard to the NCAA Tournament. This portion of the journal was completed on March 12 through 15, 1998; March 19 through 22, 1998; and March 28 and 30, 1998.

The third portion of the journal included a series of questions that were to be completed daily March 4 through 31, 1998. The daily journal questions are provided in Table 2.2. The daily journal questions were phrased to elicit written personal narratives, a form of discourse organized around consequential events experienced by the teller (Riessman, 1991; Tepper, 1997). Several of the questions were phrased to elicit more specific story-type narratives. Story-type narratives are more likely than other narrative types to focus on experiences that hold deep meaning because they include a protagonist or main character, inciting conditions, and culminating events (Riessman, 1991, 1993). Further, in this section of the journal, we avoided questions asking "Why?," such as "Why did this event have an impact on you?" because they

TABLE 2.2
Daily Log Questions and Topics

Date	Question/Topic
March 4th	What is your most memorable experience involving UK basketball? Tell your story below.
March 5th	Describe your feelings when UK won the 1996 NCAA Championship. Where were you when they won? What did you do after the game?
March 6th	What is your favorite UK basketball tradition? Describe it in as much detail as possible.
March 7th	Who had the biggest impact on you becoming a Wildcat fan? Tell your story below.
March 8th	Which player in UK basketball history do you feel most attached to? Write about your attachment below.
March 9th	What was the most disappointing event in Wildcat basketball history? How did it affect you?
March 10th	What is your favorite UK basketball team ever? Tell your story below.
March 11th	Who are UK's biggest basketball rivals? How do you feel about these teams?
March 12th	Which UK basketball game had the biggest negative effect on you? Tell your story below.
March 13th	Which UK basketball game had the biggest positive effect on you? Tell your story below.
March 14th	Are there any other sports teams that you feel the same about as you do the Wildcats? Tell your story below.
March 15 th	What was the best UK basketball team that you can remember? How did their success affect you?
March 16 th	How has your involvement as a Wildcat fan changed over time?
March 17th	What is your most memorable UK basketball game ever? How did it affect you?
March 18th	Describe your typical emotional feelings and reactions during a UK basketball game.
March 19th	Describe Wildcat memorabilia that you have collected. What is its significance to you?
March 20th	What was the worst UK basketball team that you can remember? How did their lack of success affect you?
March 21st	Describe what it means to you to be a Wildcat fan.
March 22nd	Do you have any superstitions associated with UK basketball? For example, a lucky hat or a lucky pre-game meal?
March 23rd	What was the biggest win ever in UK basketball in your memory? What impact did it have on you?
March 24th	Ticket Trivia—What are some of your favorite ticket stories? For example, what was the most you ever paid for a ticket? The hardest ticket you ever got? Your best seats? Your worst seats?
March 25th	Describe your feelings when UK lost the 1997 NCAA Championship game. Where were you when they lost? What did you do after the game?
March 26th	You were asked to participate in this study because you were identified by someone as an avid UK basketball fan. Why do other people think you are a big UK fan?
March 27th	What was the biggest loss ever for UK basketball in your memory? What impact did it have on you?
March 28th	How do you feel about the recent discussions of a new on-campus basketball arena?
March 29th	Who is the biggest Wildcat basketball fan that you know? Describe them.
March 30th	Reflect on the 1997–98 UK basketball season. Overall, how do you think the Wildcats did?
March 31st	What are your expectations for the 1998–99 basketball season?

have the potential to force rational explanations (Thompson, Locander, & Pollio 1989).

The final section of the journal focused on demographic information. This information is summarized in Table 2.3.

The Sample

A total of 30 journals were distributed to avid UK Wildcat fans during the first two days of March. All participants received a UK pen and pencil set for agreeing to participate in the study. These individuals were either self-identified as avid UK fans or were identified by other UK fans or the authors as avid UK fans. An effort was made to include a diverse group of UK fans in the sample. Of the 30 journals that were distributed, 20 were completed and returned to the authors. The sample profile is provided in Table 2.3. The sample included 10 men and 10 women, ranging in age from 22 to 59. The participants had lived in the Commonwealth of Kentucky for various lengths of time ranging from 6 to 58 years. A variety of occupations were represented in the sample (see Table 2.3). Participants also had varied affiliations with the University. The sample included individuals with no formal affiliation with the University other than being a fan and individuals who categorized themselves as varying combinations of current students, graduates, UK employees, and members of the Alumni Association.

Respondents also reported how many UK basketball games they attended during the 1997 to 1998 season. Their responses ranged from zero to 22 games. It should be noted that attending UK basketball games is probably not a strong indicator of fan interest because it is difficult to obtain tickets. In fact, there is some sentiment within the Commonwealth suggesting that the most avid UK fans do not even attend the games. Finally, participants reported the number of hours they spend each week watching basketball and sports in general on TV. Responses ranged from 4 to 15 hours of basketball viewing and from 4 to 20 hours of general sports viewing.

Method of Analysis

The textual data from these responses were analyzed using a *hermeneutic* or part-to-whole analysis (Thompson, Locander, & Pollio 1989). Each participant's journal was first read to relate each part or response to the overall journal. Once the individual parts were understood in the context of the participant's overall journal, the parts were reviewed across all participants to look for common categories or themes. These categories and themes suggested

TABLE 2.3
Sample Characteristics

Participant No.	Gender	Age	Years a KY Resident	Occupation	UK Affiliation	Games Attended in 1997–98 Season	Hours spent watching TV b-ball per week	Hours spent watching TV sports per week
1	Female	53	39	Typesetter/bookkeeper	Fan	1 Home	6–8	12–15
2	Male	22	20	Student	Current student	2 Home	4	8
3	Male	37	36	Banker	Graduate, donor, alumni association	None	15	20
4	Female	43	32	Physician	Graduate, UK employee, donor, alumni association	3 Home	15	20
5	Male	28	24	Graduate student	Current student, graduate	3 Home	10–14	18–20

(Continued)

TABLE 2.3
(Continued)

Participant No.	Gender	Age	Years a KY Resident	Occupation	UK Affiliation	Games Attended in 1997–98 Season	Hours spent watching TV b-ball per week	Hours spent watching TV sports per week
6	Male	28	24	Logistics manager	Graduate donor alumni association	5 Home	6–8	10–12
7		33	33	Office manager	Graduate alumni association	8 Home	9	12
8	Female	34	33	Staff assistant	Graduate UK employee	None	4	4
9	Female	59	58	Admissions officer	Graduate UK employee	None	5	5
10	Male	29	6	Hospital administration	Current student	None	5–6	10
11	Male	29	29	Account executive	Graduate	1 Home	6	7
12	Male	24	24	Real estate	Current student	None	4	8

13		24	6	UK administration	Current student, graduate, UK employee, alumni association	9 Home 4 Away	6	10
14	Female	24	16	Graduate student/bartender	Current student, Graduate, alumni association	1 Home 1 Away	6	10
15	Female	22	22	Student	Current student	None	2–4	2–4
16	Female	55	54	Medical technologist	Graduate, alumni association	None	4	8
17	Male	28	10	Editor	Graduate	3 Home	8	15
18	Female	29	28	Medical technologist	Graduate	13 Home 9 Away	8	8–10
19	Male	25	12	Sports publishing/journalism	Graduate, alumni association	1 Home	10–15	15–20
20	Male	45	16	Professor	Graduate, alumni association	None	8	8

relevant literature that we consulted to assist in shaping the description. The following discussion of the results describes these emergent themes, grounding them in excerpts taken from the journals (Spiggle, 1994). These journal excerpts are referenced by a participant number that links the excerpt to the demographic profile of the participant (see Table 2.3) as well as to the date of the journal entry (see Table 2.2).

ROLES OF THE SPORTS FANATIC

The emergent themes revolve around the roles enacted by individuals as they supported the UK basketball program. The fanatical UK basketball fan enacts a variety of different roles in the process of supporting the UK basketball program. The broad themes that emerged in the process of analyzing our data were labeled as follows:

Game participation
Social events surrounding games
Fan contests
Role conflicts ensuing from the fan identity
Social connectedness ensuing from the fan identity
Life lessons and decisions tied to the fan identity

Each of these emergent themes and relevant sub-themes is subsequently discussed.

Game Participation

Many of the participants in our study viewed themselves as active participants in the game. From a role theoretic perspective, game participation manifests itself in a variety of ways over time. It is possible to break down the fan's role-related activities across time much like one would for an actual participant in the game at hand. Through the course of data analysis, the following game participation roles emerged: the informational role, the team member role, and the team assistance role.

Informational Role. For many of our participants, one of the key characteristics of being a fanatical UK basketball fan involves their level of knowledge concerning current and upcoming events associated with the UK basketball program. During the SEC and NCAA Tournaments, one of the focal points of preparing for upcoming games involves gathering as much information as possible regarding the UK team and their opponents. Sources of information mentioned by our participants include newspapers, programs on national TV networks such as ESPN and CNN, local television sports news, the UK coach's show, sports talk radio call-in shows, *The Cats' Pause* (a publication devoted solely to UK sports), and various sports-related Internet sites. The accumulation of knowledge concerning the UK basketball program in effect validates that a person is indeed a fanatical follower of the program. The pursuit of information related to the UK program allows the participant to more effectively perform evaluating and assimilating activities (Holt, 1995) as they proceed through the consumption process.

In many cases, our participants specifically discussed activities related to scouting UK's next opponent in the tournament. Many of our participants make it a point to watch games of upcoming opponents and read as much information as they can about future opponents as the Cats advance through the tournament. For example, one participant wrote "Watched the UCLA/Michigan game to see who our next opponent is. We analyzed each team and hoped that UCLA would win" (#5—3/14). Interestingly, CBS's local television coverage of the NCAA Tournament seems to reflect this; it often includes coverage of games involving UK's next opponent during the NCAA Tournament each year.

In addition to the informational role that is largely enacted before a UK game, our data also suggest that multiple game participation roles are often played by our participants during the course of a UK basketball game. Interestingly, these game participation roles are enacted whether a fanatic is attending a game in person, watching a game on television, or listening on the radio. These emergent roles or themes focus on the fans' role as a team member and as a team assistant.

Team Member Role.   Many fanatics identify so strongly with their team that they feel as if they are team members. The team member role manifests itself in several different ways, including personalized attributions for the team's experiences, projections of team members' emotions onto themselves, and experiences of physical responses similar to those of players. First, it was not uncommon for our participants to write about successes and failures experienced by the UK basketball program as if they were part of the team. When Kentucky won, they said, "we won." When great successes were achieved, these events were often referred to as something "I always wanted to accomplish." For example, when asked about the 1996 National Championship game, one participant responded "It was the proudest moment that

I can remember because all my life I've always wanted a National Championship" (#2—3/5). Another participant wrote the following about the 1978 National Championship team:

> They brought back the glory of the '40s and '50s when UK dominated college basketball. It vindicated all my years of being a loyal UK fan!! It was great to dominate college basketball the entire year. We were the pre-season #1 and finished the year #1. (#4—3/15)

Team support of this nature has been referred to as "basking in reflected glory," or BIRGing and has been demonstrated experimentally (Cialdini et al., 1976). *BIRGing* is the tendency for individuals to publicly announce their association with successful teams. It may manifest itself through referring to teams in the first person or inclusively or in the apparel one wears. Interestingly, one of our participants even noted the widespread existence of the BIRGing phenomenon during the tournament each year when he noted, "It's always funny when UK wins. It seems that everyone you see has on a UK shirt, hat, etc" (#6—3/7).

Participants also reported a variety of emotional responses that one might typically associate with an actual team member. Many fanatics feel that they are in fact a part of the team, and as a result, experience many of the same emotional ups and downs a player or coach might feel during the course of a season. For example, when asked about his typical behavior during a UK game, one participant wrote:

> I get a little nervous prior to tip off. Once the game has begun I am as intense as the coach or players. I yell at good plays, big runs and even bad calls. When the game begins, my world around me stops. I also get very angry when the Cats get beat, I do not verbalize it but I get very quiet and irritable. Once the Cats pull off a big win there is a feeling of satisfaction. (#3—3/18)

Aside from emotional responses associated with fanaticism, many participants reported physiological responses during UK basketball games. For example, one male participant, age 28, wrote the following about his reactions to a typical UK game:

> I get fairly nervous, as if I have "butterflies" like the players. I always expect UK to win, but I feel the same whether they play Murray State or North Carolina. At the end of close games I am exhausted. I pretty much block out everything and everyone during a game—that's why I prefer to watch the games alone.

I think the reason why I constantly get invited to UK parties is that when I do go, my intensity during the game is entertaining to watch. (#6—3/18)

When describing his typical emotional feelings and reactions during a UK game, another participant wrote:

Before 1996, I use to get so emotional during UK games. There were times even in high school where I thought about crying because UK lost a regular season basketball game. If they won I was in a good mood for the rest of the day and nothing seemed to bother me, but if they lost I would get depressed and could be a miserable human being. (#2—3/18)

In discussing a memorable UK game, another participant wrote: "... I was very nervous about this game and how we would play. I felt very sick during the whole game. I couldn't believe that we were losing!" (#7—3/22). While writing about another game, the same participant wrote: "... My emotions ranged from disbelief to sickness to euphoria" (#7—3/13).

Many of our participants reported postgame experiences similar to those one would expect of a player. These fans described emotional and physical symptoms similar to an athlete after participating in an athletic event. For example, when describing her reactions to UK's victory over Stanford in the 1998 NCAA semi-final game one participant wrote: "When the game was finally over everyone was hugging and teary-eyed. I was completely exhausted" (#1—3/28). In describing his postgame activities following the UK victory over Stanford in the 1998 NCAA semi-final game, one respondent wrote:

What a game.... If someone had told me in January that we'd be playing in the final, I would never have believed it.... We are now in the final. Unbelievable. Watched Utah beat UNC. They will be tough. After that game, we did midnight bowling. Everyone seemed physically and mentally exhausted. Doing something like bowling was perfect to those of us that were wiped out. (#5—3/28)

In summary, for many fanatics, their point of reference and their emotional and physiological responses during and after the game are very similar to those one would expect of an athlete who had actually participated in the contest. The emotions and physical outcomes associated with UK games that were reported by our participants could be those of the actual participants in the athletic event.

Team Assistance Role.   Almost as an extension of considering oneself a part of the team, many participants made reference to their efforts to help the team during the course of a game. These efforts directed toward helping the team came in several different forms, including the traditional role of the fan, superstitions, and special game attire. First, one aspect of the team assistance role encompassed traditionally accepted fan activities. Cheering, supporting, and leading the team to victory were all common duties associated with being a fanatic that were mentioned by our participants. One male participant, age 37, went so far as to explicitly define the role of a UK fan by writing "... The fan's job is to help motivate the coaches and players and give them a reason to be proud to wear the blue and white" (#3—3/21). When asked to describe her behavior during a UK game another participant wrote: "I'm a screamer and a clapper. I don't sit still very long. I like to yell at the referees, even though they can't hear me" (#1—3/18).

Aside from taking great pride in their level of support for the UK basketball team, many participants wrote of superstitions or quirks they have regarding how their personal behavior contributes to the success of the UK basketball team. In almost all cases, these superstitions were seen as being helpful to the UK cause. For example, one participant wrote "I have to wear my game hat. It is a blue hat with the white K on the front. I wear it to the games as well as when I watch the games on television. When they are getting beat I turn the hat around backwards to help them start a rally" (#3—3/22).

Another participant wrote:

> As far as superstitions go I don't have a lucky hat or pregame meal, but I am very superstitious as far as watching UK games. If I'm watching a game and UK starts to do something good, at that moment whatever I did or however I was sitting, I will remain in that same position or continue doing that same action for the rest of the game, as long as they keep playing well. (#2—3/22)

When asked about any superstitions he might have regarding UK basketball games, one participant wrote:

> I don't have any superstitions that I always follow no matter what. But I do like to wear my UK hat (Yes, it is lucky.). When I attend games I also like to have a pre-game beer in the Civic Center. When I watch a game at home, I always sit on the floor in front of the TV. I never sit in a chair. (#6—3/22)

Another participant had some specific rules for watching UK basketball games at home on television. She wrote the following regarding the fans' role in helping the UK team to victory:

If watching a game at home, you should be wearing a UK shirt. If someone comes in to watch the game, and the team suddenly starts playing badly, that person is asked to leave the room (inherited this superstition from my dad!). (#4—3 / 22)

Many of our participants made note of special attire they wore when watching UK basketball games. For these fans, this attire seemed to take on a uniform-like quality. In essence, their UK game watching attire took on the role of a uniform worn by a team member while serving as a superstitious aid to the UK team. For example, when asked about any superstitions she might hold, one participant wrote:

I like to wear something "UK blue" and my UK accessories. I usually watch the game with my best friends at their house or at home if it's a late game on ESPN. I really don't have any superstitions. (#7—3 / 22)

In preparing for the 1998 Final Four semi-final game, another participant reported "I also broke out the UK shorts and UK jersey that I wear for Final Fours only now" (#6—3 / 28). Finally, another participant who was a member of the UK Pep Band while attending UK wrote:

I usually wear a Kentucky sweatshirt or t-shirt on the day of games. However, I did have one unusual superstition. I had two blue and white shakers that I took with me to games as a member of the band. I attached one to the end of my trombone slide. I kept the other in my back pocket. I remember sitting on the bus the afternoon before the Duke game thinking, "I forgot one in the hotel." We were already enroute to the Spectrum and couldn't turn around. I was so superstitious about that shaker (or pompom) that for awhile I thought that it was the reason we lost. (#5—3 / 22)

In summary, UK fans see themselves as helping the UK basketball team to victory in several different ways. The first way is through traditional behaviors associated with being a fan. These behaviors include activities such as cheering, supporting, and motivating. A second, less traditional, means of helping the UK team is through any number of different and unique superstitious behaviors that in actuality have little or nothing to do with the success or failure of the team. A third mechanism of team assistance that emerged built on the earlier discussion of the team member role. Some of our participants made a conscious effort to select attire for UK games that took on a uniform-like quality. The uniform-like quality of their attire served to unite them with the team while serving as a means of fulfilling a superstitious behavior. Although these fans in some cases recognized that their superstitions or quirky behaviors probably had little to do with the outcome of the game, these patterned and habitual behaviors were still enacted.

Social Events Surrounding Games

Another key aspect of the fanatic's role pertains to the social dimensions of the activities associated with being a fan. Earlier work has recognized the importance of the social aspects of fan consumption behavior. For example, Holt (1995) identified socializing and communing as the two main activities associated with consumption as play. In our conceptualization of fanatical consumption, the social context of the fanatic's role plays a key part in the life of many of our participants. This is especially true during the month of March when the NCAA Tournament is being held. Themes associated with the fan's role in creating social events surrounding the game include planning and coordination, preparation, treatment of the game as a social event, participation in postgame social activities, and the nonsocial role.

Planning and Coordination.   Some of our participants take the role of planning and coordinating social events associated with game days very seriously. They view the planning and coordinating of social activities as a key part of their role associated with UK basketball. For example, one of our participants wrote of her duties as a social event planner and coordinator repeatedly throughout the NCAA Tournament.

I made reservations on 3/3 for a group of us at Willie's restaurant to watch the game. My friends and I always watch the first game there and sit at the same table every year. I will wear my traditional UK outfit there (KY blue stirrup pants, turtleneck, and musical cardigan and matching KY blue shoes and other accessories). (#7—3/6)

I made reservations for the same group of us to watch the game at Barleycorn's. (#7—3/12)

I made my famous cookies for game day for the party at my best friend's house. (#7—3/14)

Preparation.   Earlier in our discussion of the emergent theme of game participation, we discussed the sub-theme of the informational role. Although gathering information is clearly a pervasive aspect of fanatical behavior for many of our respondents, another aspect of game preparation emerged in the course of our data analysis as well. For several of our participants, socializing was an important aspect of their game preparation activities. Specifically, for some of our fanatical participants, alcohol played a large role in the social activities associated with UK basketball game day. For example, one respondent wrote the following regarding his preparation for the Final Four games that were held on Saturday evening:

> Started drinking around 2:30 preparing for the game, where I decided I would watch the game at my fraternity house. . . . Got really drunk and partied with all the other drunks down on the corner of Woodland and Euclid. Got home pretty early to catch the end of the Utah upsetting of UNC. (#2—3/28)

And the championship game held on Monday night:

> Went to class all day, and around 6:30 came home and started getting ready for the game. Went back to the Fraternity house to watch the game, so I would be close to Woodland and Euclid. . . . Went to Woodland and Euclid and partied till latenight. Thought it was a great game and can't believe that UK won their 7th National Championship. (#2—3/30)

Another respondent wrote the following regarding her preparation for the final game:

> My friends and I got to Two Keys Tavern at noon. We began playing drinking games. We reserved the last table in the bar. We had 9 $\frac{1}{2}$ hours to drink and wait for the game to start. (#14—3/30)

Treatment of the Game as a Social Event.   For many UK basketball fans, besides being athletic competitions, UK games are considered social events. Holt (1995) noted the importance of communing and socializing to consumption behavior for fans attending an athletic event. Our data suggest that the social aspects of fanatical consumption are possibly even more important for fans who are unable to attend the event in person. For example, one of our participants wrote the following when asked about any superstitions she might have regarding UK basketball:

> I don't necessarily have any superstitions, more like traditions. For every big game, I go to Two Keys Tavern to watch it and (hopefully) to celebrate with other UK fans. During the NCAA Tournament at work we have come up with

a few. After our first win in the Tournament we all decided to wear the same shirts for every game, hoping that they are good luck. We sat in the same seats for every game. My manager wouldn't let a bartender off work tonight because he worked every other tournament night, and we have won. (#7—3/22)

Similarly, when asked to describe her feelings when UK won the NCAA title in 1996, one of our respondents wrote:

PURE ELATION!! I had been boasting all year that UK would definitely win the championship and I did *not* want to have to eat my words. Traditionally, my friends have a party for every UK game and this night was no exception. As soon as they won, we called our friend who lives in Lexington and told him that he had to stand in line the next morning for the victory celebration tickets. Of course, we woke our friend up with an early morning call and he was able to procure the tickets for us. My friends and I went to Lexington the next afternoon, had a late lunch at O'Charley's and headed to Rupp Arena for the welcome home celebration. That celebration was like no other! The pride and excitement of Kentucky filled the air. It was interesting to hear the players and coaches discuss their NCAA experience. I hated to see the celebration end, but did purchase several clothing items to remember the night and championship. (#7—3/5)

Participation in Post Game Social Activities.   Some of the more memorable experiences our participants wrote of pertained to their postgame social activities. One of the traditions associated with big UK basketball victories is the postgame rendezvous of fans at the corner of Euclid and Woodland Avenues, an intersection a few blocks from campus. This intersection is flooded with celebrating UK fans after big victories. Several of our participants wrote of their postgame experiences at this intersection following the 1996 NCAA Championship game.

It was a tough game, but we won. I remember getting a chill down my back when they had clinched it. . . . We heard a noise coming from downtown Lexington. Campus had turned into a party. We drove down to join the crowd in anticipation of further success. . . . Again, I had chills. My eyes actually watered. I thought back to my undergraduate days. . . . As I watched us win, the final seconds actually were anti-climactic as I had run through the previous cycle of emotions. That did not, however, impede me from enjoying the celebration in downtown Lexington. (#5—3/4)

It was a strange feeling of elation with emotion as I saw sixteen years of heartache and tears replaced by this joy. . . . Afterwards, we joined the mob of students at the corner of Euclid and Woodland Ave. While this was a real thrill, it seemed that emotionally I hit my peak at the time when I flashed back to all the prior years. The tension had gone but the initial thrill of victory had hit. It was an unbelievable evening all around. (#5—3/5)

The 1996 National Championship game celebration. We began our festivities at Two Keys Tavern at 3:00 P.M. that afternoon. We remained at 2 Keys until the end of the game, at which time a guy next to us purchased 10 bottles of champagne. We toasted to the CATS victory and headed out to the corner of Euclid and Woodland. I had a great time. However, the drunks got out of control. People began to throw glass bottles and light the street on fire. At this point, my girlfriend and I walked 2 miles back to our apartment. It was awesome! (#14—3/4)

We were with many other UK students at the "World Famous Two Keys Tavern." There were several TV stations present and my friends and I were interviewed several times. It was so crowded that it was nearly impossible to get a drink. After the game, we headed to celebration corner (Euclid and Woodland). It was crazy!!! I have never seen anything like it. One of my friend's cars got overturned. Crowd control from the police was horrible. Glass bottles were flying everywhere. Some of my friends (not me) showed their chests while standing on shoulders. It was very similar to Mardi Gras or the Derby Infield, but crazier. (#14—3/5)

And the 1998 NCAA Championship game:

It was a tough game the whole way through. However, we came back after getting 12 behind. We are the national champions! I cannot believe it. . . . With one minute left and UK up by 7, I couldn't sit or stand still. I was so excited I didn't know what to do. (#5—3/30)

Called home to talk to my parents (and wish my mom a happy B-day). Then I went to the intersection of Euclid and Woodland Ave. to celebrate with 11,000 friends of mine. I had a couple of victory cigars. This is one of the greatest feelings in the world, and words cannot adequately describe the euphoria. (#5—3/30)

We ran out of the Keys after the buzzer onto the street. My friends and I had our picture taken by the newspapers. I proceeded to walk 2 blocks down the crowded street with her standing on my shoulders. (I wasn't feeling much pain by this point and time.) We fell down a couple of times. We then got separated from the rest of our group. We hung out at celebration corner until we got tired of being pushed around. We walked back to Tolly Ho and ate *lots* of food. We left campus about 2:30 A.M. and things were still really wild. It was an exciting, fun, satisfying, crazy, night! (#14—3/30)

Nonsocial Role.   Interestingly, although for many of our participants UK basketball is a social event, for some of our participants, watching UK basketball is a solitary activity or an activity that is engaged in with only a limited number of other fans. Several of our participants wrote of the nonsocial aspects of their support for UK. For example, when asked to describe his pregame activities, one respondent wrote: "I did the usual pre-game newspaper analysis and watched ESPN. I also took calls inviting me to a couple of parties for the game. As usual, I prefer to watch alone . . . " (#6—3/15). When this respondent reported with whom he watched the game, he wrote: "None, even though I'm always asked to go to a bar or party to watch the game I like to watch UK by myself" (#6—3/7). Another respondent described where he watched the tournament games as follows: "I usually don't like to watch UK games anywhere else except in my house" (#2—3/7), and "Sat in my family room where I watch all UK games" (#2—3/8).

Reasons for watching UK basketball alone varied. For example, some of our participants held the superstition that UK played better when they watched the game at home by themselves. Others noted that they like to watch UK basketball games alone because when watching, they like to study the game and immerse themselves in the action. They reported that this is simply impossible when watching the game in a social setting.

Others acknowledged that they are simply so intense during a game that the social activity enjoyed by some is a distraction from the game for them. For example, one of our respondents wrote the following regarding the UK–Duke game played on March 21, 1998, which he watched at home.

I was extremely nervous prior to game. The way Duke came out and took a lead on UK, I knew it would be tough to come back. When they got 17 points behind in second half I thought it was over. I had to go in my office and watch by myself because I was so irritable to others. The feeling of believing started edging back every time they cut the lead. There were yells of excitement in my office as well as downstairs. It could not have been any sweeter revenge than the way this happened. As in 1992, the win was in their hands and we took it away as they did to us then.

As the game ended, there were a lot of cheers and yells in the house. My son and daughter took turns jumping in my arms with the excitement of the win. The telephone rang off the hook to see if I had survived the win. People know how intense a fan I am. I listened to Billy Packer eat his words about how UK was just not strong enough. Take this one to the ACC archives Billy. Listened to the post-game and watched highlights several times on ESPN and CNN. (#3—3/21)

Fan Contests

Although one generally associates fanaticism with the ardent support of a sports team, our data suggest that there may be a number of other contests in the minds of sports fans associated with the actual athletic competition. In addition to the athletic contest, other contests mentioned by our participants and described below include the fan support contest, the traditional powers contest, the knowledge contest, the grief giving contest, and the adversity contest.

Athletic Contest.   Not surprisingly, the contest that is first and foremost in the mind of many UK basketball fans is the game itself. When asked about his favorite UK basketball tradition, one of our participants perhaps put it best when he wrote: "The tradition I love most of all is winning" (#6—3/6).

Fan Support Contest.   A second contest of importance to many of our participants was the fan support contest. This contest seems to exist on two different dimensions. First, for many of our participants it was important that UK had the strongest, most loyal fan following overall and at the various tournament sites. Second, several of our participants wrote of the level of their own personal support for the UK basketball program. One of our participants responded to the question "Who is the biggest Wildcat basketball fan that you know?" as follows:

> It would have to be me! I take great pride in knowing that I'm the biggest Wildcat fan. I'll never miss a game on television unless its out of my control and if its not televised then I'll listen to it on the radio. I'm usually a nervous wreck before any UK game although this past year I was a lot more subdued. (#2—3/29)

Other fans wrote of the fan support contest as it relates to the fan support of competing schools. For example, our participants wrote the following about the SEC Tournament held just before the NCAA Tournament each season.

> Put blue K hat on (game hat). Put UK shirt and jacket on to show our colors. Go to Jock and Jills drinking well to congregate with hundreds of UK fans from all over. Seemed like a large indoor tailgate party. . . . Felt much anxiety about this game as I do everytime we play Arkansas. I would rather lose to just about anyone except Arkansas. . . . I like to be as loud as the Arkansas fans. Relieved this one is over. (#3—3/7)

The 1994 SEC tournament at the Georgia Dome. The final game with Arkansas. The competition of the Cat fans vs. the Arkansas fans to see who can cheer the loudest. The change of emotions of conceding defeat to the excitement of the dramatic overtime win. (#3—3/4)

Traditional Powers Contest.   Many of our participants expressed concern over the success or joy over the lack of success of other top quality basketball programs. Programs that served as focal points in this regard were Duke University, University of North Carolina, and University of Arizona among others. Reasons for focusing on these teams varied. For example, the focus on Duke dates back to the 1992 NCAA Tournament. In this game, Christian Laettner hit what has become known simply as "The Shot" as time expired to knock UK out of the tournament and send Duke to the Final Four.

Our participants' focus on the success, or lack thereof, of the University of North Carolina is based largely on the all-time wins totals of the two schools. At the time our data were collected, the UK basketball program held a narrow lead in the number of all-time wins for a basketball program over the University of North Carolina. The competition for the highest number of all-time victories is viewed as a very important contest by many of our participants.

Obviously, I did not want Arizona to win and I'm happy that they'll be watching the games at home this weekend! I saw just a little of the NC-Conn game, but I was rooting for UConn. I hate North Carolina! Even though Dean Smith is no longer the coach, I hate the fact that he broke Rupp's winning records. (#7—3/21)

Perhaps two of the greatest games in NCAA basketball tournament history have been played between Duke and UK. The first of these games occurred in the 1992 NCAA Tournament. In this game, Christian Laettner hit "The Shot" as time expired to knock UK out of the tournament and send Duke to the Final Four. The second game occurred during the 1998 NCAA Tournament and ended in a dramatic UK come from behind victory. This win sent UK to the Final Four and knocked Duke out of the tournament. Nearly every participant wrote passionately about the 1992 Duke–UK game and its impact on them, then and now. For example, one of the participants was a member of the UK Pep Band during the 1991 to 1992 basketball season. He wrote the following about the immediate impact of the loss to Duke:

The loss against Duke was the most disappointing event for me. UK, comprised of only one NBA player, played Duke, which had 4. The teams played in one of the greatest games ever. It was tight the whole way through. Duke shot at least 60% in the 1st half but only lead by 2 points. The game went to overtime but Kentucky lost on a last second buzzer beater by Duke's Christian Laettner.

I was at that game in the pep band. I remember the feeling of overwhelming elation when we went up by 1, then shock and sorrow after we lost. I remember the people of Philadelphia expressing their sentiment after that game. The bums didn't even ask us for money that night. We snuck on to the roof of the hotel and played "My Old Kentucky Home" that night. I just remember being depressed for about one week. I felt like doing nothing for 1 week. When I did, I was just going through the motions and not really into it. (#5—3/12)

Another participant who was a student in 1992 during the first UK-Duke game wrote the following when asked about his most memorable UK basketball game.

The most memorable game would be the 1992 game vs. Duke in the Regional Final. I remember it most because CBS won't let us UK fans forget—the shot has been on CBS' college basketball intro ever since. The night of the game also was on my birthday and I was hosting a huge birthday/UK game party. We were all so fired up during the game and especially after Sean Woods made his shot. In a way I'm glad Duke won because some of us probably would have been arrested that night for the excessive partying. Even though I was disappointed with the result, that team was the biggest over achieving group I have ever seen. They far exceeded anyone's expectations. It was the greatest game I ever saw. I still hate Christian Laettner. (#6—3/17)

Another female participant, age 53, who watched the 1992 Duke game at home on television wrote of the following reaction to that loss: "I sat on the back deck and cried for $\frac{1}{2}$ hour. I can't stand the sight of Christian Laettner to this day. When he stomped Timberlake in the stomach when he was on the floor, I just about put my fist through the TV" (#1—3/27).

In addition to the expected immediate impact such a loss might have on a fan, other participants wrote of much more enduring effects that the 1992 Duke loss and more specifically Christian Laettner's shot had on them. For example, a female participant, age 43, wrote "Losing to the arrogant Duke (and Christian Laettner) just didn't seem fair. It made me not want to watch basketball any more!—and I didn't watch much until recently." In another entry the same participant wrote "The 1992 loss to Duke was the hardest loss I've ever had to bear. (I still won't watch a pro game if Christian Laettner is playing!)" (#4—3/9). When UK and Duke played again in the 1998 NCAA

Tournament, memories of the 1992 game were still vivid for many of our participants. One of our participants wrote the following about the 1998 UK-Duke NCAA Tournament game.

> I went to my parent's house to watch the game. I watched the 1992 game there and must exorcise the demons. . . . I thought UK was done at about the 14 minute mark. . . . I couldn't believe they came back. What a game. . . . I still hate Christian Laettner. (#6—3/22)

In summary, although UK fans have many rivals when it comes to UK basketball, few of these rivals are hated and despised like Duke. Interestingly, when asked about UK's biggest rivals, very few of the participants listed Duke. The list of biggest rivals included teams like Indiana University, Tennessee, Arkansas, and North and South Carolina, but not Duke. So, although the 1992 Duke game was often cited as the single most disappointing event or the event with the biggest negative impact on an individual, Duke is generally not considered to be one of UK's great rivals. It seems that along with a rivalry comes a certain amount of tradition and respect for a program and its fans. In the case of Duke, there is very little evidence of this. Duke and Christian Laettner are seen as enemies to be hated and despised.

Knowledge Contest.   For many of our participants, one of the key characteristics of being a fanatical UK basketball fan involves their level of knowledge concerning the UK basketball program and the game of basketball in general. This knowledge pertains to UK basketball and the sport of basketball in general in the past, present, and future. When asked to describe what it means to be a Wildcat fan, one of our participants wrote:

> It means you're knowledgeable not only about UK basketball history but about *basketball* too. It means you are a fan whether we win or lose. I guess there's some arrogance about being a Wildcat fan because we're the #1 basketball program in NCAA history (most wins; most NCAA appearances). (#4—3/21)

One of the key ways in which our participants demonstrated their basketball knowledge was through predicting the outcome of NCAA Tournament games. Although the ultimate focus of UK fans is on the success of UK, many of our participants were also involved in NCAA pools. These contests are viewed as a competition of basketball knowledge. Interestingly, some of our participants expressed feelings of conflict when filling out their NCAA brackets. This conflict revolved around being loyal to UK and predicting them to win the entire tournament while being realistic in their predictions. Others simply acknowledged that a true UK fan will always pick UK to win the NCAA Tournament. In reflecting on his selections for the NCAA Tournament brackets, one participant wrote: "Of course I always pick UK as champion and work backwards" (#6—3/9).

Throughout the tournament participants periodically reflected on the status of their tournament brackets and their demonstration of basketball knowledge. For example, participants wrote, "My NCAA bracket is looking awful" (#6—3/13), and "My b-ball pools are shot after all of the upsets today" (#7—3/12).

Grief Giving Contest. For a number of our participants it was extremely important for UK to be successful in relative terms. That is, in their minds, the success of UK was partially determined by whether UK proceeded further in the tournament than other traditional basketball powers or other teams in their locale. For example, several of our participants living in the greater Cincinnati area expressed great concern over whether UK would be relatively more or less successful than the University of Cincinnati (UC) basketball team. The source of this concern was that if UC proceeded further in the tournament than UK, they would receive a great deal of grief and aggravation from friends and co-workers, whereas if UK advanced further than UC in the tournament, they would be able to "dish out" grief and aggravation to their friends and colleagues who supported UC. For example, the following excerpts were included in the journals of participants from the Cincinnati area.

> It would kill me if UC goes farther in the tournament that UK! I would never hear the end of it! I hate to admit it, but it is a good possibility if they can get past Utah. . . . I truly believe that anything is possible in March and if they want the NCAA championship bad enough, they can attain the goal. GO CATS! (#7—3/9)

> I went to the UC-UL game tonight and UC, unfortunately, won. I repeatedly hear from UC fans that since they beat UL and UL beat us, UC would definitely defeat UK. I'm so sick of hearing this! UK has a much tougher schedule than UC and more rounded conference to play in. (#7—3/5)

> Since I live in the Cincinnati area, I am happy that UC lost. UC fans are so preoccupied with UC vs. UK. It's great to see them knocked out again. My brackets are a mess with the Big 10 and Pac 10 success and the SEC stinking it up. (#6—3/14)

> UC looked flat. . . . I couldn't believe that the W. Virginia player shot a 3-pointer to win the game. I thought that they would go for the tie. I'm glad that they

didn't! Today was a great day! I can't wait to see the people at work on Tuesday night to rub this loss in! (#7—3 / 15)

Participants also wrote of similar concerns regarding other teams playing in the tournament against UK and against other opponents as well. For example, one participant wrote the following concerning the UK victory over Duke in the 1998 NCAA Tournament:

I would have been totally crushed if UK lost to Duke, not to mention all of the teasing I would get from a loss. I was screaming and jumping up and down in front of the TV (as was everyone else!) the last 5 minutes of the game. What a turn-around! All of a sudden, we could do no wrong! We hit several "3-pointers" to bring us back into the game and finally take the lead! Duke was definitely shocked and stunned! I think that the Duke players are nasty! They were acting so cocky because they were ahead by so much, but they counted us out and fell prey to our pressure. It was a big mistake for Duke to use all of their time-outs. I think that really hurt them in those last 5 minutes. I told my boyfriend that free throw shooting would be very important to the outcome of this game and I was right. (I couldn't believe Allen Edwards missed a critical free throw, even though he did play very well.) Needless to say, I was euphoric after the game. Victory is sweet! (#7—3 / 22)

Another participant wrote of the grief exchanged with others throughout the tournament:

I read the paper and watched the pregame shows. I also talked to a lot of co-workers who were giving me crap about Utah. (#6—3 / 30)

Finally, when asked to write of their reactions to the 1996, 1997, and 1998 NCAA Championship games (a UK win, loss, and win, respectively), participants provided the following comments. Interestingly enough, when asked of their feelings regarding each of these games, participants at some point reflected on the amount of grief they either dished out or experienced.

The 1996 champs were awesome. . . . 1996 was the best I remember. I had a lot of fun that year. I was in my final year at IU so I had a good time with all my classmates who were avid IU fans. They were just waiting for UK to stumble so they could give me grief. It never happened. (#6—3 / 15)

A great feeling of sadness overcame me. I just couldn't believe that we were losing and couldn't pull the win out. Arizona couldn't miss a shot and it seemed that we couldn't make a shot. I had been bragging to all my friends that we would repeat as national champions and it was so disappointing that we didn't. I received a lot of phone calls from my friends. Some of them were sympathetic and others were not so nice. They had a great season and I was proud of them for their efforts, but it was a real let down after the 1996 championship. I was at my best friend's house and I spent the night there. I went to bed right after the game. I just couldn't watch Arizona celebrate. It was too depressing for me. (#7—3/25)

Obviously, we are the BEST! I always want UK to be the national champion, but after some of their losses this year, I really wasn't sure that they could pull it out. . . . Tubby could run for governor and easily win. There's nothing more important to a KY fan than the national championship and the bragging rights that go along with it. . . . I cannot wait to "rub it in" to my UC friends and I'm going to do it a lot! Victory is sweet and life is good in Kentucky! (#7—3/30)

Adversity Contest.   The trials endured to support UK are worn as a badge of honor by avid UK fans. Our participants wrote of many of their trials and tribulations associated with getting tickets to UK games, traveling to UK games, and attending UK games. When asked about her most memorable experience involving UK basketball, one participant wrote:

My most memorable experience involving UK basketball is the first time I was able to attend basketball ticket distribution as a freshman attending UK. My best friend and I decided to stand in line for tickets because they were distributing U.K.–UL tickets and we definitely did not want to miss that game! We got up very early (6 or 7 A.M.) and walked down to Memorial Coliseum for the tickets. Little did we know that first time! You stood in line to get into the Coliseum and were then issued a number. Then after everyone was assembled in line by number, we were sent back outside to wait in line again for another couple of hours. My friend and I did not bring anything but ourselves (no money, no homework, no games, no blankets and it was cold!). People came prepared to "camp out" for tickets and we learned from them to bring the necessary items for the next time. We made some interesting friends while waiting, but best of all, we got lower level tickets (Section #31, row E) to the game and vowed always to attend distribution for the great seats we had to the games. One can get very spoiled sitting in those seats, but *any* seat in Rupp Arena is a great one! (#7—3/4).

Many participants wrote of difficulties experienced and hardships endured while traveling to UK basketball games. For example, when asked about his most memorable experience involving UK basketball, one father participating in our study wrote of such an experience with his son.

...the trip to see UK vs. Ole Miss in February 1996 with my eight year old son. Hitting the road at 4:30 A.M. traveling six hours through the snow and ice covered roads to Oxford, Mississippi. Watching the excitement of my son being able to get close to the players at courtside. The excitement of a packed small arena away from Lexington was also a new experience. (#3—3/4)

Other participants described similar hardships.

I think it is because I make an effort to attend games every year. Everyone here watches all the games, but I try to go to a few. I even try to plan my business travel around the games. I've made it to games when the interstates have been shut down due to weather. Another reason is my habit to watch games alone so I'm not interrupted. (#6—3/26)

My only trip to an SEC tournament. The tournament was in Lexington. We had a terrible snow storm. We went up a little bit early and got there before the storm. Some of our friends didn't make it. Kentucky "killed" all opponents by a large margin. The Hog Calls slowed down after we clobbered them. (#1—3/4)

One of our participants, who was a UK undergraduate student at the time of our data collection, went on a spring break camping trip during the first week of the NCAA Tournament. He described the lengths to which he went to hear the UK game on the radio while camping.

At this point I knew there was no way I was going to be able to watch the UK–St. Louis game, b/c we were in the middle of mountains, 5 miles away from our car. (#2—3/14)

I was very excited to hear that UK won b/c knowing that the game is over, but not knowing whether or not UK won was one of the worst feelings in the world. We all celebrated around the campfire. (#2—3/14)

Found out what time UK and UCLA played and an hour before the game myself and 3 others hiked down the side of a mountain in complete darkness and hiked about 1 ½ miles to our motor home where we drove it to an open field where we could pick up the game on radio. . . . After the game, we drove back to our campsite and informed the other 6 people with us that UK won "big." Everyone was excited and we spent the rest of the night partying around the campfire, celebrating UK's win. (#2—3/19)

Role Conflicts Ensuing From the Fan Identity

The role of the UK fan often leads to conflict with other aspects of life. Two prominent sources of role conflict experienced by many of our participants were related to family and work issues.

Fan–Family Role Conflict. Fan–family role conflict generally arose in situations where the participant experienced conflicting expectations regarding his or her role as an avid UK fan versus as a family member. When asked why she was considered an avid UK fan by others one of our participants wrote:

> My life revolves around UK's basketball schedule. I make sure that I can either go to or watch all of the games. I went so far as to bring a mini-TV to one of my friend's wedding receptions to watch the game. I was the most popular person there besides the wedding couple. . . . (#7—3/26)

The same participant experienced fan–family role conflict during the 1998 NCAA Tournament when a major horse race was scheduled at the same time as the UK semi-final game versus Utah. The participant wrote the following about this predicament:

> My boyfriend bought tickets to the Jim Beam stakes and we are going to the race track all day with one small (MAJOR!) conflict—UK tips off at 5:42 P.M. and the race goes off at 5:40 P.M. I'm going to bring my little TV to the track, because I don't want to miss any of the game. I wanted to leave the track early, but that's not fair to my boyfriend. We will be racing home after the stake race to finish watching the game. (#7—3/28)

Interestingly, this conflict was resolved when the stakes race was cancelled due to inclement weather.

The fan–family role conflict experienced by our participants as a result of UK basketball arose from a variety of sources. Participants experienced fan–family role conflict when UK basketball games took place during their children's athletic events:

> I had a junior pro game to coach out of town. I got back home right at tipoff time. I read all the sports pages about the UK vs. UCLA game. (*Louisville Courier, Evansville Courier* and *USA Today*). Listened to pre-game show on way home. (#3—3/19)

Participants reported conflicts that arose as a result of family members telephoning and interrupting the UK game:

> I was furious that a friend and my sister called me during the game! I said, "Don't you know the game is on?!" They didn't. (#4—3/7)

Participants also reported family role conflicts when family vacations and UK basketball placed simultaneous demands on their time:

> We spent the day at MGM and Magic Kingdom in Disney World—hurried back to watch the game. (Left Magic Kingdom early to get back by 10 P.M.) We didn't get to see much of the game! When we got ahead by 20 points the TV station switched to Valpo vs. U. of R.I. (#4—3/20)

Finally, respondents even reported conflicting demands that arose between UK basketball games and church attendance. For example, one respondent wrote:

> Ate breakfast and went to Sunday School; skipped the service and sermon to get home for the game. . . . The 2 lop-sided wins should send a message to the NCAA Committee! (#4—3/8)

Fan–Work Role Conflict.   A second major source of role conflict arose from issues pertaining to work. Many of our participants experienced conflict between their work roles and their UK fan roles during the tournament. This was particularly evident in the early rounds of the NCAA Tournament because many of those games are played on Thursday and Friday afternoons. Several of our participants wrote the following about UK tournament games that conflicted with work schedules:

> This is a work day. We called in for lunch to be delivered at work. We took a two hour lunch to watch the entire game. . . . I had to go back to work. I still went back to the break room to see other scores every 45 minutes or so. Also to see highlights of UK's game to see what the sports commentators were saying. (#3—3/12)

> Had to work at a special function for my job. We had the radio on listening to the pre-game show. My shift was done 30 minutes before game time, just enough time to get home get my game hat on and plop down in front of the TV. (#3—3/14)

I was at work doing normal things. We piped the game to my office through the Kentucky Telecare Network, calling it an "experiment in fast motion video over the T 1/2 lines." Aren't euphemisms great? (#5—3/12)

I was upset that I had to attend a meeting. I had planned to take a little TV to work or take a long lunch. My boss, who is not a UK fan, had the nerve to visit a customer on Friday afternoon and take me.... I watched the Arkansas/Tenn game because it is UK's next opponent.... Glad to see the fast pace of the Ark/Tenn game. These guys will be tired tomorrow. (#6—3/6)

I brought a small TV to work to keep tabs on the games. (#6—3/12)

I have to work during the game tonight. I hope that I'm not busy so I can watch it without interruptions.... I wasn't happy that I had to work tonight, because I like to focus all of my attention on the CATS, but I couldn't get out of working. I did see most of it though.... I'm looking forward to Sunday's game to get our revenge against Duke! (#7—3/19)

Old UK fans may disagree, but the 1996 championship team was the best.... I was suppose to have a class that night but my professor had tickets and cancelled.... (#5—3/15)

Social Connectedness Ensuing From the Fan Identity

Among the main benefits associated with being avid UK basketball fans are the bonds they experience as a result of their passion for UK basketball. There are several different types of bonds that emerged through the interpretation of our data. UK basketball serves as a bonding mechanism along the following dimensions for our participants: within family, in state pride, in travels elsewhere, and with their youth.

UK Basketball and Family Bonds.   UK basketball is a family affair. Parents and grandparents pass their love for the Wildcats down to subsequent generations. UK fans fondly recollect experiences from years gone by that link UK basketball and loved ones. One participant wrote of her grandfather passing along his love for the Wildcats to her when she was just a young girl.

Growing up in this part of the country basketball is just part of your life....
But while I was somewhat aware of UK glory days earlier, my grandfather
really got me interested in the Cats when I was around 10 or 11 (early 50's). We
both followed closely (just radio in those days) and made bets with each other.
Being terribly naïve I bet that first year after the suspension year they would

go undefeated—and they did! So I was hooked. These of course were still the Rupp years and there were still great teams to follow. (#9—3/7)

When asked who had the biggest impact on you becoming a Wildcat fan, more than half of the participants in our study listed their father as the single person most responsible for their fanaticism about UK basketball. Other participants listed their parents, mother, grandparents, or siblings as principle influences. One participant wrote:

My dad was definitely the biggest impact on me becoming a Wildcat fan. I am a short person and was short for my age as a kid. My dad taught me how to play basketball and we would watch all the games together. In the middle of the winter at halftime of the games we would go outside and play. I was always Kyle Macy. My dad would take me to games in Rupp Arena whenever he could get tickets. It was always a great time that I will always cherish. (#18—3/7)

Similarly, another participant wrote the following when asked who the biggest influence was on his becoming a UK basketball fan:

I would have to say my father. . . . I remember watching many games with him and learning the way of the game with him. . . . For his knowledge and wisdom, my father had the biggest impact on my becoming a UK fan. (#5—3/7)

Although subsequent generations fondly recollect having Wildcat mania passed down to them by parents and grandparents, it is also true that passing along this love for UK is a memorable moment in one's life. When asked about his most memorable experience involving UK basketball, one father participating in our study wrote of such an experience with his son.

. . . the trip to see UK vs. Ole Miss in February 1996 with my eight year old son. Hitting the road at 4:30 A.M. traveling six hours through the snow and ice covered roads to Oxford, Mississippi. Watching the excitement of my son being able to get close to the players at courtside. The excitement of a packed small arena away from Lexington was also a new experience. (#3—3/7)

A love for UK basketball links generations and is often a very memorable and cherished part of the life of a Wildcat fan. In this respect, being a UK basketball fan would seem to be a very healthy activity as is it creates and strengthens bonds that may not have existed otherwise.

UK Basketball and State Pride Bonds.   UK basketball fans have a great pride in the basketball program of their university. Further, the successes of the UK basketball program are often generalized to the Commonwealth of Kentucky. For example, after UK won the 1998 NCAA title, one of our participants wrote:

> To see the emotion of all of the players was an overwhelming feeling for me. They deserved this championship because they never, ever gave up. I couldn't be happier for all of them and the entire state of Kentucky. (#7—3/30)

Another respondent wrote the following regarding her favorite UK basketball tradition:

> Maybe we take it too seriously sometimes, but there is a real sense of pride throughout the state and with UK fans living elsewhere. They really support the team with their presence wherever they play. (I can't personally do this but I'm happy others can). They remember great teams and individuals. In earlier years this state had little else to be proud of sometimes so having a young guy from a small town in the hills make a big success was major to his town. Athletics in general is more of a business now but it's still important. Big Blue fans just don't forget and they truly care. Love and pride in the Cats is a unifying factor in the state. (#9—3/6)

UK Basketball and Traveling Bonds.   One of the unique aspects of being a UK fan is that no matter where you travel, if you find another UK fan you are bound to have found someone with whom you have an instant bond. Weinberg (1997) wrote of traveling Europe and running into the UK basketball team and its traveling entourage during the summer of 1995. He marveled that even in Italy one could connect with strangers based solely on the common bond of UK basketball. Similarly, one of our participants wrote of this bond as he described what it means to him to be a UK basketball fan.

> I can be in another town wearing a UK shirt and invariably someone always comes up to speak with me. This comradery solidifies my feelings of the UK faithful. (#5—3/21)

UK Basketball and Bonds with Their Youth.   Most of the participants felt especially strong levels of identification with UK basketball teams from their youth, particularly their days as college students. The common bond of knowing that these players were on campus attending classes when the participants were seemed to strengthen feelings of being a part of the team. When asked about her favorite UK team, one female participant, age 59, directly acknowledged this in writing "It's very special to have a championship team when you are a student yourself so I guess my favorite was the 1958 NCAA champ . . . " (#9—3 / 10) Similarly, another current male student wrote:

> My most memorable experience with UK basketball was when they won the national championship [in 1996]. Although there are a lot of memorable experiences involving UK, this is probably the most memorable because I was a student at UK and felt a part of the team winning. I was able to celebrate with everyone in the streets at Woodland and Euclid. Also the time prior to UK winning the championship, the last one that they won is 1978 I was only 1 year old, so this championship meant a lot to me because of how much I love UK basketball and how long I've followed them. (#2—3 / 4)

When asked about her favorite UK player and team, one of our respondents wrote:

> As a group, I felt closest to the senior group from 1975 (Grevey. . .). I started college at UK in 1973 and got to see all of their home games. They brought so much excitement to the campus! I guess Kevin Grevey, with his beautiful left-handed shot, was my favorite of the group. It was heartbreaking to see them lose to UCLA in Wooden's final game in the NCAA final. (#4—3 / 8)
>
> (I'll never forget being up in Dayton when they upset #1 IU to win the Mideast Regional!). The students were crazy about them and all the players had fan following (I was a member of "Grevey's Gorillas"). (#4—3 / 10)

Another respondent wrote this about her favorite UK player:

> Kyle Macy is one of my favorite players in UK history. He is the first player I really remember following in the games. (I was still in high school when he played at UK.). . . One day, of course, I think it would be great for him to be the head coach at UK, . . . I'll follow him wherever he coaches or in whatever else he pursues. (#7—3 / 8)

Life Lessons and Decisions Tied to the Fan Identity

Wildcat Mania stretches beyond the basketball court and reaches into the lives of true Wildcat fans. Three emergent themes were identified in this regard.

UK Basketball as a Life Lesson.   Several of the participants in our study wrote about lessons of life they learned through UK basketball. Many UK basketball fans take events from UK basketball and transfer those experiences into their own lives. Often these lessons are a result of UK basketball events occurring quite some time ago. UK fans take the experiences of their team and transfer these experiences into their own lives. Lessons reported by participants included the ideas to "never give up," "stay positive and determined and it will pay off," and "you can't be a fair weather fan."

Several participants wrote of the UK–LSU game played in 1994. In this game, UK was down by 31 points in the second half and came back to win. When asked "Which UK basketball game had the biggest positive effect on you?," one participant wrote: "It showed me that staying positive and being determined will pay off in the end" (#10—3/13). In response to the same question, other participants wrote:

> Probably the never give up game of February 1994. The greatest comeback of all time. UK was 31 points down against LSU and came back to win 99–95. The never gave up playing defense, pressing and hitting threes they fought their way back when everyone pretty much thought it was hopeless. So no matter how bleak it seems in life there's always a chance and you should NEVER GIVE UP. (#18—3/13)

> The game against LSU when UK came back from 31 points down in the second half and won. I had given up and was so upset that UK was getting beat so bad that I had gone to my room to watch the rest of the game by myself. It was the most amazing game that I had ever seen, that team played so hard to fight back and it paid off in the end. (#2—3/13)

> I believe this game was in 1994 or 1995 vs. LSU in New Orleans when UK posted a 31 point comeback win in the 2nd half. I remember it being the late game on ESPN. I was actually going to turn off the TV and go to bed—something I never do. When UK started the comeback I had my hand on the "off" switch. I'm glad I kept the faith. If anything, the long term effect is that the game is never over until the horn sounds. This is the case for either team playing. I watch every game until the bitter end. (#6—3/13)

Another participant wrote of the same basic life lesson learned from the 1995 SEC Tournament finals in a game UK played against Arkansas.

> A lot of the Cats' fans left but I told myself I had to stay with them all the way to the end. After their next come back the game was theirs. I was proud to be a Wildcat fan and it taught me to never give up on the Cats because it is not over until the final tick of the clock. (#3—3/13)

Other participants took lessons they learned from UK basketball and transferred them to their outlook on life. For example, when asked about her favorite UK basketball team, one participant responded:

> The 1992 team. The Untouchables. . . . They had the game won but Christian Laettner made an unbelievable shot. He should not have been in the game after kicking Timberlake he should have been kicked out. . . . As I have heard coaches all my life say as well as Pitino, as long as you work hard, good things will happen. (#3—3/10)

UK Basketball and Major Life Decisions.   Several of the participants noted the impact of UK basketball on major life decisions they had made. The strength of the loyalty these fans hold for UK is evident in the entries of several participants. It is worth noting that there was not a question included in the journal that specifically addressed the issue of UK basketball and major life decisions. Yet several of the participants wrote on this topic. The impact of UK basketball on major life decisions included medical school choices, job changes, and career decisions.

A female physician noted that UK basketball was one of the reasons she attended medical school at UK. She wrote "Part of why I stayed at UK (nine years of college including medical school) was to go to the games (students went free in those days). We'd wait in line for tickets and usually had seats in the first 5–10 rows!" (#4—3/26). Another participant whose chosen career is in banking was considering changing employers. Ultimately, one of the decision criteria revolved around UK basketball. He wrote the following:

> The best ticket story is in 1994 I was contemplating changing employers for advancement opportunities, the pay was equal at both places. The new employer said he would add SEC tickets to my package if I would change. That was four years ago and the tournaments have been great. (#3—3/24)

Finally, one participant wrote of the impact UK basketball, specifically the 1992 Duke game, ultimately had on his chosen career.

> Losing to Duke had the biggest negative effect on me. At the end of that game, I had gone from complete elation to utter depression. It was UK's first tournament off probation and the team was known for giving 110% on the field. I was a junior, and as I've mentioned before, I traveled with the team as a band member. After that game, I remember sitting on the floor of my hotel room in Philadelphia in disbelief. For the next week, I went to classes but halfheartedly. I took the MCAT the next Saturday, but didn't care how I did.

I remember watching the final four and final game thinking we should have been there (it was in Minneapolis). Once the season ended, I had returned to normal (more or less). (#5—3/12)

As is evident from these excerpts, UK basketball often has a tremendous impact on the lives of its fans. The bond associated with UK basketball and its allure impact some fans' major life decisions concerning events such as schools to attend, jobs to accept, and even professions to pursue.

DISCUSSION AND IMPLICATIONS

The findings of this research provide the first detailed qualitative assessment of fanaticism and its implications for the broader context of life. Six broad themes emerged through the textual data analysis procedures employed.

1. Game participation
2. Social events surrounding games
3. Fan contests
4. Role conflicts ensuing from the fan identity
5. Social connectedness ensuing from the fan identity
6. Life lessons and decisions tied to the fan identity

The nature of these themes provides an indication of the strength and breadth of the impact of fanaticism on individual beliefs, identity, perceptions, role-related issues, social behaviors, and decision-making.

Managerial Implications

There are a number of managerial implications that arise from this chapter. Our chapter provides detailed data with regard to the nature of the attraction fanatical fans feel toward the object of their fanaticism. For sports marketers, as well as marketers in general, who are interested in developing a strong Integrated Marketing Communication (IMC) program, this information should prove to be extremely beneficial. Sports marketers should be able to use the thematic results of our research to develop effective appeals and messages targeted toward potential fans and consumers. In a broader sense, our findings should benefit marketers interested in using the sports marketing vehicle as a means of promoting their product. The rich understanding of fanaticism provided by our chapter suggests appropriate messages and appeals that might be used in an effective IMC program.

Our chapter also is indicative of the importance and viability of pursuing an affinity marketing strategy. Financial services and events marketers, among others, have built on the marketing advantages provided by identifying consumer affinities for sports teams, universities, activities, and lifestyles. Our research provides strong evidence for these and other practitioners of the vast impact that these affinities (or fanatical followings) have on a consumer's life.

The strength and breadth of the impact of fanaticism also speaks to the viability of sponsorship as a promotional tool. Our research indicates that the fanatical feelings and followings of consumers are pervasive throughout their lives. Effectively executed sponsorships can build on and potentially extend these fanatical feelings to the sponsoring brand. This is an issue that has seemingly been understood by marketers for some time; however, our research provides strong evidence of the pervasiveness of the impact of fanaticism on an individual's life.

Research Implications

This research provides the first use of the journaling method in the investigation of consumption issues. The methods employed in this study were ideal for the initial investigation into the issue of fanaticism as it broadly affects a consumer's life. Future researchers might consider using and refining the journaling method in other contexts characterized by fanaticism. For example, it would be interesting to employ the journaling methodology with participants who fanatically follow the sport of NASCAR. Issues of interest might include the nature of the impact of NASCAR fanaticism on consumer decision-making and consumption. The journaling method might also be applied to broader consumer decision-making contexts to investigate loyalty and consumption communities, issues that have been investigated previously through other research methods (Oliver, 1999; Schouton & McAlexander, 1995).

The research issues considered here also merit further examination through other research methods. For example, investigating the issue of fanaticism through survey methods might provide additional insights into the phenomenon. The rigorous development of a psychometrically sound measure of fanaticism is imperative in order for quantitative empirical research to advance in this realm. In a broader sense, the development of sound measures in the field of sports marketing is vital not only to the progress of research on fanaticism but also to the development of the field of sports marketing.

Psychometrically sound measures of constructs relevant to the field of sports marketing will allow for the rigorous investigation of any number of research issues central to the advancement of our knowledge in the field of sports marketing.

REFERENCES

The American Heritage Dictionary (1985). Boston: Houghton Mifflin.

Belk, R. W. (1992, December). Moving possessions: An analysis based on personal documents from the 1847–1869 Mormon migration. *Journal of Consumer Research, 19,* 339–361.

Cialdini, R. B., Borden, R. J., Thorne, A., Walker, M. R., Freeman, S., & Sloan, L. R. (1976). Basking in reflected glory: Three (football) field studies. *Journal of Personality and Social Psychology, 34,* 366–375.

Fisher, R. J., & Wakefield, K. (1998). Factors leading to group identification: A field study of winners and losers. *Psychology and Marketing, 15*(1), 23–40.

Holt, D. B. (1995, June). How consumers consume: A typology of consumption practices. *Journal of Consumer Research, 22,* 1–16.

Oliver, R. L. (1999). Whence consumer loyalty? *Journal of Marketing, 63* (special issuee), 33–44.

Riessman, C. (1991). Beyond reductionism: Narrative genres in divorce accounts. *Journal of Narrative and Life History, 1*(1), 41–68.

Riessman, C. (1993). *Narrative Analysis.* Newbury Park, CA: Sage.

Schouton, J. W., & McAlexander, J. H. (1995, June). Subcultures of consumption: An ethnography of the new bikers. *Journal of Consumer Research, 22,* 43–61.

Spiggle, S. (1994, December). Analysis and interpretation of qualitative data in consumer research. *Journal of Consumer Research, 21,* 491–503.

Tepper, K. (1997). Categories, contexts, and conflicts of consumers' nonconformity experiences. In R. W. Belk (Ed.), *Research in Consumer Behavior* (Vol. 8, pp. 209–245). Greenwich, CT: JAI.

Thompson, C., Locander, W. B., & Pollio, H. R. (1989, September). Putting consumer experience back into consumer research: The philosophy and method of existential-phenomenology. *Journal of Consumer Research, 16,* 133–146.

Weinberg, B. (1997). *Portrait of a Writer as a Young Fan.* Louisville, KY: Sulgrave Press.

"We Are Number One!" The Phenomenon of Basking-in-Reflected-Glory and Its Implications for Sports Marketing

Vassilis Dalakas
Berry College

Robert Madrigal
University of Oregon

Keri L. Anderson
Berry College

Valparaiso, Indiana is the site of Orville Redenbacher's success and home to the Valparaiso University basketball team—the Cinderella team of the Sweet 16 during the 1998 NCAA National Basketball Tournament. The team's success did not go unnoticed in the community; most of the town's 26,000 residents spent their time discussing the team's amazing run and purchasing team apparel. Stores stocking the college's merchandise could not keep the shelves filled; requests came from not only locals but also outside enthusiasts. Even staunch Kansas fans, bitter at the Rhode Island team that ousted them from the tournament, were requesting Valparaiso apparel. An association with a team strong enough to impact an entire town is not uncommon in sports.

People's desire to associate with successful teams and make such an association public is known as *basking-in-reflected-glory* (BIRG). This concept was first introduced by Cialdini et al. (1976). In this chapter, we take a closer look at this phenomenon in the context of sports. First, we describe the original studies that introduced BIRG, then we lay out the theoretical framework that can explain the phenomenon and discuss the conditions that make it more or less likely to emerge, and, finally, we examine its implications for sports marketing.

BASKING-IN-REFLECTED-GLORY: THE ORIGINAL STUDIES

The basic premise of BIRG is that individuals try to associate themselves with other individuals or groups who are successful. In academic research, BIRG was the result of a research program involving three different studies, in the context of college football (Cialdini et al., 1976).

The first study used college students in seven universities with strong Division I football programs (including Michigan, Notre Dame, Ohio State, and Southern California) during the 1973 football season. The study examined the relationship between the outcome of a Saturday football game and students wearing clothing bearing their school's logo or name the following Monday. It was hypothesized that students would be more likely to wear clothes that made their association with the school obvious on the days following a victory. Because of the school's team success, it was expected that students would be more eager to publicize their association with the school. The results confirmed the hypothesis showing that students more often wore clothing with their school's logo or name on Mondays following a victory than on Mondays after a loss or a tie.

The second study was conducted during the 1974 football season using students in a university with a strong football program. Midway through the football season, randomly selected undergraduates were called for short telephone interviews. All interviews began with a survey of general questions about the university. Halfway through the interview, the experimenters informed the subjects either that they performed very well on the survey (personal success condition) or that they performed very poorly (personal failure condition). Then, subjects were asked to describe the outcome of one of their team's specific games, either victory or *non-victory* (loss or tie). The researchers hypothesized that subjects would tend to use "we" describing victories more than losses. They also expected this tendency to be higher among those subjects who had "failed" the survey test. The results confirmed both hypotheses, showing that a sense of personal failure increased the subjects' tendency to associate themselves with a positive source and reduced their tendency to associate with a negative source.

The third study also used students at one university with a major football program, but not the same university as in study 2. Similar to study 2, experimenters randomly called students after their school's football season ended. The experimenters identified themselves as representatives of either an on-campus agency or an agency out-of-state. All students described the outcome of two of their football team's games during the preceding season. One game was an important victory whereas the other was an important non-victory. The researchers hypothesized that subjects would use a "we" response more often when describing a victory and a "non-we" response when describing a non-victory. They also predicted that this tendency would be stronger when the subjects described the outcome to the representatives from the out-of-state agency rather than the ones from their university. Because BIRG was suggested to operate as an ego-management mechanism, the researchers expected that people would be more concerned about the image they portray to outsiders. The findings provided additional support for the phenomenon of BIRG by showing a higher use of "we" (nearly twice as often) to describe a victory rather than a non-victory. However, not significant support was found for the hypothesis that such tendencies would be stronger when interacting with outsiders rather than people of the subjects' own university. It is possible that people saw the game and the victory as a way to "bond" with the people from their own school.

In summary, all three studies by Cialdini et al. (1976) demonstrated people's tendency to engage in behaviors that associated with successful others. The inclination for such BIRG was suggested to originate from fans' perceptions and expectations that others will view them as more successful because of the association with the successful team.

THEORETICAL BACKGROUND OF BASKING-IN-REFLECTED GLORY

From an emotional standpoint, people's desire to associate with successful groups can be traced to the work of Ortony, Clore, and Collins (1988), who explored how human emotions arise. Ortony et al. suggested that, individuals often experience emotions as a result of the behavior and actions of other people or groups with which they are associated. More specifically, when one associates with other groups, successful behavior by these groups reinforces positive emotions for the person, whereas unsuccessful behavior by these groups reinforces negative emotions for the person. People prefer to experience positive emotions more than negative ones; consequently, they would tend to associate with people or groups that are successful rather than unsuccessful.

Heider's classic work on balance theory (1958) has similar implications. The theory maintains that people prefer balance and harmony rather than imbalance. One of the ways that such balance is achieved is through consistency in the attitudes or dispositions people have toward different objects that form unit relations in some way. For example, if one feels very positively about the environment, one would be more likely to feel similarly positive feelings toward companies that have an active environmental agenda.

Success is viewed more positively than failure; therefore, people have a more positive disposition toward successful groups. Consequently, under the premises of balance theory, by associating with successful groups one increases one's chances of being perceived more positively by others. Heider (1958) noted that people like to form a "unit relationship" with others they perceive to be of great worth to them. Therefore, a groups' success increases the "value" of a group to an individual and can increase the strength of a unit formation between others and that specific group.

The work by Ortony et al. (1988) highlighted the affect-like qualities of the phenomenon of BIRG. Other research (Hirt, Zillmann, Erickson, & Kennedy 1992; Wann & Branscombe, 1990) implied that the affective dimension of BIRG is quite strong. Madrigal (1995) conceptualized BIRG as a transient affective state, specific to a sporting event outcome. His findings indicated that although BIRG and enjoyment are both expressions of positive affect, they are not identical constructs. In this light, BIRG is seen as a form of the emotion of pride. In this case, sports fans use the accomplishments of their team, rather than their own actions, to derive a sense of accomplishment and a feeling of pride.

BASKING-IN-REFLECTED-GLORY AND CUTTING-OFF-REFLECTED-FAILURE IN SPORTS

According to Heider's balance theory (1958), which was discussed earlier, if one has a positive disposition toward a specific source, then one would tend to have a similarly positive disposition toward objects that are somehow connected to that source. Therefore, under this theory, by associating with a successful sports team, fans essentially expect that they will appear to be more successful themselves. Based on this premise, Cialdini et al. (1976) proposed that BIRG operates as an ego-enhancement mechanism and results from people's desire to increase their self-esteem.

In 1986, Snyder, Lassegard, and Ford introduced the concept of cutting-off-reflected-failure (CORF), which operates under the same mechanism as BIRG and is essentially its corollary. Also inspired by Heider's balance formulations, the originators of *CORF* suggested that because people value success more than failure, unsuccessful groups have a negative image; therefore, individuals will want to distance themselves from such groups. Consequently, whereas individuals BIRG in order to increase their own image, they may also tend to CORF in order to protect their image from the damage of being associated with unsuccessful others.

In the context of sports, BIRG and CORF can explain how fair-weather fans may follow a team when it is winning but distance themselves from the team in the hard times of losing. Anecdotal evidence regarding the Minnesota Twins baseball team public announcer noticeably illustrates this point. During losing periods, he would introduce the team by saying "ladies and gentlemen, *your* Minnesota Twins," whereas during winning times the introduction would change to "ladies and gentlemen, let's welcome *our* Minnesota Twins!" This tendency is supported by a high correlation between a team's winning record and fan attendance (Baade & Tiehen, 1990). In the months following their 2001 World Series Championship, the Arizona Diamondbacks baseball organization realized immediate benefits of winning the championship with an expected boost of $3.8 million to $4.7 million in season ticket revenue and a similar $4 million to $5 million increase in sponsorship revenue (King, 2002). Interestingly, the organization realized the potential of diminishing BIRGing tendencies once the new season would start; Scott Brubaker, the senior vice president of marketing and sales, noted, "We're trying to maximize what we did in November and strike while it's hot. You're only world champions for a few weeks once the season starts. After that, you're whatever it says you are in the standings" (cited in King, 2002, p. 3).

Because sports allow for a clear distinction between success and failure, winners and losers, they present a context that is very conducive for BIRG and CORF tendencies to emerge. Consequently, sports fans often seem to "jump on the bandwagon" by following teams more when they are successful and trying to publicize their support of the team more after victories. Sloan's comprehensive work on the motives of sports fans (1979) noted that one of the strongest motivations for following sports, in general, is people's desire for achievement and success. The fact that sports usually provide a clear outcome of success or failure reinforces one's desire for achievement. Sports give fans an opportunity for vicarious achievement through specific athletes or teams, every time these athletes or teams compete. In that case, a fan sees the athletes or the team as an extension of him- or herself and views the team's victories as personal victories. More importantly, a fan tends to publicize his or her support of the team and bask in the team's victories, even if his or her contribution to the team's success may be minimal or nonexistent.

THE MODERATING ROLE OF TEAM IDENTIFICATION

Although a team's performance can impact fans' tendencies to BIRG or CORF, there are cases in which team performance is not the only determining factor. It is not uncommon for certain traditionally losing teams (e.g., Major League Baseball's Chicago Cubs) to be very popular and have a large base of loyal fans that proudly publicize their association with the team, independent of the team's record. Wann and Branscombe (1990) found that the level of identification of fans with a sports team moderated the fans' reactions to wins and losses in regard to a fan's tendency to BIRG or CORF. In their study, they administered a questionnaire that assessed students' level of identification with their university's men's basketball team and examined the students' tendency to BIRG or CORF pertinent to the basketball team's performance. It was expected that high team identification would lead to higher likelihood of BIRG and lower likelihood of CORF compared to fans with lower levels of team identification. Indeed, the results showed that fans who were highly identified with their team (diehard fans) tended to BIRG a lot with their team's victories but tended to CORF less than low-identification (fair-weather) fans after team losses.

As discussed earlier, BIRG and CORF can explain the phenomenon of fair-weather fans jumping on the bandwagon of a team's success. A diehard fan, however, would follow a team, independent of the team's record and not just when the team experiences success. Hirt et al. (1992) noted that developing strong allegiances with a sports team can be risky for a fan because it makes it very difficult to disassociate from the team when the team is unsuccessful. Using the example from our introduction, highly identified Valparaiso fans continued to be loyal to their team and showed their affiliation even after the team was eliminated in the 1998 tournament; the rest of the country, however, soon lost interest and stopped following the team (while jumping on the bandwagon of other Cinderella stories like Gonzaga). The team becomes so salient for a highly identified fan that he or she defines his or her own identity in relation to the team, and the sports team essentially becomes part of the fan's self-identity (Belk, 1988). Social identity theory (Hogg, Terry, & White, 1995) suggests that, in addition to their individual characteristics (personal identity), individuals identify themselves in terms of group memberships or associations, that is, social identities. Social identity implies that group members are able to vicariously experience the group's successes or failures (Ashforth & Mael, 1989).

Given people's desire to maintain a positive image in the eyes of others, highly identified fans may struggle between trying to maintain such a positive image and not CORFing from their favorite team after losses. Research has identified a coping mechanism for dealing with this challenge, blasting (Cialdini & Richardson, 1980; End, 2001). The notion of *blasting* describes a fan's attempt to be perceived positively even after his or her team loses by saying derogatory things about (blasting) the opponents. The assumption is that by putting down the competition, a fan would still be perceived in a positive light despite his or her team's loss. In a study of Internet message boards for National Football League (NFL) fans, End (2001) found that fans used the Internet for BIRGing and for blasting their opponents and the opponents' fans. Interestingly, a greater proportion of blasting messages were posted after victories rather than losses, suggesting that, in some respects, blasting may operate as an extended form of BIRGing. The fact that sports provide a clear distinction between "in-groups" and "out-groups" reinforces the idea that a victory over an opponent offers an opportunity for favorable comparison to that group.

OTHER INFLUENCES ON BIRG

Although BIRG and CORF can be witnessed in numerous cases among sports fans, they are not the only reasons that fans are attracted to specific teams. Vicarious achievement is only one factor attracting fans to sports. Kahle, Kambara, and Rose (1996) proposed that attending sporting events is primarily motivated by one's internalization of the event, the desire to seek a unique self-expressive experience, and the desire for camaraderie. Moreover, factors such as similarity and shared values between a fan and a team can be important in making certain teams more attractive to specific fans than others (Fisher & Wakefield, 1998). For example, NFL teams such as the Pittsburgh Steelers and the Chicago Bears have a tough, no frill image that makes them quite popular with most residents in the Midwest United States. On the other hand, the San Francisco 49ers have a more sophisticated look as a team, more consistent with the image of West Coast fans.

As discussed earlier, strong team identification can moderate a fan's tendency to BIRG or CORF, explaining the popularity of some losing teams. Consistent with social identification theory, every person categorizes all groups as ones he or she belongs to or likes (in-groups) or ones that he or she does not like and does not belong to (out-groups). In the context of sports, the concept of an out-group is very interesting because it usually refers to traditional hated rivals of one's favorite team. Because highly identified fans develop a very strong and well-defined understanding of what teams they hate, it is safe to assume that any success of those teams will be very unwanted by the fan. Moreover, the fan will have no desire to BIRG for victories of teams he or she dislikes. Consistent with the notion of in-group versus out-group, fans never enjoy the successes of teams they hate and have little desire to support these teams or show any affiliation with them when they are successful. Therefore, although BIRG can offer fans the opportunity to improve their self-image by associating with a successful team, in most cases, fans tend to bask only in the success of those groups that are, at least moderately, important to their identities (Wann & Branscombe, 1990). Usually, this involves their own favorite teams, but it is not unlikely for highly identified fans to also BIRG because of the loss of a hated rival (disposition theory of sportsfanship; Zillmann, Bryant, & Sapolsky, 1979). For example, San Francisco 49ers fans may take an opportunity to BIRG and show their association with the 49ers after a big rival, such as the Dallas Cowboys, suffers a loss. As End (2001) found, blasting rival teams and their fans (and consequently, BIRGing in the victory of whoever played these teams) is relatively common in the world of sports. This tendency is particularly common in U.S. collegiate sports that have long-lasting rivalries among teams. Indicative are the T-shirts and bumper stickers with statements such as, "my favorite team is Indiana and whoever plays Purdue," Indiana's major rival, that are available for most teams and their rivals.

The premise that fans usually BIRG only when the successful team is one that is of some salience to them is important. It is very unlikely for a fan to BIRG every time a different team wins the championship. For example, we cannot expect a fan to BIRG in the Super Bowl victories of the Dallas Cowboys in 1993, 1994, and 1996, the San Francisco 49ers in 1995, the Green Bay Packers in 1997, the Denver Broncos in 1998 and 1999, the Saint Louis Rams in 2000, the Baltimore Ravens in 2001, and the New England Patriots in 2002. Such behavior would be almost comical and would likely elicit ridicule by most people, fans and non-fans alike. Norms among sports fans suggest that switching team allegiance frequently because of a team's winning record is not acceptable behavior and not something a real fan would do. Fans usually look down on fair-weather fans who switch allegiances easily and only follow a team when it is winning. Given that, according to Cialdini et al. (1976), the primary motivation for one to BIRG is to improve one's self-image, one needs to be careful how often, and more importantly, for how many different teams, one BIRGs. It is possible that a person's extreme desire to be seen in a positive way may lead him or her to change allegiances easily and BIRG for many different teams. Such tendencies, however, are likely to backfire by making a fan violate unwritten rules about fan loyalty. Therefore, norms within the sports fan community may also moderate one's tendencies to BIRG, at least regarding the number of different teams a fan BIRGs for.

IMPLICATIONS FOR SPORTS MARKETING AND ADVERTISING

The concept of BIRG has interesting implications for marketers and advertisers; knowing in what ways fans like to demonstrate their association with a winning team can be helpful in designing product offerings and marketing campaigns. Our discussion about the implications of fans' tendency to BIRG looks at licensed merchandise, advertising campaigns, fundraising campaigns, and sponsorship. We also suggest ways that losing teams may encourage BIRGing behaviors among their fans (and, thus, capitalize on all of the BIRGing implications), and we highlight the need to strengthen fan identification with the teams, independent of winning or losing records.

An area with wide potential for commercially benefiting from people's tendency to BIRG is sales of licensed merchandise bearing a team's name or logo. After all, fans' wearing of clothing with the team name or logo was the first illustration of how people BIRGed in the very first study about this topic (Cialdini et al., 1976). Along the lines of licensed merchandise, teams can reap the benefits of people's desire to BIRG by offering merchandise that not only bears a team's name or logo but also communicates a team's victory and success. Shortly after a team wins a championship, it is quite common for a wide range of product offerings celebrating the championship to become readily available for purchase. For example, right after the Maryland Terrapins won the NCAA basketball championship in 2002, a wide range of different items bearing the team's logo and mention of the championship were available to purchase. Items included clothing, pins, watches, videos, mugs, blankets, and so on. Immediate availability of such items right after an important victory is critical in order to capitalize on fans' (die-hard and fair-weather alike) desire to BIRG in the team's success.

Capitalizing on immediate wins is not limited to those selling licensed merchandise. A recent study (Platow, et al., 1999) revealed increases in pro-social behavior after a victorious game among highly identified and BIRGing fans. Researchers collecting donations for the Salvation Army found that fans of the winning team (as apparent from clothing) gave significantly larger donations after the game than other spectators. Similarly, collectors who wore apparel associated with the winning team received much larger donations from the like-minded fans. Such behavioral tendencies offer meaningful implications for fundraisers in general, but especially in colleges and universities. Running fundraising campaigns shortly after a victorious season by one of the school's sport teams may generate more funds because it offers an opportunity to alumni and friends to form an association with a winning team and BIRG through that association.

Corporate sponsorship may also be an effective way to capitalize on BIRG. Establishing a direct association between a team enables a company to elicit positive responses from the team's fans (Dalakas, Kropp, Shoham, & Florenthal, 1997; Dalakas, Rose, & Aiken, 2001; Madrigal, 2000, 2001). Therefore, sponsors can capitalize by having their name or logo appear on licensed merchandise commemorating team victories. They may also run promotions tied to the team's victories or use advertising themes that highlight the team's success. Highly identified fans are more likely to notice the sponsor's ads (Dalakas et al., 2001) and more likely to BIRG (Wann & Branscombe, 1990). An interesting twist regarding sponsorship and BIRG pertains to many sporting events and championships that have title sponsors. This is especially relevant (but not limited) to collegiate football with Bowl games having title sponsors (e.g., FedEx Orange Bowl, Tostitos Fiesta Bowl, Nokia Sugar Bowl). Future research could examine fans' tendency to BIRG (or CORF) right after winning (or losing) one of these events through temporary increase (or decrease) of consumption of products offered by the title sponsor of the sporting event.

Given that a team's performance can have an impact on how likely people are to BIRG, what can a losing team do to make fans BIRG and, consequently, to still attend games and buy licensed merchandise? During losing seasons or extensive slumps, sports marketers may emphasize previous successes of the team, if any, as a source of BIRG, increasing motivation to stay with the team (taking pride in a successful past and anticipating a successful future). Also, sports marketers may look for additional reasons, besides the team's performance, that may make fans BIRG and capitalize on such factors. Highlighting individual successful performances by members of a team can provide such additional sources of BIRG, likely to retain fan interest and maintain sales of licensed merchandise. For example, although the Seattle Mariners struggled during the 1998 baseball season, the performance by Ken Griffey, Jr. in his pursuit to be the youngest player to hit 300 home runs and Alex Rodriguez's pursuit of a 40–40 season (40 home runs and 40 stolen bases) were reasons for the fans to BIRG and remain interested. Highlighting such individual accomplishments may be a wise move for struggling teams because it can keep fans motivated to attend games and buy licensed merchandise (pertinent to the successful individual players). It is noteworthy that when Mark McGwire was chasing Roger Maris's home run record, the Saint Louis Cardinals fans BIRGed because of McGwire's performance rather than the team's overall performance (which was relatively mediocre that season). The impressive individual performance of one player provided an excellent opportunity to fans for BIRGing when the team's performance was offering few reasons for celebrating.

Another way to increase BIRG and reduce CORF is to focus on fans who identify with attributes other than or in addition to team statistics. Although winning games or having star players excel may provide the ultimate BIRGing experience, teams can win in other aspects as well. Marketers should play up the other aspects that attract fans to the team or sport. Shared values, a reputation for determination or toughness, and existence as a local tradition are some of the many aspects with which fans may identify. Perhaps the team is the league's most community-involved. Or maybe the team faces handicaps suffered by no others; the Green Bay Packers, for example, face a number of challenging hardships due to the extremely cold weather in the region and their being in a small market. Many fans BIRG on the toughness of the Green Bay team as a result of this. It is not a coincidence that the Packers fans are considered among the most loyal in the league; from 1989 to 1998, the Packers filled 97.4% of the seats at their 80 home games, despite playing in the league's smallest market and coldest weather (Thomas, 1999). It is worthwhile to note that during that period, the team went to the Super Bowl only twice and won it only once. Whatever significant element that makes the team unique can be positioned as a win that is likely to make fans BIRG.

From the standpoint of a sports team, strong fan identification may be beneficial in multiple ways. Marketers for sports teams should make conscious efforts to increase team identification, which, in turn, will increase tendencies to BIRG and reduce tendencies to CORF. Because of their deep commitment to their team, highly identified fans are considered to be of utmost economical value to a team, providing fan equity (Gorman & Calhoun, 1994). Naturally, highly committed fans will spend more money on the team by purchasing tickets, licensed merchandise, and similar activities. The benefits, however, do not end there. Teams with highly identified fans can leverage this commitment in their sponsorship proposals and their pursuit of sponsors. A team with highly identified fans is extremely attractive to potential sponsors; a loyal and identified fan base can provide a sponsor with a successful sponsorship investment (Dalakas et al., 1997, 2001; Madrigal 2000, 2001). Marketers of sports teams should consciously encourage development of strong identification.

This issue is particularly relevant for U.S. professional sports, where relocation of sports teams and increasing ticket prices alienate many fans (Burton & Howard, 1999).

In conclusion, BIRG and CORF are interesting and fascinating phenomena that are common throughout the world of sports. Understanding these phenomena provides interesting insight into consumer behavior, especially within the context of sports, and thus can be useful and relevant to sports marketers.

REFERENCES

Ashforth, B. E., & Mael, F. (1989). Social identity theory and the organization. *Academy of Management Review, 14*(1), 20–39.

Baade, R. A., & Tiehen, L. J. (1990). An analysis of Major League Baseball attendance: 1969–1987. *Journal of Sport and Social Issues, 14*(1) 14–32.

Belk, R. (1988, September). Possessions and the extended self. *Journal of Consumer Research, 15,* 139–168.

Burton, R., & Howard, D. (1999, Spring). Professional sports leagues: Marketing mix mayhem. *Marketing Management, 8*(1), 37–46.

Cialdini, R. B., Borden, R. J., Thorne, A., Walker, M. R., Freeman, S., & Sloan, L. R. (1976, September). Basking in reflected glory: Three (football) field studies. *Journal of Personality and Social Psychology, 34,* 366–375.

Cialdini, R. B., & Richardson, K. D. (1980). Two indirect tactics of image management: Basking and blasting. *Journal of Personality and Social Psychology, 39,* 406–415.

Dalakas, V., Kropp, F., Shoham, A., & Florenthal, B. (1997). Special sports identities: A cross-cultural comparison of the commercial implications of team identification. In S. M. Smith (Ed.), *Sixth Symposium of Cross-Cultural Consumer and Business Studies* (pp. 275–279). Provo, UT: Brigham Young University.

Dalakas, V., Rose, G., & Aiken, K. D. (2001). Soft drinks, auto repair, and baseball: Sports fans' perceptions of sponsors and fans' intentions toward the sponsors. In B. Ponsford (Ed.), *Proceedings of the Association of Marketing Theory and Practice Conference* (pp. 114–118). Jekyll Island, GA: Association of Marketing Theory & Practice.

End, C. M. (2001, March). An examination of NFL fans' computer mediated BIRGing. *Journal of Sport Behavior, 24,* 162–181.

Fisher, R. J., & Wakefield, K. (1998). Factors leading to group identification: A field study of winners and losers. *Psychology and Marketing, 15*(1), 23–40.

Gorman, J., & Calhoun, K. (1994). *The Name of the Game: The Business of Sports.* New York: Wiley.

Heider, F. (1958). *The psychology of interpersonal relations.* New York: Wiley.

Hirt, E., Zillmann, G., Erickson G. A., & Kennedy, C. (1992, November). Costs and benefits of allegiance: Changes in fans' self-ascribed competencies after team victory versus defeat. *Journal of Personality and Social Psychology, 63,* 724–738.

Hogg, M. A., Terry, E. J., & White, K. M. (1995). A tale of two theories: A critical comparison of identity theory with social identity theory. *Social Psychology Quarterly, 58*(4), 255–269.

Kahle, L. R., Kambara, K., & Rose, G. M. (1996). A functional model of fan attendance motivations for college football. *Sport Marketing Quarterly, 5*(4), 51–60.

King, B. (2002, February 25–march 3). D-backs ride series high with fans, sponsors. *Street and Smith's Sports Business Journal, 3.*

Madrigal, R. (1995). Cognitive and affective determinants of fan satisfaction with sporting event attendance. *Journal of Leisure Research, 27*(3), 205–227.

Madrigal, R. (2000). The influence of social alliances with sports teams on intentions to purchase corporate sponsors' products. *Journal of Advertising, 29*(4), 13–24.

Madrigal, R. (2001). Social identity effects in a belief-attitude-intentions hierarchy: Implications for corporate sponsorship. *Psychology and Marketing, 18*(2), 145–165.

Ortony, A., Clore, G. L., & Collins, A. (1988). *The Cognitive Structure of Emotions.* New York: Cambridge University Press.

Platow, M. J., Durante, M., Williams, N., Garrett, M., Walshe, J., Cincotta, S., Lianos, G., & Barutchu, A. (1999, June). The contribution of sport fan social identity to the production of prosocial behavior. *Group Dynamics, 3,* 161–169.

Sloan, L. R. (1979). The motives of sports fans. In J. H. Goldstein (Ed.), *Sports, Games and Play: Social and Psychological Viewpoints.* (219–262). Hillsdale, NJ: Lawrence Erlbaum Associates.

Snyder, C. R., Lassegard, M. A., & Ford, C. E. (1986). Distancing after group success and failure: Basking in reflected glory and cutting off reflected failure. *Journal of Personality and Social Psychology, 51*(2), 382–388.

Thomas, G. S. (1999). NFL's best fans back the pack. *Street and Smith's Sports Business Journal, 1*(40), 1, 16–18.

Wann, D. L., & Branscombe, N. R. (1990, August). Die-hard and fair-weather fans: Effects of identification on BIRGing and CORFing tendencies. *Journal of Sport and Social Issues, 14,* 103–117.

Zillman, D., Bryant, J., & Sapolsky, B. S. (1979). The enjoyment of watching sports contests. In J. H. Goldstein (Ed.), *Sports, Games and Play: Social and Psychological Viewpoints* (297–335). Hillsdale, NJ: Lawrence Erlbaum Associates.

4

Risky Sports: Making the Leap

Aviv Shoham
University of Haifa

Gregory M. Rose
University of Washington, Tacoma

Lynn R. Kahle
University of Oregon

High-risk sports have become popular (Celsi, Rose, & Leigh, 1993). Whereas many leisure activities entail low levels of personal risk, risky sports (such as parachuting and skydiving) are riskier than most leisure sports because the probability of a serious injury (or even death) is higher. Which individuals are psychologically predisposed to engage in risky sports? Once they begin to practice, how best can their continuous practice be anticipated? For marketers, how should service providers segment the population? How should they identify individuals highly pre-disposed to engage in risky sports? How should they advertise to such individuals? Such questions have been the topic of a multi-stage, programmatic study, conducted in Israel over 4 years. This chapter was written in an effort to describe, summarize, and synthesize the results of this research stream.

Marketing scholars have studied risky sports with an academic interest that parallels the popularization of such sports (Celsi, 1992; Price, Arnould, & Tierney, 1995). Two recent articles discuss risky sports from an experiential perspective in the contexts of rafting (Arnould & Price, 1993) and skydiving (Celsi et al., 1993). These studies have resulted in a well-developed understanding of the hedonic aspects of consumption of risky sports. In contrast, Shoham and associates have been involved in a programmatic effort to study risky sport consumption using an empirical paradigm (Florenthal & Shoham, 1997; Shoham, Rose, & Kahle, 1998, 2000). This chapter integrates and synthesizes both types of research: the descriptive and interpretive study of risky sports practice and the empirical study of risky sports, covering both the general population and practitioners of risky sports. Thus, the contribution of this chapter is in combining both theoretical perspectives (and the results of studies based on both) into an integrative model and in suggesting the managerial implications of this model.

PSYCHOLOGICAL AND THEORETICAL BACKGROUND

In this section we review the literature on risk-taking behavior. This literature is divided into two types. First, we review papers on the psychological determinants of risk-taking (Zuckerman, 1983a, 1983b, 1984). Second, we discuss and synthesize the hedonic aspects of consuming risky sports (Celsi et al., 1993). Subsequent to each building block of our model, we discuss the findings of our research. Figure 4.1 provides a model of risky sport consumption behavior, which is based on the two approaches to the study of risky sport and on our programmatic research effort. The model identifies personality and individual facets first. Then it examines attitudes about risky sport attributes. It uses these attitudes to predict future behavioral intentions. Intentions are followed by a decision to start practicing a given risky sport, followed, in turn, by the level of commitment to the chosen sport.

Psychological Determinants of Risk-Taking

We begin this section with a brief discussion of the main psychological determinants of risk-taking behavior. In the next section, we synthesize the various approaches and explain how the model in Figure 4.1 was developed.

Most previous research about psychological determinants of risk-taking behavior assumed that all individuals possess a personality trait that determines whether they will be positively or negatively inclined to engage in high-risk activities (Lyng, 1990). Models that assume that such a trait is a personality risk-taking disposition view it as a bipolar risk-seeking tendency. On the other hand, intrinsic motivation models search for psychological factors that cause individuals to take risks (Lyng, 1990).

Sensation Seeking. Most previous research has used personality disposition models by studying individuals that value risk-taking. Researchers

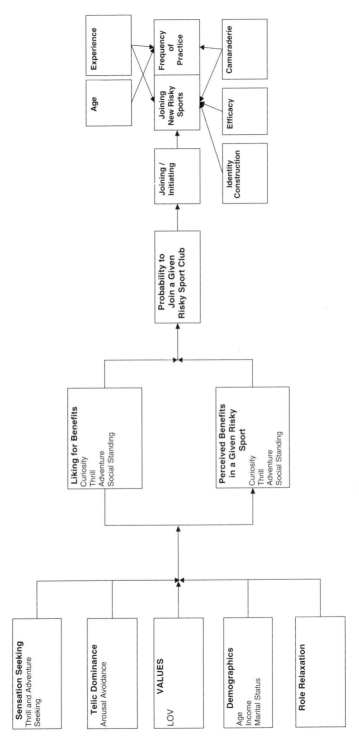

FIG. 4.1. Model of risky sport consumption.

83

following this tradition have developed and used the Sensation Seeking Scale (Zuckerman, 1983a, 1983b, 1984; Zuckerman, Kolin, Price, & Zoob, 1964), which has four subdimensions (thrill and adventure seeking, experience seeking, disinhibition, and boredom susceptibility).

In a summary of their research, Zuckerman, Buchsbaum, and Murphy (1980) identified several behavioral outcomes to sensation-seeking in general and to its thrill and adventure seeking (TAS) subdimension: greater sexual activity, drug use, smoking, and participation in dangerous activities (Burns, Hampson, Severson, & Slovic, 1993; Severson, Slovic, & Hampson, 1993).

Telic Dominance. Telic dominance is a second, state-based theory developed to explain risk-taking (Apter, 1976, 1982; Smith & Apter, 1975). Telic dominance suggests the existence of two stable arousal states: one in which individuals attempt to gain arousal, which is felt as pleasant, and one in which individuals try to reduce arousal, which is seen as unpleasant. Telic dominance is commonly operationalized along three subdimensions: arousal avoidance, serious-mindedness, and planning orientation (Murgatroyd, Rushton, Apter, & Ray, 1978). Although telic dominance is based theoretically on individual states, its operationalization has been based on personality traits (Murgatroyd et al., 1978). Telic dominance and its arousal avoidance subdimension are different for individuals practicing risky sports and for the general population (Kerr, 1991).

In sum, given how telic dominance has been operationalized (rather than theorized), it is relatively close to the approach used in the sensation-seeking research tradition. The two are discussed jointly in the remainder of this chapter.

Reference Groups. The influence of important others in individuals' reference groups affects the probability of initiating risky sport activities (Fishbein & Ajzen, 1975). In general, the impact of significant others in reference groups has been studied extensively (Ryan & Bonfield, 1975). In the context of this chapter, one potentially important influence is recognized, that of role-relaxation (an individual trait). Kahle (1995) suggested that some individuals are more role-relaxed and that these individuals tend to emphasize functional attributes over peer-group acceptance (Kahle & Shoham, 1995).

Values. Values are stable (and desirable) end-states (Kahle, 1983) that affect attitudes and behaviors in multiple behavioral domains (Beatty, Kahle, Homer, Utsey, & Keown, 1993; Homer & Kahle, 1988), including risk-taking behavior (Grube, Weir, Getzlaf, & Rokeach, 1984). We show later that values differ between individuals with a low- versus a high-propensity toward engaging in high-risk sports.

Activity Attributes.   The next part of the model includes the perceived benefits of a risky sport. Such sports are preferred over other leisure activities to the extent that they possess large quantities of desirable attributes that produce desirable consequences (Fishbein & Ajzen, 1975). Two outcomes are discussed in previous research. First, the extent to which an individual values activities that are curiosity arousing, thrilling, and adventurous and enhance social standing affects the probability of practicing risky sports. The choice of these four attributes is based on the hedonic consumption literature. The second influencing factor is the extent to which risky sports have these four attributes. These two factors are seen as interacting to determine the future probability of engaging in high-risk sports. This is based on the logic that such sports will be preferred when the four attributes are desirable and abundant (Fishbein & Ajzen, 1975). The more that individuals value activities that enhance social standing, and satisfy curiosity, adventure, and thrill needs and the more they perceive risky sports to have such attributes, the higher their probability of engagement in risky sports.

Hedonic Consumption

The popularity of this approach to the study of consumer behavior dates to the 1970s (Holbrook, 1978). Hirschman and Holbrook (1982) defined *hedonic consumption* as those facets of consumer behavior that are based on multiple senses, fantasy, and emotional aspects of consumers' experience with products. Hedonic consumption focuses on the psychological experience that is felt during product use. Several such aspects are important in determining the probability of future consumption of high-risk sports (Arnould & Price, 1993; Celsi et al., 1993).

Celsi et al. (1993) discussed skydiving as involving several emotions (e.g., thrill, pleasure, and flow) experienced by skydivers as they engage in the act. The researchers viewed skydiving as a drama, which follows a scripted, dramatic model. The motives that guide an individual change from external (e.g., reference groups) to internal over time, and the individual normalizes what was considered to be, a priori, a frightening sport (Arnould & Price, 1993). Celsi, Rose, and Leigh (1993) discussed four motivators—curiosity, thrill seeking, social status, and adventure—also recognized by Arnould and Price (1993).

A SYNTHESIS

Zuckerman's Sensation Seeking Scale

As noted previously, Zuckerman (and associates) studied sensation-seeking and its behavioral outcomes for more than two decades. Numerous such behaviors are general and can be extended to risky sports. For example, sensation-seeking individuals use more drugs more often than other individuals (Zuckerman, Buchsbaum, & Murphy, 1980). Such indirect relationships (through perceived benefits and risks) have been documented in the contexts of drug taking and gambling (Burns et al., 1993; Zuckerman, 1974). Additionally, in a different context, Hymbaugh and Garrett (1974) found that the higher the sensation-seeking tendency of individuals, the higher the probability that they would engage in parachuting. Similarly, Celsi, Rose, and Leigh (1993) identified thrill- and adventure-seeking, curiosity, and the desire for social status as important motives for initiating high-risk sport activities.

The most consistent finding in previous research concerns the role of the adventure-seeking subdimension of sensation-seeking (Zuckerman, 1983b). Thus, Figure 4.1 includes a positive link between TAS and the liking and perceived potential of risky sports to satisfy curiosity, adventure, and thrill needs.

We conducted two studies that included thrill and adventure seeking as an explanatory variable (Shoham, Rose, & Kahle, 1998). In one, we surveyed the general population in Israel to assess its impact on the populations' liking for and perceived potential of risky sports to satisfy curiosity, adventure, and thrill needs. In the second, we assessed these relationships in a sample of individuals in their first day of practice of the sport (Shoham, Rose, & Kahle, 1998).

Findings from the first study provided some support to the links in Figure 4.1. The impact of thrill- and adventure-seeking on liking of and perceived potential to deliver the three benefits was positive and reached significance for curiosity and thrill needs. The second study provided additional support for the role of thrill- and adventure-seeking in explaining curiosity arousing and adventure. In sum, on the basis of previous studies and our own studies in two populations, thrill- and adventure-seeking play an important role in explaining the importance of the four attributes of high-risk sports and the perceived potential of such sports to satisfy these needs. The implications of these findings are discussed in the "Implications" section of this chapter.

Arousal Avoidance

Of the three subdimensions of telic dominance, arousal avoidance has been the most consistent predictor of risk-taking behavior. Arousal avoidance negatively affects the liking for activities that can satisfy curiosity, adventure, and thrill (in general) and on the potential of high-risk sports to satisfy these needs. Svebak, Kerr, & Stoyva (1980) showed that high levels of arousal could be pleasant to some people, especially in the context of leisure activities, such as sports and entertainment. High arousal excites and pleases (Apter, 1976, 1982). Svebak and Kerr (1989) documented that individuals who engage in low-risk sports score higher on arousal avoidance than individuals who engage in high-risk sports. This pattern is consistent across low-risk (e.g., sailing and surfing) and high-risk sports (e.g., parachuting and gliding; Kerr & Svebak, 1989). Thus, the model includes a negative link between arousal avoidance and the liking for and perceived potential of risky sports to satisfy curiosity, adventure, and thrill needs.

We included arousal avoidance in three of our studies (Florenthal & Shoham, 1997; Shoham et al., 1998, 2000). The former two supported the role of arousal avoidance in explaining the importance of thrill, adventure, and curiosity arousing needs and the potential of risky sports to deliver these benefits. Apparently, thrill- and adventure-seeking effects all three, non-social needs, as linked in Figure 4.1.

Individuals were also found to differ in their attitudes towards high-risk sports on the basis of their arousal avoidance tendencies in the third, experiment-based study. Thus, arousal avoidance plays a role opposite from the one played by thrill- and adventure-seeking. Although they provide strong support to the links in Figure 4.1, these opposite effects may suggest that the two capture opposite points on comparable scales.

Age

The impact of age on the probability to initiate high-risk sport activities can be seen as either positive or negative. On one hand, older people may be unfit for the physical demands of such sports. To the extent that this is the factor determining the impact of age, the probability of entering risky sports should decrease with age. In other words, the older the individuals, the less likely they are to start practicing high-risk sports. On the other hand, older individuals should have had more opportunity to face workplace- and family-related tensions. Thus, they may be looking more for the catharsis value made possible by practicing risky sports (Celsi et al., 1993).

In sum, age can affect liking for and perceived potential of risky sports to satisfy social standing, curiosity, adventure, and thrill needs negatively or positively. Which is the stronger influence is an empirical question, best answered with data. The model includes a negative link between age and the intermediate outcomes on the basis of our research.

Our study in the general population found that older individuals are less likely to perceive the four benefits of high-risk sports as important and as provided by such sports (Shoham, Rose, & Kahle, 1998). The impact was negative and significant for all four benefits. The second study (of individuals just initiating risky sport activities) provided additional support to the negative role of age (Shoham, Rose, & Kahle, 2000). It affected all but one (social standing) of the four benefits of high-risk sports. This impact could not be assessed in Florenthal and Shoham (1997), who used an age-homogeneous sample of students.

In sum, age negatively affects the perceived importance of the four needs and the potential of risky sport to deliver them. Thus, the physical fitness impact seems to be stronger than the argument that older individuals have had more opportunity to face workplace- and family-related tensions, which would make the catharsis value more important.

Group Influence

Earlier, we provided a preliminary discussion of the impact of role-relaxation on consumption of high-risk sports. It should affect an individual's liking for and perceived potential of risky sports to satisfy curiosity-arousing, adventure, and thrill needs.

The potential impact of the trait of role-relaxation was recognized first by Kahle (1995) and Kahle and Shoham (1995). Role-relaxed consumers are not affected by social influences in purchasing and consuming goods (Kahle, 1995). Kahle and Shoham (1995) found differences between high- and low–role-relaxed consumers. In the context of values, the stronger the role-relaxed trait, the less important the socially defined values and the more important the independence-oriented values (Kahle, 1983). In a consumption-related context, the more role-relaxed the consumer, the lower the importance of fashion-based product attributes (e.g., the product being exciting and stylish; Kahle & Shoham, 1995).

In the context of the perceived benefits of high-risk sports, more role-relaxed consumers should place a lower value on social aspects of consumption (compared to less role-relaxed consumers). In other words, role-relaxed consumers would place a lower value on benefits that arise from being members of a given reference group, including a risky sport group. Thus, the model in Figure 4.1 includes a negative link between the extent to which individuals are role-relaxed and the liking for and perceived potential of high-risk sports to satisfy social needs.

Support for the importance of role-relaxation was provided in Shoham, Rose, and Kahle (1998). The impact of being role relaxed on the importance of social standing needs and the potential of risky sports to provide this benefit was negative and significant. This impact provides support to the general arguments made by Kahle (1995) and the generic findings reported by Kahle and Shoham (1995). In other words, being role relaxed has specific, as well as general, attitudinal and behavioral implications.

The Impact of Personal Values

Rokeach (1973) posited that *personal values* are beliefs about preferable modes of behavior and end-states that affect attitudes and behaviors. His list included 36 values: 18 instrumental values (e.g., being broadminded and independent) and 18 terminal values (e.g., freedom and happiness). These values can be ordered by their importance to consumers (Grube et al., 1984). Kahle and associates developed a different approach to values, the "List of Values" (LOV; Beatty, Kahle, Homer, & Misra, 1985; Homer & Kahle, 1988; Kahle, 1983; Kahle, Beatty, & Homer, 1986). LOV includes nine values: sense of belonging, fun and enjoyment in life, warm relationships with others, self-fulfillment, being well respected, excitement, security, self-respect, and sense of accomplishment.

Values are stable, slow-evolving, desirable end-states (Kahle, 1983) that play an important role in shaping behaviors in multiple contexts. These contexts include gift giving (Beatty et al., 1985; Beatty et al., 1993), shopping behavior, spending tendencies, nutrition attitudes (Homer & Kahle, 1988), and the importance of fashion attributes (Rose, Shoham, Kahle, & Batra, 1994). Values can be used to explain and predict a wide variety of attitudes and behaviors because of their abstract nature (Rose et al., 1994; Williams, 1979). They guide consumers in selecting which situations to enter and how to behave in these situations (Kahle, 1983). Consumers enter situations (and behave in these situations) in ways that are consistent with their values.

Values have been shown to affect risk-taking behaviors. Values affect smoking behavior (Grube et al., 1984), and the values of those who cheat on exams differ from those of non-cheaters (Hensehl, 1971). These choices are related to risk taking and depend on differing values of smokers and cheaters (compared to non-smokers and non-cheaters). Thus, the model in Figure 4.1 includes a link between the importance of personal values and the future propensity to engage in high-risk sports.

The empirical work by Shoham, Florenthal, Rose, and Kropp (1997), Shoham, Kahle, Kropp, and Rose (1997), and Shoham, Kropp, and Rose (1998) is closely related to this theoretical discussion and provides support to the link depicted in Figure 4.1. Shoham, Florenthal et al. (1997) documented that the LOV profiles of high-risk sports practitioners differed from the profiles of the general population. In a small-scale study of Israeli students, Shoham, Florenthal et al. (1997) found that three of the nine values in the LOV differed significantly between thrill-seeking and thrill-avoiding individuals. Additionally, Shoham, Rose, and Kahle (1998) reported that the value profiles of the Israeli population differed for individuals with either a low or a high future probability of engaging in high-risk sports. The differences for the importance of security and excitement observed were intuitively reasonable. People who report a high level of future probability to engage in high-risk sports can be expected to value personal security less than low-probability individuals. Additionally, as noted before, high-risk sports provide practitioners with a high level of excitement. Therefore, the observed positive impact of excitement is not surprising.

Three other values (sense of belonging, warm relationships, and being well respected) are external values. All three were valued less by high-probability individuals than by low-propensity individuals. Individuals may have perceived high-risk sports as potentially harming social standing, which would account for the differences observed. Two internal values (sense of accomplishment and self-respect) were related negatively to the future probability of engagement. High-risk sports may have been perceived as enhancing these two values less than other activities.

Attitudes and Expected Benefits of Risky Sports

In combination, one's attitudes about the benefits of engagement in a given activity and the potential of such an activity to satisfy needs should both have an impact on the probability that an individual will engage in this activity (Achenbaum, 1966; Beatty & Kahle, 1988). In the more specific context of high-risk sports, attitudes about the potential benefits of these sports and their perceived potential to satisfy the four needs discussed earlier (curiosity arousing, thrill, adventure, and social standing) should affect the probability of engaging in such sports at some future time. The theory of reasoned action posits that all three components of attitude (affective, cognitive, and behavioral) will be consistent (Ajzen & Fishbein, 1980; Fishbein, 1966, 1967;

Fishbein & Ajzen, 1975). Applied to our context, the affective component addresses how individuals generally feel about thrilling, curiosity arousing, adventurous, and social standing enhancing activities. Cognitively, it is important to study the extent to which individuals believe that risky sports can deliver these four benefits. The future behavior component, as applied to risky sports, assessed an individual's intent to engage in high-risk sports. In sum, liking for activities that satisfy the need for curiosity arousing, adventure, social standing, and thrill is positively linked to one's perception that risky sports possess these attributes (see Fig. 4.1).

The two constructs (liking for and recognition of the benefits of risky sport activities) operate jointly. Their impact was included in the two samples in Shoham, Rose, and Kahle's study (1998). Only the impact of curiosity arousing (but not the other three benefits) was significant in explaining the probability of future consumption of high-risk sports in the general population. Shoham, Rose, and Kahle (1998) attributed this limited support for these relationships to the fact that many in the general population do not recognize some of the benefits of high-risk sport until they are closer in time to actually participating in such sports. In support of this argument, means for three of the four benefits (except social standing enhancement) were significantly higher for people just beginning to practice high-risk sports than for the general population in the second study reported by Shoham, Rose, and Kahle (1998). In sum, the results based on the two samples support the proposed link between liking for and recognition of the benefits of risky sport activities, and the future probability of consumption of such activities depicted in Figure 4.1 with these relationships becoming stronger as the individual approaches initial risky-sport participation.

CONTINUOUS INVOLVEMENT IN HIGH-RISK SPORTS

We turn now to the second part of Figure 4.1—predicting two behavioral outcomes beyond Arnould and Price's (1993) and Price, Arnould, and Tierney's (1995) satisfaction outcome. We discuss the frequency of engagement in one's high-risk sport and the future probability of engaging in new risky sports. This section of the article synthesizes the previously reported qualitative research and our own research. Figure 4.1 provides a framework that integrates the drama-form (Celsi et al., 1993), the danger-neutralization and peer-identification theory (Brannigan & McDougall, 1983), and the extraordinary experience approach (Arnould & Price, 1993; Price et al., 1995). These approaches share four explanations to the consumption of risky sports: the need for identity construction, efficacy, camaraderie, and experience (Arnould & Price, 1993; Brannigan & McDougall, 1983; Celsi et al., 1993; Price et al., 1995). Notably, the individuals to whom this part of the model applies already practice high-risk sports. Previous research has demonstrated that participants have high sensation-seeking and low arousal-avoidance scores. Therefore, the model does not posit relationships between these two psychological traits and the continuous involvement in risky sports.

The Need for Identity Construction

Identity construction is the first important motivating factor used to predict continuous involvement in risky sports (Arnould & Price, 1993; Celsi et al., 1993). This factor operates by providing a context for personal change and the means to organize a new identity. Initiation into the risky sport group tends to follow a well-defined structure, somewhat similar to a rite of passage (Celsi et al., 1993). Actual participation is perceived as a special and unique experience. The opportunity for identity construction becomes a powerful motive in our times, as adult roles are, in many cases, routine, bureaucratic, and difficult-to-change.

Arnould and Price (1993) identified extension (and renewal) of self as related to satisfying river rafting experiences. This extension makes it necessary for practitioners to acquire the sport's jargon. Newcomers to flights on ultralight planes use terms such as *air pockets, lowering the nose, throttle,* and *flaps.* These terms are then used to signify an acceptance into and understanding of the special in-group of practitioners (Celsi et al., 1993). Brannigan and McDougall (1983) discussed similar self-gratification aspects of involvement in risky sports. Thus, due to the role of identity construction in explaining continuous participation and satisfaction, Figure 4.1 includes a positive link between identity construction and the frequency of engagement in a high-risk sport and the probability of engaging in other risky sports in the future.

Shoham, Rose, and Kahle (2000) provided support for this link in Figure 4.1. The impact of the satisfaction of identity construction needs by a high-risk sport on the mean future probability of entering new high-risk sports was positive and significant as expected. Notably, it did not affect the mean frequency of practicing the present high-risk sport. This unexpected finding was attributed to a potential ceiling effect, somewhat similar to diminishing returns discussed in economics. In other words, once the need is satisfied (at a given level of practice), it does not influence frequency of practice but does influence the probability of engagement in additional high-risk sports, as was found (Shoham et al., 2000).

The Need for Efficacy

Efficacy is the second important motive for continuous involvement in high-risk sports (Celsi et al., 1993). It is commonly defined as being based on a desire to develop skills that deliver personal satisfaction and social status within the practicing community. Consumers are often motivated to stay involved because they get better at their practiced risky sport (Brannigan & McDougall, 1983). Standards of excellence also tend to shift and become increasingly more demanding with increased expertise. This shift raises the bar because self-expectations rise. This process maintains the importance of efficacy *over time* (Brannigan & McDougall, 1983; Celsi et al., 1993).

Arnould and Price (1993) also supported the importance of efficacy. Rafting guides help clients to acquire new skills. Mastery evolves throughout the rafting trip and becomes ever more demanding. A single river-rafting trip, which can last a few days, provides an opportunity for individuals to satisfy efficacy needs throughout the trip. In other sports (e.g., skydiving), these needs are satisfied over numerous occasions because of the short time each incidence takes. Thus, Figure 4.1 links (positively) the perceived satisfaction of efficacy needs in a risky sport and the frequency of engagement in this sport and the future probability of engaging in other risky sports.

Shoham et al. (2000) provided limited support for this link. The impact of the satisfaction of efficacy needs (like the finding for identity construction needs) by a high-risk sport on the mean future probability of entering new high-risk sports was negative and significant, as expected. Here, too, it did not affect the mean frequency of practicing the present high-risk sport. Similar to the argument for identity construction, this finding can be explained by a potential ceiling effect. Stated differently, once the need for efficacy is satisfied at a given level of practice of a high-risk sport, it does not influence the frequency of practice of this sport. However, it influences the probability of engagement in additional high-risk sports, as was found (Shoham et al., 2000).

The Need for Camaraderie

Celsi et al. (1993) recognized group camaraderie as one of three motives (flow, communitas, and phatic communion) in their discussion of high-risk sport consumption. *Communitas* is seen as a sense of community that goes beyond mundane social norms and conventions. It provides a sense of camaraderie for people from diverse backgrounds. Thus, practitioners of risky sports see the jointly practiced activity as sacred, rather than profane (Belk, Wallendorf, & Sherry, 1989). In other words, for communitas to develop, shared experiences need to move beyond everyday life; they need to provide a sense of shared ritual. Many practitioners of risky sports recognize the irrelevancy of their *external* roles in the context of the sport. Newly acquired expertise, combined with one's specialized role within the group, separates the mundane from the experience of high-risk sports. This makes communitas an important theme in satisfying rafting trips (Arnould & Price, 1993). As they raft down white-water rivers, practitioners develop feelings of group membership. The group is united by its devotion to a single goal. Rafters dispose of personal possessions in favor of shared possessions that are relevant to attaining the group's goals. Rafting guides reinforce teamwork, further strengthening the process (Brannigan & McDougall, 1983).

Communitas is also manifested in satisfying the need for identity construction and efficacy (Arnould & Price, 1993; Brannigan & McDougall, 1983; Celsi et al., 1993; Price et al., 1995). Initiation processes—rites of passage (Celsi et al., 1993)—determine the extent to which identity construction needs are met. Identity construction takes place within groups with common risky sport interests and goals. Notably, efficacy also involves the development of skills and expertise, which differentiate experienced practitioners from novices and from non-participants (Arnould & Price, 1993). Consequently, efficacy contributes to practitioners' professional standing in the high-risk sport community.

In sum, there is a positive link between the satisfaction of camaraderie needs (within a group of practitioners) and the frequency of engagement in a high-risk sport and the future probability of engaging in additional risky sports. Such a link is included in Figure 4.1.

Shoham et al. (2000) provide strong support for the link between the satisfaction of camaraderie needs and the two outcome measures in Figure 4.1. The impact of the satisfaction of camaraderie needs by a high-risk sport on the mean future probability of entering new high-risk sports was positive and significant as expected. It also positively effected the mean frequency of practicing the present high-risk sport. This finding differed from the limited impact of the two needs discussed earlier. Why is the need for camaraderie not subject to a ceiling effect like the other two? Shoham et al. (2000) attributed this finding to the fact that it is based on the high order, transcendent motive of communitas (Celsi et al., 1993). This need remains important and operative even for experienced and expert practitioners of high-risk sports.

The Impact of Experience in a High-Risk Sport

Experience in a high-risk sport is an important determinant of present and future consumption of the same sport. It may also affect the probability of entry into new high-risk sports. Celsi et al. (1993) discussed the need for efficacy and identity construction, which is based on developing the skills and terminology of the sport (Arnould & Price, 1993). As practitioners become more knowledgeable about their sport, their attention shifts from risk-related anxiety to improved performance (Celsi et al., 1993). Furthermore, sustained participation in a risky sport provides individuals with opportunities to construct new selves (Belk, 1988). This opportunity depends on being committed to new life tasks resulting in plans for implementation. Continuous involvement in the sport is a form of such commitment (Celsi et al., 1993).

Arnould and Price (1993) traced the evolution of the themes they identified—communitas, communion with nature, and extension and renewal of self—over a river-rafting trip. These themes changed throughout the trip as opportunities for their manifestations accumulated. Consequently, experience is an important element of the high-risk sport consumption experience. Notably, gaining expertise and experience is a gradual, progressive process. Mastery at a given level leads to a desire for greater challenges (Celsi et al., 1993). In sum, experience should be related positively to the frequency of engagement. This link is included in Figure 4.1.

Importantly, experience in a given sport should negatively effect the probability of consumption of *new* high-risk sports. Although experience and expertise in one sport effect the frequency of engagement in that sport, they cannot be easily transferred to other high-risk sports. The individual starts practicing newer risky sports from scratch. Therefore, Figure 4.1 links experience in one sport and the probability to enter other sports negatively.

In line with this link, Shoham et al. (2000) found that experience in one high-risk sport has a negative impact on the probability that an individual will enter other such sports. In a non-risky sport, it is noteworthy that Michael Jordan's phenomenal success as a basketball superstar was not matched by his success as a baseball player. This serves as an example of the difficulty involved in transferring expertise from one sport to another.

Additionally, experience in a given sport has a negative impact on the frequency of engagement in the same sport (Shoham et al., 2000). This may be attributable to two potential explanations. First, it may be that the impact of experience is due to its relationship with age (discussed later). The more experienced the practitioners, the older they tend to be (by definition). Thus, experienced, older practitioners may be less fit for the demands of frequently practicing their sport. Second, experienced practitioners may have already benefited from satisfaction of two needs (identity construction and efficacy). As noted earlier, to the extent that these needs are subject to a ceiling effect, they may have a lesser impact on frequency of practice.

In sum, experience reduces the probability of entry into new, high-risk sports. It also reduces the frequency of engagement in the practiced high-risk sport.

The Impact of Age

As noted in the discussion about the impact of age on future engagement of non-practitioners, practitioners' age can have opposite effects on practitioners' behavioral tendencies. Older individuals may be less fit than young individuals for the physical demands of risky sports. Thus, age may negatively effect the frequency of practice of the sport and the probability of entering new high-risk sports in the future. On the other hand, some needs discussed by Celsi et al. (1993) may be important for older individuals. Older practitioners may have had more opportunity to experience the tensions in their workplace, causing them to look for the catharsis that can be gained from high-risk sports. Older practitioners may also have had more years to develop the skills relevant to risky sports, thus reducing the risks. Given these potentially conflicting roles, the impact of age is best viewed as an empirical question, best answered with data. In the next section, we provide the results of our study as they bear on this question.

Age had a positive and significant impact on the frequency of practice of a high-risk sport, but its negative impact on the probability of engagement in new sports failed to reach significance (Shoham et al., 2000). Apparently, the negative impact of the physical demands of high-risk sports discussed earlier was weaker than the impact of the need for the catharsis value of high-frequency practice. The two influences may have been balanced for the probability to engage in new high-risk sports. This may be due to the fact that individuals have less knowledge about the physical requirements of a new, as yet non-practiced high-risk sport. Alternatively, they may see the catharsis value as stronger in new activities, compared to presently practiced sports.

Summary

In sum, the perceived potential of the sport to fulfill the needs for identity construction and camaraderie and the future probability of engaging in additional risky sports are related positively. The impact of the need for efficacy on entry into new sports is negative. The impact of the need for camaraderie (but not efficacy and identity construction) on the frequency of practice of a given, high-risk sport is positive. The relationship between experience in a risky sport and the frequency of engagement in this sport is negative, as is its relationship with the future probability of engaging in additional high-risk sports. Finally, the impact of age on the frequency of practice (but not entry into new sports) is positive.

MANAGERIAL IMPLICATIONS

The discussion about managerial implications is divided into two sections. First, we discuss the implication of the model for the general, non-practicing population. Then, we shift the emphasis and discuss the implications for practitioners of high-risk sports. The second part of the discussion includes two subsections. A discussion of the implications for maintaining membership in a given sport and increasing its practice frequency is followed by a discussion of the implications on how best to attract individuals from one high-risk sport to another. Both parts emphasize advertising implications.

Implications for Non-Practitioners

Thrill and Adventure Seeking and Arousal Avoidance. As noted earlier, both psychological traits affect the future probability of engagement in high-risk sports. Both can be used as psychographic bases of segmentation. In other words, service providers could (and should) target individuals who are thrill, adventure, and arousal seekers. Additionally, advertising themes should emphasize the thrills and adventures inherent in the practice of risky sports. The end result of advertisements and promotions should be one of high arousal to exposed individuals.

The type of advertising discussed above has an additional benefit through its potential impact on present practitioners. As noted in the literature review section, practitioners tend to be arousal and thrill seekers, compared to the general population. Thus, even though the themes discussed here are targeted to the general population, they may also effect practitioners' sub-population by their very nature.

Demographics. Age was found to result in lower liking for adventurous, curiosity satisfying, social standing enhancing, and thrilling experiences. Older individuals do not recognize the potential of high-risk sports to provide satisfaction of these needs. The managerial implication for service providers is that segmentation and targeting of young non-practitioners is feasible and desirable. All components of the marketing mix should reflect this focus.

In addition, advertising should use the types of media read, watched, and listened to by younger adults. Themes can emphasize young adults in the process of experiencing and enjoying the high-risk sport consumption act. Additionally, to encourage a cohort phenomenon, clubs could group classes and activities on the basis of practitioners' ages.

As noted by Shoham, Rose, and Kahle (1998), age was positively correlated with income. The impact of income, through its correlation with the probability of future engagement in risky sports, was negative. Thus, the pricing structure for practicing any given risky sport should consider the lower income of the target, age-based segment. Special prices for young members—membership initiation fees, classes, and equipment rentals—should help in courting membership. Some of the initial costs for young members can be deferred. Lower prices can go a long way in reducing the costs of initiating a high-risk sport activity, especially for sports that require expensive equipment (e.g., gliding).

Apart from the main model in Shoham, Rose, and Kahle (1998), post-hoc mean comparisons showed that married individuals with children were less likely to engage in high-risk sports than singles. This finding, in combination with finding on the impact of age, can be used to fine-tune service providers' segmentation and positioning efforts. In other words, individuals in early family-life-cycle stages should be the prime target segment.

Neither gender nor education were significantly related to the future probability of engagement in risky sports. Thus, neither should be used as a segmentation basis. Additionally, advertising and promotion should be gender- and education-free.

Benefits of High-Risk Sports.   Earlier, we noted that only the curiosity satisfying potential of risky sports was significant in predicting future probability of consumption. However, Shoham, Rose, and Kahle (1998) showed that adventures and thrills are more important for people with a high probability of engagement in the future, as well as for people just initiating high-risk sport activities. Thus, all three risky sport themes should be emphasized in service design and provision. These emphases may be more crucial initially, until the novelty for practitioners wears off. Service providers' advertising and promotion need to recognize and emphasize the potential of high-risk sports to provide benefits such as interesting, curiosity arousing experiences, adventures, and thrills. These themes play an especially important role in motivating people who are seriously considering initiating a high-risk sport.

Florenthal and Shoham (1997) provided additional insights into potential strategies to affect non-practitioners. They noted that a single exposure to additional information about the risks and benefits of practice affected the cognitive but not the behavioral intention component of the general population's attitudes about high-risk sports. This suggests two implications. First, advertising can be planned to change the cognitive component of the general population's attitude. Informational advertising on the various benefits of high-risk sports' are desirable. However, the impact failed to affect the behavioral intention components of attitude. Thus, it may be necessary to reach potential customers with multiple exposures and, possibly, multiple executions highlighting the benefits of practicing high-risk sports.

Implications for Practitioners

Maintaining Membership and Activity Levels.   Shoham et al. (2000) identified two major determinants of maintaining membership and enhancing practice frequency. Older consumers tend to practice more frequently than young consumers do. Thus, older club members are a preferred target segment for frequency enhancing marketing strategies. As noted in the discussion about the general population, age-homogeneous groups of practitioners may be organized for club activities. Such targeting would make it possible to facilitate the camaraderie needs of these consumers in an age cohort setting. As older consumers tend to avoid arousal, thrill, and adventure, advertising and promotion should de-emphasize these attributes of high-risk sports. Rather, they should emphasize the potential of the sport to provide satisfaction of other needs. The most important of these needs is the need for camaraderie, which should be heavily stressed and advertised.

The second group of frequent practitioners includes the less experienced individuals. This would suggest experience as a second segmentation theme. Experience-homogeneous groups can be organized. Activities and advertising can then account for the type of individuals with less experience in the sport. Hopefully, these would carry through to increased frequency and result in heavier use of firms' products and services.

Obviously, practitioners can be segmented on the basis of the two characteristics of age and experience discussed above; such fine-tuning of advertising and promotion may give special emphasis to older beginners. As noted in the discussion about the general population, income is low and is an important determinant of future probability of engagement for younger beginners. This necessitates a cost-reduction strategy for the target segment. The opposite holds for practitioners. The older, less experienced individuals who are members of this target group can probably afford the cost of frequent engagement in their chosen high-risk sport. Thus, prices can be de-emphasized in positioning and advertising. In other words, firms can charge premium prices for this higher-income group.

Attracting Individuals From One High-Risk Sport to Another.   Providers of any high-risk sport products can benefit from reaching for practitioners of another high-risk sport. Such individuals have already "crossed the barrier" once (Shoham et al., 2000). Prime candidates for a "switching" strategy include the young, inexperienced practitioners of one high-risk sport. Whereas they crossed the threshold, they are not yet fully committed to their chosen sport. They have less expertise and have invested less, psychologically and monetarily in the just-joined sport.

Special pricing is an example of a strategy designed to potentially effect such individuals. Lower initial prices, as well as low cross-membership prices, are two forms of potentially effective strategies to attract young, inexperienced practitioners from one sport to another. Comparative advertising can also be used fruitfully. Such advertising would directly compare and highlight the benefits of the non-practiced sport over the practiced sport.

The potential of a risky sport to satisfy identity construction and camaraderie needs affected the probability of switching (Shoham et al., 2000). Advertising campaigns should illustrate how these needs are effectively satisfied by the new sport. Such campaigns should emphasize these needs. For example, visual elements should depict the practice environment in a group setting. This would provide cues about the potential of the new sport to satisfy camaraderie needs. Because the impact of efficacy-enhancing strategies affects switching negatively, it should be de-emphasized in advertising targeted at potential switchers.

Directions for Future Research

Several limitations of our research should be recognized. The data in the empirical studies by Shoham and associates were based on Israeli respondents. Shoham et al. (2000) note that the generalizability of their findings should be a minor limitation. Their main study's sample means on arousal avoidance were similar to the populations in Kerr (1991) and Kerr and Svebak (1989). Shoham, Rose, and Kahle's (1998) means on the Sensation Seeking Scale were comparable to those reported by Hymbaugh and Garrett (1974) and by Cronin (1991). Thus, the populations surveyed in this research stream are similar to the Australian, German, and U.S. populations surveyed in previous research. However, as Shoham, Rose, and Kahle (1998) noted, additional studies in other countries are needed before the cross-cultural generalizability of the findings can be fully determined.

Future probability of joining risky sport activities in our research was self-reported. Some individuals who self-reported a high level of probability may not practice any high-risk sport in the future. Conversely, individuals with low self-reported future probability may start practicing anyway. As Shoham, Rose, and Kahle (1998) noted, the relationship between self-reported future probability and actual behavior should be addressed in future, longitudinal research. Such research can be used to assess the strength of the relationship between the future probability (at the present time) and actual behavior (in the future).

Another interesting direction for future research involves the relationships between the practice of high-risk and other leisure and non-risk sport activities. Are practitioners of high-risk sport a high-probability target group for service providers of other, non-risky sports? A related question involves the potentially enhancing role of an opportunity to practice a risky sport as a part of a leisure package that includes other, non-related components. Finally, although Florenthal and Shoham's experiment (1997) provided preliminary insights, how best should marketers attempt to influence future probability of consumption of high-risk sports? A single exposure, as in Florenthal and Shoham (1997) was instrumental in influencing attitudes, but it failed to carry through to the behavioral intention measure. Additional experiments are needed to assess the impact of different messages, at varying exposures, on engagement probability.

Summary and Conclusion

This chapter synthesized the diverse models used in previous research about high-risk sports. Sensation-seeking, arousal-avoidance, role-relaxation, and demographics were found to affect the perceived benefits of risky sports and the probability of joining or participating in a risky sport. Curiosity-arousing plays an important role in early stages of the adoption process. Thrill and adventure gain importance as individuals move closer to joining a high-risk sport. Thus, differing perceived benefits influence behavioral intention in early and late stages of adoption. Finally, age, experience, and the need for efficacy, identity construction, and camaraderie affect the frequency of engagement in a high-risk sport. They also play a role in predicting whether practitioners of one high-risk sport will also practice additional risky sports. Although we have learned a lot about risk taking and participation in sports, substantial work still remains for future research.

ACKNOWLEDGMENT

This research was supported in part by the Technion V.P.R. Fund.

REFERENCES

Achenbaum, A. (1966). Knowledge is a thing called measurement. In L. Adler & I. Crespi (Eds.), *Attitude Research at Sea* (pp. 111–126). Chicago: American Marketing Association.

Ajzen, I., & Fishbein, M. (1980). *Understanding Attitudes and Predicting Social Behavior.* Englewood Cliffs, NJ: Prentice-Hall.

Apter, M. J. (1976). Some data inconsistent with the optimal arousal theory of motivation. *Perceptual and Motor Skills, 43,* 1209–1210.

Apter, M. J. (1982). *The Experience of Motivation.* London: Academic Press.

Apter, M. J. (1965). Influence of models' reinforcement contingencies on the acquisition of imitative responses. *Journal of Applied Social Psychology, 1,* 589–595.

Arnould, E. J., & Price, L. L. (1993, June). River magic: Extraordinary experience and the extended service encounter. *Journal of Consumer Research, 20,* 24–45.

Beatty, S. E., & Kahle, L. R. (1988, Summer). Alternative hierarchies of the attitude-behavior relationship: The impact of brand commitment and habit. *Journal of the Academy of Marketing Science, 16,* 1–10.

Beatty, S. E., Kahle, L. R., Homer, P. M., & Misra, S. (1985). Alternative measurement approaches to consumer values: The list of values and the rokeach Value Survey. *Psychology and Marketing, 3,* 181–200.

Beatty, S. E., Kahle, L. R., Homer, P., Utsey, M., & Keown, C. (1993). Gift giving behaviors in United States and Japan: A personal values perspective. *Journal of International Consumer Marketing, 6*(1), 49–66.

Belk, R. R. (1988, September). Possessions and the extended self. *Journal of Consumer Research, 15,* 139–168.

Belk, R. R., Wallendorf, M., & Sherry, J. F. Jr. (1989, June). The sacred and the profane in consumer behavior: Theodicy on the odyssey. *Journal of Consumer Research, 16,* 1–38.

Brannigan, A., & McDougall, A. A. (1983). Peril and pleasure in the maintenance of a high risk sport: A study of hang-gliding. *Journal of Sport Behavior, 6*(1), 37–51.

Burns, W. J., Hampson, S. E., Severson, H. H., & Slovic, P. (1993). Alcohol-related risk taking among teenagers: An investigation of contribution factors and a discussion of how marketing principles can help. In L. McAlister & M. L. Rothchild (Eds.), *Advances in Consumer Research* (vol. 20, pp. 183–187). Provo, UT: Association for Consumer Research.

Celsi, R. L. (1992). Transcendent benefits of high-risk sports. In J. F. Sherry, Jr. & B. Sternthal (Eds.), *Advances in Consumer Research* (vol. 19, pp. 636–641). Provo, UT: Association for Consumer Research.

Celsi, R. L., Rose, R. L., & Leigh, T. W. (1993, June). An exploration of high-risk leisure consumption through skydiving. *Journal of Consumer Research, 20,* 1–23.

Cronin, C. (1991). Sensation seeking among mountain climbers. *Personality and Individual Differences, 12,* 653–654.

Fishbein, M. (1967). Attitude and the prediction of behavior. In M. Fishbein (Ed.), *Readings in Attitude Theory and Measurement* (pp. 477–492). New York: Wiley.

Fishbein, M. (1966). The relationship between beliefs, attitudes, and behavior. In S. Feldman (Ed.), *Cognitive Consistency* (pp. 199–223). New York: Academic Press.

Fishbein, M., & Ajzen, I. (1975). *Belief, Attitude, Intention, and Behavior*. Reading, MA: Addison-Wesley.

Florenthal, B., & Shoham, A. (1997). The impact of persuasive information on changes in attitude and behavioral intention toward risky sports (Working Paper). Haifa, Israel: Technion—Israel Institute of Technology.

Grube, J. W., Weir, I. L., Getzlaf, S., & Rokeach, M. (1984). Own value system, value images, and cigarette smoking. *Personality and Social Psychology Bulletin, 10,* 306–313.

Hensehl, A. M. (1971). The relationship between values and behavior: A development process. *Child Development, 42,* 1997–2007.

Hirschman, E., & Holbrook, M. B. (1982, Summer). Hedonic consumption: Emerging concepts, methods, and propositions. *Journal of Marketing, 46,* 92–101.

Holbrook, M. B. (1978, November). Beyond attitude structure: Toward the informational determinants of attitude. *Journal of Marketing Research, 15,* 545–556.

Homer, P. M., & Kahle, L. R. (1988). A structural equation test of the value-attitude-behavior hierarchy. *Journal of Personality and Social Psychology, 54,* 638–646.

Hymbaugh, K., & Garrett, J. (1974). Sensation seeking among skydivers. *Perceptual and Motor Skills, 38,* 118.

Kahle, L. R. (1995). Role-relaxed consumers: A trend for the nineties. *Journal of Advertising Research, 35*(2), 66–71.

Kahle, L. R. (1983). *Social Values and Social Change: Adaptation to Life in America*. New York: Praeger.

Kahle, L. R., Beatty, S. E., & Homer, P. M. (1986). Alternative measurement approaches to consumer values: The list of values (LOV) and the values and life style (VALS). *Journal of Consumer Research, 13,* 405–409.

Kahle, L. R., & Shoham, A. (1995). Role-relaxed consumers: Empirical evidence. *Journal of Advertising Research, 35*(3), 59–62.

Kerr, J. H. (1991). Arousal seeking in risk sport participants. *Personality and Individual Differences, 12,* 613–616.

Kerr, J. H., & Svebak, S. (1989). Motivational aspects of preference for, and participation in, "risk" and "safe" sports. *Personality and Individual Differences, 10,* 797–800.

Lyng, S. (1990, January). Edgework: A social psychological analysis of voluntary risk taking. *American Journal of Sociology, 95,* 851–886.

Murgatroyd, S., Rushton, C., Apter, M., & Ray, C. (1978). The development of the Telic Dominance Scale. *Journal of Personality Assessment, 42,* 519–528.

Price, L. L., Arnould, E. J., & Tierney, P. (1995). Going to extremes: Managing service encounters and assessing provider performance. *Journal of Marketing, 59*(2), 83–97.

Rokeach, M. (1973). *The Nature of Human Values*. New York: Free Press.

Rose, G. M., Shoham, A., Kahle, L. R., & Batra, R. (1994). Social value, conformity, and dress. *Journal of Applied Social Psychology, 24,* 1501–1519.

Ryan, M. J., & Bonfield, E. H. (1975, September). The Fishbein extended model and consumer behavior. *Journal of Consumer Research, 2,* 118–136.

Severson, H. H., Slovic, P., & Hampson, S. (1993). Adolescents' perception of risk: Understanding and preventing high risk behavior. In L. McAlister & M. L. Rothchild (Eds.), *Advances in Consumer Research* (vol. 20, pp. 177–182). Provo, UT: Association for Consumer Research.

Shoham, A., Florenthal, B., Rose, G. M., & Kropp, F. (1997). The relationship between values and thrill- and adventure-seeking in Israel. In B. G. Englis & A. Olofsoon (Eds.), *European Advances in Consumer Research* (vol. 3, pp. 333–338). Provo, UT: Association for Consumer Research.

Shoham, A., Kahle, L. R., Kropp, F., & Rose, G. M. (1997). Personal values and the consumption of risk. In P. M. Herr & J. Kim (Eds.), *Proceedings of the Society for Consumer Psychology*. Washington, DC: Society for Consumer Psychology.

Shoham, A., Kropp, F., & Rose, G. M. (1998). Personal values as predictors of the probability of future consumption of sports. In C. Pechmann & D. Grewal (Eds.), *Proceedings of the Society for Consumer Psychology*. Austin, TX: Society for Consumer Psychology.

Shoham, A., Rose, G. M., & Kahle, L. R. (1998). Marketing of risky sports: From intention to action. *Journal of the Academy of Marketing Science, 26,* 307–321.

Shoham, A., Rose, G. M., & Kahle, L. R. (2000). Practitioners of risky sports: A quantitative examination. *Journal of Business Research, 47,* 237–251.

Smith, K. C. P., & Apter, M. J. (1975). *A Theory of Psychological Reversals.* Chippenham, UK: Picton Press.

Svebak, S., & Kerr, J. H. (1989). The role of impulsivity in preference for sports. *Personality and Individual Differences, 10*(1), 51–58.

Svebak, S., Kerr, J. H., & Stoyva, J. (1980). High arousal can be pleasant and exciting. *Biofeedback and Self-Regulation, 5,* 439–444.

Williams, R. M. Jr. (1979). Change and stability in values and value systems: A sociological perspective. In M. Rokeach (Ed.), *Understanding Human Values: Individual and Societal* (pp. 15–46). New York: Free Press.

Zuckerman, M. (1974). The sensation seeking motive. In B. A. Maher (Ed.), *Progress in Experimental Personality Research.* New York: Academic Press.

Zuckerman, M. (1983a). *Biological Bases of Sensation Seeking, Impulsivity and Anxiety.* Hillsdale, NJ: Lawrence Erlbaum Associates.

Zuckerman, M. (1983b). Sensation seeking and sports. *Personality and Individual Differences, 4,* 285–293.

Zuckerman, M. (1984). Sensation seeking: A comparative approach to human trait. *The Behavioral and Brain Sciences, 7,* 413–471.

Zuckerman, M., Buchsbaum, M. S., & Murphy, D. L. (1980). Sensation seeking and its biological correlates. *Psychological Bulletin, 88,* 187–214.

Zuckerman, M., Kolin, E. L., Price, L., & Zoob, I. (1964). Development of a sensation-seeking scale. *Journal of Consulting Psychology, 28,* 477–482.

II

Sports Celebrity Endorsements

Sports produce celebrities. People often want to associate themselves with these star athletes and celebrities. After all, most sports stars apparently achieve their success through remarkable skill and intense effort. Sports stars often embody many of the personal attitudes society admires. Marketers have tapped into this phenomenon by using sports celebrities to endorse products of many different forms, from shoes for sports to unseen underwear. Chapter 5 looks historically at the use of celebrities in print media, clarifying what trends dominate the field. Chapter 6 looks at whether clutter adds confusion to endorsements. Chapter 7 considers two of the most successful athletes, Magic Johnson and Mark McGwire. The depth and breadth of the celebrity appeal has critical importance for how consumers respond to the celebrities.

The Strategic Use of Celebrity Athlete Endorsers in Print Media: A Historical Perspective

Melinda J. Jones
The University of Notre Dame

David W. Schumann
The University of Tennessee

Let's begin with a "word-association" exercise. Reply with the first thing that comes to mind . . .

Michael Jordan

What came to mind? Phenomenal basketball player? Chicago Bulls? Number 23? Washington Wizards? Retirement(s)? Comebacks? Nike? Gatorade? Hanes?

Michael Jordan is known not only for his athletic prowess but also for putting his face, name, and body in and on products. Although it may be true that Jordan is an anomaly, both on the court and as an endorser, using famous athletes to endorse products is certainly not a new phenomenon. This chapter presents the findings from a content analysis of general readership magazines. The results from this study reveal that famous athletes have been used to endorse products and services since at least the 1930s. Moreover, this form of promotion has experienced a number of interesting transitions.

Let's try the word association exercise again . . .

"Joe DiMaggio"

Baseball? New York Yankees? Marilyn Monroe? Mr. Coffee? Avon? Probably long forgotten, in the early 1950s, "Joltin' Joe's" face appeared in Avon ads in an attempt to promote men's toiletries.

The unique role that athletes play in society makes them extremely marketable commodities. In the early recorded games in Olympia (Greece), winning athletes were considered heroes who made their hometowns famous, such as Milo of Kroton and Diagoras of Rhodes (Crane, 1996). The modern Olympic movement has also produced athletes who have been perceived as heroes (e.g., Jessie Owens, Wilma Rudolph). Indeed, within our modern society, one could argue that, with scant few exceptions, athletes continue to be likely candidates to attain hero status.

Given the fact that professional athletes typically represent the positive characteristics that companies also want to project (success, special talent, confidence, and motivation), athletes can be very appropriate as product endorsers. Athletes typically convey a winning attitude, healthy appearance, and general appeal. However, along with this positive representation, there are several other factors that need to be considered when using an athlete to endorse a product: their importance and potential impact on consumer attitudes and sales, as well as the risks involved with pairing an athlete with a product or brand.

IMPORTANCE/IMPACT

Philip Knight, founder of Nike, Inc., appears to have recognized the importance of celebrity athlete endorsement. Beginning with track star Steve Prefontaine, Nike has accumulated a remarkable lineup of professional athletes (e.g., Michael Jordan, Tiger Woods, & Bo Jackson) (Goldin, 1996). Although most sports marketers will acknowledge that the impact of using athletes as endorsers cannot easily be measured in terms of revenues or sales, they rely on the belief that athletes have the power to enhance the image of their product (Oneal, Finch, Hamilton, & Hammonds, 1987).

Although it may be difficult to measure an athlete endorser's success in terms of revenue and sales, it appears possible that other related impact measures may be affected. Agrawal and Kamakura (1995) analyzed stock price movements and found that press releases announcing celebrity endorsement contracts resulted in an increased return. A famous face in an advertisement can help build a recognizable image for a company or its products and has been known to boost viewer recall (Sasseen, 1984). Indeed, if there is a "fit" between the athlete and the product, a celebrity endorser's stamp of approval can bring added value to a brand's equity as well as create an emotional bond (Bradley, 1996).

RISKS

The use of spokespersons and other kinds of endorsement affiliations are considered powerful marketing tools, and some athletes have worked promotional wonders for the products they endorse. However, many companies have come to learn that linking their corporate or brand image to an individual athlete is risky. Public perception of athletes can change, sometimes rather rapidly. Moreover, the cost to maintain a sponsorship relationship with a star athlete could become overly expensive or a spokesperson who is used fairly often can become overexposed (Swenson, 1987).

Some controversy exists over the popularity of celebrity athletes and the money expended to them to endorse products. According to Richard Leonard of the Zandl Group, aggressive inquiries by the media of anyone in the limelight have brought athletes back down to a more realistic level. Although athletes may continue to be perceived as heroes, no longer are they considered allusive, untouchable beings. Numerous incidents have contributed to consumers' growing skepticism of athletes. Athlete endorsers have been tarnished by reports of exorbitant salaries, lucrative endorsement deals, legal violations, and unpopular antics, all of which serve to attenuate their credibility as spokespersons. Changing consumer attitudes toward athletes have motivated some marketers to use more realistic advertisements featuring anti-heroes who tell the truth (Jensen, 1993a).

The risks involved in using celebrity athletes as endorsers has created a movement toward event sponsorship (Walley, 1987) with marketers becoming more conservative in their selection of athlete endorsers. However, even with these concerns, it is unlikely that marketers will ever stop using athletes as endorsers (Actman, 1994). *Forbes* magazine stated that in 1998, "the 40 highest paid athletes pulled in $360 million in salary and winnings (to go along with $281 million in endorsements)" (Spiegel & Gallagher, 1999).

It has been found that the use of celebrity endorsement appeals may generate more positive feelings among younger consumers than older consumers, thus younger consumers may be prime targets for celebrity endorsement appeals (Frieden, 1984). However, a study conducted by *Advertising Age* counterargues this claim. In actuality, teens' buying habits and loyalties may have little to do with the paid endorsements by media-hyped athletes. According to *Advertising Age*, the characteristic deemed most important to young consumers in their assessment of products is quality. The study reflects that young people may be more skeptical than they were in the past, and today they are more likely to discount advertising's persuasive power. Teenagers seem to regard advertising as a form of entertainment rather than as a source of information. Furthermore, young people do not seem to be as willing to admit that their favorite stars have any impact on their purchases (Jensen, 1993b).

In sum, there is a long history of athletes becoming heroes in our culture. However, employing heroes as endorsers has had mixed results. There are documented instances where an athlete endorser has directly increased the bottom line of a company (e.g., Michael Jordan and Nike). There are also documented instances where companies have had to dissolve a relationship with an athlete because of negative public perception (e.g., O. J. Simpson and Hertz, Dennis Rodman and Converse). Where does one begin to explore these seemingly vulnerable relationships? The study presented in this chapter was an effort to better understand this phenomenon by considering its history. A content analysis was conducted to examine the changing demographics of athletes over time, the level of "fit" between athletes and the products they endorse, and how the use of athletic endorsement has changed creatively and strategically.

METHODOLOGY

A content analysis was conducted on general readership magazines in order to examine the following questions:

- Have there been trends in the use of athletes as endorsers over time?
- What is the degree of congruence between athletes and the products they endorse? Has that changed over time?
- What promotional strategies are used with athlete endorsers? Have they changed over time?

Sampling

Ten general readership magazines (Table 5.1) were chosen based on their demographic profiles (i.e., gender, age, marital status) according to the *Standard Rate and Data Service*. The demographics across the selection of magazines included both male and female readership, with ages ranging from 15 years of age and up. Eight of the 10 magazines were analyzed from their original date of publication, which ranged from 1850 to 1980 (2 magazines were

TABLE 5.1
Magazines Included in the
Study

Magazines (first year of publication)

Harpers (1850)
Good Housekeeping (1885)
Ladies Home Journal (1900)
Saturday Evening Post (1905)
Time (1925)
Business Week (1930)
Life (1940)
Seventeen (1950)
Esquire (1960)
Glamour (1980)

analyzed based on first available edition). The sampling procedure employed four different years per decade for each magazine (e.g., 1960, 1963, 1965, 1967), examining three issues each year. The three issues per year were varied. For the years ending with 0 and 5, issues were drawn from January, May, and September, whereas for the years ending with 3 and 7, issues were drawn from March, July, and November. The sampling of weekly publications employed random selection within the months assigned. The monthly publications were limited to one choice. For each magazine, the sampling process included all selected issues from the first available date through 1997.

Process

The process was initiated by locating the ads in the original magazines or on microfilm, counting the total number of ads in each issue, and photocopying each ad that contained a celebrity athlete endorser. A coding scheme was developed that would provide insights to the three research questions posed in this study. The following codes were employed in the study: magazine, month, year, name of athlete, sport, product type, product gender, source gender, race, identified quadrant of the Foote, Cone, and Belding (FCB) Grid, creative strategy, sport congruence, gender congruence, and message reinforcement. Independent coding was performed by the two authors, and differences were

TABLE 5.2
Data by Decade

Decade	Total Issues	Total Ads	Total Athlete Ads
1920	53	5,993	1
1930	75	5,799	21
1940	82	8,937	11
1950	90	11,041	10
1960	105	9,718	19
1970	111	8,315	24
1980	119	10,440	52
1990	120	8,745	29
Total	755	68,988	167

noted and resolved through discussion. Inter-coder reliability was found to be no less than 85% on all codes. Interpretation of the data included frequency analysis as well as the examination of potential trends over time.

Overall, the sample included a total of 852 issues and 73,290 ads (going back to the earliest publication in 1850). Table 5.2 provides a breakdown by decade from 1920 forward (the first appearance of an athlete endorser occurred within the 1920s).

RESULTS

Question 1: Have there been trends in the use of athletes as endorsers over time?

Six elements of using athlete endorsers were employed to examine the potential for trends over time in general readership magazines. The six elements include:

1. The relative frequency of athlete endorser usage
2. The sport represented
3. The gender of the athlete
4. The ethnic orientation
5. The type of product advertised
6. The gender orientation of the product that was endorsed by the athlete.

Each element is considered both overall and as it has appeared in each of eight decades[1].

Relative Frequency

A 1984 Madison Avenue article (Sasseen, 1984) claimed that the use of sports celebrities was increasing. The article claimed that in the early 1960s, 1 of every 15 ads (6%) featured a sports celebrity, and in the early 1980s, the number was estimated to be closer to 1 in 5 (20%). These results represent athlete endorsements across all types of media. Although the study presented in this chapter considers only those athlete endorsements found in the print media, specifically in general readership magazines, the results demonstrated great fluctuation in the use of athlete endorsers over time.

Recently, some of the top footwear companies have begun to streamline their endorsement budgets, cut back the corporate roster of endorsers, and in many cases return to the era when the product, not the player, is the star of the show (Business: Tripped up, 1998; Bhonslay, 1998). Ads are beginning to focus on brand heritage, technology, and everyday athletes (Harder look at sports stars, 1998). In particular, both Nike and Reebok have introduced strategies that rely less on the use of their so-called role model athletes and more on sports participation and the product itself. "It appears as if the 'heyday' of athletes as professional endorsers has come and gone" (Tedesci, 1998). An interesting question is whether this trend may simply reflect promotion within the United States. For example, Reebok plans to continue to use athletes to endorse products in the United Kingdom (Reebok UK stars stay, 1998).

Recall that the result of the Madison Avenue study (Sasseen, 1984) reflected a significant level of endorser advertising (20%). In our study, the incidence of athlete endorsement was significantly lower. Table 5.3 contains the number of ads per issue by decade, as well as the percentage of athlete ads as a function of total ads by decade. The percentage ranges from approximately .02% to .5% of total ads. Thus, athlete endorsement in general magazine advertising, as a subset of total media effort, is significantly smaller. The larger percentage reported from the Madison Avenue study most likely reflects the increase in sports broadcasting and sport specific magazines.

A number of conclusions can be drawn from the results of our study. First, the number of ads per issue, although fluctuating, has decreased significantly from the 1940s and 1950s (see Table 5.3). This is an interesting finding that suggests that magazines are either employing more space per ad (e.g., more

---

[1] Only one advertisement including an athlete endorser was found during the 1920s in this sample.

TABLE 5.3
Relative Frequency

Decade	Ads/Issue (#)	Athlete Ads/Total Ads (%)
1920	113.08	0.0167%
1930	77.32	0.3621%
1940	108.99	0.1231%
1950	122.68	0.0906%
1960	92.55	0.1955%
1970	74.91	0.2886%
1980	87.73	0.4981%
1990	72.88	0.3316%

full page and multi-page ads) or less advertising space is being allocated per issue. Further study is needed to examine the reasons behind this trend. Second, the use of athletes as product endorsers in print advertising has fluctuated, resulting in trend blocks. More specifically, the data illustrates that a period of increased usage (1930), was followed by a period of little usage (1940 through 1960), followed again by increased usage (1970 through 1990s). However, on closer examination, the ratio of using this type of advertising is quite diminutive. During the decade of 1980s, in which the largest percentage of athlete endorser advertising was found, only .5% of the ads featured athlete endorsers. Overall, this study found that athletes appeared in only .34% of the ads that were sampled from the 10 magazines. Further study might uncover several reasons for these fluctuations. Advertising themes and strategies might have been altered to accommodate for marketplace changes (i.e., political or economic conditions, social or cultural trends). For instance, times of war, periods of recession or depression, or the importance of placing idol status on athletes could impact a marketer's decision to use an athlete to endorse a product.

Sports Represented

As Table 5.4 reports, 28 different sports were represented in the overall sample. Three sports appeared an average of 10% of the time. Overall, football players appeared in advertising 15.3% of the time, golfers 14.9% of the time, and baseball players 13% of the time. Three other sports, tennis (9.3%), racecar

TABLE 5.4
Sports Represented in Product Endorsement

Sport	Number of ads with sport represented by athlete endorser	Percent of ads with sport represented by athlete endorser
Football	33	15.3
Golf	32	14.9
Baseball	28	13.0
Tennis	20	9.3
Race Car Driving	19	8.3
Basketball	12	5.6
Gymnastics	9	4.2
Track/Field	9	4.2
Ice Skating	8	3.7
Hockey	6	2.8
Rodeo	6	2.8
Swimming	5	2.3
Boating/Sailing	3	1.4
Diving	3	1.4
Huntsman	3	1.4
Skiing	3	1.4
Polo	2	.9
Volleyball	2	.9
Weightlifting	2	.9
Wrestling	2	.9
Biking	1	.5
Boxing	1	.5
Bowling	1	.5
Bull Fighting	1	.5
Dog Sled	1	.5
Fishing	1	.5
Horse racing	1	.5
Sportsman	1	.5

driving (8.8%), and basketball (5.6%) appeared in more than 5% of the total ads sampled. The 22 remaining sports appeared in less than 5% of the total ads sampled.

The advent of each of the dominant sports (sports represented in more than 10% of the advertising sampled) is interesting to consider. Golfers first appeared in the 1930s as product endorsers. Both men and women golfers were represented and primarily endorsed equipment for their sport. Based on the sample employed in this study, golfers may have been the first major source of athletic endorsers to appear in print advertising. The consistent use of tennis players and golfers over time may be due, in part, to the worldwide recognition of these sports. These players appear to be marketable both domestically and internationally.

Football players began to appear in print advertising in the 1950's, almost two decades after the National Football League came into existence. Although it might be expected that baseball heroes such as Babe Ruth might have been prominent in print advertising earlier in the century, the sampling employed in this study found that only a few baseball players were used as product endorsers before 1950 (i.e., Red Rolf in 1937 and Mike Barbark, George Stirnweiss, Hank Borony, and Nick Etten in 1945). Baseball players appeared to enjoy endorsement status during the 1960s and 1970s, but consistent with the literature, there has been a scarcity of marketable baseball stars in recent years. Baseball may suffer from a charisma problem, which may be the reason that very few athletes have the credibility to endorse a product not associated with sports gear (Adler, 1993). This slump may be attributed to baseball players' image, compared to other sports (Liesse, 1991). In light of the baseball strike of 1994 to 1995 and the threatened strike in 2002, many fans may be questioning player's allegiance to anything, much less to a product they might use.

Forbes magazine claimed that most athletes endorsing products played individual sports (Newcomb and Palmeri, 1990). Although the findings from the study presented in this chapter echo this claim to some extent, it appears that athletes from team sports have also benefited from endorsement deals (individual sports were represented in 60% of the athlete-endorsed ads). Although representation of different sports in product endorsement has waxed and waned over the decades, there appears to be no discernable pattern.

Gender

Although male athletes have clearly dominated product endorsement in general readership magazines overall, there is a clear trend toward greater female athlete endorsement. As Table 5.5 illustrates, over the past three decades, the number of ads employing female athlete endorsers has increased significantly. Indeed, in the decade of the 1990s, over 60% of the print ads sampled in this study employed female athletes.

This trend toward more equal representation may be due to a number of factors. First, women's participation in sports has steadily increased over

TABLE 5.5
Female Athletes As Product Endorsers

Decade	Percent of ads with female endorsers	Number of ads with female endorsers	Number of total athlete ads
1920	0	0	1
1930	9.5	2	21
1940	9.1	1	11
1950	0	0	10
1960	0	0	19
1970	32	8	24
1980	19.2	10	52
1990	60.7	17	29

time. With the passage of Title IX in 1972, female participation in team sports such as softball, basketball, volleyball, and soccer has risen significantly. Over the past decade, sporting goods equipment manufacturers such as Nike and Reebok have increased their use of women athletes by signing endorsement deals with many top professionals (Lustigman, 1995). In 1997 Reebok took a further step by introducing signature footwear tied to a set of famous female athletes in basketball and soccer (Jensen, 1997). Overall, however, the use of female athletes as endorsers still inadequately represents their contribution to and participation in sports.

Ethnic Differences

Whites appear to have dominated athlete endorsements in print advertising and continue to do so. As Figure 5.1 reflects, in this sample, until the decade of the 1970s, white athletes were the only group to be represented in print advertising. It has only been during the past three decades that other ethnic groups have been represented in athletic endorsements within this medium. However, it is interesting to note that the ethnic representation of athletes as product endorsers does not parallel the ethnic representation in sports, especially for blacks. During the 1996 to 1997 season, 79% of the players in the National Basketball Association, 66% of the players in the National Football League, and 17% of the players in Major League Baseball were black (Lipchick, 1997). However, according to our sample of print advertisements

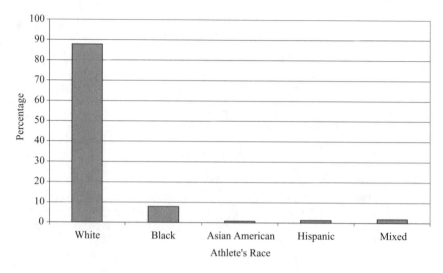

FIG. 5.1.   Percentage of race representation.

during that same time period, black athletes only appeared in 15.8% of the athlete-endorsed advertisements.

Product Type

Each product was coded into 1 of 12 product categories adapted from the Simmons Market Research Bureau framework (Table 5.6). Athletes were primarily found to endorse appliances, garden care, sports/leisure, and household products (36%). This large percentage is likely skewed by the inclusion of sporting goods products in that product category. The personal care product category was also found to be a popular category (26%) followed closely by the jewelry, luggage, and apparel category (24%). An analysis of each of these 3 categories over time revealed no discernable trends except for the fact that the latter decades found greater employment of athlete endorsers across all 3 product categories.

Product Gender

All products in the study were coded either as male oriented, female oriented, or undifferentiated. Coding was conducted based on appropriate product gender orientation at the time the advertisement appeared. For example, in the 1950s, life insurance might have been considered a male-oriented product, whereas in the 1990s, it has been considered equally appropriate across gender.

TABLE 5.6
Product Categories

Product Categories	Count	Percent
Appliances, Garden Care, Sports/Leisure, Household	36	21.4
Health Care, Beauty Aids, Personal Products	26	15.5
Jewelry, Luggage, Men's/Women's Apparel	24	14.3
Travel, Investments, Insurance	21	12.5
Automobiles, Cycles	19	11.3
Alcoholic Beverages, Tobacco	17	10.1
Coffee, Milk, Juice, Water	12	7.1
Games, Computers, Books, Telephones	11	6.5
Dairy products, Baking, Cereal, Pizza	1	0.6
Soup, Sauces, Meat	1	0.6
Restaurants, Shopping	0	0
Candy, Snacks	0	0

As Table 5.7 reflects, during the past five decades, the proportion of male products appearing in general magazines has decreased while the proportion of women's products and undifferentiated products has increased. In fact, in this sample, the last two decades revealed the majority of athlete-endorsed ads were for undifferentiated products. An article in *Advertising Age* claimed that athletes typically promote traditionally masculine products, but they also

TABLE 5.7
Product Gender: Row Count (Row Percent)

Decade	Male Count (%)	Female Count (%)	Undifferentiated Count (%)	Total Ads
1920	0 (0)	0 (0%)	0 (100%)	1
1930	11 (53.4%)	1 (4.8%)	9 (42.9%)	21
1940	3 (27.3%)	1 (9.1%)	7 (63.6%)	11
1950	8 (80%)	0 (0%)	2 (20%)	10
1960	14 (75%)	0 (0%)	5 (25%)	19
1970	11 (44%)	5 (20%)	8 (36%)	24
1980	9 (17.3%)	14 (28.8%)	27 (53.8%)	52
1990	6 (21.4%)	3 (10.7%)	20 (67.9%)	29

have been found to promote toothpaste, shampoo, spray paint, and candy bars (Ads bank on athletes to ring up those sales 1979). In our study, each of these products would have been coded as an undifferentiated product.

Question 2: What is the level of congruency between athletes that serve as endorsers and the products they endorse?

Congruency has proved to be a difficult construct to nail down. Several definitional approaches have appeared in both the advertising and psychology literature. One approach considers congruence as a "matching" or "fit" between the source and the product or brand. For example, Kanungo and Pang (1973) examined the fit between product gender and physical characteristics of the source. Hawkins, Best, and Coney (1983) viewed congruence as a matching of person, source, and audience personalities. Misra and Beatty (1990) stated that congruency exists when "highly relevant characteristics of the source are consistent with the highly relevant attributes of the brand" (p. 162). In sum, it is not always clear who might be successful as a product endorser. It may be that athletes work best as spokespeople when there is a logical connection between the endorser and the product. This connection may be a demonstrable attribute such as ruggedness or even an intangible quality such as wholesomeness (Howard, 1977).

A second approach considers the congruence between the source and the advertising message. Petty and Cacioppo (1981) viewed congruence in terms of a source and a concept about the product shared by the source (either directly or inferred). For example, attractive models are often used to represent products that promote enhancement of one's appearance. Kahle and Homer (1985) termed this the *match-up hypothesis*, borrowing from their Social Adaptation Theory. This definition suggests a match between the source and the message that has the potential to give the product perceived characteristics above and beyond its physical attributes. Kamins and his colleagues (Kamins, 1990; Kamins and Gupta, 1994) remarked that the message conveyed by the image of the celebrity and the image of the product must converge and be internalized by the audience in order create perceived congruence.

In this study, *congruency* is examined three different ways. First, gender of the athlete is compared to the gender orientation of the product. Second, the sport represented by the athlete is considered as it relates to the advertised product (Is this product typically used in direct conjunction with participation in the sport?). Third, the establishment or reinforcement of some congruence of the athlete to the product through the message is examined.

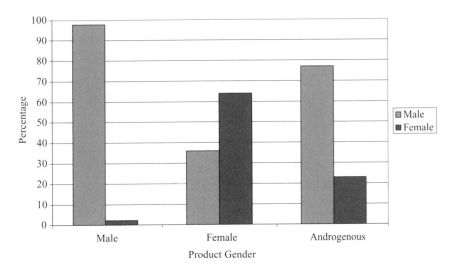

FIG. 5.2.   Source gender × product gender.

Gender Congruency

Figure 5.2 reflects the degree of congruence for male products and female products. Undifferentiated products are also included in the figure and demonstrate the high level of male endorser dominance, but they are not relevant to the discussion of gender congruency. There exists a high level of congruence between male-oriented products and male athlete endorsers (e.g., Stan Musial/aftershave; A.J. Foyt/motor oil). There is, however, relatively less congruence between female products and female athlete endorsers (Dorothy Hamill/shampoo; Cathy Rigby/feminine protection). This finding, however, can be traced to the study's methodology and sampling procedures and may not be a true reflection of reality. This particular finding resulted from a single large campaign (Merlin Olsen/flowers), each ad in the campaign coded separately. Although typically purchased by males, flowers were coded as a female product, given the receiver of the product is typically female.

Sport Congruency

Sport congruence, defined here, reflects whether the represented sport was directly related to the product. It was operationally defined by an affirmative response to one or both of the following questions: Would athletes in this sport be likely to employ this product in their training or performance? Would you be likely to consistently find this product in an athlete's training bag or locker? A consistent finding emerged from the data. Only one out of three print advertisements employing athlete endorsers were viewed as being sport congruent (e.g., golfers/golf clubs). In the majority of ads, there seems to be no direct relationship between the product and the sport represented in the ad (e.g., Arthur Ashe/tires; Lenore K. Wingard/cigarettes). Given this interesting finding and the growing interest in the concept of congruence, how else might congruency be established? Message establishment or reinforcement seemed to be the next logical place to look.

Message Establishment or Reinforcement

Given the large number of ads that did not tie the sport to the product, it seemed important to consider the extent to which the specific athlete was tied to the product. Print advertisements employing athlete endorsers were coded into one of the following four categories:

1. An obvious connection between the athlete and the product existed.
2. An obvious connection between the athlete and the product existed and was also reinforced directly within the message.
3. No obvious connection existed between the athlete and the product, nor was it established within the message.
4. No obvious connection existed between the athlete and the product, but a connection was established within the message.

Seventy-three percent of the ads were coded as having no obvious connection between the athlete and the product (categories 3 and 4). It is interesting to note that only 30% of these non-connected ads employed the message to establish the connection. Of the remaining 27% of the ads that *did* make an obvious connection between the athlete and the product (categories 1 and 2), nearly half (48.2%) of the ads employed the message to reinforce the connection.

In sum, when congruence is examined in terms of gender, sport, and message establishment and reinforcement, only gender congruence is consistently found to exist. Given the intuitive belief that congruency between athlete endorsers and products has the potential to create a positive audience response, future research is needed to explore further factors that might contribute to a congruent relationship.

Question 3: What advertising strategies are found most often among athlete endorsed advertisements?

Two types of strategies were examined in this study. The first strategy employed the FCB Grid (Foote, Cone, and Belding) which classifies four advertising planning strategies in a 2×2 matrix based on level of consumer involvement with a product (high vs. low) and information processing requirements (feeling vs. thinking) (Berger, 1986). Each quadrant is separately defined to represent a certain type of planning strategy based on the type of product being promoted. Products placed within Quadrant I are informative products that elicit high involvement and thoughtful consideration. Quadrant II also contains high involvement products, but these products are more likely to evoke affective responses. Quadrant III encompasses products that are habitual, evoking some thought yet are of low involvement, whereas Quadrant IV contains low involvement products that trigger relatively affective responses.

Figure 5.3 provides a picture of the FCB Grid along with the proportion of athlete endorser ads represented in each quadrant. What is particularly interesting is the domination of high involvement products in this analysis. The highest proportion of ads, 42.2%, exists in Quadrant I (high involvement/thinking) followed by Quadrant III (high involvement/feeling) with 24.4% of the ads. Further analysis of the involvement variable by itself shows an intriguing picture over time (Figure 5.4). Although celebrity athlete endorsement in earlier decades favored low involvement products, by the 1960s athlete endorsement of high involvement products were more common. Since the 1960s, however, the ratio of high to low involvement products

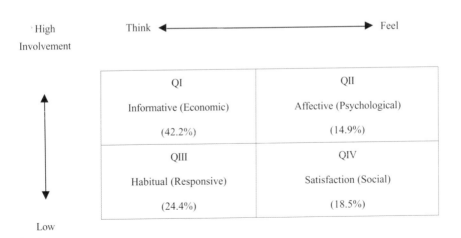

FIG. 5.3.   FCB grid results.

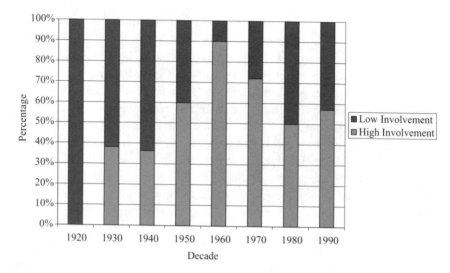

FIG. 5.4.   High vs. low involvement dimension.

employing athlete endorsers has become more equal in nature. The same examination of time was explored for the thinking/feeling dimension. In that case, there was no change over time with two-thirds of the products endorsed by athletes being located within the thinking dimension.

Advertising Strategy

Two types of advertising strategy were investigated. The first used a dichotomous variable ads that were informational versus transformational in nature (Laskey, Day, & Crask, 1989). Informational advertising is defined in terms of its ability to provide the target audience with factual and relevant brand data in a clear and logical manner. Transformational advertising seeks to associate the brand use experience with a unique set of psychological characteristics. As Figure 5.5 reflects, informational advertising strategy dominated athlete endorser advertising and has since the early decades. However, the findings of this study clearly suggest a trend toward greater use of transformational advertising.

The second advertising strategy examined in this study concerns the use of a statement of endorsement, defined as a claim made by the athlete regarding the product/service. Figure 5.6 suggests that these statements were more likely to be employed in earlier decades. It is noteworthy that

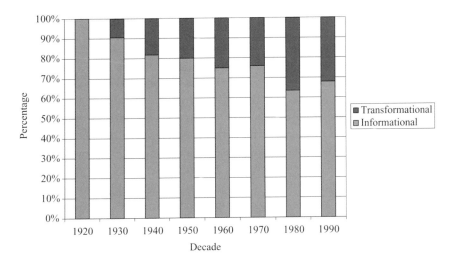

FIG. 5.5.   Basic advertising strategy.

during the 1960s, at a time when high involvement products endorsed by athletes were proportionally at their peak (see Fig. 5.3), the use of statements of endorsement was at a low point (only 24% of ads employed them). Since then, there has been a steady rise in statements of endorsement. At present, 50% of the ads containing celebrity athletes appear with such statements.

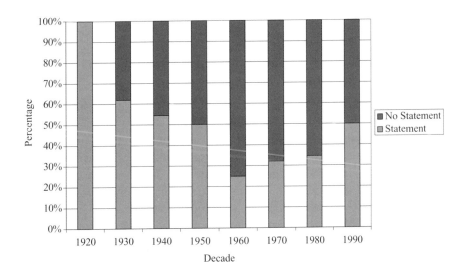

FIG. 5.6.   Statement of endorsement.

Methodological Limitations

As in any type of content analysis, there are certain methodological limitations. In general, relative to the total number of ads, there were relatively few athlete endorsed ads. Although 852 magazine issues were sampled with a total number of ads exceeding 73,000, the actual number of ads with athlete endorsers was less than 1% of that (167). Thus, although the sampling frame was quite extensive, the total number of athlete ads included in the analysis was relatively small. On one hand, it is possible that some major campaigns were not captured in this sampling process. On the other hand, it is also possible that a single campaign that ran during one of the sampled years could have skewed the data. Similarly, campaigns designed around specific athletic events (e.g., Olympics) may or may not be reflected in the data, depending on the years sampled. Finally, it must be noted that the results and conclusions from this data only represent the print magazine media for general readership. It is quite possible that a higher incidence of athlete endorsed ads might be found in other media forms (e.g., television, sports-related magazines).

DISCUSSION

The research presented in this chapter attempted to respond to questions regarding the historical use of athletes as endorsers. Specifically, demographics, congruency, and product and advertising strategies were explored. The content analysis revealed findings that led to a number of interesting conclusions. These will be presented next and will be followed by a comparison of results between this study and a similar historical study of *Sports Illustrated*.

Study Conclusions

Frequency. The use of celebrity athletes has seen periods of increased usage throughout the years, although the percentage of athletes promoting products in general readership magazines is still relatively low. The Madison Avenue study in the 1980s suggested a higher ratio of athlete-endorsed ads to total ads. This discrepancy in the actual use of athlete endorsers in advertising may be due to the greater prevalence of athletes appearing in other media forms not considered in this study.

Sporting events that are broadcast on TV coupled with magazines targeted at sports fans probably fuels a feeling of connectedness that fans have with athletes. Advertising agencies take full advantage of this felt connectedness, associating products with famous athletes and basing their media purchasing on the media preferences of this audience. Thus it is highly likely, when combined with sports specialty media, the percentage of athletes endorsing products is significantly higher than what is found in considering general readership print media.

Diversity. White male athletes have dominated the print media. However, in the past decade, female athletes, as well as athletes representing other ethnic groups, have begun to emerge. Quite possibly, with the increased recognition of women in sport and the introduction of more professional sports for women (e.g., women's professional basketball and soccer), this trend toward equal gender representation may continue. The previously mentioned data regarding the discrepancy between ethnic representation in professional sports and ethnic representation in athletic endorsement suggests the possibility that historical societal prejudices still exist and may be reflected in media targeted to the general public.

Sport Prevalence. Twenty-eight different sports were represented in the athlete-endorsed ads captured in this study. Although there were several decades when a particular sport appeared to be popular in athlete endorsement (e.g., ice skating in the 1990s or gymnastics in the 1980s), overall, the top six sports (baseball, tennis, football, basketball, golf, and car racing) have been consistently represented over time.

Strategy. This study also revealed a number of findings related to product categorization and advertising strategy in general readership magazines. Over time, the products endorsed by celebrity athletes tend to fall within Quadrant 1 of the FCB Grid (high involvement/thinking). In addition, whereas Quadrant IV (low involvement/feeling) products were found to be fairly numerous in the early years of the study, these types of products have dropped off significantly. There has been a noticeable and distinct trend toward the use of more psychologically based transformational advertising. The importance of having the athlete provide some type of statement of endorsement also seems to be making a comeback. This trend could be due to the growing skepticism of consumers who may doubt whether or not the athlete actually uses the product and if he or she is simply lending his or her name or face in order to reap the financial benefits.

Congruency. The concept of congruence was also examined in this study. Two types of congruence between the athlete and the product were considered: gender and use of the product in the sport. The results reflected the presence of gender congruence, with female-oriented products tending to be endorsed by female athletes and male products dominated by male athletes. The likely use of the product in the sport represented revealed no congruency finding. Finally, the strategy of establishing congruence via message establishment/reinforcement was employed in less than one-third of the ads sampled. Taken together, with the exception of gender congruency, these findings suggest that the majority of ads do not depend on some direct link among the athlete, the sport, and the product advertised.

A *Comparison* to Sports Illustrated

In an effort to avoid any potential bias in the type of advertising, this study examined print media that was targeted toward the general population as opposed to sports-targeted media. However, Jones and Schumann (2000) used a similar content analysis strategy to conduct a case study of advertisements appearing in *Sports Illustrated* since its inception in 1955. The data from the general readership magazine study were reanalyzed using only data from 1955 forward in order to conduct an accurate comparative study.

The comparison between the general readership magazine results and the *Sports Illustrated* case study yielded some interesting similarities and differences. Not surprisingly, the usage of athlete endorsers was greater in *Sports Illustrated* than in general readership magazines. However, it is interesting to note that although the usage in general interest magazines increased from 1970 to 1990, it was not until the 1990s that athlete endorser usage increased dramatically in *Sports Illustrated*. Although the overall percentage of ads containing athletes was greater in *Sports Illustrated* (3.8%), this number is still low compared to the claims made in the Madison Avenue study (Sasseen, 1984).

The comparison also revealed that the sports most often represented in *Sports Illustrated* were similar to the findings from the general readership magazine study (i.e., baseball, tennis, football, car racing, basketball, and golf). Sports Illustrated has also seen a switch from male-oriented products to undifferentiated products. Another similarity found in the comparison is the location of athlete endorsed products on the FCB Grid (see Fig. 5.3). The type of products appearing in Quadrant I (high involvement/thinking) are also primarily advertised in *Sports Illustrated*. There also appears to be a trend toward psychologically based transformational advertising.

The comparison also revealed several differences. Although the general readership magazines are beginning to recognize the importance and the potential of using female athletes, *Sports Illustrated* continues to emphasize male athletes in its advertising (i.e., only 3.2% of the athlete endorser ads sampled since 1955 contained women athletes in the ads). This could be due to the fact that *Sports Illustrated* is primarily targeted to male readers and there are an increasing number of specialty magazines targeted toward specific sports for both men and women. Related to this, although *Sports Illustrated* has also seen athlete-endorsed advertisement dominated by white athletes over time, black athletes have been represented more in Sports Illustrated ads than in the general readership magazine ads (13.5%).

The results for congruence also differed between *Sports Illustrated* and the general readership magazines. Interestingly, 57% of the ads in *Sports Illustrated* were found to be sport congruent, compared to 31.8% of the ads in the general readership magazines. Also, 54% of the ads in *Sports Illustrated* were found to have an obvious connection between the athlete and the product, compared to 26.4% of the ads in the general readership magazines. Finally, statements of endorsement were found in only 18.3% of the time in *Sports Illustrated* compared to 35.7% of the time in the general readership magazines. From 1960 to 1975, statements of endorsement appeared more often, yet there is an apparent trend toward not using this type of strategy.

THE FUTURE OF ATHLETE ENDORSEMENT

Although the three major sports—basketball, football, and baseball—will probably always be popular among all age groups, the popularity and following of some sports appears to be changing. The 1990s saw a growth of previously less popular sports (e.g., NASCAR) as well as new sports (e.g., extreme sports, and eco-challenge type sports). The most popular sports over time have also seen an increase in the number of young athletes in the sport. For example, Tiger Woods (golf) and Serena Williams (tennis) have the ability to appeal to younger consumers. The newly popular sports may provide an opportunity for marketers to reach distinct target audiences as well, through either specialty magazines or promotional campaigns found in general readership magazines.

The main question remains whether there are other factors that might be useful in predicting the success or failure of a particular promotional campaign employing a celebrity athlete endorser. In particular, future research could examine political, economic, social or cultural trends that are occurring within the marketplace and compare this to the usage and success of athlete endorsers. It is possible that the strategic use of athlete endorsers could be conditioned by uncontrollable, macroenvironmental issues in the marketplace.

Additionally, future research could help identify added congruency factors that could be used to establish or reinforce a three-way connectedness among the athlete, product, and audience. Relatedly, it would be also interesting to identify how the message could be better employed to help facilitate this connectedness.

Finally, perhaps the traditionally studied celebrity endorser factors (e.g., credibility, trustworthiness, expertise, attractiveness, familiarity) should be reexamined as to their effectiveness in the context of sports promotion. Are these same factors the ones that will influence the sports audience of the future, or will they be replaced by new ones (e.g., daring, affect provoking, perceived lifestyle)? What is clear is that the use of celebrity athletes as product endorsers will most likely continue. Moreover, there will likely be many more questions that are posed in the future regarding the overall effectiveness of this form of promotion.

Let's end with one last word association task . . .

LeBron James

REFERENCES

Actman, H. (1994). Marketers cautious in athlete selection. *Sporting Goods Business, 27*(8), 30.

Adler, J. (1993). Good field, no pitch. *Newsweek, 121*(15), 65.

Ads bank on athletes to ring up those sales. (1979). *Advertising Age, 50*(36), S.

Agrawal, J., and Kamakura, W. A. (1995). The economic worth of celebrity endorser: An event study analysis. *Journal of Marketing, 59*(3), 56–62.

Berger, D. (1986). Theory into practice: The FCB grid. *Marketing and Research Today, 14*(1), 35–47.

Bhonslay, M. (1998). Power of professional endorsers slipping fast. *Sporting Goods Business, 31*(9), 30.

Bradley, S. (1996). Marketers are always looking for good pitchers. *Brandweek, 37*(9), 36.

Business: Tripped up. (1998). *The Economist, 348*(8075), 63.

Crane, G., Ed. (1996). *Perseus 2.0: Interactive Sources and Studies on Ancient Greek Culture*. New Haven, Yale University Press.

Frieden, J. B. (1984). Advertising spokesperson effects: An examination of endorser type and gender on two audiences. *Journal of Advertising Research, 12*, 33–41.

Goldin, G. (1996). Nobody roots for a product. *World Business, 2*(6), 22.

Harder look at sports stars. (1998). *Advertising Age, 69*(3), 24.

Hawkins, D. I., Best, R. J., and Coney, K. (1983). *Consumer Behavior: Implications for Marketing Strategy*. Plano, Tx, Business Publications.

Howard, N. (1977). Playing the endorsement game. *Dun's Review, 110*(2), 43.

Jensen, J. (1993a). Bad role model can make good ad. *Advertising Age, 64*(40), 10.

Jensen, J. (1993b). Sneaker ads on the wrong track. *Advertising Age, 64*(50), 3.

Jensen, J. (1997). Reebok readies women's signature shoes. *Advertising Age, 68*(14), 3.

Jones, M. J. and Schumann, D. W. (2000). The strategic use of celebrity athlete endorsers in *Sports Illustrated*: An historical perspective. *Sport Marketing Quarterly, 9*(2), 65–76.

Kahle, L. R., and Homer, P. H. (1985). Physical attractiveness of the celebrity endorser: A social adaptation perspective. *Journal of Consumer Research, 1*(March), 954–961.

Kamins, M. A. (1990). An investigation into the "match-up" hypothesis in celebrity advertising: When beauty may be only skin deep. *Journal of Advertising, 19*(March), 4–13.

Kamins, M. A., and Gupta, K. (1994). Congruence between spokesperson and product type: A matchup hypothesis perspective. *Psychology and Marketing, 11*(6), 569–586.

Kanungo, R. N., and Pang, S. (1973). Effects of human models on perceived product quality. *Journal of Applied Psychology, 57*(2), 172–178.

Laskey, H. A., Day, E., and Crask, M. R. (1989). Typology of main message strategies for television commercials. *Journal of Advertising, 18*(1), 36–41.

Liesse, J. (1991). Endorsement slump: Baseball stars fail to connect with ad deals. *Advertising Age, 62*(15), 3.

Lipchick, R. (1997). Racial Report Card. Northeastern University: Boston, Center for the Study of Sport in Society.

Lustigman, A. (1995). Team spirit. *Sporting Goods Business, 28*(6), 44.

Misra, S. and Beatty, S. E. (1990). Celebrity spokesperson and brand congruence. *Journal of Business Research, 21*(2), 159–173.

Newcomb, P. and Palmeri, C. (1990). Throw a tantrum, sign a contract. *Forbes, 146*(4), 68.

Oneal, M., Finch, P., Hamilton, J. O. C., and Hammonds, K. (1987). Nothing sells like sports. *Business Week, 3014*, 48.

Petty, R. and Cacioppo, J. (1981). *Attitudes and Persuasion: Classic and Contemporary Approaches.* Dubuque, IA, Brown.

Reebok UK stars stay. (1998). *Marketing*, 4.

Sasseen, J. (1984). Jocks run faster, jump higher and sell better. *Madison Avenue, 25*(11), 92.

Spiegel, P., and Gallagher, L. (1999). The real money player. *Forbes, 163*(6), 220.

Swenson, C. A. (1987). Endorsements are a powerful marketing tool. *Sales & Marketing Management in Canada, 28*(3), 8.

Tedesci, M. (1998). The end of an era? *Sporting Goods Business, 31*(3), 24.

Walley, W. (1987). Sports marketing: Companies learn to play the game. *Advertising Age, 58*(48), S1.

The Effects of Multiple Product Endorsements by Celebrities on Consumer Attitudes and Intentions: An Extension

Ainsworth A. Bailey
The University of Toledo

Catherine A. Cole
The University of Iowa

Recent research has pointed to the fact that advertisers often spend millions of dollars annually on celebrity endorsers, with the aim of influencing consumers' perceptions and purchase intentions (Tripp, Jensen, & Carlson, 1994). This stream of research has established that, among other things, celebrities make advertisements believable (Kamins, Brand, Hoeke, & Moe, 1989), aid in the recognition of brand names (Petty, Cacioppo, & Schumann, 1983), enhance message recall (Friedman & Friedman, 1979), create a positive attitude towards the brand (Kamins et al., 1989), and create a distinct personality for the endorsed brand (McCracken, 1989). Ultimately, celebrity endorsements are believed to generate a greater likelihood of customers choosing the endorsed brand (Heath, McCarthy, & Mothersbaugh, 1994; Kahle & Homer, 1985; Kamins et al., 1989; Ohanian, 1991), and messages delivered by well-known personalities achieve a high degree of attention and recall for some consumers. Agrawal and Kamakura (1995) concluded that, on average, the impact of the announcements of celebrity endorsement contracts on stock returns is positive and suggested that celebrity endorsement contracts are generally viewed as a worthwhile investment in advertising. Given this information, one can safely argue that celebrity endorsements are here to stay.

The increasing use of celebrity endorsers, however, has spawned another phenomenon, that of using a celebrity in multiple advertising campaigns to endorse multiple products. The quintessential multiple product endorser is Michael Jordan who, according to Lipman and Hinge (1991), has endorsed products for approximately 14 companies. Jordan was named the richest athlete for 1997 by *Forbes* magazine, with most of his income, $47 million, coming from product endorsements. Tripp et al. (1994) investigated the effects of multiple product endorsements by celebrities on consumers' attitudes and purchase intentions. They found that the number of products a celebrity endorses negatively influences consumers' perceptions of endorser credibility and likability, as well as attitude toward the ad. In addition, the number of exposures to the celebrity has an impact on attitude toward the ad and purchase intentions, although the number of products endorsed by the celebrity and the number of exposures to the celebrity operate independently on consumers' attitudes.

There are, however, a number of issues relating to multiple product endorsements that remain unresolved and warrant attention. Our objective in this study is to build on the research on multiple product endorsements set in motion by Tripp et al. (1994). This is particularly important, given the preponderance of advertisements featuring celebrities, especially from the world of sports; the tarnishing of the image of sports celebrities as a consequence of recent public cases involving well-known sports celebrities (e.g., O. J. Simpson, Mike Tyson, Latrell Sprewell), and the massive advertising budgets that are usually allocated to this enterprise. We begin by presenting a review of the literature on celebrity endorsements and by identifying relevant hypotheses. We then subject our hypotheses to empirical investigation. We present the results and discuss their implications for advertising managers and researchers in advertising and consumer psychology, as well as posit possible future research directions.

BACKGROUND

As mentioned earlier, advertisers who use celebrities make their advertising more believable, more memorable, and more distinctive. Kamins et al. (1989) linked the effectiveness of celebrity endorsement to the process of social influence. They cited the work of Kelman (1961), who suggested three processes of social influence that, when pursued, facilitate the potential that an individual will accept influence from another person or group: compliance involves acceptance of persuasive influence from a source in order to obtain a favorable reaction. Internalization occurs when a person accepts what someone, else says because the ideas are congruent with his or her value system. *compliance, identification,* and *internalization. Identification,* a particularly important process, results from an individual adopting the behavior of another person or group. Because individuals aspire to be like certain persons or members of certain groups, they adopt the behavior of these people or group members, thereby enhancing their self-esteem. In other words, much of celebrity endorsement is based on the notion that members of the audience who are exposed to a celebrity in an advertisement will want to be like the celebrity and therefore use the product in the ad. Marketers have realized this and have capitalized on the use of various celebrities in advertising. For example, Gatorade revived a campaign featuring Michael Jordan in which doting admirers express the wish to be "like Mike."

According to McCracken (1989), celebrities' effectiveness as product endorsers stems from the cultural meanings with which they are endowed. His thesis was that the endorsement process depends on the symbolic properties of the celebrity endorser. Distinctions of status, class, gender, and age, as well as personality and lifestyle types, are represented in the pool of available celebrities, "putting an extraordinarily various and subtle pallet of meanings at the disposal of the marketing system (p. 312)." Based on his view, an endorsement succeeds when an association is fashioned between the cultural meanings of the celebrity world on the one hand, and the endorsed products on the other. The best endorsements, consequently, derive their efficacy from the successful transfer of meaning.

Researchers have investigated when celebrities are effective. Friedman and Friedman (1979) found that celebrity endorsers, when compared to professional experts or typical consumers, enhanced brand name and advertisement recall and, therefore, should be used when recall is the advertiser's goal. Similarly, they stated that if the major risk inherent in the purchase of a product is social or psychological, the advertiser should choose a celebrity. They argued that trustworthiness is probably the major dimension underlying source credibility. In the absence of trustworthiness, other qualities possessed by the communicator may not be effective in inducing attitude change.

Although a number of the studies have focused on when to use celebrity endorsers to endorse single products, the question of when to use a celebrity to endorse multiple products has not been addressed. Tripp et al. (1994) are among the few researchers who have looked closely at multiple product endorsements. They set in motion a research program, which we hope to extend, given the increase in advertisements featuring celebrities, especially from the world of sports. A number of issues that were not addressed in the Tripp et al. (1994) study are investigated in this chapter, in an effort to extend the generalizability of their results. For example, does familiarity with a celebrity endorser matter in the case of multiple product endorsements? Does the condition under which consumers process information affect their responses to the use of a celebrity to endorse multiple products? Our study uses male and female sports celebrities, and we take into account the levels of familiarity participants have with these celebrities. Here, familiarity is operationalized as the extent to which the celebrity in an advertising spot is identifiable by the participants and whether the participants have seen him or her in previous advertising spots.

HYPOTHESES

Central to our investigation is attribution theory (Kelley, 1973), which suggests that trait inferences may result in consumers' evaluating multiple product endorsers less favorably than single product endorsers (Mowen & Brown, 1981; Tripp et al., 1994). As the number of product endorsements increases, there will be a decline in the strength of source effects. This decline occurs because, as Tripp et al. (1994) postulated, "The multiple product endorser may be viewed as a single but non-independent (i.e., a confederate) source of relatively predictable information, presumably activating negative causal attributions." (p. 544)

From the foregoing, we posit the following hypotheses.

H1a. As the number of product endorsements increases, there will be a decline in the consumers' perceptions of the sport celebrity's credibility (trustworthiness and expertise).

H1b. As the number of product endorsements increases, there will be a decline in consumers' attitudes toward ads featuring a multiple-product endorser.

H1c. As the number of product endorsements increases, there will be a decline in consumers' purchase intentions for a brand endorsed by a multiple-product endorser.

We tested whether these effects hold for both familiar and unfamiliar celebrity endorsers. On the one hand, we predicted that highly familiar sports celebrity endorsers would be more effective than relatively unfamiliar sports celebrity endorsers. *Familiarity* refers to the extent to which the participant can identify the sport celebrity and has been exposed to him or her in previous ads.

Familiarity breeds contempt. Consumers begin to question the motives of the endorser (Is he/she just doing this for the money?), as well as the credibility and the endorser's expertise in each successive product category. However, familiarity with the source does create some degree of trust (To know me is to trust me.). This effect results from the fact that consumers make inferences that if, an endorser is being used by several companies, then he or she must be good, even honorable. This could help to attenuate decline in source effects due to other factors such as concerns about source expertise. Keller (1998) argued that the use of well-known spokespersons is often viewed advantageously by advertisers because a rich memory trace often already exists in long-term memory for that person, containing positive affect, belief, and so on.

We argue that the difference in the effectiveness of familiar and unfamiliar sports celebrity endorsers becomes greater as the number of product endorsements increases. This is because as Tripp et al. (1994) noted, based on their Study 2, it seemed unlikely that more familiar celebrity endorsers (e.g., Michael Jordan) are subject to a decline in favorableness across multiple endorsements. However, the evaluations of unfamiliar celebrities should decline, owing to the fact that there is no transference of affect or any degree of trust that has been developed between the consumer and the celebrity. As a result, we make the following prediction.

H2a. As exposure to the same endorser increases, consumers' perceptions of the credibility of unfamiliar celebrities will decline more rapidly than will their perceptions of the credibility of familiar sport celebrities. This may be moderated by the gender of the endorser.

H2b. As exposure to the same endorser increases, consumers' attitudes toward the ads featuring unfamiliar celebrities will decline more rapidly than will their attitudes toward the ads featuring familiar sport celebrities. This may be moderated by the gender of the endorser.

H2c. As exposure to the same endorser increases, consumers' purchase intentions for brands featuring the unfamiliar celebrities will decline more rapidly than will their purchase intentions for brands featuring familiar sport celebrities. This may be moderated by the gender of the endorser.

Literature in the popular press suggests that gender of the celebrity endorser could be important. In a 1995 article in *The Wall Street Journal*, writer Kevin Goldman claimed that according to a ranking of TV endorsers compiled by Video Storyboard Tests in New York, women endorsers were perceived to be more credible that men. He reported that according to one industry person, "Now if you need to speak to a woman consumer, you hire a woman." (p. B1) However, survey respondents were merely asked to name which show business celebrity was "most convincing and believable," and product affiliations were not provided. The article also quoted the president of Video Storyboard Tests, David Vadehra, as saying that advertisers may be turning away from male entertainers in favor of male athletes. He said, "It's becoming obvious to advertisers that if you want to sell to men, use a jock" because "athletes represent something to which men aspire: perfection." (p. B1)

These opinions, however, have not been subjected to empirical investigation. Consequently, we analyzed our data in an effort to determine whether celebrity gender plays a role in consumers' responses to multiple product endorsements by celebrities. Findings should prove useful to advertisers, in terms of selecting celebrity endorsers for their products.

Our study also took into consideration the processing conditions under which consumers form their attitudes and judgments, in an effort to better understand the consequences of allocation of processing resources and motivation on consumers' attitudes to, and perceptions of, multiple product endorsements. Whereas Tripp et al. (1994) assumed "that readers of print ads exert at least a moderate level of cognitive effort," (p. 545) we manipulated the processing conditions: systematic processing versus heuristic processing of information. We expected that, consistent with Fazio's motivation & opportunity as determinants (MODE) model and other dual-process models such as the elaboration likelihood model (ELM; Petty, Cacioppo, & Schumann, 1983), and Gilbert's (1989) characterization-correction model, we would see differences in consumers' attitudes and perceptions under systematic processing conditions compared to heuristic processing conditions. The heuristic-systematic model (HSM) of Chaiken (1980) and Chaiken, Liberman, and Eagly (1989) supports this thesis.

Our study also brought to bear on this discussion findings from research in the area of social cognition relating to information processing. Gilbert (1989), Gilbert and Hixon (1991), and Trope and Alfieri (1997) have shown that when participants are placed under cognitive load, this affects their information processing capacity. Fazio's (1986) MODE model posits the importance of motivation and opportunity to process to the outcome of information processing. Sanbonmatsu and Fazio (1990), in a test of the MODE model, showed that in the absence of time pressures and given high fear of invalidity,[1] people

---

[1]As per Kruglanski's theory of lay epistemology, participants are assumed to be under burden to engage in making correct decisions when they are told that their decisions will be subject to scrutiny.

will engage in more systematic processing of information. Under cognitive load and low fear of invalidity, people engage in more heuristic processing of information.

In general, the allocation of processing resources to a decision or judgment task will impact the quality of the decision or judgment made. The ELM (Petty & Cacioppo, 1981, 1986), with its distinction between central and peripheral route routes to persuasion, and the HSM (Chaiken, 1980, 1987; Chaiken et al., 1989) are consistent with the MODE model, in its emphasis on the distinction between heuristic or peripheral processing and systematic processing or systematic processing. These dual-process theories, according to Chaiken and Maheswaran (1994), regard systematic (systematic) processing as more effortful and capacity limited than heuristic processing. They, therefore, assume that heuristic processing predominates when motivation or capacity for effortful processing is low. Thus, although systematic processing implies that "people have formed or updated their attitudes by actively attending to and cognitively elaborating persuasive argumentation," heuristic processing implies that "people have formed or changed their attitudes by invoking heuristics such as 'experts can be trusted,' 'majority opinion is correct,' and 'long messages are valid messages' " (Chaiken & Maheswaran, 1994, p. 460). This discussion leads to the following hypotheses.

H3a. Consumers who process information in a systematic manner will have lower perceptions of the sport celebrity's credibility (trustworthiness and expertise) than consumers who process information in a heuristic manner. H3b. Consumers who process information in a systematic manner will have a less favorable attitude toward the ad than consumers who process information in a heuristic manner. H3c. Consumers who process information in a systematic manner will have lower purchase intentions than consumers who process information in a heuristic manner.

The following interaction also should be observed.

H4. There will be an interaction of processing condition and the number of product endorsements such that as the number of product endorsements increases, systematic processing leads to a greater decline in the consumers' perceptions of the sport celebrity's credibility and trustworthiness, attitude toward the ad, and purchase intentions than does heuristic processing.

Additional differences in our study include the fact that we used two unfamiliar brands, Grace's Raisin Bran and Neal and Massey's Fresh Stick Ultimate deodorant; one moderately familiar brand name applied to a different product category, Sunkist orange juice; and a familiar brand, Kodak Advantix 200 camera and film. Both brands used in the Tripp et al. (1994) study were well-established brands (Kodak camera and Visa credit card). The results should have implications for new products or brands, as compared to brands with which consumers are already familiar and for which they may already have very strong preferences.

PRETEST

To determine whom we would use as familiar male and female sports celebrities, we passed out a questionnaire to an experimental group of undergraduate marketing students, asking them to name male and female entertainment and sports celebrities whom they had seen in ads for any product. Sixty-three undergraduate students participated in this pretest. All 63 participants named Michael Jordan as one male sport celebrity they had seen in ads, with Grant Hill, Shaquille O'Neal, Tiger Woods, and Hakeem Olajuwon being among others who were frequently cited. On average, these participants were better able to recall male sports celebrity endorsers than the other types of celebrities. On average, male participants recalled 6.6 male sport celebrity endorsers, whereas women participants, on average, recalled 3.9 male sport celebrity endorsers. As a result of this pretest, we used basketball player Grant Hill as the familiar male sport celebrity, tennis player Todd Martin as the unfamiliar male sports celebrity, tennis player Monica Seles as the familiar female sports celebrity, and tennis player Amanda Coetzer as the unfamiliar female sport celebrity.

In addition, in a follow-up, 27 undergraduate marketing students rated the level of familiarity with the celebrities we chose on a 7-point Likert scale anchored by *very unfamiliar with* (1) and *very familiar with* (7). They also answered "Yes/No" to the question, "Have you seen this person in ads for other products?" The results proved consistent with our classification of familiar and unfamiliar sport celebrities. Average rating on the 7-point scale for Grant Hill was 6.26, for Todd Martin was 2.52, for Monica Seles was 6.19, and for Amanda Coetzer was 2.07. In the case of the dichotomous response item, we allotted a score of 1 to the celebrity if participants indicated that they had seen him or her in previous ads. Otherwise, they obtained a score of 0. These scores were then averaged; a score of 1 was the maximum and 0 the minimum. For the most part, participants had seen Grant Hill in previous advertising spots, as he averaged 0.81. Fewer participants had seen Monica Seles in an ad (average = 0.37). Only one participant indicated seeing Todd Martin in an ad, whereas none of the participants had ever seen Amanda Coetzer in any ads. These results validated our choices of familiar and unfamiliar sports celebrity endorsers. A focus group discussion was also held with 25 undergraduate marketing students to determine the likability of, and attitudes toward, the endorsers and the appropriateness of their endorsing the products.

STUDY 1

Method

Design

Our design was a mixed factorial design. The first three factors, type of celebrity (male or female sport celebrity), level of familiarity or product endorser (high versus low), and processing condition (heuristic versus systematic) were between-subjects factors. The fourth factor, number of product endorsements/exposures, was a within-subjects factor. The design was, therefore, a 2 (type of celebrity: female and male sports celebrities) × 2 (level of familiarity: high/low) × 2 (processing condition: heuristic versus systematic) × 4 (number of product endorsements to which subject is exposed) mixed factorial design.

Participants

Participants were 160 undergraduate seniors and juniors enrolled in introductory marketing classes at The University of Iowa.

Procedure

The principal study took place in a laboratory setting, with participants processed in groups of 20. On arrival at the experimental lab, each subject was given one of eight possible booklets containing the stimuli. Each booklet contained four ads for different products endorsed by the same celebrity. Appendixes A through D contain further details about the booklets. The image of the celebrity appeared in each ad. After each exposure to an ad, participants completed the measures for endorser credibility and trustworthiness, attitude toward the ad, and purchase intentions. Following this, they were asked to recall the product categories and the brands in each product category, as well as complete a thought-listing exercise, listing their thoughts from the time they started up to that point in the study. They then completed a scale that was used to measure the effectiveness of the processing manipulation and answered a question about the true purpose of the experiment. They were then debriefed and thanked for their participation.

Independent Variables

The independent variables of interest were *type of celebrity* (male versus female sport celebrity), *level of familiarity with the sport celebrity endorser, processing condition* (systematic versus heuristic), and *number of product endorsements.* The method of selection of the familiar and unfamiliar male and female sports celebrity endorsers was discussed earlier.

The manipulation of processing conditions is as follows. In the heuristic processing conditions, participants learned that advertisers on the East Coast would use the print ads. In the systematic processing condition, participants learned that advertisers in their area would use the print ads. In addition, the advertisers of the products were interested in their honest opinions. They were asked to indicate whether they would be willing to participate in a follow-up discussion of their ideas.

As a manipulation check of the processing in which participants engaged, we utilized an index formed from items 1 (*effort*), 2 (*care*), and 5 (*motivate*) contained in Appendix C.

Dependent Variables

The dependent variables of interest were the consumers' perceptions of the sport celebrity's credibility (trustworthiness and expertise), attitude toward the ad, purchase intentions, and brand name recall. The scales used to measure these are contained in Appendix B. These dependent variables are of interest because advertisers need to consider whether using a sport celebrity in multiple product endorsements could hurt, rather than aid, the fortunes of their products. Whether a sport celebrity doing multiple product endorsements aids a brand warrants investigation.

Results

Manipulation Checks.   We checked the manipulation of processing condition (Table 6.1). We used a composite index formed from three items in Appendix C. There were no significant differences in processing conditions. We did a t test analysis on the familiarity scale and found that subjects found our familiar sport celebrity endorsers more familiar than our unfamiliar sport celebrity endorsers ($t = 6.10$, $p < 0.01$). We were disappointed that

TABLE 6.1
Analysis of Variance Results for Attitudes Toward the Ad,
Purchase Intentions, and Source Credibility

	d.f.	A_{ad}	PI	Cred
Source		F	F	F
		(P<)	(P<)	(P<)
Between-subjects effects				
Familiarity (F)	1	1.59	.05	1.36
		(.21)	(.82)	(.25)
Gender of Celebrity (G)	1	.37	1.06	.56
		(.55)	(.30)	(.45)
Processing (P)	1	.39	2.49	0.0
		(.54)	(.11)	(.96)
F × G	1	3.56	.1	.01
		(.06)	(.76)	(.94)
F × P	1	.02	.1	.27
		(.89)	(.76)	(.60)
G × P	1	.37	.19	.73
		(.54)	(.67)	(.39)
F × G × P	1	.0	.66	.21
		(.95)	(.42)	(.64)
Within-subjects effects				
Exposure (E)	3	2.12	5.0	2.17
		(.09)	(.01)	(.09)
E × F	3	1.33	1.51	.43
		(.26)	(.21)	(.44)
E × G	3	.10	.23	.25
		(.27)	(.87)	(.85)
E × P	3	2.48	.9	.25
		(.06)	(.441)	(.85)
E × F × G	3	3.91	29.48	6.16
		(.01)	(.01)	(.01)
E × F × P	3	0.57	1.01	9.76
		(.64)	(0.39)	(0.00)
E × G × P	3	2.88	.60	1.21
		(.04)	(.60)	(.31)
E × F × G × P	3	.22	.92	.13
		(.882)	(.43)	(.94)

A_{ad}, attitude toward the ad; Cred, perception of credibility of celebrity; PI, purchase intentions; Recall 1, recall of familiar brand; Recall 2, recall of unfamiliar brand.

the processing manipulation did not work. It means that we were unable to test H3a through H3c and H4.

Changes in Attitudinal Variables as Number of Endorsements by Same Spokesperson Increases.

Hypotheses H1a through H1c contended that we would see declines in consumers' (a) perceptions of a sports celebrity's credibility, (b) attitude toward the ad, and (c) purchase intentions as the number of product endorsements increased. Support was found for H1a. Between the first and second exposure, credibility increased but then declined thereafter ($F = 2.93$, $p < 0.04$). The effect of exposure on attitude toward the ad was not significant. In the case of purchase intentions, there was a significant effect ($F = 5.29$, $p < 0.01$). However, contrary to our prediction, purchase intentions actually increased as the number of product endorsements increased.

Changes in Gender and Spokesperson Familiarity Effects on Attitudinal Variables as Number of Endorsements by Same Spokesperson Increases.

For all three attitudinal variables, the three-way interaction among number of product endorsements, spokesperson familiarity, and gender was significant (attitude toward the ads: $F = 3.91$, $p < .01$; purchase intentions: $F = 29.48$, $p < .01$; and source credibility $F = 6.16$, $p < .01$).

To better understand what changes are occurring, we first look at changes in credibility ratings, ad evaluation, and purchase intentions as number of product endorsements (exposures) increases. We do this first for familiar then unfamiliar celebrities.

For female familiar celebrity endorsers, there were no significant changes in credibility as exposures increased, but as exposures increased from one to two attitudes toward the ad became significantly more favorable ($t = 2.4$, $p < .05$) and purchase intentions ($t = 7.17$, $p < .01$). For male familiar celebrity endorsers between one and two exposures there was a significant increase in credibility ($t = 2.98$, $p < .01$) and a significant decrease in purchase intentions ($t = 2.31$, $p < .02$) but no significant changes in attitudes toward the ad. Purchase intentions went back up between three and four exposures ($t = 2.6$, $p < .01$).

For the unfamiliar female celebrity, credibility increased significantly between the first and second exposure ($t = 2.62$, $p < .02$), whereas purchase intentions decreased significantly ($t = 3.29$, $p < .05$). Interestingly, between the third and fourth exposure, for the unfamiliar female celebrity, even though credibility decreased significantly ($t = 2.3$, $p < .02$), attitudes toward the ad actually became more favorable ($t = 2.87$, $p < .01$) as did purchase intentions ($t = 3.5$, $p < .01$). For the male unfamiliar celebrity endorsers, credibility did not change significantly between exposures, but between exposures 1 and 2, attitude toward the advertisement improved ($t = 2.35$, $p < .02$) as did purchase intentions ($t = 4.69$, $p < .01$).

From this analysis, we see some trends consistent with H2a through H2c. As exposures increase, the changes in credibility, attitudes toward the ad, and purchase intentions are less dramatic for familiar than unfamiliar spokespeople. Of the contrasts comparing male and female familiar endorsers at different exposure levels, only five showed significant differences. Of the contrasts comparing male and female unfamiliar endorsers at different exposure levels, however, seven showed significant differences. This suggests more volatility in the ratings of unfamiliar celebrities.

We also look at familiarity effects holding gender and exposure levels constant. For male endorsers, attitudes toward the ads and purchase intentions, at the first exposure and fourth exposures, were lower for unfamiliar than familiar endorsers ($p < .05$ for all contrasts). In addition, on the second exposure, the familiar endorser was seen as more credible than the unfamiliar endorser ($p < .03$). Thus, a generalization from this analysis is that familiar male endorsers are more persuasive than unfamiliar male endorsers.

For ads featuring female endorsers, only at the fourth exposure did source familiarity affect attitudes toward the ad, such that when female endorsers were unfamiliar, subjects had more favorable attitudes toward the advertisement than when they were familiar ($p < .03$). In addition, unfamiliar endorsers generated higher purchase intentions at one exposure ($p < .01$) and at the fourth exposure than familiar endorsers ($p < .02$). This suggests that unfamiliar female endorsers may be more persuasive than familiar female endorsers.

Thoughts-Listing Exercise

As part of the study, near the end of the survey, we asked participants to list the thoughts that were going through their minds from the time they started the study until that point in the study. This exercise was completed after they had been exposed to the four ads featuring the sport celebrity and had completed the scales and the recall of brand names. This thoughts-listing exercise represented a variation on the Study 2 that was conducted by Tripp et al. (1994). In their work, Tripp et al. (1994) conducted semi-structured interviews with 10 subjects who had participated in their initial study. As was the case with these authors, our principal aim was to see whether we could obtain feedback on the kinds of attribution processes that might operate when participants are exposed to a sport celebrity endorsing multiple products.

The authors reviewed these comments and found several themes. First, a number of participants expressed doubt that the athletes in the ads really used the products they were endorsing. In addition, participants thought that the athletes in the ads were doing the endorsements for the money, and did not genuinely believe the product claims. Third, many participants indicated that they would not necessarily like or purchase a product simply because it is endorsed by a sport celebrity. They expressed doubt about the athletes' knowledge about certain product categories (such as food products). Finally, they indicated that in the case of athletes who were not household names, they were unlikely to be swayed by these athletes.

From an examination of a sample of about 30 scripts, we concluded that the thoughts could be listed under certain broad themes. These included credibility of the celebrity, concerns about expertise/knowledge of the celebrity, familiarity with the celebrity, fit between the celebrity endorser and the product endorsed, motivations of the celebrity endorser, the likely influence of celebrities on consumer decision-making, as well as doubts as to whether the celebrity, in fact, used the product he or she was endorsing. Table 6.2 provides some quotes from participants.

Many of these views seem consistent with those found in the Tripp et al. (1994) study. For example, these authors noted that, "All informants stated that celebrities endorse products because they are paid for those endorsements. To some extent, all informants questioned whether the endorser used or even liked the products endorsed" (p. 543). One of their subjects opined, "I would figure Michael Jordan was a specialist about maybe tennis shoes or basketball shoes, but I don't honestly think he knows more about Hanes briefs or Wheaties than I do" (p. 543). The quotes cited in Table 6.2 bear an uncanny resemblance to some of the views expressed by subjects in the Tripp et al. (1994) study, further supporting some of their conclusions regarding concerns about endorser sincerity, the impact of the number of products endorsed by a celebrity, and attributions of trust.[2]

---

[2]Shortly after the data collection stage of our study, an ad by Sprite began running on television in the Iowa City area. In this advertising spot, shot, ostensibly, in a locker room, Grant Hill emerges, holding aloft a bottle of Sprite in his right hand. He remarks, "Hi. I'm Grant Hill, professional basketball player for the Detroit Pistons. You know, when I get thirsty, I reach for a Sprite." (A smaller image of Hill, holding a money bag instead of a bottle of Sprite in his right hand, pops up to the right of the screen, then disappears). "You see," Hill continues, "Sprite refreshes me like nothing else," (The small image pops up again, this time holding a moneybag in either hand, and a cash register clinks and clinks), "because it is the only drink with that cool, crisp, refreshing taste," (He takes a sip), "that satisfies even my manliest thirst. Yes, that's Sprite for you." (He takes a big gulp, as the cash register continues to clink and the money piles up). IMAGE IS NOTHING. THIRST IS EVERYTHING. OBEY YOUR THIRST flashes across the screen, and the voiceover exhorts us, "Drink Sprite 'cause you like it, not because an athlete says he does."

TABLE 6.2
A Sample of Participants' Comments
on Celebrity Endorsements

Theme	Comments
Credibility of the celebrity	"Also, I don't' buy into a lot of celebrity endorsements because I don't see them as very trustworthy. (They are paid to read a scripted response)." "Why choose her (Monica) as the celebrity of choice? What in the hell does she know about cameras? Celebrities don't always make the best people for selling something, as they usually aren't experts or usually important."
Concerns about expertise/knowledge	"He was an unqualified person to make any kind of valid critic because he has no knowledge of the product. Athletes typically have no knowledge of the products they endorse." "It seemed to me Monica wouldn't know much about the best cameras and films."
Familiarity with the celebrity	"I was wondering why they were using Todd Martin, because he is not that well-known of a celebrity. Most companies use people like Andre Agassi and Jimmy Connors." "I don't know who the tennis player (Amanda) is. I never heard of her. So I was hesitant toward the ads." "Who is Todd Martin, and why should I believe anything he says?"
Fit between celebrity and product endorsed	"Knowing Grant Hill from a sports perspective, I couldn't see him in a couple of these ads." "I was more convinced on the deodorant because Amanda is a tennis player, therefore it is more believable that the deodorant works."
Motivations of the celebrity (sincerity)	"Grant Hill is doing it for the money." "I was thinking does this person actually use all of these products or does she just endorse them for the money?" "The star (Grant Hill) probably doesn't really use the brands he's advertising, he's just being paid to advertise them."
Celebrity influence on decision making	"I feel no influence to buy a product because a particular celebrity is in its advertisement. The product wouldn't (doesn't) seem any better/worse because of the celebrity." "I don't think that I could ever buy cereals just because it was endorsed by a tennis player." "I was thinking that just because Grant Hill likes the product, it doesn't mean I will."
Doubts about product use by celebrity	(See "Motivations" above) "I don't think she really eats raisin bran. She was just paid enough to pretend." "Didn't believe for a second that she actually used the products. If she did, it was because she got them all for free and got paid to do it."

STUDY 2

As a result of the thoughts expressed by participants in the thoughts-listing exercise, we decided to further explore the target audience's responses to the use of sports celebrities in multiple product endorsements. A group of 13 undergraduate students who had participated in Study 1 were asked to participate in a follow-up focus group discussion of the issue. Of this number, 9 participants showed up for this initial discussion. The discussion lasted 32 minutes and was tape-recorded for later transcription. In addition, notes were also taken by the moderator, one of the authors.

The focus group discussion bore out most of the themes that emerged in the thoughts-listing exercise. The fit between the endorser and the product that he or she endorses came up again for discussion. At least two participants indicated that multiple product endorsements by a sport celebrity would not matter seriously to them if they perceived that the celebrity used the products or it was a product that was used in the sport with which the celebrity was associated. One participant used the example of Monica Seles and tennis-related products such as tennis shoes, tennis balls, and tennis rackets. His opinion was that if she endorsed all these products then he was more likely to be convinced about her claims about these products. According to this participant, "You see her using a tennis racket, but you kinda wonder if she drinks that orange juice."

Another participant argued that in the case of goods that he bought with great frequency and that did not cost a lot, if he went to the store and saw the brands that he had seen in an ad featuring a sport celebrity, he was likely to try these brands. However, in the case of an item such as a camera, he was less likely to be swayed by the sport celebrity's opinions, but would be more likely to seek advice from a friend who knew about cameras or from a salesperson at the store.

There was an interesting perspective from one participant on the issue of familiarity with the sport celebrity. In reference to Grant Hill, the participant indicated that if a sport celebrity is as popular as Grant Hill is, the participant may be inclined to believe him and may be influenced to purchase a product that he endorses. This, the participant reasoned, resulted from the fact that he perceives someone such as Hill as having a lot of money; therefore, Hill was not doing the endorsement for the money but because he believed in the product. He cited the case of Todd Martin, who he concluded was unfamiliar and was likely to "grab any endorsement that he can get from any company" because many companies did not use him.

When asked whether the gender of a celebrity was a factor in their decision, a female participant remarked that she might be swayed by a female sport celebrity endorser pitching products designed for women. Other participants remarked that gender was not a factor where such products as cereal and orange juice, "which are used by both sexes," are concerned. Nor did they think that female endorsers were necessarily more credible than male endorsers, or vice versa. One participant reiterated that gender was not a factor as long as he could perceive that the sport celebrity could be associated with the product because he or she used it in a sport-related environment.

Overall, the views expressed in the thoughts-listing exercise and in this follow-up focus group discussion tend to overlap on the major themes such as perceived fit between the celebrity and the product endorsed, which is a recurring theme in research on the use of celebrities in advertising. In addition, concerns regarding the sincerity of celebrity endorsers, whether they use the products they endorse, their motivations for doing endorsements, and their ability to influence people to like or purchase a product all seem to pervade discussions on the use of sport celebrities to endorse multiple products.

DISCUSSION AND DIRECTIONS
FOR FUTURE RESEARCH

We found that the effects for familiar endorsers seem to be more stable across different exposure levels than the effects for unfamiliar endorsers. In addition, we saw evidence that for male endorsers, familiar celebrities were often more effective than unfamiliar celebrities. In contrast, for female endorsers, the opposite seemed to hold. In our focus groups, participants indicated that they thought that they would be more likely to be swayed by known than unknown athletes because they would trust the known athlete's motives more than the unknown one. In future research, we will continue to investigate the differences between familiar and unfamiliar endorsers.

We found some differences for male and female celebrities. There are two possible reasons for these effects that deserve further investigation. Perhaps the female familiar athletes were less familiar than the male familiar athletes were. In addition, in future research, we wish to test whether the effect of gender of the celebrity is moderated by the gender of the target audience.

From our focus groups emerged another important variable that we plan to incorporate into future research: the importance between the match of the celebrities' expertise and their endorsement. Celebrity endorsers who endorse products related to their areas of expertise appear to be more persuasive than celebrity endorsers who endorse products outside this area of expertise.

We contribute to the theory about the effects of product endorsers on consumer evaluations and purchase intentions by explaining why the consequences of using multiple product endorsers should depend on stimuli characteristics (familiarity and gender). In addition, we look specifically at sports celebrities because they are usually the ones who are featured in these multiple endorsements and because they function in an environment that may be becoming hostile to sport heroes.

Finally, in Study 1, we theorized that processing conditions—systematic versus heuristic—influenced the effects that sport celebrities might have on consumers' attitude toward ads, purchase intentions, and perceptions of the credibility of the sport celebrity endorser who endorses multiple products. Although there was no support for this hypothesis in this initial study, we believe that it is a factor that deserves further investigation.

APPENDIX A

Marketing Research Project: Systematic Processing Condition

We have been asked by a company that operates in Iowa, mainly in college towns such as Iowa City-Coralville, Cedar Rapids, Ames, and Des Moines, to assist it with some marketing research. The company is thinking of carrying some additional products in its stores, which sell an assortment of goods and which target the college populations in these towns. The company is testing some print ads that it intends to place in local newspapers and magazines. Whether it uses these ads or not will be based on the written feedback obtained from students in these cities including students at the University of Iowa.

In addition, within the next week, a selected sample of students who are participating in this part of the study will be called and asked to participate in a focus group to further discuss the company's advertising strategy. Participation in the second part of the study is completely voluntary, but you will be paid for your time.

Before you continue, please indicate whether you would be willing to further assist the company by participating in a follow-up discussion of the company's advertising. Then if you want to be considered for the focus group, please write in your name and telephone number. Before we give you the questionnaire packet, we will collect these sheets. We will not be able to match your name to your questionnaire. Your responses are anonymous.

1. Are you willing to participate in a follow-up discussion of your ideas?

Yes _____ No _____

If yes, please print your name _____

If yes, please print your phone number _____

If yes, please print three days of the week and times of day which are best to reach you _____

_____

_____

For now, we ask that you take your time in reviewing the ads and responding to the questions. Please give us your honest feedback, as this will be beneficial to the company. After each ad there is a short questionnaire. Once you have completed the questionnaire that relates to that ad, DO NOT turn to it again for the remainder of the study.

Marketing Research Project: Heuristic Processing Condition

We have been asked by a company that operates in the Northeast, mainly in college towns, to assist it with some marketing research. The company is thinking of carrying some additional products in its stores, which sell an assortment of goods, and which target the college populations in these towns. The company is testing some print ads that it intends to place in local newspapers and magazines in the Northeast. Whether it uses these ads or not will be based on the written feedback obtained from many students from all over the country.

In addition, within the next week, a randomly selected sample of students who are participating in this part of the study may be called and asked to participate in a focus group to discuss student spending patterns for food, beverages, housing, and recreation. Participation in the second part of the study is completely voluntary, but you will be paid for your time.

Before you continue, please indicate whether you would be willing to further assist the company by participating in this follow-up discussion. Then if you want to be considered for the focus group, please write in your name and telephone number. Before we give you the questionnaire packet, we will collect these sheets. We will not be able to match your name to your questionnaire. Your responses are anonymous.

1. Are you willing to participate in a follow-up discussion of your ideas?

Yes _____ No _____

If yes, please print your name _____

If yes, please print your phone number _____

If yes, please print three days of the week and times of day which are best to reach you _____

_____

_____

For now, we ask that you quickly review the ads and respond to the questions. We are not interested in your thoughtful analysis; instead, we are interested in your immediate reaction to each advertisement. After each ad there is a short questionnaire. Once you have completed the questionnaire that relates to that ad, DO NOT turn to it again for the remainder of the study.

APPENDIX B

PLEASE DO NOT TURN BACK TO THE AD

Using the scale below, please indicate your overall reaction to the advertisement that you just saw.

Unfavorable	1	2	3	4	5	6	7	Favorable
Bad	1	2	3	4	5	6	7	Good
Unappealing	1	2	3	4	5	6	7	Appealing
Not Likable	1	2	3	4	5	6	7	Likable

Using the scale below, please rate the probability that you would purchase the brand in the ad the next time you make a purchase in this product category.

Very Unlikely	1	2	3	4	5	6	7	Very Likely
Improbable	1	2	3	4	5	6	7	Probable
Impossible	1	2	3	4	5	6	7	Possible
Would Not	1	2	3	4	5	6	7	Would Seriously

Consider Seriously Consider

Using the scale provided below, please rate your attitudes to the celebrity in the ad that you just saw, in terms of his/her trustworthiness and the level of expertise with the product or product category.

Dependable	1	2	3	4	5	6	7	Undependable
Honest	1	2	3	4	5	6	7	Dishonest
Reliable	1	2	3	4	5	6	7	Unreliable
Trustworthy	1	2	3	4	5	6	7	Untrustworthy
Sincere	1	2	3	4	5	6	7	Insincere
Expert	1	2	3	4	5	6	7	Not an expert
Experienced	1	2	3	4	5	6	7	Inexperienced
Knowledgeable	1	2	3	4	5	6	7	Not knowledgeable
Qualified	1	2	3	4	5	6	7	Unqualified
Skilled	1	2	3	4	5	6	7	Unskilled

In the first part of this experiment, you were exposed to print ads for four products endorsed by a sports celebrity. Please answer the following questions about this person.

1. What is the name of the sport celebrity in the print ads to which you were exposed?

_____

2. How familiar are you with the sport celebrity you saw in the print ads?
Very Unfamiliar   1   2   3   4   5   6   7   Very Familiar

3. I have seen this person before in ads for other products.
Yes _____ No _____

In the first part of this experiment, you were exposed to ads for four brands from four different product categories. Below, list the product categories and the brands from these categories for which you saw ads.

Product Category	Brand Name

In the space below, please write down whatever was going through your mind between the time you started and the time you finished the experiment. Please list the thoughts that occurred to you. You can list as many as you can recall. Do not worry about spelling, punctuation, or grammar.

APPENDIX C

Before you turn in the booklet, please answer the following questions for us.

1. How much effort did you expend reviewing the ads?
Not Very Much   1   2   3   4   5   6   7   Very Much

2. How carefully did you think about the advertisements?
Not Very Carefully   1   2   3   4   5   6   7   Very Carefully

3. How quickly did you form an opinion about the advertisement?
Not Very Quickly   1   2   3   4   5   6   7   Very Quickly

4. How challenging, in terms of time and effort, was it for you to review the ads and make your decisions?
Not Very Challenging   1   2   3   4   5   6   7   Very Challenging

5. How motivated were you to complete the study?
Not Very Motivated   1   2   3   4   5   6   7   Very Motivated

6. What is your gender? Male_____ Female _____

Note. The first five items from the above list were formed into a composite index to measure the processing manipulation.

APPENDIX D

CONDITIONS/CELLS

1. **High Familiarity, Male Sport Celebrity, Systematic Processing** (Ad featuring basketball player Grant Hill; participants under no need to recall 8-digit number but told that results will be compared.)

2. **High Familiarity, Female Sport Celebrity, Systematic Processing** (Ad featuring tennis player Monica Seles; participants under no need to recall 8-digit number but told that results will be compared.)

3. **High Familiarity, Male Sport Celebrity, Heuristic Processing** (Ad featuring basketball player Grant Hill; subject required to recall 8-digit number but not told of comparison of results.)

4. **High Familiarity, Female Sport Celebrity, Heuristic Processing**
(Ad featuring tennis player Monica Seles; participants required to recall 8-digit number but are not told that results will be compared.)

5. **Low Familiarity, Male Sport Celebrity, Systematic Processing**
(Ad featuring tennis player Todd Martin; participants not required to recall 8-digit number but told of comparison of results.)

6. **Low Familiarity, Female Sport Celebrity, Systematic Processing**
(Ad featuring tennis player Amanda Coetzer; participants not required to recall 8-digit number but told of comparison of results.)

7. **Low Familiarity, Male Sport Celebrity, Heuristic Processing**
(Ad featuring tennis player Todd Martin; participants required to recall 8-digit number but not told of comparison of results.)

8. **Low Familiarity, Female Sport Celebrity, Heuristic Processing**
(Ad featuring tennis player Amanda Coetzer; participants required to recall 8-digit number but are not told of comparison of results.)

REFERENCES

Agrawal, J., & Kamakura, W. A. (1995, July), The economic worth of celebrity endorsers: An event study analysis. *Journal of Marketing, 59,* 56–62.

Atkins, C., & Block, M. (1983, February/March). Effectiveness of celebrity endorsers. *Journal of Advertising Research, 23,* 57–61.

Chaiken, S. (1980). Heuristic versus systematic information processing and the use of source versus message cues in persuasion. *Journal of Personality and Social Psychology, 39,* 752–766.

Chaiken, S. (1987). The heuristic model of persuasion. In M. P. Zanna, J. M. Olson, & C. P. Herman (Eds.), *Social Influence: The Ontario Symposium* (vol. 5, pp. 3–39). Hillsdale, NJ: Lawrence Erlbaum Associates.

Chaiken, S., Liberman, A., & Eagly, A. H. (1989). Heuristic and systematic information processing within and beyond the persuasion context. In S. Uleman & J. A. Bargh (Eds.), *Unintended Thoughts: Limits of Awareness, Intention, and Control* (pp. 189–211). New York: Guilford.

Chaiken, S., & Maheswaran, D. (1994). Heuristic processing can bias systematic processing: Effects of source credibility, argument ambiguity, and task importance on attitude judgment. *Journal of Personality and Social Psychology, 66,* 460–473.

Cole, C., Ettenson, R., Reinke, S., & Schrader, T. (1990). The elaboration likelihood model (ELM): Replications, extensions, and some conflicting findings. In M. E. Goldberg, et al., G. Gorn, & R. Pollay (Eds.), *Advances in Consumer Research* (vol. 17, pp. 231–236). Provo, UT: Association for Consumer Research.

Fazio, R. H. (1986). How do attitudes guide behavior? In R. M. Sorrentino & E. T. Higgins (Eds.), *The hand book of motivation and cognition: Foundation of social behavior* (pp. 204–243). New York: Guilford Press.

Fazio, R. H. (1990). Multiple processes by which attitudes guide behavior: The MODE model as an integrative framework. In M. P. Zanna (Ed.), *Advances in Experimental Social Psychology*, (vol. 23, pp. 75–109). New York: Academic Press.

Forkan, J. (1995, November 17). Commercial actors squeezed by stars, "Real People." *Advertising Age*, 142.

Friedman, H. H., & Friedman, L. (1979, October). Endorser effectiveness by product type. *Journal of Advertising Research, 19*, 63–71.

Gilbert, D. T. (1989). Thinking lightly about others: Automatic components of the social inference process. In J. S. Uleman & J. A. Bargh (Eds.), *Unintended Thoughts: Limits of Awareness, Intention, and Control*, (pp. 189–211). New York: Guilford.

Gilbert, D. T., & Hixon, J. G. (1991). The trouble of thinking: activation and application of stereotypic beliefs. *Journal of Personality and Social Psychology, 60*, 509–517.

Gill, J. D., Grossbart, S., & Laczniak, R. N. (1988). Influence of involvement, commitment, and familiarity on brand beliefs and attitudes of viewers exposed to alternative ad claim strategies. *Journal of Advertising, 17*(2), 33–43.

Goldman, K. (1995, October 12). Women endorsers more credible than men. *The Wall Street Journal.* p. B1.

Heath, T. B., McCarthy, M. S., & Mothersbaugh, D. L. (1994). Spokesperson fame and vividness effects in the context of issue-relevant thinking: The moderating role of competitive setting. *Journal of Consumer Research, 20*, 520–534.

Hennessey, J. E., & Anderson, S. C. (1990). Interaction of peripheral cues and message arguments on cognitive responses to an advertisement. In M. E. Goldberg et al. (Eds.), *Advances in Consumer Research.* (vol. 17, pp. 237–243). Provo, UT: Association for Consumer Research.

Homer, P. M., & Kahle, L. R. (1990). Source expertise, time of source identification, and involvement in persuasion: An elaborative processing perspective. *Journal of Advertising, 19*(1), 30–39.

Kahle, L. R., & Homer, P. M. (1985). Physical attractiveness of the celebrity endorser: A social adaptation perspective. *Journal of Consumer Research, 11*, 954–961.

Kamins, M. A., Brand, M. J., Hoeke, S. A., & Moe, J. C. (1989). Two-sided versus one-sided celebrity endorsements: The impact on advertising effectiveness and credibility, *Journal of Advertising, 18*, 4–10.

Keller, K. L. (1998). *Strategic Brand Management.* Upper Saddle River, NJ: Prentice Hall.

Keller, K. L. (1987, December). Memory factors in advertising: The effect of advertising retrieval cues on brand evaluations. *Journal of Consumer Research, 14*, 316–333.

Kelley, H. H. (1973). The processes of causal attribution. *American Psychologist, 28*, 107–128.

Kelman, H. C. (1961). Process of opinion change. *Public Opinion Quarterly, 25*, 57–78.

Lane, R., & McHugh, J. (1995, December 18). A very green 1995. *Forbes, 156*, 212–232.

Lipman, J., & Hinge, J. B. (1991, July 12). Will Michael Jordan jump to Gatorade? *The Wall Street Journal*, B3.

McCracken, G. (1989, December). Who is the celebrity endorser?: Cultural foundations of the endorsement process. *Journal of Consumer Research, 16*, 310–321.

Misra, S., & Beatty, S. E. (1990). Celebrity spokesperson and brand congruence. *Journal of Business Research, 21*, 159–173.

Mitchell, A. A., & Olson, J. C. (1981, August). Are product attribute beliefs the only mediator of advertising effects? *Journal of Marketing Research, 18*, 318–332.

Mowen, J. C., Brown, S. W. (1981). On explaining and predicting the effectiveness of celebrity endorsers. In K. B. Monroe (Ed.), *Advances in Consumer Research* (vol. 8, pp. 437–441). Ann Arbor, MI: Association for Consumer Research.

Ohanian, R. (1990). Construction and validation of a scale to measure celebrity endorsers' perceived expertise, trustworthiness, and attractiveness. *Journal of Advertising, 19*(3), 39–52.

Ohanian, R., (1991, February/March). The impact of celebrity spokespersons' perceived image on consumers' intention to purchase. *Journal of Advertising Research, 31*, 46–54.

Pechmann, C., & Stewart, D. W. (1988). Advertising repetition: A critical review of wearin and wearout. In J. H. Leigh & C. R. Martin, Jr. (Eds.), *Current Issues and Research in Advertising* (vol. 11 [1], pp. 285–329). Ann Arbor, MI: University of Michigan School of Business Administration.

Petty, R. E., & Cacioppo, J. T. (1979). Issue involvement can increase or decrease persuasion by enhancing message-relevant cognitive responses. *Journal of Personality and Social Psychology, 37*, 1915–1926.

Petty, R. E., & Cacioppo, J. T. (1981). *Attitudes and Persuasion: Classic and Contemporary Approaches*, Dubuque, IA: William C. Brown.

Petty, R. E., & Cacioppo, J. T. (1983a). *Attitude Change: Central and Peripheral Routes to Persuasion*. New York: Springer-Verlag.

Petty, R. E., & Cacioppo, J. T. (1983b). Central and peripheral routes to persuasion: Application to advertising. In L. Percy & A. Woodside (Eds.), *Advertising and Consumer Psychology* (pp. 3–23). Lexington, MA: Lexington Books.

Petty, R. E., & Cacioppo, J. T. (1984). The effects of Involvement on Responses to Argument Quantity and Quality: Central and Peripheral Routes to Persuasion", *Journal of Personality and Social Psychology, 46*, 69–81.

Petty, R. E., & Cacioppo, J. T. (1986). The elaboration likelihood model of persuasion. In L. Berkowitz (Ed.), *Advances in Experimental Social Psychology* (pp. 123–205). New York: Academic Press.

Petty, R. E., Cacioppo, J. T., & Schumann, D. (1983, September). Central and peripheral routes to advertising effectiveness: The moderating role of involvement. *Journal of Consumer Research, 10*, 135–146.

Sanbonmatsu & Fazio. (1990). The role of attitudes in memory-based decision making, *Journal of Personality & Social Psychology, 59*, 614–622.

Shatel, T. (1991, May 19). Off-course activities take toll on trevino. *Chicago Tribune*, p. 2.

Sherman, S. P. (1985, August 18). When you wish upon a star. *Fortune. 112*, 132–136.

Tripp, C., Jensen, T. D., & Carlson, L. (1994). The effects of multiple endorsements by celebrities on consumers' attitudes and intentions. *Journal of Consumer Research, 20*, 535–547.

Trope, Y., & Alfieri, T. (1997). Effortfulness and flexibility of dispositional judgment processes. *Journal of Personality & Social Psychology, 73*, 662–674.

Zaichkowsky, J. (1985). Measuring the involvement construct. *Journal of Consumer Research, 12*, 341–352.

Magic Johnson and Mark McGwire: The Power of Identification With Sports Celebrities

Michael D. Basil
University of Lethbridge

William J. Brown
Regent University

In November 1991, Earvin "Magic" Johnson of the Los Angeles Lakers basketball team held a press conference to announce that he had contracted HIV and was retiring from professional basketball. The news of his infection spread quickly, and instantly the world had a well-liked, high-profile celebrity who demonstrated that heterosexuals were at risk for AIDS. This appeared to be a potentially critical event in people's perception of the disease. The press quickly predicted that Magic would be immensely effective in conveying this risk to the public. They speculated that his charisma would personalize the concern to other heterosexuals who had otherwise rationalized that the AIDS risk was limited to gay men. Magic's immediate interviews with the press, public service announcements, and appointment to the President's AIDS Council reinforced this hope (Anonymous, 1992; Baker, Lepley, Krishnan, & Victory, 1992; Fumento, 1992).

In September 1998, Mark McGwire, closely pursued by Sammy Sosa, crushed home run after home run. In the end, both broke Roger Maris's 37-year home run record and became heroes in the process. In this case, the news media made two interesting facts known about McGwire: he is a strong advocate and supporter of child abuse prevention programs, and he used a muscle-building dietary supplement, Androstenedione (McGregor, 1998;

Turner, 1998; Verducci, 1998a, 1998b). Thus, in this case, Mark McGwire's influence could have positive and negative consequences: against child abuse and in favor of steroid use.

This chapter reviews a series of four studies that explored the effects of these events in shaping people's perceptions and behavioral intentions. The first was a survey administered a week after Magic Johnson's press conference. The second was an experiment that assigned classes to watch a tape of the press conference or to engage in an interpersonal discussion about HIV and AIDS. The third was a survey conducted 1 year after the news conference. The fourth was a survey immediately after the 1998 baseball season. The results of each study show that identification with the celebrity determined the effects, shaping personal concern, perceptions, and behavioral intentions. They reveal that a sports celebrity can be immensely effective in advocating behavior. But this hinges on the extent that people identify with that celebrity. The theoretical literature and the four studies are reviewed next.

THEORY

A variety of theories and research suggest that a sports celebrity can be very effective in marshalling concern about an issue or influencing behavior. These include a theory of parasocial identification and a theory of identification with sports teams. Both of these approaches will be reviewed with a focus on understanding the potential of a sports celebrity to affect attitudes toward AIDS, child abuse, and steroid use.

The Importance of the Spokesperson

It is commonly accepted that who speaks on behalf of an issue or product is very important. The belief in the importance of the speaker in persuasion has a long history. Aristotle, in his book *Rhetoric*, claimed that to ensure success, a persuader should choose a source that is similar to the audience, yet high in status. He proposed that ethos was "the speaker's power of evincing a personal character . . ." (1941, p. 1318). Aristotle claimed that ethos is the largest determinant of the success of a persuasive attempt.

From the earliest social science studies of persuasion, as far back as the Yale studies (Hovland, Janis, & Kelley, 1953), research has examined the importance of the speaker. The results generally show that, as Aristotle postulated, credibility is one of the most important factors in persuasion. Quite a few subsequent researchers have confirmed the importance of credibility (Chaiken &

Maheswaran, 1994; Wu & Shaffer, 1987). Despite general agreement on the importance of credibility, there are problems with the somewhat circular definition used to define the concept. Here we propose that theories of parasocial identification and identification with sports teams offer an explanation for the power of sports celebrities.

Identification

One approach to understanding endorser effects rests on a theory of drama. In 1950, Burke proposed that successful drama requires that the audience identify with a character or characters. Through identification, audiences are more likely to become involved in the drama and, consequently, to be more moved by the performance. Burke concentrated on dramatic performances and did not apply his theory to the process of persuasion.

By the 1950s, with the diffusion of television, people began to take note of the mediated experience. Most relevant among these, Horton and Wohl (1956) began taking note of clinical psychology patients who felt a sense of intimacy with TV personalities. They referred to the imaginary relationship between a TV viewer and TV personalities as a *parasocial relationship*.

In 1961, Kelman proposed a more general model of behavior change. He proposed that there are three ways in which behavior change occurs. The first of these he labeled *compliance*. Compliance occurs when someone has power over you. The second form of behavior change he labeled *identification*. He proposed that identification occurs when a person likes or wants to be like someone else. The third process, *internalization*, occurs when a person adopts basic values of another. This process can best be seen in successful parenting. Kelman, however, he did not identify the conditions under which identification takes place, and he did not write within the context of the highly mediated world fostered by the information explosion of the late 20th century. Yet thinking through his predictions, it seems likely that compliance and internalization require longer-term face-to-face interaction; therefore, only identification can occur in situations in which a person does not have direct contact with the other person. This theory suggests that to the extent that people identify with media personalities, these personalities may create behaviors through a process of identification.

It fell to another scholar, Bentley (1964), to further articulate the role of audience involvement in increasing the effects of drama on an audience. He also suggested that even real life issues, such as a celebrity facing a real world challenge such as a divorce, a kidnapped child, or a rare disease, may invoke a similar response.

With concern about the potential of the mass media, Bandura began investigating how children might imitate behaviors seen on television. Based on this research he proposed a theory of social learning (1977) and later, social cognitive theory (1986). These theories propose that one way people learn is through observing others. Bandura identified the conditions under which people learn behaviors. He found that people are more likely to perform modeled behaviors to the extent that they identify with the person modeling the behavior. Therefore, identification does appear to be important in learning and in shaping actual behavior.

Through studying TV, researchers began to discover that repeated exposure to media figures through the mass media creates a sense of friendship or intimacy in media users (Levy, 1979). Audience members commonly look to media personalities as "friends" and those with whom they feel "comfortable." Evidence of parasocial relationships has been observed between TV viewers and newscasters, talk show hosts, and soap opera stars (Levy, 1979; Rubin & McHugh, 1987). Therefore, this line of research suggests one mechanism through which parasocial identification can occur—repeated media exposure.

Adding the areas of identification and celebrity together, it appears that behavioral effects are more likely when people develop a sense of identification with the model. Therefore, the theories of Horton and Wohl (1956), Kelman (1961), and Bandura (1977, 1986) all suggest that identification is a powerful process that can occur through media personalities. One of the main processes through which identification with celebrities can occur is the exposure that occurs through repeated TV exposure.

Basking in Reflected Glory

In the case of sports celebrities, there is another way that identification may develop. Theorists have proposed that fans see "their" team as an extension of themselves. One proposed mechanism for this process is called "Basking In Reflected Glory" (BIRG; Cialdini, Borden, Thorne, Walker, Freeman, & Sloan, 1976). In this situation, fans come to identify with teams that win. As evidence for this, Cialdini et al. found that fans use terms such as "we won" to refer to the team's performance on a previous day and are more likely to wear the team's apparel following a win.

The tendency to BIRG may help to explain an additional mechanism through which people may come to develop an imagined association with a successful team. The literature suggests that the BIRG phenomenon has many qualities that may shape associated affective responses. For example, Wann and Branscombe (1990) observed that the BIRG phenomenon determines a fan's sense of enjoyment derived from following a winning team. Some research suggests that the BIRG phenomenon is not entirely determined by winning and losing (Branscombe & Wann, 1991). Specifically, they found that a fan's identification with a team was not related to that team's professional record. These studies may help explain the behavior of fans who continue to remain loyal to mediocre teams.

To the extent that an attitude toward a team is established, this attitude may be seen to apply to phenomena such as affect transfer and balance (Heider, 1958). Thus, a positive attitude toward a sports team is likely to transfer to a particular sports celebrity. This affect may also transfer to products or issues endorsed by the sports celebrity (McCracken, 1989).

Because of the importance of sports figures as figures of identification (Fowles, 1992), sports seems an especially likely area to investigate the importance of identification. Zillmann and Paulus (1993) stated that the defining characteristic of fans is the formation of imaginary alliances in which fans perceive themselves to be members of an existing group. This approach, then, supports the importance of identification with the group of athletes that make up a sports team. It is quite reasonable, then, that identification with a particular member of a sports team is possible and even likely.

Previous Research on Magic Johnson's Effectiveness

There have been several studies that have examined the effects of Magic Johnson's announcement on people's sexual behaviors. Generally, these have found varying reactions, depending on the population under study and which effects were assessed. Most of the studies assessing attitudes have found moderately strong effects (Brown, Baranowski, Kulig, Stephenson & Perry, 1996; Graham, Weiner, Guiliano & Williams, 1993; Penner & Fritzsche, 1993; Pollock, 1994; Wanta & Elliott, 1995; Whalen, Henker, O'Neil, & Hollingshead, 1994; Zimet, Lazebnik, DiClemente, & Anglin, 1993). Meanwhile, others found significant self-reported changes (Hollander, 1993), whereas research that focused on actual behavior found more limited effects (Kalichman, 1994). Of course, findings that more significant changes occur on attitudes than on behaviors are consistent with hierarchy of effects theories (Batra & Ray, 1983; McGuire, 1981). Given the limitations of the power to observe behavioral outcomes, it is critical to include a measure of the underlying process.

In this case, research on the effects of sports celebrities should examine people's identification. To the extent that behavioral outcomes are contingent on identification, research would be more likely to reveal the underlying process through which these effects occur as well as actual behavioral effects.

News Diffusion

In November 1991, as a result of his public news conference and subsequent publicity surrounding his HIV diagnosis, Magic Johnson was thrown into the public eye as a spokesperson for AIDS. In one study of the diffusion of the news of his HIV diagnosis, Basil and Brown (1994) found that neither people's overall interest in the AIDS issue nor the source of the news predicted telling others. Gender, however, did show a relationship to spreading the news, but being a fan made people much more likely to tell others. Because this study found that involvement with basketball, and not AIDS, was the critical determinant of diffusion, it supports the notion that identification with Magic determined the effects of his announcement. Because heterosexual males, who had previously distanced themselves from the disease, are likely to be basketball fans, they may be the more likely to be influenced through Magic's announcement. If identification works in the ways that Burke (1950), Kelman (1961) and Bandura (1977, 1986) described, then the level of this identification should determine the effectiveness of the message.

H1: Identification with celebrities determines their effectiveness as spokes-people.

STUDY 1

In our first attempt to investigate the effects of identification, we studied 391 undergraduates drawn from speech classes at the University of Hawaii the week after Magic Johnson's announcement (Brown & Basil, 1995). We examined the extent to which these respondents knew about or identified with Magic, and their concern and intended condom use and intention to get an HIV blood test. The correlational relationships of knowledge of Magic on attitudes and behaviors were very close to zero (the correlations ranged from $-.02$ to $.11$, the betas between $-.01$ and $.00$).

These results demonstrated no relationship between knowledge and these attitudinal or behavioral outcomes. Knowledge of a celebrity, in this case Magic Johnson, was not related to the effectiveness of the celebrity as a spokesperson. This suggests that few effects accrue directly from whether a person is familiar with a celebrity or not.

The next analysis examined the effect of identification. The relationships between identification and the other outcomes showed significant correlations around $.2$. Specifically, the beta was $.35$ ($p < .001$) to personal concern,

.15 ($p < .01$) to perceived risk, .31 ($p < .001$) to perceptions of heterosexual risk, .30 ($p < .001$) to intended behavioral change, and .02 (insignificant) to intention to get an HIV blood test. Overall, the results suggest that the effects of the message depended on how much the audience member identified with Magic Johnson. Consistent with Bandura's theory, the results of this study suggest that attitude and behavior change are contingent on viewers' level of identification with the spokesperson. The more people identified with Magic, the more likely they were to embrace the attitudes that Magic advocated. People's intentions to make the changes in behavior that Magic advocated were also contingent on their identification with him.

These survey results, of course, were correlational. Therefore, it is possible that another variable may have determined identification with Magic as well as attitudes about AIDS and behavioral intentions. Traditionally, causality is established through strict control and randomization over all other factors while experimentally manipulating the variable or variables in question.

STUDY 2

If identification determines the process of persuasion, we reasoned that it should be possible to experimentally manipulate these effects. That is, through manipulating some aspect of the message to the audience or the medium through which that communication occurred, it should be possible to induce a feeling of identification with the message source.

In an experimental application of the research discussed earlier, we attempted to manipulate 361 college students (also at the University of Hawaii). We measured their social and personal risk perceptions for AIDS by involving them in additional communication about Magic Johnson (Basil & Brown, 1997). This experiment took place 2 weeks after the original news conference. It used a modified Solomon four-group design to compare pre-post and post-test only control groups with a group shown a media message of Magic's news conference and a group whose members interpersonally discussed the news. We proposed that this approach could not only test causality but also as a critical test of the impersonal impact hypotheses (predict that mass media stories determine social risk perceptions), interpersonal discussion (affects personal risk perceptions), and differential impact hypothesis (predicts that when the message makes use of a dramatic portrayal the mass media can affect both social and personal risk perceptions).

The results showed that people's attitudes were generally not affected by viewing the media message. Further, contrary to predictions, the interpersonal discussion condition showed the lowest social risk perceptions (5.8 versus overall 6.2, $p < .02$), but there was no difference between personal risk perceptions (4.8, $p > .10$). However, consistent with the identification approach, people's social and personal risk perceptions depended on their existing levels of identification with Magic Johnson (betas $= .20$ and $.16$, respectively, both $p < .02$). Therefore, consistent with the survey findings, this experiment suggests that message effects hinge on identification with Magic Johnson. Further analyses also revealed that people's identification with Magic Johnson mediated their perceptions of both social and personal risk so that the effectiveness of his message depended on whether or not the viewer identified with him as being similar to him or her. Specifically, the relationship between interpersonal communication and social risk perception dropped from .37 ($p < .001$) to .04 (not significant) when identification was included in the model. Similarly, the relationship between interpersonal communication and personal risk perceptions dropped from .37 ($p < .001$) to .02 (not significant) when identification was included. Therefore, the effects of interpersonal communication in reducing both social and personal risk perceptions were strongly mediated by identification with Magic Johnson. In sum, when people saw themselves as similar to Magic, although interpersonal communication generally served to reassure participants, identification served to reduce people's ability to rationalize away their fears. When people did not identify with Magic, the interpersonal discussion was very powerful in allowing participants to allay their concerns.

STUDY 3

The next question was to see if the mediated relationship between identification with Magic Johnson still held a year later. In a sample of 147 college students at the University of Hawaii, a questionnaire similar to the one administered a year earlier was distributed (Basil, 1996). The analysis showed that people's identification with Magic again correlated with people's personal concern about AIDS, their risk perceptions, and their behavioral intentions. These findings were consistent with those found a year earlier. Here, the path coefficient between identification and sexual behaviors was .14. The mediated path through identification showed a significant contribution to the prediction of sexual behaviors over and above more direct effects. Again, Magic's influence hinged on how much people identified with him.

This finding demonstrates the lasting importance of identification. Thus, identification with a celebrity appears to determine the extent to which a person is persuaded by the celebrity. In this case, identification with Magic Johnson related to people's beliefs and intentions, even a year after the publicity surrounding his announcement occurred.

STUDY 4

After these Magic Johnson studies, we wondered about the generalizability of these results to other sports celebrities. When Mark McGwire broke the home run record in 1998, this seemed like a natural follow-up. In this case we used a survey to examine the relationship between identification and two behavioral outcomes: one positive and one negative (Brown, Basil, & Bocarena, 2003). The positive outcome would arise from McGwire's statements against child abuse (McGregor, 1998). The negative ones would arise from his use of the steroid Androstenedione (Turner, 1998; Verducci, 1998a, 1998b).

In this case, we had two parts to our sample: students from four universities and a survey posted on the Internet. The survey also revealed high levels of parasocial identification with the celebrity. Again, the level of identification was an important predictor of these outcomes. Specifically, the relationship between identification and speaking out against child abuse was significant and positive ($r = .39$, $beta = .36$, $p < .01$). Meanwhile, the relationship between identification and intention to use steroids was also significant and positive ($r = .39$, $beta = .45$, $p < .01$).

These findings demonstrate a remarkably consistent relationship between identification on both positive and negative outcomes. They also replicate the Magic Johnson findings with a different celebrity. Therefore, the power of identification established with Mark McGwire appears very consistent with that found in the earlier studies for Magic Johnson.

CONCLUSIONS

There are two general conclusions that can be drawn from the four studies. First, a sports celebrity can be a very effective spokesperson in advocating behavioral compliance. Magic Johnson's announcement that he was HIV-positive was a powerful and lasting event that altered people's personal concerns about HIV, increased social and personal risk perceptions, and altered people's behavioral intentions. In these cases, identification with Magic Johnson appears to operate as if a trusted friend had been diagnosed with HIV. The size of these changes was comparable to changes that occurred in response to long-term HIV-related interventions in specific communities. Although it is likely that some of the behavioral changes will dissipate over time (Kalichman, 1994), so would any other intervention. Even the effect of being personally diagnosed with HIV likely partially dissipates over time.

In the case of Mark McGwire, identification predicted attitudes and behavioral intentions toward two distinct issues: concern about child abuse and intention to use steroids. Identification appeared to have strikingly similar effects, regardless of whether the potential modeling was positive or negative.

Thus, the power of identification seems to hold across at least two major sports figures (one involved in basketball, one in baseball) almost 7 years apart and across three different public health outcomes (HIV / AIDS, steroid use, and child abuse). With both celebrities, these effects depended on individuals' level of identification with them. This means that to be effective in persuading a targeted group, it is necessary to select a source with whom the group identifies. In the case of most celebrities, viewers probably already have an existing level of identification with that celebrity. Some of this identification likely results from the BIRG phenomenon, a level of identification with the team that the celebrity plays for and represents in the public's mind. Other parts of this identification likely result from aspects of the particular celebrity's personality and the way the celebrity is seen by the public. A virtual unknown from a victorious team immediately following a victory will have some power by virtue of the BIRG phenomenon. Other athletes, by virtue of their personality, poise, and name recognition would likely also have potential. When an athlete has both, such as a Super Bowl most valuable player with personality, he or she will likely be the most effective. Still other athletes, such as Chicago Bulls star Dennis Rodman, may have some positive team BIRG effects and, to some viewers, negative personal identification. Thus, the effects of particular sports celebrities may enhance or detract from overall BIRG effects.

Further research should examine to what extent each of these factors determine an athlete's persuasive power. It should also examine whether identification with non-sports models also determines people's responses to other forms of advocacy and advertising. Thus, although this research suggests that identification with a known other follows predictions derived from identification, further research should examine whether the identification process for other celebrities is actually the same as that for sports celebrities. Specifically, it should examine whether these effects also depend on people's levels of identification with the celebrities. In other research we have conducted using this approach, we have shown a similar result in people's reactions to the death of Princess Diana (Brown, Basil, & Bocarnea, in press). In the case of Princess Diana, identification was related to their ownership of Princess Diana memorabilia, their mass media use after her death, their feelings of grief, and their level of blaming the press for her death. Therefore, the identification we found with sports celebrities also appears to hold for other celebrities.

Those with an eye to the practical implications of this research might wonder how public relations people, advertisers, and marketers can influence the audience. These results suggest that the effectiveness of celebrities hinges on the breadth and depth of their appeal. To the extent that a large portion of the audience closely identifies with a celebrity, that celebrity would be effective in a broad appeal. Limited-appeal celebrities, meanwhile, are best left to regions or channels where most or all of the audience identifies with that celebrity or the team that the celebrity represents. Further, establishing the breadth and depth of people's identification with celebrities is likely a more predictive measure of their power than the traditional "Q" measure.

REFERENCES

Anonymous. (1992). Exchange with reporters prior to a meeting with Magic Johnson (interview with George Bush). *Weekly Compilation of Presidential Documents, 28*(33), 87–89.

Aristotle. (1941). *The Basic Works of Aristotle.* New York: Random House.

Baker, J. A., Lepley, C. J., Krishnan, S., & Victory, K. S. (1992). Celebrities as health educators: Media advocacy guidelines. *Journal of School Health, 62,* 433–436.

Bandura, A. (1977). *Social learning theory.* Englewood Cliffs, NJ: Prentice-Hall.

Bandura, A. (1986). *Social Foundations of Thought and Action: A Social-Cognitive Theory.* Englewood Cliffs, NJ: Prentice-Hall.

Basil, M. D. (1996). Identification as a mediator of celebrity effects. *Journal of Broadcasting and Electronic Media, 40,* 478–495.

Basil, M. D., & Brown, W. J. (1994). Interpersonal communication in news diffusion: A study of "Magic" Johnson's announcement. *Journalism Quarterly, 71,* 305–320.

Basil, M. D., & Brown, W. J. (1997). Marketing AIDS prevention: The differential impact hypothesis versus identification effects. *Journal of Consumer Psychology, 6,* 389–411.

Batra, R., & Ray, M. (1984). How advertising works at contact. In L. Alwitt & A. Mitchell (Eds.), *Psychological Processes and Advertising Effects: Theory, Research, and Applications* (pp. 13–43). Hillsdale, NJ: Lawrence Erlbaum Associates.

Bentley, E. (1964). *Life of the Drama.* New York: Antheneum.

Branscombe, N. R., & Wann, D. L. (1991). The positive social and self concept consequences of sports team identification. *Journal of Sport and Social Issues, 15,* 115–127.

Brown B. R. Jr., Baranowski, M. D., Kulig, J. W., Stephenson, J. M., & Perry, B. (1996). Searching for the Magic Johnson effect: AIDS, adolescents, and celebrity disclosure. *Adolescence, 31,* 253–258.

Brown, W. J., & Basil, M. D. (1995). Media celebrities and public health: Responses to "Magic" Johnson's HIV disclosure and its impact on AIDS risk and high-risk behaviors. *Health Communication, 7,* 345–370.

Brown, W. J., Basil, M. D., & Bocarnea, M. (in press). Social influence of an international celebrity: Responses to the death of Princess Diana. *Journal of Comunication*.

Brown, W. J., Basil, M. D., & Bocarena, M. C. (2003). The influence of famous athletes on health beliefs and practices: Mark McGwire, child abuse prevention, and Androstenedione. *Journal of Health Communication, 8*, 41–57.

Burke, K. (1950). *A Rhetoric of Motives*. Englewood Cliffs, NJ: Prentice-Hall.

Chaiken, S., & Maheswaran, D. (1994). Heuristic processing can bias systematic processing: Effects of source credibility, argument ambiguity, and task importance on attitude judgment. *Journal of Personality and Social Psychology, 66*, 460–473.

Cialdini, R. B., Borden, R. J., Thorne, A., Walker, M. R., Freeman, S., & Sloan, L. R. (1976). Basking in reflected glory: Three (football) field studies. *Journal of Personality and Social Psychology, 34*, 366–375.

Fowles, J. (1992). *Star Struck: Celebrity Performers and the American Public*. Washington, DC: Smithsonian Institution Press.

Fumento, M. (1992). Do you believe in Magic? *The American Spectator, 25*(2), 16–23.

Graham, S., Weiner, B., & Guiliano, T., & Weiner. (1993). An attributional analysis of reactions to Magic Johnson. *Journal of Applied Social Psychology, 23*, 996–1003.

Heider, F. (1958). *The Psychology of Interpersonal Relations*. New York: Wiley.

Hollander, D. (1993). Publicity about Magic Johnson may have led some to reduce their risky behavior, request HIV testing. *Family Planning Perspectives, 25*, 192–194.

Horton, D., & Wohl, R. R. (1956). Mass communication and parasocial interaction: Observations on intimacy at a distance. *Psychiatry, 19*, 215–229.

Hovland, C. I., Janis, I. L., & Kelley, H. H. (1953). *Communication and Persuasion*. New Haven, CT: Yale University Press.

Kalichman, S. C. (1994). Magic Johnson and public attitudes towards AIDS: A review of empirical findings. *AIDS Education and Prevention, 6*, 542.

Kelman, H. C. (1961). Processes of opinion change. *Public Opinion Quarterly, 25*, 57–78.

Levy, M. (1979). Watching television news as parasocial interaction. *Journal of Broadcasting, 23*, 69–80.

McCracken, G. (1989). Who is the celebrity endorser? Cultural foundations of the endorsement process. *Journal of Consumer Research, 16*, 310–321.

McGregor, E. J. (1998). Mark McGwire is a hero for more than his homers. *Sports Illustrated, 89*(12), 22.

McGuire, W. J. (1981). The probabilogical model of cognitive structure and attitude change. In R. Petty, T. Ostrom & T. Brock (Eds.), *Cognitive Responses in Persuasion*. Hillsdale, NJ: Lawrence Erlbaum Associates.

Penner, L. A., & Fritzsche, B. A. (1993). Magic Johnson and reaction to people with AIDS: A natural experiment. *Journal of Applied Social Psychology, 23*, 1035–1040.

Pollock, P. H., III (1994). Issues, values, and critical moments: Did "Magic" Johnson transform public opinion on AIDS? *American Journal of Political Science, 38*, 426–448.

Rubin, A. M., & McHugh, M. P. (1987). Development of parasocial interaction relationships. *Journal of Broadcasting and Electronic Media, 31*, 279–292.

Turner, M. J. (1998, September 28). McGwire and steroids. *U.S. News and World Report*, 5.

Verducci, T. (1998a, September 14). Making his mark. *Sports Illustrated*, 28–33.

Verducci, T. (1998b, October 5). The greatest season ever. *Sports Illustrated*, 38–53.

Wann, D. L., & Branscombe, N. R. (1990). Die-hard and fair-weather fans: Effects of identification on BIRGing and CORFing tendencies. *Journal of Sport and Social Issues, 14*, 103–117.

Wanta, W., & Elliott, W. R. (1995). Did the "Magic" work? Knowledge of HIV/AIDS and the knowledge gap hypothesis. *Journalism and Mass Communication Quarterly, 72,* 312–322.

Whalen, Henker, O'Neil, & Hollingshead (1994).

Wu, C., & Shaffer, D. R. (1987). Susceptibility to persuasive appeals as a function of source credibility and prior experience with the attitude object. *Journal of Personality and Social Psychology, 52,* 677–688.

Zillmann, D., & Paulus, P. B. (1993). Spectators: Reactions to sports events and effects on athletic performance. In R. N. Singer, M. Murphey, & L. K. Tennant (Eds.), *Handbook of Research on Sport Psychology* (pp. 600–610). New York and Toronto and New York: Macmillan.

Zimet, G. D., Lazebnik, R., DiClemente, R. J., Anglin, T. M. (1993). The relationship of Magic Johnson's announcement of HIV infection to the AIDS attitudes of junior high school students. *Journal of Sex Research, 30,* 129–134.

III

The Consequences of Sponsorship

Sponsorship in its various forms dominates sports marketing. This topic looms large in many conversations about sports marketing. It is with good reason, therefore, that we have more chapters in this section than in any other. Chapter 8 presents a thoughtful overview regarding mechanisms through which sponsorship can influence consumers. Chapter 9 discusses the outcomes of sponsorship on two campuses. Chapter 10 provides evidence regarding how consumers think about sponsorship, and Chapter 11 looks at what happens with stock prices when sponsorship deals are announced. Chapter 12 reviews the literature on team identification and how that relates to responses to corporate sponsors.

Seven Psychological Mechanisms Through Which Sponsorship Can Influence Consumers

John W. Pracejus
University of Alberta

Gaining commercial advantage through association with an event is a complicated proposition. These events (sports or otherwise) are culturally bound and meaning laden. They can invoke in consumer audiences complex scripts and multiple associations. Events can vary in size and prestige. Some associations represent a strong fit between brand and event, whereas other associations are less logical. Consumers can vary greatly in their involvement in and knowledge of a single event, and sponsors of an event can vary in the amount of presence they have relative to other event sponsors.

Given the number of factors that can be involved in a sponsorship association, any attempt to study the **way** sponsorship works is likely to provide an incomplete picture of the process. At present, very little conceptual or empirical work has addressed how it works. It is proposed here that there are, in fact, multiple **ways** in which sponsorship works.

Seven distinct mechanisms are proposed through which sponsorship functions to impact brand equity, brand positioning, and other relevant marketing variables of interest. The mechanisms are not mutually exclusive, thus two or more may function in any given sponsorship association. Together, however, they represent a reasonably complete set of ways sponsorship works.

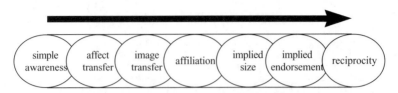

FIG. 8.1.   Increase in required cognitive elaboration.

These seven mechanisms can be ordered by the amount of consumer cognitive elaboration required for the mechanism to function. They are listed in increasing order of cognitive elaboration needed: simple awareness, affect transfer, image transfer, affiliation, implied size, implied endorsement, and reciprocity. The relationships among mechanisms are depicted in Fig. 8.1.

The only of these mechanisms to receive significant direct acknowledgment are simple awareness, affect transfer, and, to a lesser extent, image transfer. Evidence for the existence of the affiliation, implied size, implied endorsement, and reciprocity mechanisms is largely intuitive or anecdotal. The seven mechanisms are described individually in the following sections.

SIMPLE AWARENESS

. . . mere repeated exposure of the individual to a stimulus is sufficient condition for the enhancement of his attitude toward it. (Zajonc, 1968, p. 1)

Awareness, as a mechanism through which sponsorship is likely to function, is widely accepted by practitioners and academics alike. A typical explanation of how this mechanism might function is as follows. A consumer goes to an event or watches it on TV and is "exposed" to the brand name. Because repeated exposure to an object has been found to lead to positive affect toward the object (Zajonc, 1968), the consumer feels better about the brand. This good feeling then has all sorts of benefits to the brand, including, but not limited to, greater attention paid to subsequent commercial communications (and may reduce counterarguing, see Pracejus, 1995) and greater chance of inclusion in the consideration set. Although there is little doubt that such things take place, to end here with awareness ignores the rich possibilities involved in the association. In short, if simple awareness were the only mechanism in operation, then it would, for example, make no difference whether a brand name was seen on the side of a racecar or on the side of a barn.

As mentioned earlier, there is little doubt that awareness functions as an important mechanism in sponsorship. However, examples of simple awareness, with little or no chance of cognitive elaboration by the consumer, are not easy to cite. One that comes close is the practice of soft drink bottlers paying for convenience store signage, provided it prominently displays the appropriate brand logo. This example meets the criterion for simple awareness because of the low likelihood of elaboration by a store patron as to the origins of the large "Coke" logo on the "ABC Beverage" sign. Even if there were some attribution on the part of a customer, it is unlikely that he or she would have enough involvement with the store to care that the owners received a new sign courtesy of the local Coke bottler. The most likely impact (if any) is that the customer may have high top-of-mind awareness of Coke as he or she faces soft drink selection. There is little or no difference between the logo appearing on the sign and on the side of a nearby building. The only things accomplished are simple exposure-based familiarity with the brand and awareness.

Despite the relative simplicity of this mechanism, considering how it functions allows predictions about sponsorship associations to be made. For example, it is expected that the more frequently a sponsor's name is encountered by a consumer in the context of an event, the more positive feelings he or she has toward the brand. It is also expected that the increase in positive feelings from this kind of exposure will be greater for less familiar brands. (These and subsequent propositions are formally stated in Table 8.1.)

AFFECT TRANSFER

Affect transfer in a sponsorship context is analogous to affect transfer in an advertising context, whereby one's attitude toward the ad transfers to one's attitude toward the brand, with little cognitive mediation (MacKenzie & Lutz, 1989; MacKenzie, Lutz, & Belch, 1986). As a mechanism through which sponsorship may function, affect transfer refers to positive feelings toward an event transferring to the sponsoring brand through the sponsorship association. This mechanism requires no real cognitive elaboration. It does not even require conscious awareness of the association, although such awareness might be beneficial to the transfer taking place.

Affect transfer is a mechanism that has received some mention in the sponsorship literature, although much of it is rather vague. In an article that reported significant differences in demographic and lifestyle variables among several Hallmark events, Roslow, Nicholls, and Laskey (1992) noted, "Hallmark events are attended by diverse audiences who have come together to enjoy a specific experience or entertainment. This heightened level of expectation may provide a more beneficial exposure content than traditional media" (p. 54). They elaborated, "It is probable that this form of promotion

TABLE 8.1
Summary of Testable Propositions About
the Seven Mechanisms

Mechanism	Testable Proposition
Simple awareness	P1: The more frequently a sponsored brand name is encountered by a consumer in the context of an event, the more positive feelings she or he has toward the brand.
	P2: The effect of P1 is greater for less familiar brands than more familiar brands.
Affect transfer	P3: The more positive the affective response to an event, the more positive the affective response to a sponsoring brand.
	P4: The stronger the associative linkage between the brand and the event, the stronger the impact of P3.
Image transfer	P5: Brands involved in few sponsorship activities acquire more of the image and abstract associations of an event than brands that sponsor many events.
	P6: Transfer of image from event to brand takes place more easily, and with greater magnitude, for low symbolic brands compared to high symbolic brands.
	P7: Due to a "maximum rule," sponsorship by brands with images not fully congruent with an event will not cause appreciable harm to the image of the event.
Affiliation	P8: Affiliation with a sponsored event is positively correlated with perceived prestige of the event.
	P9: Affiliation with a sponsored event is positively correlated with frequency of attendance.
	P10: Affiliation with a sponsored event is negatively correlated with one's participation in other activities.
Implied size	P11: Event sponsorship can influence the perceived size of a sponsoring firm.
	P12: The larger the perceived size of the event, the greater the impact of the sponsorship on the perceived size of the firm.
	P13: Sponsorship of an event by a large sponsor can increase the perceived size of the event.
	P14: The sponsorship impact on perceived size can have a positive impact on perceived quality of the brand.
Implied endorsement	P15: Use of the brand in the sponsored event facilitates the inferences necessary for the implied endorsement to function.
	P16: Having the sponsor's name in the event name facilitates the inferences necessary for implied endorsement to function.
Reciprocity	P17: The more involved consumers are with an event, the more likely the sponsorship is to engage reciprocity.

would benefit the advertiser from increased levels of excitement and interest associated with hallmark events" (p. 58). These authors seemed to be proposing that the positive affective responses to the hallmark event may transfer to the sponsoring brand.

Crimmins and Horn (1996) also addressed the idea of affect transfer. They discussed the transfer of positive feelings from the event to the brand in terms of Heider's (1946) elementary human calculus. They posited that, given the relative weakness of many brand beliefs, the impact of associating a lowly regarded brand with a highly regarded event should usually lead to an upward estimation of the brand. Although this seems plausible, the authors provided no data to support the assertion. The idea, however, is that the positiveness of the event can transfer to the sponsor.

Stipp and Schiavone (1996) attempted to demonstrate that attitude toward the Olympics can actually rub off onto Olympic sponsors. Through multiple regression, they found that attitude toward Olympic sponsorship in general had a significant impact, net of ad recall and ad evaluation, on sponsor's image.

Indication of an affect transfer mechanism is also found in other commercial association domains. In the context of celebrity endorsers, for example, Misra and Beatty (1990) found that the transfer of affect from spokesperson to brand was facilitated when the two were matched. In the domain of brand extensions, Rangaswamy, Burke, and Oliva (1993) proposed "affect transfer through categorization" as a method by which utility of the brand name impacts utility of the product.

Affect-transfer–like mechanisms are also found in the retail assortment domain. In a factorial design, Jacoby and Mazursky (1984) associated high- and low-quality brands with high- and low-quality stores. They attempted to determine how differential affects in the associate pair interact. They found some support for an averaging process.

Like simple awareness, the cognitively simple mechanism of affect transfer allows for basic predictions to be made. One might expect, for example, that the more a consumer likes a sponsored event, the more positive feelings will be generated about the sponsoring brand. One might also expect that the associative linkage between brand and event would facilitate the transfer of positive affect from event to brand.

IMAGE TRANSFER

The aim of sponsorship is image transfer: the transfer of personality, aura and competence . . . to the brand. (Ryssel & Stamminger, 1988, p. 111)

Although affect transfer is the process of assigning event-based affective response to the brand, image transfer refers to the assignment of abstract event associations to the brand. Image transfer is the mechanism requiring the least cognitive elaboration in which the association can be formally stated as a message. The message of image transfer is that, along some dimension, this brand is like this event.

The idea that the image or personality of an event can affect the image or personality of a brand has been alluded to several times in the context of sponsorship. Parker (1991) for example, described the relationship between sponsorship and brand image. Marshall and Cook (1992) found that 14% of respondents listed "image of sport" as the most important determinant in selecting an event to sponsor. Wolton (1988) contended that art sponsorship is used to alter or modify the image of a company, lending a human face to cold, technologically oriented companies and providing a positive association with companies, such as insurers, that are usually associated with unpleasant situations.

McDonald (1991) described what he referred to as "product relevance" (p. 36), which can be either direct or indirect. Indirect relevance is proposed to imply association at an abstract, more image-based level. A strong and traditional bank sponsoring the traditional sport of football (soccer) was given as an example of indirect relevance, where the link was tradition. Relating back to the previous discussion, in this example the message would be that this bank is like the soccer league in that they are both traditional.

Perhaps the best anecdotal evidence of how the image transfer mechanism might be used for a specific marketing objective, such as repositioning a brand, was given by Meenaghan (1991a). He stated that sponsorships can achieve specific objectives through what he called the "image by association effect" (p. 42). He gave as an example how a very American company, Gillette, was made to seem more British through its sponsorship of cricket, a traditionally British sport. He also cited the case of IVECO trucks, which, were viewed as weak European vehicles, compared to U.S.-made trucks. By sponsoring the macho sport of heavyweight boxing, IVECO was able to shift this image in a highly successful way.

More recently, Gwinner (1997) proposed a "model of image creation and image transfer in event sponsorship." He proposed that several variables would moderate the transfer of image from event to sponsoring brand. He provided a series of testable propositions about image transfer in the context of sponsorship.

The image transfer mechanism can also be found in other domains of commercial association. Within the domain of celebrity endorsers, Walker, Langmeyer, and Langmeyer (1992) investigated how products pick up some of the personality of the endorser. They found that previously unendorsed products pick up more of the personality of the endorser than do previously endorsed products. Within the sponsorship context, then, one might expect brands involved in few sponsorship activities to acquire more of the image and abstract associations of an event than brands that sponsor many events.

Within the brand extension domain, Reddy, Holak, and Bhat (1994) found that brands with high symbolic value extend better than brands with low symbolic value. If image transfer in sponsorship functions in a similar manner, one might expect that brands with high symbolic value would be less likely to have the image of the event transferred onto them.

Within the domain of combined brands Rao and Ruekert (1994) argued in favor of a maximum rule whereby the combined brand may receive the higher of the two brand perceptions on each dimension. An example of this is the association between Lays potato chips and KC Masterpiece barbecue sauce. Although the combined brand gains the desired associations of tangy and hickory smoke flavor from KC Masterpiece, an average "crispness" between the chips and the sauce is not perceived. Crispness remains at the higher of the two levels, the level of regular Lays. If image transfer in sponsorship functions in a similar way, brand images not fully congruent with an event should not cause appreciable harm to the image of the event.

In fact, anecdotal evidence of reverse image transfer, without negative impact on the brand, has been cited. Jones and Dearsley (1989 cf. McDonald, 1991) found that the image of football (soccer) was actually improved by a sponsorship by Barclays Bank during a time when football was receiving a lot of bad press. Apparently, this association transferred the perception of stability from Barclays to the soccer league without transferring rowdiness to Barclays. Perhaps positive associations are more easily transferred than negative ones. This is certainly an interesting empirical question for future study.

AFFILIATION

Affiliation, like image transfer, can be stated as a message. The message of affiliation is that this brand "is for people like me." The primary requirement for the functioning of this mechanism is that the event be perceived as "for people like me." The more this statement is perceived to be true, the more the message about the brand being "for me" will be facilitated.

Although there is no formal conceptual development of the way affiliation might function as a mechanism of sponsorship effectiveness, some authors have hinted at the idea. Meenaghan (1991b) for example, pointed out that "the (sponsorship) message is delivered by association with a socially intrusive activity" (p. 8). Parker (1991) posited that today's consumers, in addition to demanding products with desired attributes at a reasonable price, also seek products that are "for people like me." Sponsorship, he proposed, is uniquely suited to helping a brand achieve the perception of being "for people like me." No further development of these ideas, however, is presented by either of these authors.

There have been several studies of the impact of strong social affiliations such as political affiliations (Ellen, Wiener, & Cobb-Walgren, 1991) and ethnic affiliations (Deshpande, Hoyer, & Donthu, 1986) on consumer behavior. At a broader level, Westbrook and Black (1985) found that "desire for affiliations with others" is an important determinant of some people's shopping behavior. In addition to these general impacts of affiliation with a group on consumer behavior, the possibility that an affiliation with a brand or organization can be beneficially developed through the use of marketing variables has been explored.

Macchiette and Roy (1992) described *affinity marketing* as the use of group affiliation to produce a strong promotional program. The resultant *affinity groups* are said to have high levels of social bonding and cohesiveness. Members of affinity groups are also said to be committed to the objectives of the group. The authors proposed marketing generated affinity as one source of group centeredness.

An example of how marketing can take advantage of people's existing affiliations is the *affinity credit card*. Such cards bear the name and symbol of an organization to which the cardholder belongs. High levels of cardholder loyalty have been claimed for these cards (Worthington & Horn, 1992).

Bhattacharya, Rao, and Glynn (1995) investigated the correlates of social identification with an organization. They found that perceived prestige and visiting frequency are positively correlated with affiliation. They also found that participation in similar organizations is negatively correlated with affiliation. Affiliation with an event, therefore, is also likely to be positively correlated with perceived prestige of the event. Affiliation with an event is also likely to be negatively related to attendance at other events and participation in other activities.

It should be noted that in advertising, the manipulation of *affiliation motivation* has been cited as a frequently employed tactic (Zinkhan, Hong, & Lawson, 1990). These authors conducted content analysis on a sample of magazine ads from selected years between 1935 and 1985. They found that over the period studied, affiliation motivational appeals increased in frequency. The authors contrasted this increase with a decline in the use of achievement appeals.

IMPLIED SIZE

The implied size mechanism also has a message that can be stated in words. The message of implied size is that "this company is big." The cognitive elaboration required for this mechanism to occur is considerably higher than those previously listed. A consumer must, at some level, think to him or herself "this must be a big company to be able to sponsor this event."

The idea that sponsoring an event can influence the perceived size of the sponsor has been examined and has received some empirical support. McDonald (1991) explored this possibility but did not find evidence of an effect. He stated, however, that the reason sponsorship did not appear to affect perceptions of size was that most of the companies studied were already clearly perceived to be very big and important (e.g., Phillips and Cadbury). He speculated that if the sample included more small companies an impact of sponsorship on perceived size might have been found.

Rajaretnam (1994) found evidence that sponsorship can influence perceived size. In the evaluation of the experiment in which a tire maker spent almost its entire marketing budget from 1984 to 1987 on sponsorship, during this period, perceived size of company increased by 19.7%. Perceived financial health of the company, a related measure, increased by 24.6% (p. 68). Although this field experiment with no control group does not prove that sponsorship can impact the perceived size of the firm, it certainly suggests the possibility. One might expect, then, that sponsoring events that are perceived to be large would lead to more inferences about the size of the sponsoring company than would sponsoring events that are perceived to be small.

This process may also function in the opposite direction. Anecdotal evidence of the size of the sponsor affecting the perceived size of the event has been reported by Parker (1991), who proposed that Mars' sponsorship of the London Marathon was the key to persuading people that it was a "real" event.

The marketing literature provides evidence of the benefits of perceived size. Kirmani and Wright (1989) proposed the idea that "perceived advertising expense is a signal of a firm's financial strength, probable social acceptance or some other factor that defines quality in some markets" (p. 344). This idea is similar to the idea that a company could not afford to sponsor a prominent event unless it is a large, stable company. The authors did not investigate the perceived financial strength possibility, however, stating that the default attribution is the "most interesting possibility and the one we pursue most directly in this research" (p. 346).

Following up this work, Kirmani (1990) proposed that perceived costs will be used as cues to quality when they are more diagnostic than other cues.

She hypothesized that this should take place under low involvement with the product class. The hypothesis, however, was not supported. No effect of involvement was found.

It is not difficult to imagine situations under which perception of firm size would have an impact on perceived quality, yet little research has directly investigated this effect. Within the context of the banking industry, there is evidence that perceived size of a bank can affect consumer beliefs about the likelihood of receiving a loan (Leonard & Spencer, 1991). In the arena of legal services, however, there is evidence to suggest that service providers believe perceived firm size to be more important than do clients (Gaedeke & Tootelian, 1988).

Nonetheless, it seems possible that under certain circumstances, perceptions of the size of the sponsoring company can contribute to brand equity. This might take place because large brands are perceived to be of high quality in that category. Company size might imply stability, which can contribute to consumer utility for the brand through risk reduction. Perceived size may also indirectly impact brand equity by lending credibility to its other communications.

IMPLIED ENDORSEMENT

The *implied endorsement mechanism* requires even more cognitive elaboration. Its message is "this brand must be OK, or it wouldn't be allowed to be the sponsor." The implied endorsement mechanism requires the consumer to infer that the event is somehow endorsing the quality of the brand. Several examples of this can be cited. McDonald (1991) provided Seiko's sponsorship of track meets at which it is the official timer as an example of what he called "direct relevance" (p. 36). *Direct relevance* means that one might logically conclude that the official status of a sponsor implies some measure of quality.

Crimmins and Horn (1996) cited Visa and Seiko as brands that actually affected consumer perceptions of quality due to their association with the 1992 summer Olympics (as measured by DDB Needham's SponsorWatch service). Because Seiko was the official timekeeper and Visa was the only credit card the Olympics would accept for tickets, it seems that an implied endorsement may have led to the Olympic sponsorship success of these two brands.

The implied endorsement mechanism, however, does not require some official sanctioning of the sponsoring brand. As long as a consumer infers that some minimum quality level is required before an event will let a brand sponsor it, the implied endorsement mechanism can be engaged. Usage of the brand at an event, however, might certainly increase the likelihood of this type of inference. Seeing top pool players compete for large prizes on Brunswick tables at the Brunswick Tournament for example, might cause some consumers to infer a level of quality for Brunswick tables.

One might expect, therefore, that the greater the congruency between the sponsor and the event, the more likely it is that consumers will make inferences about an implied endorsement of the brand by the event. The *share of presence* a sponsor has at an event is also likely to impact implied endorsement, such that major sponsors of an event are more likely than minor ones to elicit inferences about implied endorsement. The situation most likely to lead to inferences about an implied endorsement, therefore, would be when the event has the brand name in the title and brand is actually used in the event.

The ways in which implied endorsement can impact perceptions, attitudes, and choice have been well delineated in the source effects literature. Factors affecting the ability of a source to persuade include trustworthiness (Brehm & Lipsher, 1959), expertise (Petty, Cacioppo, & Goldman, 1981), attractiveness (Landy & Sigall, 1974), and credibility (Birnbaum, Wong, & Wong, 1976). Although the literature on source effects is rich with predictive constructs, proposing the impact of these constructs in the context of sponsorship first requires some empirical investigation. For example, it is not known whether a credible event or a trustworthy event exists in the minds of consumers. If such things do exist, it is not obvious what the determinants of these source characteristics would be. Further elaboration on the role of source characteristics in sponsorship therefore, requires prior empirical investigation.

RECIPROCITY

Fans are grateful for sponsorship. Others are not. (Crimmins & Horn, 1996, p. 17)

Reciprocity is the mechanism that requires the highest level of cognitive elaboration on the part of the consumer. The message of reciprocity is "the sponsor supports events you care about, so you should patronize the sponsor." The reciprocity mechanism is engaged when a consumer makes a conscious decision to go out of his or her way to support the brands that support the events that he or she finds important. Although this may not be the most common response to sponsorship, it is certainly a powerful one.

There is some evidence to support the notion that fans of certain events demonstrate significant reciprocity (or so they claim). Crimmins and Horn (1996) presented what they called *gratitude* whereby the fan of an event goes out of his or her way to buy the products of an event sponsor. They cited a survey in which 48% of NASCAR fans said they would "almost always" purchase a sponsor's product over a closely priced competitor. Reported reciprocity for the Chicago Gospel Festival was even more impressive. As measured by "it (sponsorship) makes me more likely to buy," fan reciprocity was 82%. The authors went on to point out that it is unlikely that these effects will occur in casual observers or uninvolved spectators. Simply stated, they claimed, "Fans are grateful for sponsorship. Others are not" (p. 17). It seems reasonable, then, that the more involved consumers are with an event, the more likely the sponsorship is to elicit consumer reciprocity.

FUTURE RESEARCH USING
THE SEVEN MECHANISMS

By breaking sponsorship into these component mechanisms, it becomes possible to posit and test how audience, event, and associational factors will impact the success of sponsorship associations. A detailed discussion of these three kinds of sponsorship factors is beyond the scope of this chapter. A brief description of some factors and how they are expected to impact the functioning of the seven mechanisms, however, is provided next. The goal of this discussion is to demonstrate the usefulness of considering the multiple ways sponsorship works in conceptualizing future research in the sponsorship domain.

Audience factors, such as the personal relevance of the event to an audience member, are most likely to affect which mechanisms can reasonably be expected to function. Audience members for whom the event has low personal relevance are not likely to be affected by mechanisms requiring high cognitive elaboration. These people are, for example, not likely to engage in reciprocity, because they are not grateful for sponsor support.

Even audience members for whom an event holds low personal relevance should be affected by simple awareness. To the extent that personal relevance is a necessary precursor to cognitive elaboration, audience members for whom the event is increasingly relevant should be susceptible to successively higher elaboration mechanisms. Therefore, the higher the personal relevance of the event to an audience member, the more ways that sponsorship can impact him or her.

Factors such as the size or prestige of the event should only affect certain mechanisms while having little or no impact on others. The size of the event, for example, is likely to have a large impact on the implied size mechanism, whereas event prestige might have a greater impact on implied endorsement. Neither of them, however, is expected to have much impact on the functioning of the simple awareness mechanism (for an individual who is exposed to the association).

Associational factors, such as brand–event fit (similarity) are likely to facilitate the functioning of some mechanisms but not others. By modifying Tversky's (1977) definition of similarity, brand–event fit can be conceptualized as increasing (decreasing) with greater (fewer) overlapping attributes or associations and decreasing (increasing) with greater (fewer) non-overlapping attributes and associations. High levels of fit between brand and event, then, might facilitate image transfer, even along non-overlapping attribute and associational dimensions. (For an example of how type of relationship can impact attribute transfer, see Sedikides, Olsen, & Reis, 1993).

Fit might also facilitate the implied endorsement mechanism. A strong fit between the brand and event could make it more likely that someone would infer that the product must be good or else the event would not let the brand be an official sponsor (e.g., athletic shoes sponsoring a sporting event). A weak fit between brand and event, however, might not lead to the same endorsement inference. A bank sponsoring a sporting event, for example, should not lead to as many thoughts that "this must be a good bank or it would not be allowed to be the official bank of this event."

SUMMARY

Any attempt to study event sponsorship must consider the multiple ways that an association of a brand with an event can have an impact on consumers. Seven mechanisms and their psychological underpinnings have been proposed and discussed in this chapter. By considering the various kinds of impact a sponsorship association can have, a more efficient framework for studying the effect of audience, event, and associational factors can be developed. Such a framework should help to greatly illuminate the emerging promotional tool of event sponsorship.

REFERENCES

Bhattacharya, C. B., Rao, H., & Glynn, M. A. (1995). Understanding the bond of identification: An investigation of its correlates among art museum members. *Journal of Marketing, 59,* 46–57.

Birnbaum, M. H., Wong, R., & Wong, L. K. (1976). Combining information from sources that vary in credibility. *Memory and Cognition, 4,* 330–336.

Brehm, J. W., & Lipsher, D. (1959). Communicator-communicatee discrepancy and perceived communicator trustworthiness. *Journal of Personality, 27*, 352–361.

Crimmins, J., & Horn, M. (1996). Sponsorship: From management ego trip to marketing success. *Journal of Advertising Research, 36*, 11–21.

Deshpande, R., Hoyer, W. D., & Donthu, N. (1986). The intensity of ethnic affiliation: A study of the sociology of Hispanic consumption. *Journal of Consumer Research, 13*, 214–220.

Ellen, P. S., Wiener, J. L., & Cobb-Walgren, C. (1991). The role of perceived consumer effectiveness in motivating environmentally conscious behaviors. *Journal of Public Policy and Marketing, 10*, 102–117.

Gaedeke, R. M., & Tootelian, D. H. (1988). Understanding how clients select and evaluate law firms. *Journal of Professional Services Marketing, 3*, 199–207.

Gwinner, K. (1997). A model of image creation and image transfer in event sponsorship. *International Marketing Review, 14*, 145–158.

Heider, F. (1946). Attitudes and cognitive organization. *Journal of Psychology, 21*, 107–112.

Jacoby, J., & Mazursky, D. (1984). Linking brands and retailer images—Do the potential risks outweigh the rewards? *Journal of Retailing, 60*, 105–122.

Kirmani, A. (1990). The effect of perceived advertising costs on brand perceptions. *Journal of Consumer Research, 17*, 160–171.

Kirmani, A., & Wright, P. (1989). Perceived advertising expense and expected product quality. *Journal of Consumer Research, 16*, 344–353.

Landy, D., & Sigall, H. (1974). Beauty is talent: Task evaluation as a function of the performer's physical attractiveness. *Journal of Personality and Social Psychology, 29*, 299–304.

Leonard, M., & Spencer, A. (1991). The importance of image as a competitive strategy: An exploratory study in commercial banks. *International Journal of Bank Marketing, 9*, 25–29.

Macchiette, B., & Roy, A. (1992). Affinity marketing: What is it and how does it work? *Journal of Services Marketing, 6*, 47–57.

MacKenzie, S. B., & Lutz, R. J. (1989). An empirical examination of the structural antecedents of attitude toward the ad in an advertising pretesting context. *Journal of Marketing, 53*, 48–65.

MacKenzie, S. B., Lutz, R. J., & Belch, G. E. (1986). The role of attitude toward the ad as a mediator of advertising effectiveness: A test of competing explanations. *Journal of Marketing Research, 23*, 130–143.

Marshall, D. W., & Cook, G. (1992). The corporate (sports) sponsor. *International Journal of Advertising, 11*, 307–324.

McDonald, C. (1991). Sponsorship and the image of the corporate sponsor. *European Journal of Marketing, 25*, 31–38.

Meenaghan, T. (1991b). Sponsorship—Legitimizing the medium. *European Journal of Marketing, 25*, 5–10.

Meenaghan, T. (1991a). The role of sponsorship in the marketing communications mix. *International Journal of Advertising, 10*, 35–47.

Misra, S., & Beatty, S. E. (1990). Celebrity spokesperson and brand congruence: An assessment of recall and affect. *Journal of Business Research, 21*, 159–173.

Parker, K. (1991). Sponsorship: The research contribution. *European Journal of Marketing, 25*, 22–30.

Petty, R. E., Cacioppo, J. T., & Goldman, R. (1981). Personal involvement as a determinant of argument-based persuasion. *Journal of Personality and Social Psychology, 41*, 847–855.

Pracejus, J. W. (1995). Is more exposure always better? Effects of incidental exposure to a brand name on subsequent processing of advertising. In F. Kardes & M. Sujan (Eds.), *Advances in Consumer Research* (vol. 22, pp. 319–322). Provo, UT: Association for Consumer Research.

Rajaretnam, J. (1994). The long term effects of sponsorship of corporate and product image: Findings of a unique experiment. *Marketing and Research Today, 22,* 62–74.

Rangaswamy, A., Burke, R. R., & Oliva, T. A. (1993). Brand equity and the extendibility of brand names. *International Journal of Research in Marketing, 10,* 61–75.

Rao, A. A., & Ruekert, R. W. (1994, Fall). Brand alliances as signals of product quality. *Sloan Management Review,* 87–97.

Reddy. S. K., Holak, S. L., & Bhat, S. (1994). To extend or not to extend: Success determinants of line extensions. *Journal of Marketing Research, 3*(1), 243–262.

Roslow, S., Nicholls, J. A. F., & Laskey, H. A. (1992). Hallmark events and measurement of reach and audience characteristics. *Journal of Advertising Research, 32,* 53–59.

Ryssel, C., & Stamminger, E. (1988, May). Sponsoring world-class tennis players. *European Research,* 110–116.

Sedikides, C., Olsen, N., & Reis, H.T. (1993) Relationships as natural categories. *Journal of Personality and Social Psychology, 64*(1), 71–82

Stipp, H., & Schiavone, N. P. (1996). Modeling the impact of Olympic sponsorship on corporate image. *Journal of Advertising Research, 36,* 22–28.

Tversky, A. (1977). Features of similarity. *Psychological Review, 84*(4), 327–352.

Walker, M., Langmeyer, L., & Langmeyer, D. (1992). Celebrity endorsers: Do you get what you pay for? *Journal of Consumer Marketing, 9,* 69–76.

Westbrook, R. A., & Black, W. C. (1985). A motivation-based shopper typology. *Journal of Retailing, 61,* 78–103.

Wolton, C. (1988, May). Arts sponsorship: Harmony or discord? *European Research,* 87–96.

Worthington, S., & Horne, S. (1992). Affinity credit cards: Card issuer strategies and affinity group aspirations. *International Journal of Bank Marketing, 10,* 3–10.

Zajonc, R. B. (1968). Attitudinal effects of mere exposure. *Journal of Personality and Social Psychology, 9,* 1–27.

Zinkhan, G. M., Hong, J. W., & Lawson, R. (1990). Achievement and affiliation motivation: Changing patterns in social values as represented in American advertising. *Journal of Business Research, 20,* 135–143.

9

It's Gotta Be the Shoes: Exploring the Effects of Relationships of Nike and Reebok Sponsorship on Two College Athletic Programs

Jan Slater
Ohio University

Carla Lloyd
Syracuse University

Corporate sponsorship of sporting events is not new. These alliances go back more than 100 years, with the first advertisements appearing in the official program of the 1896 Olympics. Yet, the real growth and pervasiveness of sports sponsorship, with its overabundance of commercial sponsors, peaked in 1984 at the summer Olympics in Los Angeles (Stotlar, 1993). Since then, there appears to be no turning back. It is estimated that companies such as AT&T, Coca-Cola, McDonald's, Anheuser-Busch, Visa, and Reebok shelled out between $40 and 60 million each in cash and services for worldwide rights to align their names with and achieve worldwide exposure at the 2002 Winter Games in Salt Lake City, Utah and the 2004 Summer Games in Athens, Greece (Sandomir, 2002).

Big promoters, such as those who make athletic shoes and clothes, sponsor not only events but also entire teams and star athletes. One of the early and true fans of sports sponsorship was Nike. Nike's corporate philosophy is to support the athlete (Copetas, 1998). Basically, this support translates to paying athletes to wear Nike shoes. When Nike signed Michael Jordan as an endorser in 1984, the marketing practice of using star athletes as shoe salesmen took the sports world by storm.

Today, it is routine practice for athletic shoe and apparel companies to sponsor premier athletes and teams to showcase their products. All major professional teams currently affiliate with at least one of the top athletic shoe and clothing makers. With guaranteed multimillion dollar TV contracts for each major sport, sponsors can seize big audiences with their splashy commercials. But the exposure does not stop there. Powerful athletic brands have muscled their way into the lockerroom by plastering their logos on everything from shoes to warm-up suits to sweatbands to uniforms. This has turned the players themselves into nonstop ads.

In recent years, athletic brands have taken aim at college campuses, ushering in a whole new form of corporate involvement. A top-ranked college team has become a vital advertising medium for the likes of Nike and Reebok. Advertising placed here translates to significant sales. In 1994, for example, colleges generated an estimated $2.5 billion in retail sales for products bearing their names, logos, and mascots. This was more than the National Hockey League or Major League Baseball earned. Nike and Reebok, the primary leaders in the athletic shoe category, have long battled in the marketplace for position and market share. Now these rivals have turned to college campuses, competing for their place on college athletic teams.

Previous research in this area has focused primarily on the benefits of sports sponsorship for corporate exposure or on the general nature of "event" sports marketing. But there has been no research that has exclusively explored the relationship that these athletic shoe manufacturers are forging with college athletes and college athletic programs. That is the focus of this chapter.

OVERVIEW OF SPORTS SPONSORSHIP

Sporting events as a marketing tool are extremely popular because they appeal to a mass audience. The Super Bowl is a prime example of this. In today's overly fragmented media world, where one-on-one marketing is increasingly common, where else can an advertiser plunk down $2.1 million and buy such a massive, diverse audience? Advertising opportunities like this are few. Furthermore, there is the added benefit of fan loyalty. Sell-out crowds swarm stadiums and arenas in Ann Arbor, Green Bay, Lawrence, Denver, Lexington, Chicago, Lincoln, Buffalo, and Knoxville to root for the home team. There are so many sporting events that cable channels such as ESPN, ESPN2, and Fox Sports have popped up on already crowded cable services to serve rabid fans who want even more sports, 24 hours a day.

It is easy to understand why sport sponsorship is such an attractive alternative communication tool for corporations. In 1984, when sports sponsorship seemed to explode during the Los Angeles Olympic Games, major brands were already shifting above-the-line expenditures (main media advertising) to below-the-line promotions (Jones, 1992). Brand proliferation and main media audience fragmentation created too much clutter on the shelves, not to mention too much advertising clutter. At this time, brands searched for ways to stand out among the competitive pack and become the MVP of a category. Previous research has shown that by aligning a brand image with a sports image, the overall brand is enhanced (Martin, 1994). Furthermore, major sports, both professional and amateur, receive extensive media coverage through radio, TV, newspapers, and magazines. This allows brand marketers such as Nike and Reebok the opportunity to stretch general advertising dollars by having their logos on the athletes' clothing, thus securing coveted media exposure that they do not actually have to buy.

The growth and objectives of sports sponsorship is well documented (Abratt, Clayton, & Pitt, 1987; Abratt & Grobler, 1989; Pope, 1998; Wilson, 1998). Therefore, it is not necessary, at least for this discussion, to reproduce this overview. What is important, however, is to include a working definition of sports sponsorship and an overview of the two brands under investigation.

For this study, at least, Pope (1998) has provided the most useful definition of *sports sponsorship*:

> Sponsorship is the provision of resources (e.g., money, people, equipment) by an organization (the sponsor) directly to an individual, authority or body (the sponsee), to enable the latter to pursue some activity in return for benefits contemplated in terms of the sponsor's promotion strategy, and which can be expressed in terms of corporate, marketing, or media objectives.

Pope (1998) identified three broad objectives that are basic to how corporations evaluate the effectiveness of sports sponsorships. For starters, corporate objectives are image-based, and as such, the association increases brand awareness. Therefore, it is an excellent communications tool to reinforce the corporate or brand image by aligning that image with a successful sports team or athlete.

Second, marketing objectives focus on promoting the brand and essentially increasing sales of the brand. The sponsorship offers two potentially powerful markets: those who participate in the sport and those who are spectators. Both markets are affected by the hero persona of the top athletes who endorse sports products; as a form of idolatry and mimicry, the hero worshippers purchase the products worn by the stars.

Finally, the media objectives are realized by the opportunity for extensive and somewhat exclusive TV exposure. It is more cost-effective to sponsor events than to buy 30 seconds of airtime during the event. When Michael Jordan and the Chicago Bulls played on TV, it was basically a 3-hour commercial for Nike. In summation, a sports sponsorship is undertaken to benefit all participating parties in some way. This is not a philanthropic gesture on the part of corporations; it is a strictly commercial venture. Corporations such as Nike and Reebok reap the benefits of sports sponsorship and are masters at it. In fact, some would credit Nike for creating the phenomenon that now seems commonplace.

BACKGROUND ANALYSIS OF NIKE AND REEBOK

Of the 1200 U.S. brands tracked annually by advertising agency Young & Rubicam, Nike ranks in the top 10, among such brands as Coca-Cola, Disney, and Hallmark (Lane, 1996). The Nike "swoosh" is so familiar that sneakers and other company products no longer need to carry the name, just the logo. Phil Knight, CEO and founder of Nike, has made sneakers a disposable consumer good and transformed them into a status symbol. He makes shoes that are cool and makes it cool to be a Nike consumer (Lane, 1996).

Knight, himself an athlete, early on saw the value of aligning his shoes with teams and athletes. It has been reported that Nike does not sell shoes but sells "the athletic ideals of determination, individuality, self-sacrifice and winning" (Lane, 1996, p. 42). Knight began to sponsor athletes, one of the first being track star Steve Prefontaine, who he paid to wear Nike shoes in 1973. Nike sales were less than $3 million in 1972. By 1980, sales hit $270 million, and in 1986, sales swelled to a record $1 billion. But the running craze was fading, aerobics were taking center stage, and rival Reebok forged ahead. That's when Phil Knight the marketer was unleashed.

When Prefontaine died suddenly in 1975, Knight looked for a successor to fill the "Nike-guy" persona. He found it in Michael Jordan, who was talked out of an adidas deal to sign with Nike in 1984. When Reebok pushed into the No. 1 position, Nike used Jordan as a means to introduce shoes for other sports, helping Nike to become a leading brand worldwide.

Today, the Beaverton, Oregon-based Nike controls the athletic shoe market share with 39% and sales totaling $10.7 billion in 2002. The company operates 11 retail stores (Niketown) and sells its shoes and apparel in 20,000 retail outlets in the United States. In an annual survey by the *Sports Marketing Letter*, Nike ranked as the most widely recognized corporate sponsor in sports (Nike most recognized, 1998). Its roster of past and superstar athlete endorsers includes LeBron James, Tiger Woods, Kobe Bryant, Andre Agassi, Martina Hingis, Lance Armstrong, in addition to the venerable Jordan. Nike spent $1 billion for sponsorship and marketing activities in 2002 (Duhigg, 2003).

Reebok, the next largest athletic shoe manufacturer, is a distant number two, both in sales and spending. In 2002, Reebok's U.S. market share totaled 12% with nearly $3.1 billion in sales (McCarthy, 2003). Compared to Nike's $1 billion in spending, Reebok spent $334 million in sponsorships and marketing (Duhigg, 2003). Reebok moved away from athlete endorsements in the late 90's but has signed in recent years stars such as Allen Iverson and Venus Williams. Historically, it has been playing catch up with Nike.

Knowing that head-to-head competition with Nike and adidas would be difficult, Reebok looked to the aerobic-shoe market. The company's introduction of the Freestyle aerobic oxford in 1982 coincided with the increased popularity of aerobic exercise. The Freestyle became one of the best selling shoes in history, giving Reebok its first and only market share lead over Nike. Reebok sales went from $3.5 million in 1982 to $919 million in 1986.

Although Reebok advanced athletic shoe technology, corralled a stable of superstar athletes (Saquille O'Neal, Emmett Smith, Clyde Drexler, and Shawn Kemp), and outfitted thousands of Olympic athletes, the company could not sustain its leadership position. Reebok's market share and profits declined after 1987, whereas Nike's rebounded and continues to soar.

All athletic shoe manufacturers depend on professional athlete endorsers, but Nike was the leader in moving into the college system. As early as the 1970s, Nike hired recruiter Sonny Vaccaro to deliver college coaches to the roster of endorsers. Nike agreed to pay coaches at high-profile schools. In exchange, the school team would wear Nike. John Thompson of Georgetown was one of the first signers, supposedly earning as much as several thousand dollars in the early 1980s (Reynolds, 1998). Coaches such as Florida State's Bobby Bowden receives $225,000 per year in addition to his salary and Duke's Mike Krzyzewksi makes $1 million-plus from his Nike shoe contract (Armstrong, 1997). The $1 million salary of University of Utah coach Rick Majerus reportedly includes $500,000 from Reebok. In fact, Majerus was considered the hot prospect for the coaching job at Arizona State following his second-place finish in the NCAA Tournament. Although Majerus was very interested in the job, reports stated that he could not accept it because of his long-term contract with Reebok. Arizona State is a Nike school.

Aside from coaches' contracts, a more recent development is for schools to cut deals with shoe companies who then have the responsibility and the cost of outfitting the school's entire athletic department, hence the label Nike school. In addition to Arizona State, Duke, Georgetown, and Florida State, Nike has partnered with such colleges as Penn State, Illinois, Michigan, Colorado, North Carolina, and Miami. Florida State's deal is worth $6.2 million in cash, equipment, and apparel for the 17 varsity teams over the next 5 years. Michigan's deal gave the school $8 million in cash and equipment over 6 years; Colorado received $5.6 million over 6 years, and Penn State's deal provided $2.6 million over 3 years.

Reebok was again behind the leader in lining up colleges, but it has built an impressive roster of teams, adding sponsorships with UCLA, Texas, Iowa, Michigan State, Wisconsin, Boston College, Louisville, Georgia Tech, Brigham Young, and Utah.

This chapter looks closely at two sponsored colleges athletic programs: Syracuse University (Nike) and Xavier University (Reebok). Both schools have top 25 basketball programs with strong win-loss records. These are mid-size private universities, and although the teams appear annually in post-season tournament play they are not powerhouse college sports entities like some of those named previously. This chapter explores how each sponsorship is organized and what this relationship means to the program, the coaches, the players, and, ultimately, the fans.

RESEARCH METHOD

This research* is designed as a case study. *Case study method* has been described as the means for exploring an entity or phenomenon (the case) bounded by time and activity (a process or event), wherein the researcher collects detailed information by using a variety of data collection procedures during a sustained period of time (Creswell, 1994; Yin, 1994). It is a respected research method, especially when the objective is one of exploration (Yin, 1994), which is the intent of this research endeavor.

Two schools, Syracuse University and Xavier University, were studied, which allowed for a broader perspective and the opportunity to study both the uniqueness and the commonality of two sponsors and two programs. Furthermore, the multiple-case design is often preferred because it offers the opportunity of comparisons and quite often provides more understanding and more compelling data (Stake, 1995; Yin, 1994).

---

*Research was conducted on the Xavier and Syracuse campuses during the spring semester of 1998.

As suggested by Stake (1995), access to the cases is key in order to maximize what can be learned. Therefore, Syracuse and Xavier were selected for the case studies due to the accessibility of resources. As researchers, the first obligation then was to seek complete understanding of these two cases. This entailed obtaining multiple views, descriptions, and interpretations. As in most case study research, the depth interview became the main technique to gaining these multiple realities (Stake, 1995). In-depth interviews were conducted among coaches, players, and retailers as a means of gaining different perspectives of the sponsorship effect. In addition, this provided a cross-check mechanism to support interpretations gathered from other data and observations.

Data gathering was structured to provide a thorough understanding of what was happening with these two cases. Following an extensive review of the literature, the coaches of the two schools were interviewed first. Semi-structured interview schedules were developed as recommended for a multi-case study (Marshall & Rossman, 1995; Stake, 1995). Although it was not the desire of the researchers to impose rigid controls on the interview process, it was important to ensure that certain topics were covered across all interviews because two researchers were conducting separate interviews for each school. However, the interviews were open-ended enough to allow the respondents to add perceptions and interpretations to the process. Once the coaches' data was transcribed and coded, interview schedules were developed for the players and retailers. Six players from each team were interviewed as were the buyers and managers from the respective university bookstores.

From this data, a questionnaire was designed for administration to the general student body of each university. The instrument contained separate sections representative of the factors regarding the student's awareness of the sponsorships, involvement in sports, and attitudes and purchasing opinions as they are influenced by the sponsorships. These sections included questions regarding active and passive sports involvement, purchase behaviors, awareness of college sponsorship, spending amounts, and brand awareness. The five-page closed-ended questionnaire was administered to students across each campus (Syracuse $n = 109$; Xavier $n = 110$). Descriptive statistics were generated from this questionnaire and are included in the results section of this chapter.

COACHES FINDINGS

The Syracuse University Orangemen are members of the Big East Conference, one of the preeminent basketball conferences in the country. Big East games are televised on ESPN every Monday night, ESPN2 every Tuesday night, and

CBS on the weekends. In addition, the Big East has its own television network that regionally televises games to various East Coast markets. Syracuse plays its home games in the 33,000-seat Carrier Dome on the university campus. The team wears Nike shoes and Nike also makes the team uniforms, which display the Nike swoosh.

The Xavier University Musketeers are members of the Atlantic 10 Conference, which has recently emerged as one of the top basketball conferences in the nation. Atlantic 10 games are not televised on a set basis on national TV, but they do appear on ESPN, ESPN2, and ABC at various times throughout the season. Cincinnati's ABC affiliate WCPO's schedule includes 11 locally produced games, 8 of which are part of the Atlantic 10. The Musketeers appeared on national television five times during the 1997 to 1998 season. Xavier plays its home games at the Cintas Center, which seats 10,250. The team wears Reebok shoes and Reebok makes the team uniforms, which display the Reebok logo.

To be a Nike coach, at least for Coach Jim Boeheim, means that you are one of the top coaches in basketball. His 22-year record as Syracuse University's head basketball coach, 20 of which have been winning seasons, has secured him a solid place among the coaching elite. Boeheim has been associated with the Syracuse University basketball program for 35 years, starting as a walk-on player. Boeheim returned to Syracuse as an assistant and was named head coach in 1976. With 18 NCAA Tournament appearances, 30 NCAA Tournament wins, and two trips to the Final Four, Boeheim is ranked among the top 10 active coaches in the United States. He gives the Nike swoosh national TV exposure with regular trips to the winner's circle.

To be a Reebok coach like Coach Skip Prosser means that success has followed throughout your coaching career at different high schools and universities. In just 6 years as Xavier's head coach, Prosser has racked up an impressive record with five 20-win seasons, three NCAA Tournament berths, and two National Invitational Tournament (NIT) invitations. Prosser has ignited fans, breaking attendance records in each of the 6 years he has been at Xavier. He was named the 1996 to 1997 *Basketball Times* Mideast Coach-of-the-Year and NABC District 10 Coach-of-the-Year. Prosser has coached in 11 NCAA Tournaments in 12 years, including 7 in 8 years as a Xavier assistant, 1 as Loyola's head coach, and 3 in 6 years as Xavier's head coach. Prosser's long-running success and lively coaching style on the floor translates to large fan loyalty and exposure for Reebok.

Xavier and Syracuse share very different sorts of relationships with each of their respective shoe companies. At Xavier, it's a simple partnership between Reebok and the coach. At Syracuse, it's a more complex association between

Nike, the entire school and its various athletic programs, At Xavier, the men's baseball team, and women's basketball and volleyball teams all use Reebok. However, the relationship with the Reebok company rests primarily with the men's basketball team.

Syracuse and Nike go back 20 years. Premium products landed Nike on Syracuse University's basketball courts back then, and this quality keeps them there today. Boeheim switched from Pony to Nike in 1978 because, he said, "Nike came up with a better product and because my players liked Nike the best." It's Nike's superior products and outstanding service that keeps Boeheim renewing his contracts with Nike every 3 to 5 years. To Boeheim, Nike is quite simply the best, which has resulted in his long-term allegiance to the brand. When asked about all the benefits from an affiliation with Nike, Boeheim is emphatic about two major plusses when it comes to Nike: "They have the best product and service."

Xavier, on the other hand, came over to Reebok when Prosser came on board as head coach in 1995. Xavier had been a Nike school when Prosser was an assistant. "When I came in, I decided it was time for a change," said Prosser. Competition, exclusivity, service, and ethical corporate practices were all factors that Prosser considered when deciding whether to stay with Nike or move to Reebok. "Reebok was very aggressive in recruiting us—I felt like they really wanted us," says Prosser. Local rival, the University of Cincinnati is a larger school than Xavier, with a strong men's basketball team. It is a Nike School. Prosser said that he thought Xavier would be in the shadow of the University of Cincinnati when it came to Nike. Compared to Nike, Prosser said he thought that Reebok, with a regional office in Cincinnati, would be more accessible. Weighing the two shoe giants, it came down to which company could offer Prosser and his players the better deal. Reebok was the shoe manufacturer that came through with the best offer. Prosser says the relationship between Xavier and Reebok is good and that the company "is very accommodating." Prosser's first Reebok contract was for 3 years. He was so pleased with the service that this shoe company provided that he negotiated another contract, this time for 7 years.

Xavier never called the quality of Nike's equipment into question. Prosser pointed out, "Nike has good shoes. We had no problem with them. But I felt like Reebok was more committed to us. Whenever we need anything, they are right there."

Both coaches say it was ultimately their decision to affiliate their teams with their chosen athletic shoe company. The contractual obligations that exist between the two basketball programs and the two shoe companies are similar: both coaches are obligated to wear items that display the company name or logo; both shoe manufacturers are obligated to provide players with shoes, equipment, and uniforms; and both coaches speak at clinics that the shoe companies sponsor.

Both coaches said that their shoe sponsors are very good to them, and their players, athletic programs and schools benefit from these alliances. "Reebok is really good to our kids," said Prosser. "Reebok outfits our kids from head to toe. Obviously that means more than just sneakers." Boeheim's players receive everything from shoes and uniforms to equipment, and Boeheim said his players, too, are treated very well because "they get the best stuff."

Free clothing and gear financially benefits both universities. "This outfitting saves the university thousands of dollars—and it's clothes that the players need," pointed out Prosser. Boeheim stated the same benefits. "The athletic program gets a lot of free equipment. And the school benefits by saving on expenses."

But one of the real benefits of being a Reebok school is that it makes small schools, like Xavier, feel like they are receiving the same type of star treatment that is regularly showered on the big, prestigious programs. Reebok makes Xavier feel special, desired, and respected. "We're a top 25 basketball team," Prosser stated, "but we're probably one of the smaller schools involved in this. We're not a powerhouse program like Michigan." But Prosser's Musketeers, with their winning record and big-city location, earn high marks in Reebok's book, and as a result, red-carpet treatment. Prosser noted, "Nike certainly has more exposure, but I thought Reebok would provide us some differentiation. And they treated us better. I wanted to be special, and we're more important to Reebok than to Nike." Thanks to Reebok, the players come out the real winners, said Prosser, because "they get visibility and feel special."

So what do athletic shoe companies like Nike, Reebok, adidas and Fila gain from aligning their products with high caliber programs, players, and coaches? These two coaches said it is strong marketing. "The players themselves become the ad medium," Prosser said. They glean big-time sports media coverage for Reebok, Nike, or any shoe company. Prosser noted, "The perception is that it helps Reebok to be associated with a top-25 school" because "[Xavier] players make it on the pages of *Sports Illustrated, ESPN Magazine, USA Today* or in the NCAA tourney." All of this high-profile exposure, according to Prosser, comes at a fraction of the cost of paying for all of the time and space through advertising. " It's a lot of exposure that isn't quite the cost of advertising." Athletes are cost-effective media vehicles.

This exposure can be national, regional or local. No matter, the shoe companies' marketing programs benefit from this penetration. As Prosser stated, "Of course, we're not on national television as much as many other schools, so our exposure is often really limited to right here in Cincinnati. But with the University of Cincinnati being a Nike team, Xavier can provide exposure for Reebok that they wouldn't have in Cincinnati otherwise." A winning record ratchets up the overall efficiency of this local media penetration, as Prosser said. "When we're winning—that makes it even better."

By splashing logos, brand names, and other brand signatures on players and coaches, shoe companies are aiming to reach a lucrative and impressionable audience of young fans. These kids, who range in age from 5 to 18, strive to look and act like the college players wearing the name-brand shoes. Boeheim said that he believes the Syracuse University basketball players influence not only these young kids but also "people in the community and fans." The bottom line, according to Prosser, is for these companies "to sell shoes." Using college athletes to promote shoe sales is just one way these companies can survive in a competitive marketplace. Here is how Coach Prosser sees Reebok boosting sales thanks to his Musketeers: "The shoe business is very competitive. And they (Reebok) are trying to sell shoes to junior high kids. Reebok has the perception that if Xavier players are in Reebok shoes and clothing, then some junior high kid is going to want to be in Reebok shoes and clothing."

High-visibility college athletes help build sales in local markets, and the professional athletes provide national coverage for these shoe companies. "They can sell shoes, T-shirts, etc. right here in Cincinnati," said Prosser, "maybe not all over the country, but they can get them right here in Cincinnati. It's a 'win-win' situation all the way around. We get kids in sneakers and so does Reebok."

PLAYERS' REACTIONS TO SPORTS SPONSORSHIP

Part of this exploratory study included in-depth interviews with 12 varsity men basketball players, 6 from each school. These athletes have been playing basketball for a big chunk of their lives. The 6 Syracuse University players said they have been playing basketball between 6 and 15 years. The 6 Xavier University players, said that they have logged 6 to an astounding 18 years playing the game. All these athletes played basketball in junior high, with the majority of them lacing up Nike sneakers to hit the courts.

Xavier players said spectators and fans know that they are wearing Reebok apparel thanks to the company's logo, which appears on the uniforms and the shoes. Xavier athletes said the logo is "big enough on the shoes" so that spectators can see what brand they are wearing. One Xavier player said, "The emblems are so big, how could anyone miss it?" The Syracuse players said that spectators can readily recognize this as a Nike school because of the swoosh logo. " They can tell by the swoosh, it's the most famous thing about Nike," said one player.

Xavier players are expected to wear suits and ties when they come into the arena to play. Thus, they are not expected to actually wear Reebok shoes and apparel to the games. On the road, however, the players can wear Reebok clothing. Syracuse players don all sorts of Nike apparel, including uniform, wrist bands, socks, sneakers, shorts, tops, shooting shirts, T-shirts under uniform, tights, and warm ups. One Syracuse player said that the Nike name is "written on everything we wear."

None of the Xavier players expressed the belief that the Reebok sponsorship played a role in their decision to play for that university. "I just wanted to play," said a Xavier player. Two of the Syracuse players said that the Nike sponsorship had a "little bit of influence" in their decision to come to Syracuse. But none of them said that shoe sponsorships had any impact on their final decision about where they would play college ball. The major advantage to being a Reebok school, according to Xavier players, is that Reebok gives Xavier players more attention than they would receive from any other brand. All but one of the Syracuse players thought it was advantageous to be a Nike school.

Every one of the basketball players interviewed from Syracuse expressed the desire to be involved with Nike in some way after they graduate. One Syracuse player said he wants to be a Nike sales representative, another wants to be a Nike coach, and others have set their sites on the pros and want to wear Nike clothing when they are in the big leagues. The Syracuse athletes are fiercely loyal to the Nike brand and want this relationship to continue long after they leave Syracuse.

SURVEY RESULTS FROM STUDENTS

Students from both universities were surveyed to understand if and why they wear branded athletic gear and what influences their purchase decisions. The questionnaire was administered to a total of 219 undergraduate students. The students (82%) were between the ages of 18 and 20 years of age; 45% were freshmen, 34% sophomores, 10% juniors, and 5% seniors. Female students accounted for 59% of the respondents. Among Syracuse (63%) and Xavier (43%) students, Nike was considered the "coolest" athletic shoes; adidas was second with 30% and 35%, respectively; and Reebok lagged far behind at .9%

and 2%. Phil Knight has indeed succeeded in making and maintaining the coolness of Nike in these two groups of students.

These students are sports-minded. They are involved in sports, both as spectators and participants. More than three fourths of them (77%) play some sort of recreational sport, with nearly one fifth of them (18%) being college athletes themselves. College athletes taking part in this study are involved in a variety of varsity athletics: basketball, football, cross-country, lacrosse, soccer, volleyball, swimming, tennis, and track. In addition, 90% watch professional sports, predominantly basketball and football. When asked to identify their favorite professional athlete, 55% listed Michael Jordan and of those who identified him as their favorite, 100% could recall that he wears Nike shoes. As the numbers suggest, these students, who were attending universities where sports are a visible part of the campus scene, had made sports an active part of their own lifestyle. They played sports, watched sports, and admired the exceptional athletes who were at the pinnacle of their games.

A significant 61% of the students said they attend university basketball games, with an impressive 82% reporting that they were aware that the basketball program was sponsored by a brand of athletic shoes. Of those, a majority (72%) of the Syracuse students could correctly identify Nike as the athletic sponsor and 61% of the Xavier students could identify Reebok as the basketball team's sponsor; just about all of these students attend games to see their Orangemen or Musketeers do battle against rival teams. Little wonder then that many of these true fans know which shoe company sponsors their home team. Therefore, the exposure to players who actually become the ads has been an effective device in generating awareness of the Nike and Reebok brands, one of the major objectives of sports sponsorship.

The students surveyed also acted as walking billboards for the athletic brands they routinely wear. These students wore and purchased branded athletic gear and clothing with the school's logo, name, insignia, or mascot on it to show support for the home team. Forty-two percent wore branded hats regularly, 64% wore athletic brands of shorts, and 66% donned athletic brands of sweatshirts. But T-shirts and shoes come up the real winners. College students wore athletic shoes almost exclusively, with a staggering 92% saying they wore some type of sports shoe on a regular basis.

In the past 12 months before the survey, approximately two thirds of the students purchased branded athletic gear. The items that they purchased most often were hats (33%), sweatshirts (43%), and T-shirts (58%). Of those who made a purchase in the past 12 months, 54% of the Syracuse students purchased Nike products and 40% purchased a Champion item. Among Xavier students, 44% purchased Champion and only 33% purchased a Reebok item.

The campus bookstore was the place where the students (59%) most often shopped for athletic clothing, with the local sporting goods retailer ranking second (18%). Students may be buying at the bookstore because of convenience, in terms of location and due to the fact that students can charge bookstore purchases to their bursar's account. But whatever the reason, they are buying, and, according to the bookstores, that is the real benefit of these athletic program sponsorships: They make the cash register ring.

RETAILERS REACTION TO BRANDED MERCHANDISE

The real payoff of these sponsorships comes in overall sales of products that these two schools reap. Based on the student survey results, interviews were conducted with the buyers for the Syracuse (Gale Youmell) and Xavier (Nikki Eubanks) bookstores.

Xavier athletic wear, primarily basketball related, has always been available in the bookstore. This is important at Xavier because basketball is the leading varsity sport and its season mirrors the peak sales period for athletic merchandise. Clothing sales account for 17% of the Xavier bookstore's annual sales; 70% of those sales occur during basketball season.

Xavier University is approximately half the size of Syracuse University. With a smaller target market, Xavier must limit the number of items offered. In addition, they are held to a 1,000-piece minimum on all Reebok orders, which makes it financially and logistically difficult to carry a wide range of Reebok styles, according to Eubanks. The bookstore limits the merchandise to two jackets, two T-shirts and the replicas of the basketball players' uniforms. All other clothing merchandise is purchased through Gear, Jansport, and Champion, all of which do not have the minimum order requirement.

Eubanks conceded that Reebok is a difficult supplier. Although Reebok offers many styles of merchandise, the minimums make it impossible for Xavier to carry any more than a few. The bookstore can only place orders to Reebok twice a year, providing little margin for error in judgment. But Eubanks noted that Xavier is a very small school for Reebok, probably one of the smallest on Reebok's college roster. She explained:

> It's really a gamble for them with Xavier. We're just not that big a deal. Until now—when we're winning and gaining a national reputation—retailers finally are interested in Xavier merchandise and that helps Reebok. But before, retailers like Dick's, Dillards and Penney's just weren't interested. I mean we're not

Georgetown. We're not going to make any great impact on Reebok's sales. We don't make a difference.

So why bother with the hassles of Reebok when other manufacturers sell just as well, if not better? Because, Eubanks said, it is what the students and fans want. "They want what the players wear, and that's Reebok," she says. If not for the sponsorship, the bookstore would not carry Reebok merchandise. But because the Reebok logo appears on the basketball uniforms, students and fans want what the players have.

Syracuse contends with some of the same issues with Nike as Xavier does with Reebok. Basketball is the prime selling season, Nike is a difficult vendor, orders can only be placed twice a year, and the variety of merchandise is limited. However, Syracuse purchases 5 to 15 items per season and minimums are not an issue.

Youmell, from the Syracuse bookstore, witnessed Nike's popularity grow over the past 3 to 4 years and noted that she believed that it is the Nike style, fit, and design along with terrific advertising that helps pull the product out of the bookstore. The bookstore has its own "Niketown" as such with all the Nike merchandise displayed in one section of the store complete with Nike fixtures and signage. It makes quite a statement.

Youmell said she believes Nike is a good seller because it offers students what they want. Nike produces designs and styles that are popular and that fit the students' active lifestyle, the clothing wears well and is reasonably priced. Furthermore, by wearing official Nike Syracuse apparel, the students can show enthusiasm and pride in representing the university. But Youmell is adamant that the overriding effect of Nike's appeal is that students want what the players have. "There is a direct effect between what the players wear and what the students buy," she claimed. "Whatever is seen on the players on TV should be available in the bookstore," she added. "That's what students want." That is effective advertising.

DISCUSSION

This exploratory study aimed to show what it means to be a Nike-sponsored school compared to being a Reebok-sponsored school. By conducting in-depth interviews with coaches, athletes, and retailers and then following up with a student questionnaire, we found that sponsorship of college sports provides a powerful and meaningful association for these two brands of athletic shoes. But more particularly, we found that the effect of sports sponsorships have some definite advantages and disadvantages when it comes to college sports and athletic shoe companies. These include the following:

1. College merchandise is profitable. Sales of college products generate more than $2.5 billion annually. Items that are worn by players and coaches during the games have become popular with fans. As the bookstore managers indicated, the students want what the players wear, and because of the sponsorship contracts, Nike and Reebok receive a percentage of those sales. This is especially true for athletic shoes. The average American teenager now buys 10 pairs of athletic shoes a year: 6 for specific sports, 4 for fashion. For Nike, that translates into 6 million teenagers buying more than $1 billion worth of Nike shoes (Lane, 1996).

2. The sponsors have exclusivity, giving them elements of market-by-market domination. Geographically, Nike and Reebok have strategically placed themselves as part of the hometown team, often dominating the local market and establishing strong brand awareness and loyalty at a grassroots level. The sponsorship of local teams and athletes resonates with the loyal fans. Awareness and loyalty are created and enhanced. The students at both Xavier and Syracuse were aware of the brands sponsoring their school. In this regard, sponsorship of college teams is somewhat similar to spot-TV buying. For examples, Nike and Reebok sponsor local teams, and instead of purchasing local airtime, the brands get multiple exposures each time the team plays, whether or not the game is broadcast. This exposure grows nationally as the teams play in league and NCAA Tournaments.

3. Alignment with the nation's largest, most visible and successful college athletic programs helps the companies authenticate their brands, which in turn sells more product. By association, when the team is a winner, the brands are winners because the triumphant teams wore Nike or Reebok. The same is true for the colleges and universities. Because of the alignment with strong sports brands, schools such as Xavier and Syracuse gain respect and special treatment.

4. As market competition continues to increase and products are harder to differentiate, the associations with college teams provides a point of difference for the athletic shoe manufacturers. Teens buy the shoe styles and brands worn by the home team and the jerseys used by their favorite player. College sponsorships also provide schools with a type of differentiation. Coach Prosser made the case that Reebok distinguished Xavier in a market shared by the University of Cincinnati's powerhouse basketball team, a Nike-sponsored program.

5. Colleges and universities are facing increasing costs and fewer funding sources not only for athletics but also for other programs as well. Becoming a Nike or Reebok school provides an influx of cash while saving the costs associated with purchasing uniforms and equipment for various varsity sports programs. This is no doubt an important benefit for private schools such as Xavier and Syracuse. As Prosser pointed out, "This outfitting saves the university thousands of dollars."

6. With national brands such as Nike and Reebok, colleges and universities profit by spreading their merchandise to more retailers and over a broader distribution network. This generates more money for the universities in licensing fees and increases the national exposure of the athletic programs and the universities as well. According to Eubanks, Xavier's bookstore manager, the school's alliance with Reebok helped capture the national retail interest of retailers from Dick's Sporting Goods and J.C. Penney.

Finally, the intent of this study was to explore the relationship between these two brands and these two athletic programs. Indeed, evidence of strong relationships among the various subjects emerged from the data. But the relationships are different between each of these subjects. The coaches, the fans, the players, and the school share the brand, but they all connect to the brand differently. To understand these connections, it is important to understand the conceptual foundations of brand relationships that have been analyzed in Fournier's (1998) work on this topic.

First, for a relationship to exist, the parties must interact and depend on each other. We made this case earlier in outlining the benefits to the brands and to the schools. The schools depend on the brands for prestige as well as shoes and clothing. The brands depend on the schools for exposure and the association of a winning team.

Second, relationships have some meaning and provide some value. To understand the relationship, one must understand the meaning assigned to the relationship. In looking at the data from this study, the meaning becomes evident. The discussion of the various relationships with Nike and Reebok follow:

1. The fans, in essence the students of Xavier and Syracuse, are very aware of the Nike and Reebok sponsorships. They also considered Nike the coolest athletic shoe. These students also wear branded athletic shoes, hats, shorts, T-shirts, and sweatshirts. But the relationship is established with the school and the team, not necessarily with the brands of Nike

and Reebok. The fans are purchasing athletic gear that touts the school's logo or mascot, not necessarily the Nike swoosh. The students wear this gear because of their loyalty to the school, not necessarily the brands.

2. The schools have what Fournier (1998) called a commitment relationship with the brands. This entails a behavior that is supportive of the relationship, although it may not be the relationship desired. Both bookstore managers expressed difficulty in working with Nike and Reebok, as well as limitations these relationships imposed. However, both realized the importance of the relationships in that the students want the branded merchandise. Fifty-nine percent of the students purchase their athletic clothing at the campus bookstores. This is a profitable commitment for the schools, and it extends beyond just the bookstore.

3. The players exhibit a brand relationship that Fournier (1998) termed *self-connection*. The brands are important in how the players view themselves and determine their self-worth. If they wear the best athletic shoes and clothing, then they must be the best players. The players feel special because of the relationships established by wearing the brands, and they feel like winners, even when they are not. The bond with the players is exceptionally strong because their interactions with the brand are quite frequent, everyday in most cases. Additionally, the brands deliver an element of performance prowess. If the brand performs, the players perform. And that is a very advantageous attitude on the basketball court. Finally, the players are so dependent on the brand that most of them want to extend their time with the brand and work for them after graduation, or better yet, endorse the brand when they move up to the NBA.

4. The coaches and the brands are partners. Fournier (1998) described this as marital attachment, and it is dependent on how well the partner performs within the relationship. The interaction between the brands and the coaches are linked to the strength and satisfaction of the relationship. This includes believing the brand has a positive attitude about the school. Prosser, from Xavier, was adamant about his feelings that Reebok gave his players more attention, made them feel special, and took good care of them. "I felt like they really wanted us," he said. Boeheim said Nike treated his players very well. Furthermore, both coaches said the brand performed well and was reliable. "They get the best stuff," Boeheim stated several times. Fournier (1998, p. 365) said this a key factor in partnership which relies on "trust or faith that the brand will deliver what is desired." In the case of the coaches, they hope the brand delivers prestige, quality products, and financial rewards, not to mention a powerful association gained from being linked to a leading brand.

CONCLUSION

This chapter provides some new insight into what it means to be a Nike or a Reebok school from a variety of perspectives. We should point out, however, that research subjects taking part in this study were, to a varying degree, involved in some aspect of their university's sports program. As such, all have a vested interest in maintaining strong relationships with their college, not to mention the sponsoring brand. In other words, it may have been difficult for each of these groups to be critical of the alliance that exists between their college and its sponsoring shoe company when so much is at stake. For example, the coaches and players are the beneficiaries of these alliances and are given, in the cases of the coaches, big checks or, in the case of the players, free shoes and clothing. The retailers are also part of this alliance and have the potential to land sales. The students are part of the university and show their loyalty by attending games and donning university apparel.

We found that Nike and Reebok's sponsorship of these two college sports programs has established a powerful and meaningful association. In addition, we found these relationships to be mutually beneficial.

Returning to Pope's (1998) three main objectives of how to evaluate the effectiveness of sports sponsorship, it would seem that the Nike and Reebok partnerships with these two athletic programs have been effective. First, in terms of supporting brand image, awareness is not only increased but also enhanced by the winning traditions of the two teams. Second, marketing objectives are realized as a result of the powerful endorsements of top college athletes and teams, which parlay desires into sales among students and fans. Third, the media benefits are enormous because these alliances provide extensive and exclusive market coverage as well as national exposure.

Finally, the sports sponsorships of Syracuse University and Xavier University are beneficial to the respective schools and athletic programs. The universities have found a money source to fund not only athletic, but various programs across the campus. The teams align themselves with popular, image-laden brands. The coaches are generously compensated for that alignment financially, and the players are rewarded with a wardrobe of the most popular styles of athletic clothing while receiving special and exclusive attention from the industry's top brands. Students and fans, who are the real sports enthusiasts, can purchase and wear the most popular brand of athletic apparel while supporting the home team. And retailers find the sponsorships lucrative as the brand–school association pulls products off the shelves and puts money in the cash register. As Xavier Coach Prosser stated, this is a "win-win situation." And in sports, winning is everything.

REFERENCES

Abratt, R., Clayton, B., & Pitt, L. (1987). Corporate objectives in sports sponsorship. *International Journal of Advertising, 6,* 299–311.

Abratt, R., & Grobler, P. (1989). The evaluation of sports sponsorship. *International Journal of Advertising, 8,* 351–362.

Armstrong, J. (1997, November). Three stripes, you're in. *Sport, 88,* 84.

Copetas, A. C. (1998, February 11). Playing the sponsorship game. *The Wall Street Journal Interactive Edition.* Retrieved July 21, 2003, from http://interactive.wsj.com/archive/retrieve.cgi?id=SB8871440579093000.djm

Creswell, J. W. (1994). *Research Design: Qualitative and Quantitative Approaches.* Thousand Oaks, CA: Sage.

Duhigg, C. (2003, August 18). Refusing to sweat. *The Washington Post,* E01.

Fournier, S. (1998). Consumers and their brands: Developing relationship theory in consumer research. *Journal of Consumer Research, 24,* 343–373.

Jones, J. P. (1992). *How Much Is Enough: Getting the Most From Your Advertising Dollar.* New York: Lexington Books.

Lane, R. (1996, October 14). You are what you wear. *Forbes, 158,* 42.

Marshall, C., & Rossman, G. B. (1995). *Designing Qualitative Research.* Thousand Oaks, CA: Sage.

Martin, J. H. (1994). Using a perceptual map of the consumer's sport schema to make sponsorship decisions. *Sport Marketing Quarterly, 3,* 27–31.

McCarthy, M. (2003, April 3). Rivals scramble to topple Nike's sneaker supremacy. *USA Today,* 1B.

Nike most recognized sponsors, survey says. (1998, February 1). *The Seattle Times,* p. D7.

Pope, N. (1998, January). Overview of current sponsorship thought. *The Cyber-Journal of Sport Marketing.* Retrieved July 21, 2003 from http://www.cad.gu.edu.au/cjsm/pope21.htm

Reynolds, B. (1998, April 12). Sneaker deals not squeaky clean. *The Record,* p. S02.

Sandomir, R. (2002, February 27). Salt Lake Games end, marketing games begin. *The New York Times,* D3.

Saporito, B. (1998, March 30). Can Nike get unstuck? *Time,* 48–53.

Stake, R. E. (1995). *The Art of Case Study Research.* Thousand Oaks, CA: Sage.

Stotlar, D. (1993). Sponsorship and the Olympic Winter Games. *Sport Marketing Quarterly, 2,* 35–43.

Wilson, G. A. (1998). Does sport sponsorship have a direct effect on product sales? *The Cyber-Journal of Sport Marketing.* Retrieved July 21, 2003 from http://www.ca.gu.edu.au/cjsm/wilson.htm

Yin, R. K. (1994). *Case Study Research.* Thousand Oaks, CA: Sage.

American Consumer Attitudes Toward Corporate Sponsorship of Sporting Events

Lance Kinney
University of Alabama

Stephen R. McDaniel
University of Maryland

The proliferation of event sponsorship opportunities, the amount of money flowing from marketers into event sponsorship, and the development of a body of academic literature dedicated to investigating and cataloging various sports event sponsorship effects all attest to its acceptance by marketers as a viable marketing communication technique (Cornwell & Maignan, 1998). To date, there has been little academic research assessing public attitudes toward event sponsorship, especially as it relates to sports events. In contrast, public satisfaction with advertising is frequently assessed and the results widely disseminated (Shavitt, Lowrey, & Haefner, 1997). Studies may have been undertaken by sponsoring companies to guide their marketing decisions, but results were considered proprietary. Perhaps what is needed in the burgeoning world of sport sponsorship is a review of consumer attitudes concerning sports event sponsorship activities. Providing this type of review is the objective of this research.

Understanding consumer attitudes toward marketing activities is an important factor for managers considering a variety of communication strategies (Gaski & Etzel, 1986). With event sponsorship, several questions seem ripe for consumer review. As in all areas of marketing communication, there are controversies regarding the appropriateness of the activity. For example, is sponsorship of sports event really welcomed by fans? Some consumers may resent the intrusion of corporate marketing activities into their favorite sports, saying that sports are somehow tainted by corporate involvement. Also, several product categories are noted for the controversy they generate. For example, what do consumers think about tobacco and alcohol sponsorship of sports events?

An area of special interest for potential sponsors is how consumers perceive event sponsors' brands. Are consumers more interested in sponsoring brands? Do consumers welcome sponsors and appreciate sponsor contributions to staging events that are important to the consumer? Event organizers and sponsoring companies may perceive the sponsorship as helping stage the event and contributing to the sporting experience. Consumers may be irritated as arenas and TV screens become cluttered with logos, signage, and other brand messages. Critics are increasingly vocal about what might be perceived as the overcommercialization of sports (Real, 1996), especially as it relates to collegiate or other amateur events (McAllister, 1998).

In the following sections, a definition of sports event sponsorship is offered, along with a brief review of the scope of the industry, and common consumer and organizational objectives associated with this tactic. Research questions about consumer attitudes toward several aspects of sports event sponsorship are offered. Then the results of a national telephone survey ($n = 400$) are reported. Results are then discussed in terms of the research questions. Lastly, other event sponsorship issues are identified for additional research effort.

REVIEW OF LITERATURE

Sport Sponsorship

Sport sponsorship, sometimes known as event marketing, may be defined as "a cash or in-kind fee paid to a property in return for access to the exploitable commercial potential associated with that property" (Ukman, 1995, p. 1). Estimates note the phenomenal growth of event sponsorship as a marketing tactic; expenditures across all types of events, including sports, cultural, and others, are estimated at $9.57 billion for 2002 (IEG, 2002). This staggering figure illustrates why event sponsorship is one of the fastest growing areas of marketing communication.

A variety of consumer-oriented objectives are often associated with event sponsorship, including increasing brand awareness and brand image, as well as the ability to use promotional tie-ins and sampling at events (Cunningham

& Taylor, 1995; Levin, 1993; Schreiber, 1994; Shanklin & Kuzma, 1992). Event sponsorship strategies are also noted for their ability to associate sponsors with particular usage situations and to cut through the clutter associated with other marketing communication techniques. By carefully selecting events, marketers can gain exposure to difficult-to-reach target markets and demonstrate a commitment to supporting the target's lifestyle and interests (Jensen, 1994; Schreiber, 1994). In addition to consumer-oriented objectives, Sandler and Shani (1993) noted that other objectives can be served, including corporate image building or media exposure. Sponsorship is noted to operate differently from conventional advertising in that event title sponsorship, such as the Nokia Sugar Bowl, and arena signage viewed at the event or via TV broadcasts offer little opportunity to relay a selling message (Hastings, 1984; Ukman, 1995).

Ultimately, marketers strive to impact brand sales performance via consumer sponsorship strategies. However, unless the marketer undertakes a relevant, trackable promotion tie-in, sales impact can be difficult to assess. It is more likely that event sponsorship success will be evaluated in terms of intervening variables, including brand preference or other attitudinal measures. Marketing communication strategists at Visa USA have reported noticeable increases in brand perception resulting from event sponsorship (Petrecca, 1999), but Visa spends lavishly to tout its sponsorship efforts. Crimmins and Horn (1996) noted that additional promotion expenditures are often necessary to make the event–sponsor connection clear to consumers.

A technique often used to assess event sponsorship success is to compare the exposure generated by the event association with the cost of purchasing equivalent advertising time or space. For example, if a sponsorship requiring a $500,000 commitment produces the equivalent of $3 million of advertising exposure, the sponsorship may be considered a success, depending on the sponsor's objective. The development of more sophisticated quantification techniques is the primary challenge facing marketers wishing to undertake event sponsorship, as well as facing event marketers themselves (Friedman, 1999).

Alcohol and tobacco are noted as special cases in sports event sponsorship terms for a number of reasons. Each product category has a long association with sports, both as a sponsor and as a valued aspect of the sports viewing experience. Critics have maintained that promoting alcohol and tobacco brands via sports events produces an unsavory influence on children. It was also noted that alcohol and tobacco consumption are antithetical to the performance of many sports activities, for instance, motor sports and alcohol or tobacco and tennis (Basil et al., 1991; Hoek, Gendall, & Stockdale, 1993; Ledwith, 1984;

Pollay, 1993; Warner et al., 1986). Another criticism is that event sponsorship allows alcohol and tobacco brands to circumvent regulations governing their promotion. The international nature of many sports events allows alcohol and tobacco marketers to gain visibility where national or local laws would prohibit such presence (Cornwell & Maignan, 1998).

Research Questions

Given the small amount of available research into public attitudes regarding sports sponsorship activities, an investigation of several areas could have timely managerial and regulatory implications. This research poses the following specific research questions:

RQ1: How do American consumers feel, generally, about corporate sponsorship of college and professional sporting events?

RQ2: How do American consumers feel about tobacco and alcohol sponsorship of college and professional sporting events?

RQ3: Do American consumers think sponsor involvement decreases ticket prices for sporting events?

RQ4: Do American consumers seek sponsor brands when purchasing goods and services?

RQ5: Do American consumers support government regulation of sports sponsorship activities?

A preliminary understanding of these questions will serve event marketers as they approach potential sponsors. Firms considering a sports event strategy would also have some insight into how the public perceives this type of marketing communication. Lastly, those concerned with alcohol and tobacco sponsorship issues, on all sides of the debate, will have some understanding of how consumers perceive the questions surrounding regulation of these brands.

METHOD

A 2-week, national telephone survey was conducted during October 1998 from the research institute of a large southeastern university in the United States. Calls were made primarily in the evenings by a trained calling staff. A commercial research firm generated a universe of residential phone numbers with a random digit dialing technique. Using this method, local prefixes (excluding commercial prefixes) were used intact. Random digits were then selected to complete the seven-number sequence. Phone numbers were generated for the continental United States stratified by state to reflect proportionate representation (Alaska and Hawaii were excluded). Calls resulted in a response rate of 56%, for a total of 400 completed interviews.

The sport sponsorship questions reported here were included as a portion of a larger general public attitude survey. Other sections of the survey addressed attitudes on a variety of advertising and other marketing issues. A demographic section was included at the end of the survey with queries about the respondent's age, race, gender, income level, and education.

A number of researchers had input into the development of the full survey; however, the authors referenced here developed the sports sponsorship section. The general nature of the survey necessitated that all questions be brief and easily interpreted by the respondent. Therefore, the sports event questions were limited to the most general, yet important, issues facing sports event marketers and potential sports event sponsors. Of special interest were consumer acceptance of event sponsors, issues surrounding controversial product categories, and the relative suitability of professional sports event sponsorship as compared to college sports event sponsorship.

The sports event sponsorship section of the survey consisted of nine items, rated on Likert-type, 5-point scales (survey items can be reviewed in Table 10.2). To establish a common meaning for "corporate sports event sponsorship," respondents were provided with examples for the early sports event survey items: "Many companies sponsor college sporting events, such as the Federal Express Orange Bowl." Similarly, the Buick Challenge (golf) was used to illustrate professional sports event sponsorship.

RESULTS

Respondent demographics are detailed in Table 10.1. Just over three quarters (78.5%) of these respondents were younger than 65 years of age. This sample overrepresented females at 59.3%. Females are estimated at 51.1% of the population (U.S. Census Bureau, 1999). The sample also underrepresented non-whites, who are estimated at 25% of the population (U.S. Census Bureau, 1999). The median sample age of 43.0 years was also older than the general median age of 36.3 years (U.S. Census Bureau, 1999). The overwhelming majority had at least a high school education (87.8%), with 69.5% earning $20,001 or more annually.

TABLE 10.1
Respondent Demographic Profile

Variable	F	%[1]
Age		
18–34 years	116	27.5
35–64 years	204	51.0
65 years or more	42	10.5
NA[2]	38	9.5
Race		
White	323	80.8
Black	36	9.0
Hispanic	8	2.0
Other	14	3.5
NA[2]	19	4.8
Education		
Less than high school	25	6.3
Completed high school	98	24.5
Some college/technical	125	31.3
Completed college/technical	128	32.0
NA[2]	24	6.0
Income		
<$20,000	35	8.8
$20,001–40,000	92	23.0
$40,001–60,000	100	25.0
$60,001–80,000	46	11.5
$81,000 or more	40	10.0
NA[2]	87	21.8
Sex		
Male	163	40.8
Female	237	59.3

Note. $n = 400$.
[1]Percentages may not sum to 100% due to rounding.
[2]NA = No answer/refused.

For the following statistical analyses, the *strongly disagree/disagree* responses are combined, as are *strongly agree/agree*, to ascertain a general level of disagreement or agreement. This grouping results in categorical data suitable for chi-square analysis. Respondents who indicated they neither agreed nor disagreed with the item were excluded from statistical analysis. Full results for each survey item are shown in Table 10.2.

RQ1 addressed the appropriateness of corporate sponsorship of sports events at the professional and college levels. As for college, 53.8% of respondents expressed agreement or strong agreement for college sports event sponsorship. This level of agreement was more than twice the 19.8% disagreement level, resulting in a statistically significant difference ($\chi^2 = 62.91$, $df = 1$, $p \leq .05$). An even stronger level of support was reported for sponsorship of professional sports events; 65.8% of these respondents expressed some level of support for sponsorship at the professional level. As noted for college sports sponsorship, there is significantly more support than opposition for professional sports sponsorship ($\chi^2 = 144.95$, $df = 1$, $p \leq .05$).

RQ2 was interested in how consumers feel about alcohol and tobacco sponsorship of college and professional sports events. There was some ambivalence about beer sponsorship at the collegiate level, with 36.8% supporting these sponsorships and 49.3% opposed ($\chi^2 = 7.23$, $df = 1$, $p \leq .05$). When asked about support for beer sponsorship at the professional level, support rose to 46% ($\chi^2 = 3.68$, $df = 1$, $p \leq .05$). At both levels, college and professional, there was more opposition than support for alcohol sponsorship. When tobacco brand sponsorship was considered at the professional level, 39.6% supported tobacco brand involvement, whereas 48.8% opposed tobacco brands ($\chi^2 = 3.87$, $df = 1$, $p \leq .05$). Under current National Collegiate Athletic Association (NCAA) policies, liquor and tobacco brands may not sponsor member college sports events.

In terms of consumer benefits from sports event sponsorship, 36.1% of these respondents believed corporate involvement decreases ticket prices (RQ3). However, no significant difference was observed between these respondents and respondents reporting a belief that sponsorship does not decrease ticket prices. Most of these respondents did not believe the brands sponsoring sports events were superior; 10.8% reported that sponsor brands were better, whereas 71.5% disagreed that sponsor brands were any better than competitive brands ($\chi^2 = 179.48$, $df = 1$, $p \leq .05$). Similarly, a minority of respondents, 19.5%, reported any intention to seek out brands sponsoring their favorite teams or events (RQ4) ($\chi^2 = 95.64$, $df = 1$, $p \leq .05$).

TABLE 10.2

Consumer Responses to Survey Items[1]

Survey Item	Percentage Responding					
	Strongly Disagree	Disagree	Neither Agree Nor Disagree	Agree	Strongly Agree	No Answer
In general, how do you feel about corporate sponsorship of college sports? Would you say you . . . with this business practice?	5.3	14.5	23.8	46.3	7.5	2.8
In general, how do you feel about corporate sponsorship of professional sports? Would you say you . . . with this business practice?	2.5	10.0	18.8	55.3	10.5	3.0
Corporate sponsorship helps keep ticket prices down.	6.3	29.8	20.5	35.8	4.0	3.8
Beer companies should not sponsor college sports events.	6.0	30.8	10.5	33.8	15.5	3.5
Beer companies should not sponsor pro sports events.	7.2	38.8	12.8	24.8	12.5	4.0
Tobacco companies should not sponsor pro sports events.	5.3	34.3	8.0	31.0	17.8	3.8
The federal government should regulate corporate sponsorship of sports events.	19.8	40.8	13.8	19.8	2.0	4.0
I seek products that sponsor my favorite sports teams.	15.3	49.0	12.5	19.0	.5	3.8
Companies that sponsor sports events offer better products.	15.5	56.0	13.3	10.5	.3	4.5

Note. $n = 400$.

[1] Percentages may not sum to 100% due to rounding.

There appear to be strong feelings regarding the role of government regulation in sports event sponsorship (RQ5). These respondents opposed government intervention at nearly three times the rate of support; 60.6% opposed regulation, whereas 21.8% supported it ($\chi^2 = 73.02$, $df = 1$, $p \leq .05$).

DISCUSSION

As with any research, a number of limitations must be considered. Two states, Alaska and Hawaii, were excluded from this phone survey, thus the attitudes of consumers in these areas are not represented. This research's narrow focus on general sports event sponsorship ignores specific event sponsorship opportunities. Similar research questions for specific sporting events, such as the Olympic Games, Super Bowl, or World Cup Soccer, might produce different results.

The findings reported here should be interpreted as tentative. As noted earlier, this sample was somewhat older, with a larger percentage of whites and females than is found in the general public. Also, caution should always be used when assessing attitudes with single-item indicators, as validity cannot be ascertained. Replication must be undertaken to verify these findings against other academic research in similar areas. Lastly, public attitudes concerning sports event sponsorship may be fluid. The cross-sectional survey reported here will not capture the dynamics of attitude change in the sports event sponsorship area.

This survey of general consumer attitudes offers interesting findings for both brands considering sports event sponsorship opportunities and sports event marketers. Results for RQ1, acceptability of corporate sponsorship of sports events, suggest that although American consumers support sponsorship of college events, they are more comfortable with sponsorship in the professional arena. Managers considering college level sponsorship might be advised to consider if similar targets can be reached via professional events. Future research should investigate attitudes underlying the college–professional split. Why do consumers consider professional sports events more acceptable for corporate sponsorship?

As for beer brand sponsorship of college sports events, there appears to be more opposition than support, with more support reported for beer sponsors of professional sports events. These results suggest that beer brand marketers might also consider professional sports. They also suggest public support for the policy decisions of the NCAA; some member schools and other events restrict or refuse beer brands as event sponsors (Naughton, 1998). Similar findings are noted for tobacco brands. Despite opposition to tobacco and alcohol brands, these respondents do not support government regulation prohibiting these brands' sponsorship activities.

As for consumer advantages from sports event sponsorship, the majority of these respondents clearly do not believe ticket prices are decreased, nor do they consider sponsor brands to be superior. Respondents also report no particular intention to seek out sponsor brands. Taken together, these findings suggest that event sponsors should consider alternatives to consumer-based sponsorship objectives or try to leverage the event in other ways. For example, a sponsor could request a sponsor support program from the event producer outlining the sponsor's contribution to staging the event. As another strategy, a sponsor might also consider product sampling, thereby exposing potential consumers to the brand via use at the event. Other on-site tactics are outlined by Nicholls, Roslow, and Laskey (1994).

Future Research Areas

There are many areas to be investigated regarding event sponsorship. The research reported here deals only with American public perceptions of sports events. Clearly, more research into other types of events, including civic, cultural, and musical events, is required. Attitudes may vary by event type.

Data analysis of demographic and psychographic variables could result in more specialized profiles. Some sports or other events may be perceived as more appropriate for sponsorship, and some potential target markets may be more receptive to event sponsorship. Event producers and potential event sponsors could then investigate sports events in terms of more refined demographic and psychographic profiles. The brand's target market could then be matched to the event producer's attendees and/or viewers. There is some support in the academic literature suggesting variability based on sports interest and involvement (Burnet, Menon, & Smart, 1993).

More research is needed into the ongoing debate regarding the acceptability of potentially controversial sponsors. Although tobacco and beer in a sports context are addressed here, other product categories should also be investigated, such as "hard" liquor brands, casinos, lotteries, and other gambling activities. This type of research will allow event marketers to refine policies about the acceptability of potential sponsors. It would also allow the marketer of potentially controversial brands to sponsor events where event producers, sports fans, and members of the general public might welcome their involvement.

ACKNOWLEDGMENT

This research was supported by a research grant from Lewis Communications, Mobile, Alabama.

REFERENCES

Basil, M. D., Schooler, C. S., Altman, D. G., Slater, M., Albright, C. L., & Maccoby, N. (1991). How cigarettes are advertised in magazines: Special messages for special markets. *Health Communication, 3*(2), 75–91.

Burnet, J., Menon, A., & Smart, D. T. (1993, September/October). Sports marketing: A new ball game with new rules. *Journal of Advertising Research, 33*, 21–35.

Cornwell, T. B., & Maignan, I. (1998). An international review of sponsorship research. *Journal of Advertising, 27*(1), 1–22.

Crimmins J., & Horn, M. (1996). Sponsorship: From management ego trip to marketing success. *Journal of Advertising Research, 21*, 11–21.

Cunningham, M. H., & Taylor, S. F. (1995). Event marketing: State of the industry and research agenda. *Festival Management and Event Tourism, 2*, 123–137.

Friedman, A. (1999). The question remains: Are sponsorships selling the product? *Street and Smith's Sports Business Journal, 2*(1), 14.

Gaski, J. F., & Etzel, M. J. (1986). The index of consumer sentiment toward marketing. *Journal of Marketing, 50*, 71–81.

Hastings, G. B. (1984). Sponsorship works differently from advertising. *International Journal of Advertising, 3*, 171–176.

Hoek, J., Gendall, P., & Stockdale, M. (1993). Some effects of tobacco sponsorship advertisements on young males. *International Journal of Advertising, 12*, 25–35.

IEG, Inc. (1998). Sponsorship spending in North America. Retrieved May 21, 2003, from http://www.sponsorship.com

Jensen, J. (1994, March 28). Sports marketing links need nurturing. *Advertising Age, 65*, p. 13.

Ledwith, L. (1984). Does tobacco sports sponsorship on television act as advertising to children? *Health Education Journal, 1*, 85–88.

Levin, G. (1993, June 21). Sponsors put pressure on for accountability. *Advertising Age, 64*, S-1.

McAllister, M. (1998). College bowl sponsorship and the increased commercialization of amateur sports. *Critical Studies in Mass Communication, 15*, 357–381.

Naughton, J. (1998). Colleges eye restrictions on promotions by brewing companies. *The Chronicle of Higher Education, XLIV*, 18.

Nicholls, J., Roslow, A. F., & Laskey, H. (1994). Sports event sponsorship for brand promotion. *Journal of Applied Business Research, 10*(4), 35–40.

Petrecca, L. (1999, August 30). Visa's biggest-ever NFL push gets $50 mil budget, *Advertising Age*, pp. 1, 40.

Pollay, R. W. (1993). Pertinent research and impertinent opinions: Our contributions to the cigarette advertising policy debate. *Journal of Advertising Research, 22*, 110–117.

Real, M. R. (1996). Is television corrupting the Olympics? *Television Quarterly, 28*, 2–12.

Sandler, D. M., & Shani, D. (1993). Sponsorship and the Olympic Games: The consumer perspective. *Sport Marketing Quarterly, 2*, 38–43.

Schreiber, A. A. (1994). *Lifestyle and Event Marketing: Building the New Customer Relationship*. New York: McGraw-Hill.

Shanklin, W. L., & Kuzma, J. R. (1992, Spring). Buying that sporting image. *Marketing Management, 59–67*.

Shavitt, S., Lowrey, P. M., & Haefner, J. E. (1997). *Public Attitudes Toward Advertising: More Favorable Than You Might Think*. Urbana, IL: The Cummings Center for Advertising Studies at the University of Illinois.

Ukman, L. (1995). *The IEG's Complete Guide to Sponsorship: Everything You Need to Know About Sports, Arts, Event, Entertainment and Cause Marketing*. Chicago, IL: IEG.

United States Census Bureau. (1999). *Statistical Abstract of the United States: 1999* (119th ed.). Washington, DC: Author.

Warner, K. E., Ernster, V. L., Holbrook, J. H., Lewitt, E. M., Pertschuk, M., Steinfeld, J. L., Tye, J. B., & Whelan, E. M. (1986). Promotion of tobacco products: Issues and policy options. *Journal of Health Politics, Policy and Law, 11*, 367–392.

11

Do Sport Sponsorship Announcements Influence Firm Stock Prices?

Lance Kinney and Gregg Bell
University of Alabama

The proliferation of sports event sponsorship opportunities, the amount of money flowing from marketers to event sponsorship, and the development of a body of academic literature dedicated to cataloging various sports sponsorship objectives, strategies, tactics, and effects attest to its acceptance by marketers as a viable integrated marketing communication strategy (Cornwell & Maignan, 1998). Originally considered unusual or innovative, sports sponsorship may now be as common as more traditional marketing communication strategies as burgeoning sports leagues compete with established leagues for sports sponsorship funds. Overlapping football, basketball, baseball, and hockey seasons in the United States provided 200 professional sports events during October 2000 (Petrecca, 2000). Sports saturation has resulted in declining TV ratings, yet sports sponsorship spending continues to rise (IEG, 2002). However, some prominent sponsors are beginning to back away from sponsorship; IBM announced its long-time affiliation with the Olympics would end with the 2000 Summer Olympic Games held in Sydney, Australia (Elkin, 2000). Even marketing behemoth Coca-Cola is questioning the value of sports sponsorship relative to its escalating costs (Fatsis, 1998).

A variety of consumer-oriented objectives are often associated with sports event sponsorship, including increasing brand awareness and brand image, as well as the ability to use promotional tie-ins and sampling at sports events (Cunningham & Taylor, 1995; Levin, 1993; Nicholls, Roslow, & Laskey, 1994; Schreiber, 1994; Shanklin & Kuzma, 1992). By carefully selecting events to sponsor, marketers gain exposure to difficult-to-reach target markets and demonstrate a commitment to supporting the target's lifestyle and interests (Jensen, 1994; Schreiber, 1994). In addition to consumer objectives, Sandler and Shani (1993) noted that other objectives could be served, including corporate image-building or media exposure. Internally, event sponsorships may be used to instill pride in the organization's workforce and to motivate staff (Grimes & Meenaghan, 1998). A technique often used to assess event sponsorship success is to compare the exposure generated by the event association with the cost of purchasing similar levels of advertising time or space. For example, if a sponsorship requiring a $1 million commitment produced the equivalent of $5 million of advertising exposure, the sponsorship may be considered a success, depending on the sponsor's objective.

Many of the objectives referenced here are long-term intervening variables objectives that offer little immediate justification for the expenses of incurring the sponsorship and the subsequent expenditures required to support the sponsorship investment (Crimmins & Horn, 1996). Also, these objectives are removed from sales measures. The development of more sophisticated, quantitative evaluation techniques is the primary challenge facing marketers wishing to sponsor events (Friedman, 1999). Meenaghan (1999) also noted that corporate sponsors will be looking for more tangible proof of delivered value, if sponsorship is to sustain its rapid growth. Event study methodology (ESM) offers sponsors a more immediate, alternative assessment of a sponsorship's perceived value to the investment community.

In the following sections, a formal definition of sports sponsorship is offered, along with a brief review of ESM and its appropriateness for marketing communication strategy research. A pool of sports sponsorship announcements is gathered and ESM is applied to assess the perceived value of sports sponsorship. Results are presented and discussed, along with recommendations for future sponsorship research.

REVIEW OF LITERATURE

Sports Sponsorship

Sports sponsorship, sometimes known as *event marketing*, may be defined as "a cash or in-kind fee paid to a property in return for access to the exploitable commercial potential associated with that property" (Ukman, 1995, p. 1). Recent estimates note the phenomenal growth of event sponsorship as a marketing communication strategy. Expenditures across all types of events, including sports, cultural, and other types of events, were estimated at $24.4 billion for 2002, a 3.4% increase over 2000 spending levels. The majority (69%) of this spending is allocated to sports events (IEG, 2002). This staggering figure and double-digit growth illustrate why event sponsorship is one of the fastest growing areas of marketing communication.

Event Study Methodology

ESM offers sponsoring marketers from publicly traded firms an opportunity to move beyond consumer-based, indirect intervening variables effectiveness assessment. A more immediate indicator of the perceived value of the sponsorship could be observed in the firm's stock price as traded on any number of stock exchanges. As noted by Lane and Jacobson (1995, p. 67), ESM is believed to provide an unbiased estimate "of future long-term earnings. Excess stock return measures the difference between the actual return and the expected return if the event had not occurred."

ESM assumes a theory of efficient capital markets based on public information exchange (Fama, Fisher, Jensen, & Roll, 1969). At any given time, a publicly traded company's stock value reflects the trading public's perception of all available information about the firm. This perceived value is made tangible in the firm's stock price. New information is quickly disseminated and acted on by current and potential investors. If information is released that investors think bodes well for a firm's future, capital will rush to the firm, thereby increasing the firm's stock value. Conversely, information perceived as negative may result in selling activity, perhaps devaluing or destabilizing the firm. Of course, information could be perceived as inconsequential and produce no significant change in the firm's stock price. ESM research entails isolating the date of the information release, then examining stock prices adjacent to this time period. The excess value created by significantly positive information is called the *cumulative abnormal return*, or CAR (Agrawal & Kamakura, 1995).

ESM, Marketing, and Advertising

ESM has been used to assess the impact of marketing and advertising information. Horsky and Swyngedouw (1987) reported that company name changes produce significantly positive abnormal returns. They theorized that name changes signal to potential investors that important changes loom that should result in profitable returns. Chaney, Devinney, and Winer (1991) reported significant abnormal returns associated with new product introduction announcements for technical firms, most notably for introductions of genuine innovations, as compared to brand extensions and repositioning of existing brands. Bobinski and Ramirez (1994) reviewed the influence of investor relations advertising appearing in the *Wall Street Journal*. Overall results are inconclusive, but significant effects are noted for small-cap firms, suggesting the new visibility generated by advertising might pique the interest of investors who were previously unaware of the firm.

Agrawal and Kamakura (1995) noted significant abnormal returns associated with announcements of celebrity endorsement contracts. They wrote that "results clearly indicate a positive impact of celebrity endorsements on expected future profits, which lends objective, market level support to the use of celebrities in advertising" (p. 60). The value of the celebrity is most clearly observed in Mathur, Mathur, and Rangan's (1997) ESM analysis of Michael Jordan's return to professional basketball following his foray into minor league baseball. Jordan's announcement alone was enough to add value to firms benefiting from his endorsement.

Mathur and Mathur (1995) investigated advertising slogan change announcements for 87 firms. Although they reported no immediate, significant impact, significant effects were observed within 10 days of the announcement. Their analysis suggests that slogan changes increased firm profits from $6 to $8 million. Mathur and Mathur (1996) also noted significant wealth effects associated with the announcement of some types of client–ad agency alliances. Consolidation, new business activities, agency prestige, and account size seem to impact publicly traded ad agency stock prices.

ESM and Sports Sponsorship

We are aware of at least two other academic research inquiries into the relationship between sports sponsorship and stock prices. (Note: Mathur, Mathur, and Rangan [1997] investigated the impact of Michael Jordan's announcement as a result of his celebrity, rather than his sporting activities; however, it is difficult to separate one from the other. Similarly, Agrawal and Kamakura [1995] noted that many of the endorsements they reviewed were for sports apparel endorsed by athletes; however, their research is not sports specific.) Cornwell, Pruitt, and Van Ness (2001) used ESM to investigate the impact of winning a high profile automobile race on the winning racing team's publicly traded sponsor partners. They noted that several controllable and uncontrollable variables impact stock price, especially brand–event congruency. Sponsoring brands congruent with auto racing, such as motor oil and gasoline additives, may derive significantly more benefit than incongruent sponsor brands.

Miyazaki and Morgan (2001) investigated brands sponsoring the 1996 Summer Olympic Games in Atlanta, Georgia. Although they noted significant impact for some sponsors, they did not find a general effect. They concluded that their nonsignificant findings might indicate that the investment community thinks sponsorships are appropriately valued as acceptable activities that should enhance long-term corporate objectives. Similarly, Hilsenrath (1996) reported no significant stock impact during the Atlanta Games. Hilsenrath did not use ESM to investigate stock prices, nor was this research reported in a peer-reviewed academic journal.

Research Questions

RQ1: Does the announcement of a firm's intention to sponsor a sports event increase the stock value of publicly traded companies?

This research intended to analyze the broadest array of sports sponsorship announcements possible, rather than specific sports events. A review of extant literature did not produce a review of general sports sponsorship and stock prices; therefore, the research of Agrawal and Kamakura (1995) regarding celebrity-based advertising was adopted as the model for this research.

RQ2: Are some sports perceived by investors to be better sponsorship opportunities?

Although other ESM research has been published examining an auto race (Cornwell, Pruitt, & Van Ness, 2001) and the Olympics (Miyazaki & Morgan, 2001), the research reported here considers the possibility that investors might respond more favorably to some sports relative to others. Because companies listed on American stock exchanges are used for this research, there may be a bias toward sports most popular in America, especially American-style football, baseball, and basketball.

RQ3: Does the scope of the sponsored event increase the stock value of publicly traded firms?

The final research question addressed here concerns the scope of the sports event sponsored. Some sports events are local in orientation, drawing interest and media coverage primarily from the locale where the event is held. The largest sports events, such as World Cup Soccer tournaments or the Olympic Games, draw competitors and media from around the world, with competition continuing over an extended period of time. These extended events offer the sponsoring firm more visibility and more opportunities to meet sponsorship objectives. Few companies can afford the initial rights fees and additional funds to leverage events of this magnitude. This global sponsorship level may only be feasible for brands competing worldwide with international distribution, such as Coca-Cola. Companies seeking to enter the upper echelon of elite, international business may wish to sponsor global events as a strategy to build an international corporate image or to lay the groundwork for future international efforts. Investors may perceive a broader scope as offering more potential for a better return on the sponsorship investment. If so, the firm's stock price should reflect this perception.

The implied hypothesis of financial ESM is that the CAR of the company linked to the event is significantly greater than zero. Null and research hypotheses for each research question investigated here can be expressed as Ho: CAR = 0 and Ha: CAR ≠ 0. Attention is now turned to describing the method used to obtain sponsorship announcements.

METHOD

The Dow Jones Interactive (DJI) Business Newsstand database was used to locate sports sponsorship announcements. This on-line database covers the 50 largest circulation United States newspapers, as well as business and financial press wires. The database was searched using the keyword "sponsorship" in combination with the following terms: *football, baseball, tennis, auto racing, soccer, Olympics,* and *hockey*. An "other" category was included to account for sports events that were observed infrequently, such as yacht and horse racing. Table 11.1 details the number of sponsorship announcements for each pair of search terms.

These search terms yielded sponsorship announcements and articles in newspapers and press releases issued by sporting events, sports federations, or companies wishing to announce the sponsorship. The *event study date* is defined as the date of newspaper publication or the press release date. In the case of announcements appearing over several days in different papers, the

TABLE 11.1
Sponsorship Announcements for Each Sport Type

Sport	Number of Announcements
Olympic Games	27
Football	16
Baseball	15
Soccer	14
Basketball	10
Golf	7
Auto racing	7
Other sports*	16
Total	**112**

*This category includes announcements for sports observed infrequently, such as track and field events, bicycle or horse racing, tennis, and hockey.

earliest announcement date is used as the event study date. Multiple references to a single sponsorship were excluded, ensuring that each announcement was examined only once. During the initial search phase, all announcements located in the database were recorded.

In addition to announcement date and event–brand sponsor partners, each announcement was coded for type of sport (see the earlier search terms) and *event scope*, defined as local, national, or international. *Local sponsorships* are those that are confined to a single event and that are unlikely to generate significant media coverage or interest beyond the local region. *National sponsorships* are defined as events that are likely to generate some level of national media coverage, such as a college football bowl game or a high-profile golf tournament. Sponsorships for national sporting federations or teams are also included here. For example, in 1997 Coca-Cola announced a sponsorship agreement with the Women's National Basketball Association. This specific announcement noted that the brand was supporting the league and its many teams, rather than pairing with any particular team. In the case of the Olympics, sponsor partners could be worldwide or national sponsors. For example, Eddie Bauer sponsored the United States bobsled team at the 1994 Winter Olympic Games in Lillehammer, Norway. This would be coded as a national sponsorship. *International events* are assumed to generate significant international media coverage, as well as draw spectators and competitors from around the world, such as the Olympic Games and World Cup Soccer.

Stock price data were located using the Center for Research in Security Prices (CRSP) database at the University of Chicago. The CRSP database contains stock prices for the Dow Jones, AMEX, and NASDAQ stock exchanges. Observed event date stock prices were compared to the CRSP value-weighted portfolio of NYSE and AMEX stocks, then regressed on and compared to the value-weighted portfolio. Excess return is calculated as the actual return minus the market model expected return (Lane & Jacobson, 1995).

A full ESM statistical review is beyond the scope of this chapter. For fuller details, see Lane and Jacobson (1995) and Brown and Warner (1980, 1985). At the time of this analysis, stock prices were available through the end of the 2000 calendar year.

RESULTS

For all analyses reported here, stock prices were obtained for the 100 trading days before the actual event announcement for the sponsoring firms. Day-by-day ESM regressions were conducted for the event announcement date (denoted as day 0), and the 5 days before the event date. Regressions were also conducted for the 5 days following the event data. Announcing firms' stock prices were compared to the CRSP value-weighted portfolio as a statistical test for significant differences.

Excluding all announcements for private firms and multiple announcements for publicly traded firms yielded a total of 112 unique events for study. A total of 69 different firms were represented, and some firms were observed several times: Anheuser-Busch (9 announcements), Nike (8 announcements) Coca-Cola (7 announcements), General Motors (6 announcements), Reebok (4 announcements) and Pepsico (3 announcements). The earliest retained sports sponsorship announcement was noted for Pepsi and the America's Cup yacht race announced January 19, 1987. The most recent retained announcement was noted for Reebok and the National Football League announced on December 20, 2000.

Research question 1 addressed the possibility of a statistically significant general effect for sports sponsorship announcement similar to the celebrity effect noted by Agrawal and Kamakura (1995). There appears to be no significant

TABLE 11.2
TABLE 11.2
Returns for 112 Sports Sponsorship Announcements

Window	CAR	z-Statistic	p-Value
−5, 0	.022	.04	.97
−4, 0	.002	.06	.96
−3, 0	.0004	.01	1.00
−2, 0	.001	.01	.97
−1, 0	−.00003	−.001	1.00
−1, +1	−.001	−.04	.97
−1, +2	.001	.03	.97
−1, +3	.002	.04	.97
−1, +4	.004	.06	.95
−1, +5	.003	.05	.96

CAR, cumulative abnormal return.

general sports sponsorship announcement effect. For the 112 announcements analyzed here, 37 are associated with significantly positive returns, whereas 22 are associated with significantly negative returns. Another 53 firms' stock prices appear relatively unchanged. Table 11.2 details the cumulative abnormal return (or CAR), z-scores, and probabilities for the general analysis.

As suggested earlier, there is the possibility that investors with funds in North American stock exchanges could prefer sponsorships for popular North American sports. Therefore, each announcement was coded for sport, and separate ESM analyses were conducted for each sport, including the catch-all "other" category. It appears, however, that investors do not perceive any sport as a significant plus for sponsorship. As with the general sports sponsorship strategy, no significant results are noted for specific sports. Results for each sport, with its associated CAR, z-statistic, and p-value, can be reviewed in Table 11.3.

Of the 112 sports sponsorship announcements analyzed here, 28 were for local events, 57 for were national events, and the remaining 27 were for international events. As with sports sponsorship generally and specific sports, investors appear to have no significant preference regarding the scope of the sponsorship. Table 11.4 contains the time frame, CAR, z-statistics, and p-values for each event scope.

TABLE 11.3
Returns for Sponsorship of Different Sports

Window	CAR	z-Statistic	p-Value
Olympic Games			
−5, 0	−.003	−.07	.93
−4, 0	.003	.11	.92
−3, 0	.005	.20	.84
−2, 0	.007	.26	.80
−1, 0	.0008	.04	.97
−1, +1	−.0004	−.01	.99
−1, +2	.008	.19	.85
−1, +3	.013	.27	.79
−1, +4	.015	.27	.78
−1, +5	.009	.17	.87
Football			
−5, 0	.016	.37	.71
−4, 0	.014	.48	.63
−3, 0	.007	.46	.65
−2, 0	.003	.14	.89
−1, 0	.013	.54	.59
−1, +1	.009	.36	.72
−1, +2	.0003	.01	.99
−1, +3	.016	.31	.75
−1, +4	.028	.31	.76
−1, +5	.025	.25	.80
Baseball			
−5, 0	.024	.24	.81
−4, 0	.020	.25	.80
−3, 0	−.0007	−.01	.99
−2, 0	−.0008	−.12	.90
−1, 0	−.0039	−.11	.91
−1, +1	.011	.22	.82
−1, +2	.016	.30	.76
−1, +3	−.004	−.09	.93
−1, +4	.004	.06	.95
−1, +5	−.003	.05	.96
Soccer			
−5, 0	.017	.15	.88
−4, 0	−.001	−.02	.99

(Continued)

TABLE 11.3
(Continued)

Window	CAR	z-Statistic	p-Value
−3, 0	.006	.09	.93
−2, 0	.002	.03	.97
−1, 0	.005	.16	.88
−1, +1	−.008	−.18	.86
−1, +2	.006	.23	.81
−1, +3	−.011	−.31	.75
−1, +4	−.021	−.37	.78
−1, +5	−.020	−.35	.73
Basketball			
−5, 0	−.017	−.33	.74
−4, 0	−.014	−.33	.74
−3, 0	−.014	−.31	.76
−2, 0	−.008	−.25	.80
−1, 0	−.004	−.22	.82
−1, +1	−.002	−.12	.90
−1, +2	−.005	−.21	.83
−1, +3	−.002	−.08	.93
−1, +4	−.006	−.19	.85
−1, +5	−.004	−.10	.92
Other Sports			
−5, 0	.013	.29	.77
−4, 0	.010	.26	.79
−3, 0	.002	.05	.96
−2, 0	−.0005	−.02	.98
−1, 0	.001	.06	.95
−1, +1	−.000	−.01	.99
−1, +2	.0002	.01	.99
−1, +3	.002	.06	.95
−1, +4	.009	.23	.81
−1, +5	.007	.16	.88
Golf			
−5, 0	−.035	−.42	.67
−4, 0	−.005	−.13	.90
−3, 0	−.012	−.21	.83
−2, 0	.005	.15	.88
−1, 0	−.041	−.40	.69

(Continued)

TABLE 11.3
(Continued)

Window	CAR	z-Statistic	p-Value
−1, +1	−.054	−.40	.69
−1, +2	−.048	−.49	.62
−1, +3	−.053	−.30	.76
−1, +4	−.010	−.08	.94
−1, +5	−.031	−.19	.85
Auto Racing			
−5, 0	−.007	−.19	.84
−4, 0	−.012	−.45	.65
−3, 0	−.005	−.26	.79
−2, 0	.004	.26	.79
−1, 0	.012	.68	.50
−1, +1	.012	.44	.68
−1, +2	.006	.24	.81
−1, +3	.003	.07	.94
−1, +4	−.003	−.06	.95
−1, +5	.010	.30	.76

CAR, cumulative abnormal return.

DISCUSSION

As with any research, a number of limitations must be considered. This research's focus on general sports event sponsorship ignores specific sports event sponsorship opportunities, with the exception of the Olympics. Similar research questions for specific events or other types of sponsored events might produce different results. However, this is at least the third analysis of Olympics sponsorship to demonstrate no significant stock price effects (Hilsenrath, 1996; Miyazaki & Morgan, 2001).

ESM has a number of method-specific limitations. This method is only applicable to publicly traded firms. Information leaked before the announcement date can diminish the impact of the formal, public announcement. There is also the possibility of other "noise" affecting stock prices, such as general market fluctuation based on consumer confidence, although the ESM analytical technique should account for this. However, a sponsor brand could

TABLE 11.4
Returns for Sponsorships of Different Scopes

Window	CAR	z-Statistic	p-Value
Local			
−5, 0	.012	.22	.83
−4, 0	.004	.12	.90
−3, 0	.001	.05	.96
−2, 0	.002	.07	.94
−1, 0	.006	.26	.79
−1, +1	.006	.21	.83
−1, +2	.008	.25	.80
−1, +3	.012	.31	.75
−1, +4	.004	.06	.95
−1, +5	.021	.31	.76
National			
−5, 0	−.004	−.06	.95
−4, 0	.0003	.00	1.00
−3, 0	−.004	−.08	.93
−2, 0	−.002	−.06	.95
−1, 0	−.004	−.088	.93
−1, +1	−.005	−.09	.93
−1, +2	−.002	−.04	.97
−1, +3	−.004	−.06	.95
−1, +4	−.009	−.15	.88
−1, +5	−.010	−.13	.90
International			
−5, 0	.007	.18	.86
−4, 0	.006	.18	.86
−3, 0	.008	.27	.79
−2, 0	.008	.45	.65
−1, 0	.001	.08	.94
−1, +1	−.003	−.11	.91
−1, +2	.0003	.01	1.00
−1, +3	.005	.16	.87
−1, +4	.013	.22	.82
−1, +5	.003	.22	.83

CAR, cumulative abnormal return.

be a subsidiary of a larger firm. The sponsorship announcement could be insignificant or overwhelmed by information from other corporate partners. The method used to locate announcements could have made an impact. The DJI Newsstand will not contain sponsorships that were never announced. Perhaps some sponsorships did return significant stock price value despite no formal public announcement.

Although ESM research has uncovered significant findings for other marketing communication activities, no significant effects were observed for the sports sponsorship announcements analyzed here. There may be several explanations for these results. In the case of sports, there is often a long delay between the sponsorship announcement and the actual event. In fact, years may pass between announcement and competition. A lengthy time lag between the announcement and event could make it difficult to determine if the sponsorship was a sound, profit-building strategy. Initial nonsignificant effects could mean that investors do not expect a significant return on investment until the time of the event. Nonsignificant effects could also mean that the investor community thinks sponsorship is appropriately priced for the value delivered, as suggested by Miyazaki and Morgan (2001). If so, the firm's stock price should be stable. There is also the possibility that sports sponsorship strategies have become so common that they are accepted as a standard marketing communication activity. If sponsorship is not perceived as novel, then the firm's stock price should not be impacted. Similarly, sponsorship announcements may not be dramatic enough to capture an investor's attention. In other words, a sports sponsorship announcement is not likely to be perceived as bad news, and it may not be viewed as positive enough to impact perceptions about a firm's profit potential.

An interesting condition was reported by Mathur and Mathur (1996) that might help interpret these sports sponsorship results. They noted that the information content of the announcement appears to make a significant difference, with more informative announcements demonstrating more positive impact. The impact of information was considered as an important variable for the sports announcements investigated here. Initially, sponsorship announcements were observed for word length and size of the sponsorship rights fee. The authors abandoned these variables as impractical. It was quickly observed that rights fees are almost never reported. Instead, a disclaimer like "financial terms were not disclosed" was observed. Also, sponsorship announcements did not often warrant full editorial treatment and were frequently observed as brief components of general business articles. Under these circumstances, analysis based on the word count for the announcement could well be misleading. Still, there remains the possibility that investors could better evaluate the profit potential of sports sponsorship if more detail was reported in the announcements.

Future Research Areas

There remain several sponsorship questions that ESM could address, especially in terms of specific events. Although baseball as a general category does not appear to produce significant value, sponsoring the World Series might. As noted earlier, Cornwell, Pruitt, and Van Ness (2001) did report significant effects as a result of winning an auto race, but only under very specific conditions. ESM applied to specific sports events, rather than the generic sports sponsorship strategy, might produce different results. Of course, sports events are not the only events a firm can sponsor. Sponsorships are available for arts and civic groups, music tours, festivals, and so on. Sponsoring other types of events might produce significant effects. Lastly, the congruence concept noted by Cornwell et al. (2001) is not addressed here and may provide more insight into sports sponsorship phenomena.

Readers are encouraged not to interpret these nonsignificant results as diminishing the value of sports sponsorship. Instead, these results may best be interpreted as suggesting that sports sponsorship strategies are best undertaken as a single component of long-term, brand equity–building marketing communication strategies. Cornwell, Roy, and Steinard (2001) noted that active managers do expect financial value from sports sponsorship and integrate other strategies and tactics to support the sponsorship. Sponsorships are managed for the long term, especially as they relate to the more general brand equity elements of corporate image, brand image, and brand awareness. Therefore, not seeing immediate financial market results should not discourage marketing communication managers from sport sponsorship opportunities.

REFERENCES

Agrawal, J., & Kamakura, W. A. (1995, July). The economic worth of celebrity endorsers: An event study analysis. *Journal of Marketing, 59,* 56–62.

Bobinski, G. S., Jr., & Ramirez, G. G. (1994). Advertising to investors: The effect of financial-relations advertising on stock volume and price. *Journal of Advertising, 23*(4), 13–28.

Brown, S. J., & Warner, J. B. (1980). Measuring security price performance. *Journal of Financial Economics, 8,* 205–258.

Brown, S. J., & Warner, J. B. (1985). Using daily stock returns: The case of event studies. *Journal of Financial Economics, 41*(1), 3–31.

Chaney, P. K., Devinney, T. M., & Winer, R. S. (1991). The impact of new product introductions on the market value of firms. *Journal of Business, 64*(4), 573–610.

Cornwell, T. B., & Maignan, I. (1998). An international review of sponsorship research. *Journal of Advertising, 27*(1), 1–22.

Cornwell, T. B., Pruitt, S. W., & Van Ness, R. (2001, January/February). The value of winning in motorsports: Sponsorship-linked marketing. *Journal of Advertising Research, 41*, 17–31.

Cornwell, T. B., Roy, D. P., & Steinard, E. A., II (2001). Exploring managers' perceptions of the impact of sponsorship on brand equity. *Journal of Advertising, 30*(2), 41–51.

Crimmins, J., & Horn, M. (1996). Sponsorship: From management ego trip to marketing success. *Journal of Advertising Research, 21*, 11–21.

Cunningham, M. H., & Taylor, S. F. (1995). Event marketing: State of the industry and research agenda. *Festival Management and Event Tourism, 2*, 123–137.

Elkin, L. (2000, September 11). IBM farewell offers tribute to unknowns. *Advertising Age*, pp. 72–73.

Fama, E., Fisher, L., Jensen, M., & Roll, R. (1969). The adjustment of stock prices to new information. *International Economic Review, 10*, 1–21.

Fatsis, S. (1998, October 19). Coke doesn't swing at Yankees' first pitch to remain team's official soft drink. *Wall Street Journal*, p. B12.

Friedman, A. (1999). The question remains: Are sponsorships selling the product? *Street and Smith's Sports Business Journal, 2*(1), 14.

Grimes, E., & Meenaghan, T. (1998). Focusing commercial sponsorship on the internal corporate audience. *International Journal of Advertising, 17*, 51–74.

Hilsenrath, J. (1996, August 11). The great Olympic-sponsor challenge: Games fail to make stocks jump. *The New York Times*, p. 4.

Horsky, D., & Swyngedouw, P. (1987). Does it pay to change your company's name? A stock market perspective. *Marketing Science, 6*(4), 320–335.

IEG, Inc. (2002). Sponsorship Spending Worldwide. Retrieved May 21, 2003, from http://www.sponsorship.com

Jensen, J. (1994, March 28). Sports marketing links need nurturing. *Advertising Age, 65*, p. 13.

Lane, V., & Jacobson, R. (1995, January). Stock market reactions to brand extension announcements: The effects of brand attitude and familiarity. *Journal of Marketing, 59*, 63–77.

Levin, G. (1993, June 21). Sponsors put pressure on for accountability. *Advertising Age*, p. S–1.

Mathur, L. K., & Mathur, I. (1995, January/February). The effect of advertising slogan changes on the market values of firms. *Journal of Advertising Research, 35*, 59–65.

Mathur, L. K., & Mathur, I. (1996). Is value associated with initiating new advertising agency client-relations? *Journal of Advertising, 25*(3), 1–12.

Mathur, L. K., Mathur, I., & Rangan, N. (1997, May/June). The wealth effects associated with a celebrity endorser: The Michael Jordan phenomenon. *Journal of Advertising Research, 37*, 67–73.

Meenaghan, T. (1999). Current developments and future directions in sponsorship. *International Journal of Advertising, 17*, 3–28.

Miyazaki, A. D., & Morgan, A. G. (2001). Assessing market value of event sponsoring: Corporate Olympic sponsorships. *Journal of Advertising Research, 41*, 9–15.

Nicholls, J., Roslow, A. F., & Laskey, H. (1994). Sports event sponsorship for brand promotion. *Journal of Applied Business Research, 10*(4), 35–40.

Petrecca, L. (2000, October 9). How much is too much? *Advertising Age*, pp. 38–41.

Sandler, D. M., & Shani, D. (1993). Sponsorship and the Olympic Games: The consumer perspective. *Sport Marketing Quarterly, 2,* 38–43.

Schreiber, A. A. (1994). Lifestyle and event marketing: Building the new customer relationship. New York: McGraw-Hill.

Shanklin, W. L., & Kuzma, J. R. (1992, Spring). Buying that sporting image. *Marketing Management, 1,* 59–67.

Ukman, L. (1995). The IEG's complete guide to sponsorship: Everything you need to know about sports, arts, event, entertainment and cause marketing. Chicago, IL: IEG, Inc.

12

A Review of Team Identification and Its Influence on Consumers' Responses Toward Corporate Sponsors

Robert Madrigal

University of Oregon

Knowledge about sports spectators can be traced back to the origin of the Olympic Games in Greece, which spanned from 776 B.C. to 393 A.D. Grecian respect for athletic grace and beauty was later supplanted by the "blood-sports" of the Roman Empire. Rome's Colosseum could seat 40,000 spectators at gladiatorial events, and its racetrack attracted approximately 250,000 spectators per event (Harris, 1972). Admission was charged to these events and seating was assigned according to social status. The allure of watching sports was also evident in ancient China and Japan (Midwinter, 1986).

Zillmann and Paulus (1993) argued that athletic competition evolved in the context of the division of labor governing these early societies. Determining who was the strongest, fastest, or most enduring in a community had practical implications in ancient times because it served as a basis for task assignments. Because these talents benefitted everyone in the community, spectators had reason to cheer and support excellence. Communal comparisons gave citizens the opportunity to rejoice in the skills of their fellow citizens. Citizens also experienced a sense of vicarious achievement if they lived in a place known for its athletes. This association suggested that the citizenry was capable of securing food and shelter as well as fend off enemies.

Clearly, the need for realizing vicarious achievement through the physical prowess of athletes for the sake of survival is not a concern in modern times. Yet there still appears to be a need for people to watch sports and to form alliances with preferred athletes and teams. According to the *Sports Business Journal* ("Behind the Numbers," 2002), nearly 500 million people in the United States attended an organized sporting event in 2001, with spectator spending exceeding $22 billion. Nourished by a $6.99 billion investment by advertisers, network and cable TV networks in the United States broadcast over 1.5 million hours of sports programming in 2001.

Of interest in this chapter is the attachment that spectators form with teams and its implications for sports marketers. Attachment to a sports team represents a special form of social identification. Just as the ancients derived a sense of achievement from watching the skills of athletes representing their community, so too do today's spectators.

The purpose of this chapter is twofold. First, the underlying principles of social identity theory and their application to the context of team identification are discussed. Second, research is reviewed that considers social identity effects in the topical area of corporate sponsorship. A common assumption made by many companies is that highly identified fans will reciprocate a sponsorship investment by purchasing a sponsor's products (Crimmins & Horn, 1996).

THE CONSTRUCT OF SOCIAL IDENTITY

Social identity theory maintains that we define ourselves in part by our memberships and affiliations to various social groups (Hogg & Abrams, 1988; Tajfel & Turner, 1979; Turner, 1982). "Social identity is self-conception as a group member" (Abrams & Hogg, 1990, p. 2), wherein increased levels of identification are related to a greater sense of oneness or connectedness to a salient group. More recently, social categorization theory has emerged from social identification as a way to explain how people categorize themselves into salient groups (Turner, Hogg, Oakes, Reicher, & Wetherell, 1987). Turner, in his preface (Turner et al., 1987), noted that "self-categorization theory makes social identity the social-cognitive basis of group behavior, the mechanism that makes it possible (and not just the aspects of the self derived from group membership)" (p. ix). Social self-categorization is thought to be responsible for social identification. Social identification becomes salient for a person only when he or she is included as part of a social category. Thus, for many, being a Yankees fan is merely the byproduct of being a resident of New York City. By simply sharing category membership with other residents, regardless of whether those relationships are formalized or even known to others, a person feels a sense of identification with the team.

A person's self-concept is comprised of many self-identities, each varying along a continuum ranging from individual characteristics at the personal extreme to social categorical characteristics at the social extreme (Turner, 1982). A person is apt to behave as a group member in those situations in which social categorization is made salient and as an individual when personal identity is salient. Team identification is just one type of self-identity. What follows is a description of key themes underlying social identity theory that highlight its heuristic value and how the theme has been empirically applied in the context of team identification. This section is divided into five themes: social identity and the need for self-esteem, intergroup perception, intragroup perception, social identity and emotion, and the behavioral implications of social identity.

Social Identity and the Need for Self-Esteem

A central tenet of social identity theory is that people are motivated to maintain a positive social identity. Tajfel and Turner (1979) explicitly stated that intergroup behavior is motivated by self-esteem. When one's social identity is made salient in a situation, a positive evaluation of that person's group satisfies his or her need for self-worth or self-esteem. Consistent with balance theory (Heider, 1958), people seek associations with successful others in order to enhance their own esteem in the eyes of others. For example, Cialdini et al. (1976) found that students were more apt to wear clothes featuring their school's colors or insignia the day after a game in which their football team won rather than lost. Moreover, they also used the inclusive pronoun "we" more frequently when describing a winning effort and the exclusive pronoun "they" in describing a loss. This phenomenon was referred to as *basking in reflected glory* (BIRG). According to balance theory, people who evaluate the team positively will also evaluate a fan favorably once his or her connection to the team is made apparent. A corollary to BIRG is *casting off reflected failure* (CORF; Snyder, Lassegard, & Ford, 1986). In an effort to protect one's self image, individuals will display a tendency to distance themselves from unsuccessful groups.

An interesting study by Wann and Branscombe (1990) examined the ability of team identification to moderate sports spectators' tendency to BIRG or CORF. As might be expected, they reported that spectators who were highly identified with a team BIRGed more following a victory than those who were moderately identified, and that both high and moderate identifiers

BIRGed more than spectators with low levels of identification. More interesting, however, was the finding that although those low in identification CORFed following a loss, those who were moderately or highly identified were unable to distance themselves from the team. Thus, commitment to a sports team appears to have both positive and negative psychological consequences for sports fans. It should be noted, however, that a shortcoming of this research is that BIRG/CORF was measured using only a single-item scale.

The need for positive distinctiveness in order to maintain self-esteem also appears to motivate biased processing in sports fans that favors the in-group. Two studies were found examining the moderating effect of team identification on sports spectators' attributional processing of the causes of a preferred team's victory or defeat. Wann and Dolan (1994) reported that although high and low identifiers attributed a preferred team's victory to internal causes (success bias) and loss to external causes (failure bias), the effect was more pronounced for high identifiers. Relative to those low in identification, highly identified fans were more apt to attribute a victory to the players and fans in attendance and to interpret a loss as being the result of poor refereeing and fate. More recently, a study by Madrigal (1997) used a within-subjects approach to examine the relationship between spectators' perceptions of a preferred team's personal control over a game outcome and their assessment of the stability of the outcome over time. The results indicated that a team victory was thought to be under the control of the team and stable for both those high and low in team identification. In contrast, although both low and high identifiers felt that a loss was more controllable than stable, the difference was substantially greater for those high in identification. Thus, it appears that although highly identified fans may hold their team's players responsible for a loss, they are also more likely to maintain faith that things will improve in the future.

Intergroup Perception

Social identity theory suggests that an individual's social identification is clarified through social comparisons, especially between in-groups and out-groups (Abrams & Hogg, 1990). Social identification is enhanced through positive distinctiveness when the in-group is perceived to be different and better than the out-group on dimensions generally considered to have social value or which are important to the in-group. The need for positive identity leads in-group members to accentuate intergroup differences on those dimensions that favor the in-group. In an effort to achieve positive distinctiveness from other groups, in-group members frequently display an in-group bias. Highly identified individuals view fellow in-group members as being similar to themselves and out-group members as being different. In-group members also tend to think of out-groups as being far more homogeneous and depersonalized than in-groups (Marques, 1990). As a result of more frequent interaction with others in their own group and less with out-group members, it is easier for in-group members to develop a more complex schema for in-group members and a more simplified schema for out-group members (Linville & Jones, 1980).

Research on team identification has investigated these stereotypic behaviors. Work by Branscombe and Wann (1992; Wann & Branscombe, 1993, 1995a, 1995b) has demonstrated that highly identified fans are more likely to view other fans from the same team (in-group) in more favorable terms than fans from opposing teams (out-group). In a study of the effect of team identification on stereotyping, Wann and Branscombe (1995a) initially classified students as being either high or low in identification with their school's (University of Kansas [KU]) men's basketball team. The students were then asked to form groups of traits (i.e., positive, negative, or neutral) describing the typical fan of either KU or the University of Missouri. Study participants were also assigned to either a high or low arousal condition. The authors reported that highly identified and highly aroused individuals viewed the in-group as being more complex than the out-group. In contrast, no differences were found between the in-group and the out-group for highly identified fans in the low arousal condition. These results suggest that incidental physiological arousal can influence the complexity with which group members are perceived and that this effect is moderated by team identification.

Intragroup Perception

A positive social identity can also be maintained through intragroup differentiation. It is logical to assume that not all group members will be perceived as being equally good exemplars of a particular category. In fact, self-esteem can be protected by developing a negative attitude toward members thought to deviate from the in-group's normative standards. The situation wherein a disliked in-group member is viewed more unfavorably than an equally disliked out-group member is referred to as the *black-sheep effect* (Marques & Yzerbyt, 1988; Marques, Yzerbyt, & Leyens, 1988). Interestingly, the black-sheep effect emphasizes the need for more complex and differentiated perceptions of in-group members, thus reinforcing out-group homogeneity. Those classified as being black-sheep represent a threat to a group's positive distinctiveness and are therefore subjected to greater scrutiny and criticism.

Only one study was found investigating the black-sheep effect in the context of team identification. Wann and Branscombe (1992) conducted a study in which participants were asked to read a brief article summarizing a basketball game featuring an in-group team with author commentary. After blocking on team identification (high/low), participants were randomly assigned to one of eight conditions in which group membership of the author (fan of in-group/fan of out-group), loyalty of the author (high/low) and game outcome (win/lose) were manipulated. As hypothesized, the results revealed that the most positive mood state occurred for highly identified participants who read an article describing a victory for the in-group team by an author who was loyal to that team. In contrast, the most negative mood state was found for highly identified readers following an article summarizing a loss for the in-group team written by a disloyal fan of the same team. A similar pattern for low identifiers was not found. The results, therefore, provide evidence of a black-sheep effect only among those who were highly identified with the team.

Social Identity and Emotion

The finding that mood states were moderated by identification in the Wann and Branscombe (1992) article just discussed is not a new one. According to Pettigrew (1986), "[T]o treat intergroup contact as if it were dealing simply with cold cognition is to slight what makes the entire area of intergroup contact problematic—its heat" (p. 181). The unit formation occurring between a fan and team increases the probability of intense emotional reactions being felt during and after games featuring that particular team. For example, Sloan (1989) found that fans reported greater happiness and little anger following a preferred team's victory, whereas they reported the opposite pattern following a defeat. More recently, Wann, Dolan, McGeorge, and Allison (1994) extended this research to examine team identification's ability to moderate this effect. They reported that although highly identified fans indicated an increase in pre- to post-game positive emotions following a preferred team's victory and an increase in negative emotions following a defeat, only minimal differences were found for those low in identification. Hirt, Zillmann, Erickson, and Kennedy (1992) also found that differences in emotional reactions following a victory or loss were greatest among those most attached to the team. Interestingly, Hirt et al. found that team failure led to an even more intense negative reaction than did a manipulated personal failure. These effects led to the conclusion that highly identified fans perceive a team's success or failure as they would a personal success or failure.

The influence of team identification and affective reactions has also been integrated into a model of spectators' satisfaction with viewing a sports performance. Using structural equation modeling, Madrigal (1995) tested a model in which three cognitive antecedents (team identification, expectancy disconfirmation, quality of opponent) were related to two affective states (enjoyment, BIRG) that were, in turn, related directly to satisfaction judgments. The results revealed that of the three cognitive antecedents considered, team identification had the greatest effect on BIRG ($\beta = .56$, $p < .001$) and enjoyment ($\beta = .51$, $p < .001$). Moreover, identification's effect on summary satisfaction was wholly mediated by affect.

In a somewhat different approach, Branscombe and Wann (1992) examined the moderating effect of identification with the United States on spectators' physiological arousal during a sporting event. After blocking on identification, respondents were assigned to watch a segment from the movie *Rocky IV* in which either the American (in-group) or the Russian (out-group) won. The results indicated that although highly identified (i.e., patriotic) spectators had a significant pre- to post-film increase in blood pressure, no differences were found for subjects low in identification. In addition, collapsed across outcome, patriotic spectators perceived the opponent more negatively than did those low in identification. Further, as arousal increased for highly identified subjects, so too did derogation of Russians in general.

The Behavioral Implications of Social Identity

Referent informational influence is a form of social influence responsible for in-group conformity to group norms (Hogg & Turner, 1987; Turner, 1982). Hogg and Abrams (1988) described referent informational influence in terms of a process whereby people first categorize themselves as members of a distinct social category and assume a social identity related to that category. Next, they develop or learn the stereotypic norms associated with that category. Finally, they internalize these norms such that their behavior becomes more normative as category membership becomes more salient. Referent informational influence explains how private acceptance of group norms through the social identification associated with categorization accounts for consistency in intragroup attitudes and behaviors. Highly identified individuals do not merely conform to the observable behavior of other in-group members but, rather, to the cognitive representation of the appropriate in-group norm. For example, Hogg and Turner (1987) found that private acceptance of group norms led to conformity of behavior that was independent of surveillance.

A study by Terry and Hogg (1996) exemplified this point. Their research found that group norms had an effect on behavioral intentions to engage in health-related behaviors, but only among those most highly identified with the group and not for low identifiers. Specifically, high identifiers who also perceived greater levels of normative influence from other group members were most likely to form favorable intentions toward the behaviors. In contrast, no group norm differences were found for low identifiers. Terry and Hogg concluded that when social identification is made salient, high identifiers not only enact a group norm because others are watching, but also privately enact a group norm that is consistent with how group members ought to act in that situation. It appears, therefore, that increased levels of identification with a social group lead to behavioral intentions that are consistent with group goals and values.

Although research into institutional behavior has been conducted on the antecedents and behavioral consequences of organizational identification (Ashforth & Mael, 1989; Bhattacharya, Rao, & Glynn 1995; Dutton, Dukerich, & Harquail, 1994; Mael & Ashforth, 1992), only one study was found addressing such effects in the realm of team identification. Using data collected from two sets of hockey fans (one set from a successful team, the other from a less successful team), Fisher and Wakefield (1998) developed a structural equations model examining the antecedents and behavioral consequences of team identification. Overall, they found that team identification mediated the effect of involvement with the sport (i.e., domain involvement), team performance, and player attractiveness on a number of behaviors including attendance, purchase of licensed merchandise, and displays of team support (e.g., wearing team logo, carrying signs at games).

The model's parameters were also compared across the two samples. The underlying question here was whether team success influenced the effect of those factors leading to team identification and, subsequently, the incidence of group-supportive behaviors. The researchers found that the effect of team performance on identification was greater for fans of the successful team than for those of the less successful team. Interestingly, domain involvement had a greater influence on identification for those in the latter group. Regarding the regression path from identification to behaviors, the findings revealed a significant direct effect in each sample and no differences between groups. Specifically, across groups, the direct effect of team identification was greatest for frequency of attendance ($\beta = .41$, $p < .01$), followed by purchase of licensed products ($\beta = .34$, $p < .01$) and overt displays of support ($\beta = .28$, $p < .01$).

To recapitulate, the preceding was an overview of the principles underlying social identity theory and how these principles have been applied in the context of team identification. The next section of the chapter investigates how fans' identification with a sports team influences their support of companies aligned with that team as corporate sponsors.

TEAM IDENTIFICATION AND CORPORATE SPONSORSHIP

Sponsorship refers to "a cash and/or in-kind fee paid to a property (typically in sports, arts, entertainment or causes) in return for access to the exploitable commercial potential associated with that property" (Ukman, 1996, p. 1). Companies have increasingly turned to sponsorship in recent years due to the increased clutter and cost associated with advertising media, consumers' changing habits relative to traditional media, and a need to target specific geographic and lifestyle segments (Belch & Belch, 1995; Shimp, 1997). Expenditures on corporate sponsorship in the United States have grown from $850,000 in 1985 to over $9 billion in 2001, 67% of which was spent on sports properties ("IEG Projection," 2002).

Sponsorship relies on an associative process whereby the positive feelings consumers have toward a particular property are transferred to or "rub off" on a sponsor's brand (Gwinner, 1997; Javalgi, Traylor, Gross, & Lampman, 1994; Keller, 1993; McDaniel 1999). An underlying expectation of this process is that only those who are most highly aligned with a particular property will reward a sponsor with their patronage (Crimmins & Horn, 1996). Anecdotal evidence of such an effect may be found in industry research on NASCAR fans. Data collected from a national probability sample of 1000 individuals describing themselves as NASCAR fans indicated that 71% of the respondents said that they "almost always" or "frequently" chose brands of NASCAR sponsors over competitors simply because of the sponsorship. In addition, 42% said that they switched brands after a manufacturer became a sponsor ("Performance research," 1994).

A fan's willingness to support a preferred team's corporate sponsors is consistent with the argument outlined earlier regarding the effects of referent informational influence. In essence, fans view supporting their team's sponsors favorably because by doing so they are acting in a way that is consistent with the goals and values of the team. Madrigal (2000) considered the influence of referent informational influence in a study of fans' intentions to purchase products from corporate sponsors of a favorite team. Data were collected from 678 individuals attending a college football game. The majority of respondents were season ticket holders (65.8%) and male (62.5%).

The study's findings indicated that the largest contributor to purchase intentions was group norms, followed by team identification. Interestingly, and in contrast to the predicted disordinal interaction, a significant ordinal interaction was found. Although significant for both, group norms had a greater effect on intentions at lower levels of identification than they did at higher levels of identification. Madrigal concluded that this unexpected effect was probably due to the composition of the sample. The majority of the sample was comprised of season ticket holders, and all study respondents were physically present at the football game. It is therefore logical to assume—especially in light of the skewed distribution discovered for the team identification measure—that even low identifiers were at least moderately identified. Thus, the less significant effect of group norms on intentions found among high compared to low identifiers may simply have been due to a ceiling effect at higher levels of team identification. Regardless of the nature of the interaction, the results provide strong evidence of the normative pressure associated with referent information influence.

A second study by Madrigal (2001) also considered team identification effects on intentions to purchase products from corporate sponsors. However, rather than investigate effects associated with group norms, the article examined a belief–attitude–intention hierarchy (cf., Fishbein, 1963) related to the corporate sponsorship of the athletic teams of a large Midwestern university. Team identification was operationalized as the extent to which respondents felt a sense of connectedness to that university. In an attempt to minimize the likelihood of a skewed distribution on the team identification measure, a random-digit dialing methodology was used to collect data from 368 individuals.

The results suggested that certain beliefs about sponsorship (e.g., sponsorship lowers ticket prices for attendees, sponsorship improves a company's image), the perceived importance of a company having a good image, and team identification were all favorably related to consumers' attitudes toward buying sponsors' products. A subsequent moderated regression was conducted in which purchase intentions were regressed against attitude, beliefs, the importance of those beliefs, team identification, and the interaction of team identification and attitude. As expected, a favorable attitude toward sponsorship was positively related to purchase intentions. The perceived importance of the beliefs that sponsorship makes some events possible that would not otherwise take place and improves the company's image were also each favorably related to purchase intentions. The next variable entered into the model, team identification, was also positively related to purchase intentions.

Perhaps the most interesting finding of the study, however, was the significant Team Identification × Attitude Interaction. It revealed that attitude was more predictive of purchase intentions among those low in team identification than for those high in identification. Specifically, the analysis indicated that among those with an unfavorable attitude toward sponsorship, the purchase intentions of highly identified individuals were significantly greater than for those with lower levels of identification. It appears, therefore, that highly identified fans are more likely to form behavioral intentions that are congruent with the goals and objectives of the group (i.e., the team in this study) than they are with personal factors such as an attitude toward the behavior. In effect, team identification influences the intended course of action for those who are most highly aligned because such behavior reinforces or strengthens their identity as members of the group.

Together, these studies demonstrate the direct and indirect effects of team identification on fans' intentions to behave in a way that is supportive of a preferred team. As team identification increases, so too do intentions to purchase products from corporate sponsors. The studies also provided insights into how team identification influences the direct effects of group norms and attitudes on purchase intentions. For sports marketing practitioners, the results provide empirical evidence for the transfer of identification with a sports team to behavioral intentions to purchase products from a sponsor.

Two implications emerge regarding the role of team identification and corporate sponsorship. First, corporate sponsors would do well to emphasize their associations with sports properties in their advertising campaigns. As obvious as this proposition sounds, it is surprising just how poorly companies do at establishing this linkage in the minds of their consumers (Stipp & Schiavone, 1996; Thwaites, 1995). Using DDB Needham's Sponsor Watch Tracking data, Crimmins and Horn (1996) demonstrated that sponsors who spent more money communicating the sponsorship of the 1992 Summer Olympic Games were far more successful in developing an association with consumers than those sponsors who did not. "Brands fail because they do not seriously commit their own marketing dollars to communicate the link" (Crimmins & Horn, 1996, p. 15).

A second implication arising from the study is that sports marketers must guard the goodwill or equity engendered in their properties in order to be attractive to corporate sponsors. It is not inconceivable that fans may one day turn their backs on professional sports franchises and leagues. Player strikes, increased ticket prices, player violence, front office "extortion" to relocate their teams if tax dollars are not used to build new stadia are all recent trends that may eventually lead to diminishing fans' interest in sport. Sports marketers must seek creative ways to strengthen fans' identification with their favorite team. Fan outreach, community involvement, and special events aimed at allowing fans to meet players are only a few tactics that might be employed to meet this end.

CONCLUSION

In closing, identification with a sports team is a special form of social identity. A fan that forms a close association with a team perceives it to be an extension of self. The fan processes information related to team outcomes as he or she would information about personal outcomes. In the realm of corporate sponsorship, the results of the research reported here support the notion that increased levels of team identification are positively associated with attitudes and intentions to purchase products from sponsors of the team. By supporting a team with which fans identify, sponsors are able to tap into a reservoir of goodwill that "rubs off" on their products.

REFERENCES

Abrams, D., & Hogg, M. A. (1990). An introduction to the social identity approach. In D. Abrams & M. A. Hogg (Eds.), *Social Identity Theory: Constructive and Critical Advances* (pp. 1–27). New York: Springer-Verlag.

Ashforth, B. E., & Mael, F. (1989). Social identity theory and the organization. *Academy of Management Review, 14*, 20–39.

Behind the numbers: How U.S. sports dollars are spent. (2002, March 11–17). *Street and Smith's Sports Business Journal, 4*(47), pp. 30–39.

Belch, G. E., & Belch, M. A. (1995). *Introduction to Advertising and Promotion*, 3rd ed. Chicago: Irwin.

Bhattacharya, B., Rao, H., & Glynn, M. A. (1995). Understanding the bond of identification: An investigation of its correlates among art museum members. *Journal of Marketing, 59*, 46–57.

Branscombe, N. R., & Wann, D. L. (1992). Physiological arousal and reactions to out-group members during competitions that implicate an important social identity. *Aggressive Behavior, 18*, 85–93.

Cialdini, R. B., Borden, R. J., Thorne, A., Walker, M. R., Freeman, S., & Sloan, L. R. (1976). Basking in reflected glory: Three (football) field studies. *Journal of Personality and Social Psychology, 34*, 366–375.

Crimmins, J., & Horn, M. (1996). Sponsorship: From management ego to marketing success. *Journal of Advertising Research, 36*(4), 11–21.

Dutton, J. E., Dukerich, J. M., & Harquail, C. V. (1994). Organizational images and member identification. *Administrative Science Quarterly, 39*, 239–263.

Fishbein, M. (1963). An investigation of the relationship between beliefs about an object and the attitude toward that object. *Human Relations, 16*, 233–240.

Fisher, R. J., & Wakefield, K. (1998). Factors leading to group identification: A field study of winners and losers. *Psychology and Marketing, 15*, 23–40.

Gwinner, K. (1997). A model of image creation and image transfer in event sponsorship. *International Marketing Review, 14*, 145–158.

Harris, H. A. (1972). *Aspects of Greek and Roman Life: Sport in Greece and Rome.* Ithaca, NY: Cornell.

Heider, F. (1958). *The Psychology of Interpersonal Relations.* New York: Wiley.

Hirt, E. R., Zillmann, D., Erickson, G. A., & Kennedy, C. (1992). Costs and benefits of allegiance: Changes in fans' self-ascribed competencies after team victory versus defeat. *Journal of Personality and Social Psychology, 63*, 724–738.

Hogg, M. A., & Abrams, D. (1988). *Social Identifications: A Social Psychology of Intergroup Relations and Group Processes.* London: Routledge.

Hogg, M. A., & Turner, J. C. (1987). Social identity and conformity: A theory of referent information influence. In W. Doise & S. Moscovici (Eds.), *Current Issues in European Social Psychology* (vol. 2, pp. 139–182). Cambridge, England: Cambridge Press.

IEG Projection: Sponsorship spending will lag predicted economic rebound. (2002, December 24). *IEG Sponsorship Report, 20*(24), pp. 1, 4–5.

Javalgi, R. G., Traylor, M. B., Gross, A. C., & Lampman, E. (1994). Awareness of sponsorship and corporate image: An empirical investigation. *Journal of Advertising, 23*, 47–58.

Keller, K. L. (1993). Conceptualizing, measuring, and managing customer-based brand equity. *Journal of Marketing, 57*, 1–22.

Linville, P. W., & Jones, E. E. (1980). Polarized appraisals of out-group members. *Journal of Personality and Social Psychology, 38*, 689–703.

Madrigal, R. (1995). Cognitive and affective determinants of fan satisfaction. *Journal of Leisure Research, 27*, 205–227.

Madrigal, R. (2001). Social identity effects in a beliefs–attitude–intentions hierarchy: Implications for corporate sponsorship. *Psychology and Marketing, 18*, 145–165.

Madrigal, R. (1997). Team identification as a moderator of sports spectators' causal attributions of game outcomes. In C. Pechmann & S. Ratneshwar (Eds.), *Society for Consumer Psychology: 1997 Winter Conference Proceedings* (pp. 105–110). St. Petersburg, FL: Society for Consumer Psychology.

Madrigal, R. (2000). The influence of sponsee identification and group norms on intentions to purchase a corporate sponsor's products. *Journal of Advertising, 29*(4), 13–24.

Mael, F., & Ashford, B. E. (1992). Alumni and their alma mater: A partial test of the reformulated model of organizational identification. *Journal of Organizational Behavior, 13*, 103–123.

Marques, J. M. (1990). The black-sheep effect: Out-group homogeneity in social comparison settings. In D. Abrams & M. A. Hogg (Eds.), *Social Identity Theory: Constructive and Critical Advances* (pp. 131–151). New York: Springer-Verlag.

Marques, J. M., & Yzerbyt, V. Y. (1988). The black sheep effect: Judgmental extremity towards ingroup members in inter- and intra-group situations. *European Journal of Social Psychology, 18*, 287–292.

Marques, J. M., Yzerbyt, V. Y., & Leyens, J. (1988). The "black sheep effect": Extremity of judgments towards ingroup members as a function of group identification. *European Journal of Social Psychology, 18*, 1–16.

McDaniel, S. R. (1999). An investigation of match-up effects in sport sponsorship advertising: The implications of consumer advertising schemas. *Psychology and Marketing, 16*, 163–184.

Midwinter, E. C. (1986). *Fair Game: Myth and Reality in Sport.* Boston: Allen. Performance research quantifies NASCAR impact. (1994, January 31). *IEG Sponsorship Report, 13*(3), 3, 6.

Pettigrew, T. F. (1986). The intergroup contact hypothesis reconsidered. In M. Hewstone & R. Brown (Eds.), *Contact and Conflict in Intergroup Encounters* (pp. 169–195). Oxford, England: Basil Blackwell.

Shimp, T. A. (1997). *Advertising, Promotion, and Supplemental Aspects of Integrated Marketing Communications*, 4th. ed. Fort Worth, TX: Dryden.

Sloan, L. R. (1989). The motives of sports fans. In J. H. Goldstein (Ed.), *Sports, Games and Play: Social and Psychological Viewpoints*, 2nd ed. (pp. 175–240). Hillsdale, NJ: Lawrence Erlbaum Associates.

Snyder, C. R., Lassegard, M. A., & Ford, C. E. (1986). Distancing after group success and failure: Basking in reflected glory and cutting off reflected failure. *Journal of Personality and Social Psychology, 51*, 382–388.

Stipp, H., & Schiavone, N. P. (1996). Modeling the impact of Olympic sponsorship on corporate image. *Journal of Advertising Research, 36*(4), 22–28.

Tajfel, H., & Turner, J. C. (1979). An integrative theory of intergroup conflict. In W. G. Austin & S. Worchel (Eds.), *The Social Psychology of Intergroup Relations* (pp. 33–47). Monterey, CA: Brooks Cole.

Terry, D. J., & Hogg, M. A. (1996). Group norms and the attitude-behavior relationship: A role for group identification. *Personality and Social Psychology Bulletin, 22*, 776–793.

Thwaites, D. (1995). Professional football sponsorship—Profitable or profligate? *International Journal of Advertising, 14*, 149–164.

Turner, J. C. (1982). Towards a cognitive redefinition of the social group. In H. Tajfel (Ed.), *Social Identity and Intergroup Relations* (pp. 15–40). New York: Cambridge.

Turner, J. C., Hogg, M. A., Oakes, P. J., Reicher, S. D., & Wetherell, M. S. (1987). *Rediscovering the Social Group: A Self-Categorization Theory.* New York: Basil Blackwell.

Ukman, L. (1996). *IEG's Complete Guide to Sponsorship: Everything You Need to Know About Sports, Arts, Event, Entertainment and Cause Marketing.* Chicago: IEG, Inc.

Wann, D. L., & Branscombe, N. R. (1990). Die-hard and fair-weather fans: Effects of identification on BIRGing and CORFing tendencies. *Journal of Sport and Social Issues, 14*, 103–117.

Wann, D. L., & Branscombe, N. R. (1992). Emotional responses to the sports page. *Journal of Sport and Social Issues, 16*, 49–64.

Wann, D. L., & Branscombe, N. R. (1995a). Influence of level of identification with a group and physiological arousal on perceived intergroup complexity. *British Journal of Social Psychology, 34*, 223–235.

Wann, D. L., & Branscombe, N. R. (1995b). Influence of identification with a sports team on objective knowledge and subjective beliefs. *International Journal of Sport Psychology, 26*, 551–567.

Wann, D. L., & Branscombe, N. R. (1993). Sports fans: Measuring degree of identification with their team. *Journal of Sport Psychology, 24*, 1–17.

Wann, D. L., & Dolan, T. J. (1994). Attributions of highly identified sports spectators. *Journal of Social Psychology, 134*, 783–792.

Wann, D. L., Dolan, T. J., McGeorge, K. K., & Allison, J. A. (1994). Relationships between spectator identification and spectators' perceptions of influence, spectators' emotions, and competition outcome. *Journal of Sport and Exercise Psychology, 16*, 347–364.

Zillmann, D., & Paulus, P. B. (1993). Spectators: Reactions to sports events and effects on athletic performance. In R. N. Singer, M. Murphey, & L. Keith Tennant (Eds.), *Handbook of Research on Sport Psychology* (pp. 600–619). NewYork: Macmillan.

IV

Marketing Strategy

What strategic issues confront the sports marketer? The list is endless, and this section deals with three of the entries on the list. Licensing products has generated vast amounts of revenue for some teams as marketers take advantage of brand equity in teams and properties. Chapter 13 looks at that set of issues. In a sense, most marketing involves segmentation of one sort or another. Chapter 14 examines one method of segmentation and in the process provides a great deal of good advice about segmentation strategy. Chapter 15 looks at the classic topic of ambush marketing.

Teams as Brands: A Review of the Sports Licensing Concept

Rick Burton

Australian National Basketball League

Whereas a great deal has been recorded on sponsorship's definition and the ways in which sponsorship or team identification is thought to work, the literature is less comprehensive when acknowledging or discussing the sports marketing activity known as licensing. Irwin, Sutton and McCarthy (2002) suggested licensing programs, as engineered by teams or leagues, exist for the purpose of supporting three fundamental benefits: (a) promotional exposure, (b) profit from license application, and (c) protection against unauthorized logo usage.

Licensing is a vibrant marketing concept and draws its relevance from *fan identification*, which Sutton, McDonald, Milne, and Cimperman (1997, p. 15) defined as "the personal commitment and emotional involvement customers have with a sport organization." Mael and Ashforth (1992) suggested that when fans identify closely with a sport organization (i.e., a team) "a sense of connectedness ensues" and the fan begins to define him- or herself in relation to the organization. Wann, Hamlet, Wilson, and Hodges (1995) suggested fans come to see themselves as "extensions of the team" and Sutton, McDonald, Milne, and Cimperman (1997, p. 15) wrote of sports fans generating notably high levels of "emotional attachment and identification."

Given that all sport teams must ultimately win or lose the games they play, additional theory such as Cialdini, Borden, Thorne, Walker, Freeman, and Sloan's (1976) BIRGing work, Rooney's (1974) pride in place, or Wann and Branscombe's (1993) team identification work provided a foundation that fans clearly identify with teams and are willing to represent those teams with various behaviors. Cialdini et al. identified BIRGing as a consumer behavior that stood for basking in reflected glory and suggested that when a fan's sports team won, fans of the team usually articulated that victory in language resembling the words, "We won" and were inclined to wear team colors or licensed items bearing team logos, graphics, or trademarked words. Cialdini et al. posited the fan was able to see him- or herself as a satellite member of the team and believed (in varying degrees of commitment) that his or her avidity helped play a role in the team's success. Not surprisingly, the most visible method for reflecting the team's glory was for the fan to purchase and wear licensed clothing in public. In doing so, the fan moved one step closer to perceived team membership and achieved, through this identification, an elevation of status generally not possible in their normal jobs.

Lever (1983) wrote of this behavior and suggested sport involved people jointly by providing common symbols, a collective identity and a reason for solidarity. This supports Aaker's work (1991) as described by Gladden and Milne (1999) in discussing brand equities where "positive associations with a particular brand name (or logo/mark) adds to the value provided by the product/team" (Gladden & Milne, 1999, p. 21). Thus, teams that win frequently generate a growing willingness to BIRG and are likely to profit from increased revenue (from selling team-identified items) and increased public visibility (from fans paying for the privilege to wear the team's brand on their bodies for free).

In fact, while studying the Atlanta Braves baseball team and sponsors Coca-Cola and Auto Zone, Dalakas, Rose, and Aiken (2001) and Dalakas and Burton (2002) found that the more a fan is identified with a team, the greater the likelihood the fan would understand the role of sponsorship and support the team's sponsors in retail settings. Madrigal's (2000, 2001) comprehensive research with American college football fans also showed that highly identified fans share a norm that suggests attitudes toward properties contribute to a consumer's intentions to purchase sponsors' products. Thus, the team identification benefit not only goes beyond the team's branded image but also serves the equities of players, broadcasters, and team sponsors. It also gives credence to a popular refrain often uttered by NASCAR auto manufacturers—"Win on Sunday, Sell on Monday"—because the victory translates into retail benefit.

A team that loses, however, creates a situation called *cutting off reflected failure* (Wann & Branscombe, 1990; Wann et al., 1995) and exists as part of the social identity theory literature to explain a fan's desire to disassociate with failure or a negative event or outcome. When a team loses, many fans announce, "They (the team) lost." Constant CORFing from fans means teams not only miss out on revenue from licensed merchandise that goes unsold but also lose the generation of positive team visibility (achieved through BIRGing), which would interest sponsors. It is feasible to suggest that teams that lose consistently and start their seasons with losses (i.e., the Cincinnati Bengals of the National Football League (NFL) or Los Angeles Clippers of the National Basketball Association (NBA) will suffer from smaller crowds at their games, generate lower TV ratings, and face a more difficult time selling team advertising and sponsorships the following season.

But where did this sport branding process start? England's Football Association traces its roots to a November 1863 meeting when Eton, Rugby, Winchester, Westminster, and Harrow agreed to unite in their management of English football. Logically, each of these schools sported either a coat of arms, crest, or school insignia to differentiate the value of the educations they provided.

Six years later, in 1869, the Cincinnati Red Stockings (later known as just the Reds) became baseball's first professional team (Zimbalist, 1992) and presumably established the first American team sport brand. More than three decades later, America's Major League Baseball (MLB) was created in 1903 when two rival baseball leagues merged (Burton, 1999b; Helyar, 1994).

American football, in the form of the NFL, would not start until June 24, 1922, when the American Professional Football Association (APFA) morphed into the NFL. On that same afternoon, the Chicago Staleys became the Chicago Bears and the previously banned Green Bay Packers (dismissed from the APFA for using college players) were re-admitted into the fold as members of the new league (Burton & Crow, 2002; NFL, 1994).

It is difficult to pinpoint the first time licensed clothing was sold but one of the earliest licensing deals may have taken place in 1928 when David Warsaw, a ceramics manufacturer in Chicago, approached Philip Wrigley, owner of baseball's Chicago Cubs, and requested permission to create and sell cigarette ashtrays shaped in the configuration of Wrigley Field (Burton, 1999b). Warsaw agreed to pay the chewing gum magnate a financial royalty for every ashtray sold. As recounted by Warsaw's son Jim, Wrigley said yes, and from ashtrays the Warsaw family moved to celebrity bobble-head dolls (featuring baseball and football players), team T-shirts, and hats, and ultimately emerged in 1963 as the first licensee of the NFL when NFL commissioner Pete Rozelle created NFL Properties "to enhance consumer affinity and expand market penetration. The NFL thus became the first American sports league to launch a sport licensing program. The creation of such a group within the league (the NHL's properties arm is called *NHL Enterprises*) is designed to facilitate the organization's branding strategy through less expensive channels of marketing communication. Ultimately, licensees deliver the organization's intellectual property via logos, designs, phrases, trademarked color patterns, insignias, and icons (Irwin et al., 2002).

Since 1963, most professional sports teams in the United States, Europe, Japan, and Australia have embraced the royalty revenue generated by licensees and eager fans. In fact, according to Bernstein (2002), sport-licensed product in 2001 accounted for U.S. $10.5 billion or roughly 5.4% of the U.S. $194.6 billion American sport business industry. Table 13.1 breaks out licensing revenue by league or governing body.

In fact, for a while, sports licensing was the fastest growing area of the sports promotion arsenal and grew from $5.35-billion in 1990 to $13.8 to billion in 1996. But between 1997 and 2002, market saturation, manufacturing consolidation, and societal changes toward sport (e.g., aging Baby Boomers, advent of the Internet, declines in TV sport broadcast ratings) has meant the revenue produced from traditional sports licensing has hovered near $10 billion annually.

TABLE 13.1
Licensing Revenue by League or Governing Body

NFL	$2.5-billion
All Colleges (primarily NCAA)	$2.5-billion
Major League Baseball	$2.3-billion
NASCAR	$1.2-billion
NBA	$1.0-billion
NHL	$900-million
Other	$100-million
Total	US$10.5-billion

Source: Sporting Goods Manufacturers Association as reported in *Sports Business Journal*, March 11–17, 2002.

Many industry practitioners believe the stall in revenue growth occurred because U.S. leagues frequently granted licensing contracts to fast moving production companies like Starter, Sports Specialties, Umbro, The Hockey Company, Logo 7, and hundreds of others during the mid- to late 1990s and allowed these organizations to place team logos on any flat surface and sell items in a wide range of distribution channels. Unfortunately, as numerous licensees moved into the market, they placed logos on items reaching far beyond shirts and hats. In the NFL *Merchandise Catalog 1995*, NFL Properties president Sara Levinson revealed that the sale of NFL licensed products had reached the $3 billion mark or the equivalent of every American having spent $10 on NFL merchandise (p. 3). Levinson also noted that although the numbers were good, the NFL needed to focus on three major targets:

1. "Research exactly what it is that makes the NFL a passion, one that is shared by such a variety of demographic groups" and determine what drives or influences "their purchasing decisions."
2. "Maximize our support for all [NFL] marketing programs, by increasing the investment we make in [NFL] advertising and promotion."
3. "Explore marketing the distinct heritage and personality of each of the [then] 30 member clubs within the NFL family."

On the following two pages, nearly 300 distinct licensees were listed featuring NFL or team-identified products ranging from address labels to zipper binders. In between A and Z were products such as dog apparel (sweaters, collars, leashes, bowls, bandanas, beds, hats, and neckties) beanbag chairs, cookie jars, exercise mats, placemats, floor mats, toddler, towels, and windsocks.

In the same *NFL Merchandise Catalog 1995*, the NFL provided charts developed by research firm Morgan-Horan suggesting that, based on consumer responses, the outlook for NFL product popularity in the future was 45% "more popular," 42% "same popularity," and 11% "less popular." The next chart ("Sales Expectations for 1994/95") detailed 74% of retailers surveyed believed there would be an increase in demand for licensed sports products in the future with only 6% indicating a decrease; 19% felt their sales projections would remain the same (p. 20).

Unfortunately, as the 1990s roared to a close, many of the U.S. companies that aggressively participated in the sports licensing run-up found the process of sustainable team branding complicated at best. From a business perspective, many of the companies dedicated to stamping out team items learned the hard way that as league or team licensing and royalty agreements approached 10% of the wholesale price, margins decreased while competition increased.

Additionally, some fans logically found they could only justify a few team-identified items to satisfy their BIRGing needs. In other words, once they owned the official hat, shirt, jacket, sweat suit, Christmas tree ornament, and computer mouse pad, they were clearly team-identified. Presumably, more items owned did not give fans additional benefits at the stadium or qualify them as more important "members" of the team.

For the NFL's part, they spoke to licensees annually in a collective meeting at the Super Bowl and in the *NFL Merchandise Catalog 1995*, suggesting that retailers needed to "choose product selectively, present the product effectively and market the product strategically" (pp. 20–21). Additionally, when it came to selecting NFL-themed products, the League wanted retailers to understand that there were three distinct segments (performance, lifestyle, and family) covering trademarked categories such as NFL Pro Line (the league's most elite or prestigious label because it was the same product and apparel worn and used by players and coaches), NFL Fitness (a brand of equipment and apparel for letting fans work out like the pros), NFL Throwbacks (vintage replica items), NFL Spirit (apparel for women), NFL Classic (for everyday use), NFL Kids, NFL Pro Line Kids, NFL Baby, NFL Back to School, NFL at Home (pillows, bedspreads, wallpaper, lamps) NFL Tailgate (coolers, tablecloths, barbecue grills), NFL Pet Shop, NFL Auto, NFL Quarterback Club, NFL Trading Cards, NFL Collectibles, NFL Publishing, and NFL Films. In addition, the NFL had aggressively courted major mass merchants such as JC Penney, Champs Sports, Footaction USA, Modell's, Target, Foot Locker, Sears, and Marshall Field's.

Interestingly, although some areas of licensing have slowed down since 1995, new areas, such as computer-based gaming, have increased. In fact, all of the U.S. leagues (and certain European-based groups like Federation Internationale de Football Association (FIFA) and Formula One), have enjoyed the added royalty revenue and visibility provided in the video game category from companies such as Sony (PlayStation 2), Microsoft (XBOX), Electronic Arts, Nintendo (Game Cube), Sega, and Infogrames (Humongous). These companies have created gaming platforms or games that have provided a much-needed boost to the toy segment of the sports licensing category. This area has provided revenue not only to leagues and teams (where the club controls its own trademarked logo) but also to individual players because the child playing at home is provided the sensation of controlling any player on the field or court. According to Bernstein (2002), the NHL attributed licensed product growth of 7% in 2001 primarily to the video game category despite decreases generated when master toy licensee Hasbro dropped its entire pro sports merchandise line.

Another area where sales have surged is throwback or retro classics. In fact, *USA Today* columnist Michael Hiestand (2002, p. 3c) wrote "sports leagues and their merchandisers continually come out with new merchandise emblazoned with old team logos or the names of long-retired athletes. Such nostalgia usually produces small streams of steady sales, mainly from aging fans, but now old hand-me-downs suddenly have cachet, especially among teenagers." To capitalize on this trend, the NHL asked The Hockey Company to add apparel featuring the old designs of the NHL's six original teams (Bernstein, 2002), a group that included the Toronto Arenas, Montreal Canadiens, Montreal Wanderers, Ottawa Senators, Hamilton Tigers, and Quebec Bulldogs.

Still, despite fashion merchandising or category developments, the wisest teams seek to cultivate and grow their fan base and branding potential locally, regionally, and globally. Perhaps no current professional sports team stands out more illustratively than Manchester United (MU). This British soccer team has emerged within the last 5 years as the most global of sports brands by aggressively marketing their brand assets at games, at stadium retail outlets, on their websites, through product penetration around the stadium (including the largest mass and chain retailers), and with satellite departments in major cosmopolitan department stores around the world.

MU, in fact, has licensed stores (The Theatre of Dreams outlet) within FJ Benjamin Holdings department stores in Singapore with plans to open more in Kuala Lumpur and Jakarta. The agreement with FJ Benjamin also provides coverage for Malaysia, Brunei, and Indonesia and first rights in Burma/Myanmar, Cambodia, Laos, the Philippines, and Vietnam and sees to it that MU items as varied as key chains and replica kits are sold all over Asia (Burton, 2003).

Likewise, major global events like the Olympics (IOC), World Cup (FIFA), and Formula One (FIA) have learned to develop semi-permanent retail settings in airports, malls, and primary intersections to capitalize on impending the arrival of a major sports event. For the Salt Lake City Olympic Games, the Salt Lake Organizing Committee (SLOC) arranged 70 licensing agreements to produce Salt Lake Olympic merchandise. In doing so, SLOC produced $500 million in gross retail sales with 75% of the revenue generated in the 6-month window before and during the Games (Salt Lake a shining success, 2002).

A downside for these teams and leagues, however, has been the knowledge that counterfeiters are stealing their brand logos and mass-producing easy-to-screen items such as shirts, hats, banners, and towels. Because of the lucrative nature of illegally producing valuable brand trademarks, leagues and teams regularly employ large groups of lawyers and investigators to chase down counterfeiters and vigorously attempt to protect all trademarked intellectual property rights (including logos, jersey designs, names, player faces, and player likenesses). In fact, in 2001, the four American major leagues (NFL, NBA, MLB, and NHL) joined the Motion Picture Association of America (MPAA) to back the Digital Millennium Copyright Act and attack the makers of illegally produced DVDs. The leagues took this action after learning MLB had invested $500,000 in the MLB Authentication Program because the Federal Bureau of Investigation (FBI) had broken up a network of forgers who sold more than U.S. $100 million of fake souvenirs and collectibles across 15 U.S. states. According to one source, during this 3-year sting, the FBI discovered nearly 90% of all American baseball memorabilia sold was counterfeit (Burton, 2003).

But the licensing news is not all bad. As of 1998, leagues such as the NBA were creating their own outlets such as the NBA Store (to sell NBA-licensed merchandise) on Fifth Avenue in New York City and NBA City (a restaurant with an expansive gift shop) in Orlando, Florida. Both stores were firsts for U.S. sports leagues. Another first-mover in the United States was television network ESPN (owned by the Disney Corporation), which launched the ESPN Zone restaurant in Baltimore in 1998 and as of January 2003 offered seven more eateries in New York, Chicago, Atlanta, Las Vegas, Washington D.C., Denver, and Anaheim. All of these outlets worked hard at selling the "ESPN experience" by including multiple TV screens showing ESPN, ESPN2, and ESPN Classic programming, framed displays of sport memorabilia, and a gift shop offering network T-shirts and hats to hungry customers waiting for their cheeseburgers. ESPN marketers could only project that while waiters poured glasses of Coke, Chivas, and Coors Light, consumers would revel in the experiential marketing experience provided by the ESPN brand.

That ESPN is aggressively marketing its brand should not strike readers as unusual. In the last 30 years, many sport organizations have borrowed traditional branding strategies from organizations such as Coca-Cola, Nike, McDonald's, Visa, and Budweiser to make their brands stand out and thus enhance their licensing potential. The NFL, NBA, New York Yankees, Dallas Cowboys, Notre Dame, Michael Jordan, Tiger Woods (PGA), Anna Kournikova (WTA), David Beckham and Jeff Gordon and the late Dale Earnhardt (NASCAR) are contemporary examples of heavily branded entities. As sports brands they are (or have) high awareness and generally conjure images of excellence, excitement, and passion.

These "brands" and the emergence of new "brands" such as 13-year-old soccer phenomenon Freddie Adu and high school basketball star LeBron James have combined athletic excellence with partnered sponsorships or endorsements to achieve superior brand equities worth millions of dollars. LeBron James, was the No. 1 draft choice during the NBA's 2003 draft, was widely reported to have signed a 7-year endorsement deal with Nike for more than $90 million.

These leagues, teams, and individuals (working as business entities or in partnerships with agencies and agents) relentlessly promote logos, nicknames, broadcasts, licensing arrangements, endorsements, and online websites. And frequently, the sports world's print and electronic mass media serve as a willing, and usually free, delivery partner. Instead of paying for brand impressions, sports leagues, teams, and star athletes benefit from almost daily coverage and public relations efforts designed to provide local and national media outlets with a steady display of familiar brand assets: uniforms, hats, helmets, trademarks, logos, insignias, and faces. Combined, this relentless marketing builds huge brand awareness helping to sell licensed items and generate royalty revenues. That can lead to millions in sponsorship and advertising revenue.

FUTURE RESEARCH NEEDS

An interesting element of this discussion, however, is why the leagues have allowed the revenue generation to stagnate at the aforementioned $10 billion mark. At issue in America may be an uncertainty as to how to penetrate new markets outside the United States and to better understand whether certain demographic segments are drawn to licensed items differently than others or are changing consumption preferences over time. Future researchers may wish, in fact, to study if, as Irwin et al. (2002) noted, babies as young as 6 months can actually "begin to form mental images of and affinity [with] logos" or whether boys are truly more desirable as consumers than girls. A 1999 white paper created by the Sporting Goods Manufacturers Association, citing a study conducted by *Sports Illustrated for Kids*, suggested 60% of boys claimed to own or possess NBA-branded apparel, compared to 37% for girls. It is likely the research did not factor in the fact the NBA (a male-only league) has existed since 1946 to 1947, whereas a league featuring female players (the WNBA) has only existed since 1997. Research may also wish to study whether children raised with computer Internet access are consuming sport differently than their parents and possibly identifying with leagues, teams, and players differently. The advent of retail Internet Websites such as Amazon.com, ebay.com, and NFL.com may change the process by which children or any fan purchases licensed items.

Finally, leagues and teams may wish to better understand why their brands are not considered among the most recognized when marketers are researching this topic. When *BusinessWeek* measured the best global brands and ranked the 100 top brands and Eight top brand portfolios, not a single league or team made any of the lists (Best global brands, 2001). Surely, the NFL, New York Yankees, or MU are as recognizable as number 100 Benetton, but perhaps they did not make the list because the criteria required a brand be seen as global in nature and derive more than 20% of sales from outside their home country. On that scale, perhaps licensing of sports brands still has a long way to go. The answer for teams in the future may lie in a stronger understanding of licensing a brand name, protecting a brand's image, and sustaining product equities. The best teams, whether MU Ferrari, or the Yankees, generally invest in the right players at the right time, and these athletes represent the short-term equivalent of marketing promotions because, if they perform to expectations, they provide a tangible benefit toward a team's return on investment. A Super Bowl or World Series, Stanley Cup victory is merely an opportunity to build and leverage the brand's legacy and licensing with fans and casual spectators.

REFERENCES

Aaker, D. A. (1991). *Managing Brand Equity*. New York: The Free Press.

Bernstein, A. (2002, August 12–18). Licensed-product sales up 7%, NHL says. *Sports Business Journal*, p. 5.

Burton, R. (1999). From Hearst to Stern: The shaping of an industry over a century. *New York Times*, p. 52.

Burton, R. (2003, January). Adding value. *Stadia, 20*, 62–66.

Burton, R., & Crow, R. B. (2002). A review of the NFL's growth in America: Which games made the biggest difference? *Football Studies, 5*(1), 77–88.

Cialdini, R. B., Borden, R. J., Thorne, R. J., Walker, M. R., Freeman, S., & Sloan, L. R. (1976). Basking in reflected glory: Three football field studies. *Journal of Personality and Social Psychology, 34*, 366–375.

Dalakas, V., & Burton, R. (2002). Direct and indirect effects of team identification on response to team sponsors. Presented at North American Society for Sport Management, Canmore, Alberta, Canada, May 29–June 1.

Dalakas, V., Rose, G., & Aiken, K. D. (2001). Soft drinks, auto repair, and baseball: Sports fans' perceptions of sponsors and fans' intentions toward the sponsors. B. Ponsford (Ed.), *Association of Marketing Theory and Practice Proceedings*, 10th ed. (114–118). Jekyll Island, GA: March.

Gladden, J. M., & Milne, G. R., (1999). Examining the importance of brand equity in professional sport. *Sport Marketing Quarterly, 8*(1), 21–29.

Heistand, M. (2002, August 19). Sports gear so out of style it's in style. *USA Today*, p. 3C.

Helyar, J. (1994). *Lords of the Realm*. New York: Ballantine Books.

Irwin, R. L., Sutton, W. A., & McCarthy, L. (2002). *Sport Promotion and Sales Management*. Champaign, IL: Human Kinetics Publishers.

Khermouch, G., Holmes, S., & Ihlwan, M. (2001, August 6). The best global brands and the 100 top brands. *Business Week*, pp. 50–64.

Lever, J. (1983). *Soccer Madness*. Chicago: University of Chicago Press.

Lowy, J. (1999, December 19). Psychologists concerned about advertisers' pitches to children. *(Memphis) Commercial Appeal*, pp. G1, G3.

Madrigal, R. (2000, Winter). The influence of social alliances with sports teams on intentions to purchase corporate sponsors' products. *Journal of Advertising, 29*(4), 13–24.

Madrigal, R. (2001). Social identity effects in a beliefs–attitude–intentions hierarchy: Implications for corporate sponsorship. *Psychology and Marketing, 18*(2), 145–165.

Mael, F., & Ashforth, B. E. (1992). Alumni and their alma mater: A partial test of the reformulated model of organizational identification. *Journal of Organizational Behavior, 13*, 103–23.

National Football League Properties. (1994). *75 Seasons: The Complete Story of the National Football League, 1920–1995*. Atlanta: Turner Publishing.

National Football League Properties. (1995). *NFL Merchandise Catalog 1995*. New York: NFL Properties.

Rooney, J. F. (1974). *The Geography of American Sport*, Reading, MA: Addison Wesley.

Salt Lake a shining success. (2002, August). *SportBusiness International, 72*, 42–44.

Sutton, W. A., McDonald, M. A., Milne, G. R., & Cimperman, J. (1997). Creating and fostering fan identification in professional sports. *Sport Marketing Quarterly, 6*(1), 15–22.

Wann, D., & Branscombe, N. (1990). Die-hard and fair weather fans: Effects of identification on BIRGing and CORFing tendencies. *Journal of Sport and Social Issues 14*(2), 103–117.

Wann, D. L., & Branscombe, N. R. (1993). Sports fans: Measuring degree of identification with their team. *International Journal of Sport Psychology, 24*, 1–17.

Wann, D. L., Hamlet, M. A., Wilson, T. M., & Hodges, J. A. (1995). Basking in reflected glory, cutting off reflected failure, and cutting off future failure: The importance of group identification. *The Journal of Social Behavior and Personality, 23*, 377–388.

Zimbalist, A. (1992). *Baseball and Billions*. New York: Basic Books.

14

SportNEST: A Nested Approach to Segmenting the Sport Consumer Market

Mick Jackowski
Metropolitan State College of Denver

Dianna P. Gray
University of Northern Colorado

Sport marketing is concerned with identifying and satisfying consumers' needs. The concept of dividing a mass market into homogeneous segments and targeting one or more with a distinct product offering and unique marketing communication is a fundamental precept of marketing theory. Market segmentation recognizes that different customer groups have different wants and needs that justify the development and offering of different products and services. The process of segmentation theoretically results in a much better understanding of users' needs, their decision criteria, and their approaches. Although much of the theory of market segmentation is appreciated and understood by sport marketers, it remains one of the more difficult marketing concepts to turn into profitable reality.

Consumer segmentation can help the sport marketer in the following areas. First, it allows an analysis of the marketplace, including a knowledge of competitors as well as how and why customers buy. Second, it can contribute to the strategic management of an organization in that it allows marketers to make intelligent choices about the fit between their company and the products and needs of each segment (Bonoma & Shapiro, 1983). "Those segments that fit the organization's capabilities are chosen for penetration. Those segments that do not suit the company's capabilities are left for others to serve" (Bonoma & Shapiro, 1983, p. 2). Third, market segmentation provides a key to improving the sport organization's competitive position. Choosing market segments that match the strengths of the sport business allows the organization to further develop its competitive advantage and fend off attacks from competitors.

A variety of approaches have been used to segment the sport and leisure markets. However, each of the traditional approaches has limitations. In an attempt to address some of these limitations, we introduce a nested sport segmentation model—*SportNEST*—to more effectively identify market segments for sport managers. SportNEST is a unique approach that integrates situational factors into market segmentation strategy and offers both a theoretical underpinning and a practical guide for identifying and understanding the sport consumer. Adapted from the works of Bonoma and Shapiro (1983, 1991), Grunig and Hunt (1984), Grunig and Repper (1992), and Dickson (1982), the SportNEST approach to segmentation can be conceptualized as a set of boxes that fit one into the other (Fig. 14.1). The variables that are easiest to access, such as demographics, geodemographics, and lifestyles form the outermost boxes, while communities, product, and person-situation variables form the three innermost boxes.

PRINCIPLES OF SEGMENTATION

A market or a market segment exists only because a researcher or a practitioner used a particular theoretical concept to identify it. The basic concept of segmentation is to divide a population or market into groups whose members are more like each other than members of other segments. In practice, *segmentation* means identifying customer groups that respond differently than other customer groups to the sport organization's competitive marketing strategies. Therefore, it is important to develop approaches that the sport marketer can apply to a population for the purpose of identifying unique and responsive segments.

Smith (1956) introduced the concept of segmentation in marketing by contrasting market segmentation with product differentiation. *Product differentiation* attempts to bend demand to the will of supply. It uses advertising and promotion to distinguish a product from competing products and, as a result, to increase demand and reduce competition for that product. In contrast, *market segmentation* works from the demand side of the market—the consumer side—and represents a rational and more precise adjustment of product and marketing efforts to meet consumers' requirements. *Segmentation*

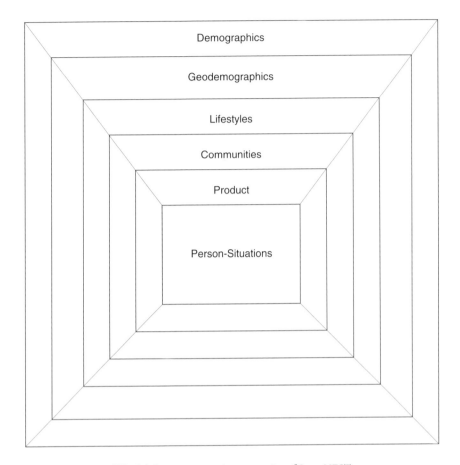

FIG. 14.1. Segmentation categories of SportNEST.

bends supply to demand by identifying lucrative segments of the market and developing products specifically to fit those segments.

Michman (1983) defined *market segmentation* as "the process of taking the mass market for consumer or industrial goods and breaking it up into small, more homogeneous submarkets based on relevant or distinguishing characteristics" (p. 127). Bonoma and Shapiro (1983) viewed *segmentation* as a "process of aggregating individual customers, prospects and buying situations into groups or as a process of dissaggregating a total market into pieces" (p. 1).

Virtually every marketing and sport marketing textbook (e.g., Aaker, 1998; Assael, 1987; Brooks, 1994; Croft, 1994; Kotler, 1991; Kotler & Andreasen, 1987; Mullin, Hardy, & Sutton, 2000; Pitts & Stotlar, 2002) contains a section covering segmentation concepts and presents a listing of various approaches for dividing or segmenting the market. The traditional listing of segmentation approaches typically includes demographics, geographics, psychographics, values and lifestyles, price sensitivity, product usage and benefits, consumption levels, and brand loyalty.

Segmentation Criteria

After using one or more of the traditional techniques listed earlier to identify potential market segments, the marketer determines an appropriate segmentation strategy and decides which segments will be targeted. If it can be identified, the sport marketer will usually try to target the most responsive segment first. Kotler (2001) suggested that the usefulness of a particular segmentation approach be assessed in terms of the following three criteria. First, the marketer must be able to measure the segment's size and purchasing power. The identification of a category, such as type and amount of media usage, is valuable only if the marketer knows how many people use that media type or its potential volume in sales. Second, the segment must be accessible. The knowledge that individuals in Cuba are likely purchasers of your athletic apparel is meaningless if national policy in that country prohibits your entry into the market. Finally, the segment must be responsive and large enough to be substantial and to service economically. Before the marketer develops a marketing plan for a specific segment, it must be determined to what extent the segment's members will respond to the mix of strategies and marketing communication presented by the sport organization.

However, all things being equal, the most critical criterion for choosing a market segment lies in its members' behavioral responses; that is, their purchase, adoption, and use of a product or service (Kotler & Andreasen, 1987). Marketers have frequently used more easily obtained, less expensive demographic, media use, and geographic variables as predictors of behavior, rather than attempting to collect behavioral information (i.e., perceptions, cognitions, or attitudes) by questioning members of a segment directly. There has also been a general lack of consideration in sport marketing research of the interaction of the person with his or her environment as a basis for defining market segments.

Research on Person–Situation Segmentation

The person–situation approach to segmentation (Belk, 1974, 1975; Dickson, 1982; Radder, 1982) explicitly segments the market by groups of consumers within usage situations and represents an important refinement of previous segmentation approaches (e.g., Adams, lifestyle research, 1982; Haley benefit segmentation, 1968; Plummer, lifestyle segmentation, 1974; Ziff, psychographics, 1977). The person–situation approach builds on benefit segmentation (Haley, 1968) because it recognizes that different people may seek different benefits and that the desired benefits can change across different usage situations.

Situational theorists posit that the physical, biological, social, and cultural aspects of the environment that an individual experiences shape his or her behavior. "Knowledge of the kinds of actual situations an individual has encountered and the physical, social and cultural contexts in which they have been embedded helps us to understand his / her world conceptions and his / her behavior in actual situations at difference stages of development" (Magnusson, 1981, p. 10).

A person–situation segmentation opportunity exists when the differential sensitivity to all or particular products and their characteristics depends on the situation *and* the person (Dickson, 1982, p. 57). The theoretical foundation for person–situation segmentation is based on the perspective that human motivations, intentions and behavior are a function of the interaction between the person and the situation, that is, each *specific situation*, and that each person views each physical and social setting somewhat differently.

Dubow (1992), in a report on occasion-based segmentation used in the private sector, and Backman (1994), in a study using Dickson's (1982) person-situation approach, report on the usefulness of the person-situation /occasion segmentation approach. "The occasion-based approach brings additional, and possibly more useful, decision-making information to the benefits segmentation party" (Dubow, 1992, p. 18).

CONCEPTUAL FRAMEWORK FOR SPORTNEST

A nested model means that the segmentation variables that are more difficult to access are located within variables that are easier to reach (Bonoma & Shapiro, 1983). Variables in the inner nests can more accurately identify a market segment. As explained by Grunig and Repper (1992), a variable in an inner nest can pinpoint a market segment precisely. "A variable in an outer nest will not be able to discriminate segments as well as those that could be identified by variables in the inner nest" (Grunig & Repper, 1992, p. 132).

Figure 14.1 illustrates the categories of SportNEST, which have been adapted for sport marketing from the fields of marketing and public relations. Overlap exists between some of these segments, as is generally the case when using any principle of segmentation.

Traditional consumer market segmentation concepts can be divided into two components (Weinstein, 1987): (a) physical attributes, and (b) behavioral attributes.

Physical attributes refer to segmenting by attributes that generally do not change. The physical attribute variables of SportNEST include (a) *demographics*, such as age, gender, household income, and so on, and (b) *geodemographics*, which is the area of the world, country, state, county, city, census tract, or zip code where you live. The characteristics from these outer segments are typically descriptive of the consumer but cannot be used to infer customers' behaviors.

Behavioral attributes refer to the criteria that are more specific to the individual, and they can be further classified as either cross-situational or situational. *Cross-situational attributes* are characteristics of the person that are more open to change but are independent of the product or service being offered. The segments of SportNEST that are cross-situational include the lifestyle and communities nests. The lifestyles segment includes the concepts of psychographics and media consumption that are used to locate segments of the mass audience based on psychological or social characteristics or both (Grunig & Repper, 1992). Lifestyles is a broader segmentation concept than communities because the segment it produces may include several communities.

Communities are defined as individuals with a common interest (Grunig & Hunt, 1984; Shoham & Kahle, 1996), such as the community of sports fans. Shoham and Kahle (1996) identified two types of sport communities: (a) *consumption*, which is people having common consumption interests, and (b) *communication*, which is people with common media habits, watching televised events and reading about sport in magazines and newspapers. Consumption communities pertain to both participant and spectator sports and are characterized by shared consumption patterns or characteristics of a product or service. Sport consumption communities, like other social groups, also have identifiable communication habits. These communication communities are similar in the types and frequency of media used by its members. Because different sports attract different types of consumption communities, this nest is an important segmentation tool for sport marketers.

The community nest may overlap with the lifestyles nest above it and the product nest within it, in that several lifestyles may be found in the same consumption community, and members of consumption communities may have different brand loyalties, identify different product benefits, and have differing product adoption and usage patterns.

Situational attributes are characteristics of the situation that could change in accordance with the nature of the situation or occasion. The segments of SportNEST that are situational include (a) product, and (b) person–situation factors. Determining the frequency by which they occur can further delineate these situational attributes. Product and usage benefits are usually determined once before the purchase and rarely change after the purchase is made. For example, long-distance runners think of situations they expect to encounter with their footwear, purchase their footwear based on these situations, and rarely develop new running situations after they purchase the product.

Also included in the product nest would be the marketing concept of adopter classes. Because we know that consumers do not adopt new products at the same rate, they can be classified according to their time frame for adopting a new product relative to other consumers. Although not all new product adopters follow this distribution, the categories of innovators, early adopters, early or late majority, and laggards (Rogers, 1962 as reported in Engel, Blackwell, & Miniard, 1995) can be used as product nest subsegments that have varying degrees of attractiveness for sport marketers. Sport marketers should focus their attention on the situational-specific innovators and early adopters in this nest. If these consumers do not accept the product, there is not much hope of other consumers supporting the product.

The innermost nest, person–situation, is concerned with the fundamental behavioral question, "why do people behave as they do?" Applied to marketing the question becomes, "why do some people purchase certain products and services and other people do not?"

It is important that information about buyers' decision processes and the underlying motivations be gathered. Although collection of this information is important, consumers do not generally wear information about their perceptions, motives, and values on their sleeve. The sport marketer should be advised that the person–situation nest is not merely a combination of demographics and situational characteristics. A more thorough investigation of sports consumers is necessary to flesh out the richness of this segment.

Situational factors in the person–situation nest may change each time the product or service is used. An example for this innermost segment would be the sport spectator who makes separate purchase decisions based on any combination of the following: (a) day of the week, (b) time of event, (c) past performance of athletes, (d) social makeup and number of people with whom the spectator will be attending the event. Furthermore, these situations, combined with personal characteristics such as attitudes and cognitions, values, and risk sensitivity (risk aversive versus risk receptive), generate person–situation factors that explain more explicitly the circumstances by which certain groups of people enjoy a specific sport product.

The level of risk a customer is willing to assume is related to other personality variables such as personal style, intolerance for ambiguity, and self-confidence. Buyers who are risk averse are not good prospects for new products or products that are unpredictable and inconsistent (Bonoma & Shapiro, 1991).

Bonoma and Shapiro (1983, 1991) suggested that marketers use the nested approach by first utilizing the easier to obtain outer segmentation variables and work inward until financial considerations prohibit further analyses. Conversely, Grunig and Repper (1992) recommended that public relations practitioners use their adaptation of Bonoma and Shapiro's model by beginning with the inner nests, which provide more important information for their field.

The variables from the outer nests are generally insufficient when used in all but the most homogeneous markets because their criteria ignore buyer–situational differences. Therefore, this chapter recommends that users of SportNEST begin with the inner nests because many of the unique elements of marketing that differentiate sport from other forms of corporate endeavor are situational in nature. Consequently, if sport managers concentrate on segmenting markets using person–situation factors, they can more definitively determine the wants and needs of their customers. Thus, the remainder of this chapter concentrates on the innermost variable of SportNEST–person–situation factors.

With respect to Kotler's (2001) criteria—ease of measurement, accessibility, and responsiveness—the SportNEST model is appropriate. Measurement is relatively easy. According to Dickson (1982), the most practical approach is to describe usage situations in terms of normally occurring situations for a specific product. For example, Major League Baseball pre-season games and opening day games describe two typical usage situations associated with the unique sport characteristic: sport is seasonal and demand for the product fluctuates. The segments identified, pre-season (spring training) attendees and opening day fans, occur at the beginning of each season at baseball stadia around the country. People who attend these games can be identified and their reasons for attending investigated.

With regard to the accessibility and responsiveness of the segments' members, although not guaranteed, reaching the aforementioned segments is feasible (Backman, 1994). Franchise's ticket records and onsite entry and exit interviews can be used to reach these naturally occurring segments.

THE SPORT PRODUCT

The basis for using person–situation segmentation in a sport marketing context is found in the sport product itself. Researchers in the field of sport marketing have identified several characteristics of sport that are generally unlike other forms of business.

Unique Aspects of Sport

Unlike most products available in the marketplace, sport cannot be sampled; the customer cannot touch, taste, or view it before the competition. Mullin, et al. (2000) identified at least seven unique characteristics of sport, which are situational in nature.

Sport Demand Tends to Fluctuate Widely.   Most sport organizations face special problems in balancing a supply of the product with consumer demand. Because sport is seasonal, it is natural that the demand for products relating to baseball will increase in the spring and decrease during the off-season. The seasonal demand concept also manifests itself on opening day, when the excitement for the team is typically high at the beginning of the season and either wanes or increases as the season progresses, depending on the team's fortunes in the division and league.

Sport Is Intangible and Subjective.   Few businesses are faced with the dilemma of such a variety of opinion regarding the performance and output of the organization. Each spectator and participant develops a singular personal assessment of the activity each time it is consumed. The athletes involved in the competition and the spectators watching it are important sources of their own satisfaction.

Consumers Personally Identify With Sport.   Cialdini, Borden, Thorne, Walker, Freeman, and Sloan (1976) coined the term *basking-in-reflected-glory* (BIRGing), a concept illustrative of sports fans vicariously living through sports when "our" team does well and distancing themselves from it when "they" fail. Cialdini et al. found that team apparel sales increased after wins and decreased following losses.

The *personal identification* of sport was further developed by Sutton, McDonald, Milne, and Cimperman (1997), who identified a "conceptual framework of fan identification and the levels, motivations and benefits of such identification" (p. 15).

The Sport Competition or Event Is Manufactured and Consumed Onsite, Resulting in an Inconsistent and Unpredictable Product.   People produce sport, and people are inconsistent. Although most businesses would fail quickly if the consumer could not rely on a consistent product, sport organizations use this characteristic to attract fans. Next weekend's football game will not be identical to the last one. Even though fans want their team to win, sport consumers thrive on not knowing what the outcome of the competition will be. Because of the skill level of the home and opposing teams, injury status of key players, even the weather, each event results in a different competitive outcome and a different response by fans.

Sport Marketers Have No Control Over the Composition of the Core Product.   Because of this reality, sport marketers concentrate on product extensions. The use of a situational segmentation model would not offer control of the core product, but it would allow the marketer to adjust the product extensions for various segments of fans.

Social Facilitation Is a Key Aspect of Sport Consumption.   With few exceptions, sport is generally enjoyed in groups of two or more people in a public setting. Hence, the interaction between individuals at the event often determines the level of satisfaction each time the event is consumed.

Prices Are Determined by the Marketer's Sense of Consumers' Wants.   It is difficult to price the individual sport product using traditional cost–benefit approaches. Additionally, because there are numerous variables involved with satisfying the sport consumer (e.g., seat location, parking ease and proximity to the stadium, in-arena services, quality and variety of food, and so on), and the sport marketer has no control over many of these variables, it is difficult for sport marketers to price the product offerings to consistently satisfy all consumers.

Elements of the Sport Product

To properly identify the situations applicable for each of the seven unique aspects of sport, these characteristics must first be connected to the specific elements of the sport product. Several sport marketing experts (Brooks, 1994; Mullin et al., 2000) have developed specific domains of the sport product to better explain its nature.

Brooks (1994) divided the sport product into tangible and intangible elements. The *tangible elements* include (a) sport, (b) participants, and (c) team.

The *intangible elements* are the psychic qualities of (a) emotions, (b) experiences, and (c) feelings. The tangible element of sport defines what game is being played. *Participants* include athletes, coaches, and environment. *Team* refers to the participants in the game and the level of competition that is involved. The intangible elements are illustrated through such things as "the *high* we get . . . the *thrill* of winning . . . the *satisfaction* (we derive) . . . (and) the *pride* we feel when our team wins" (Brooks, 1994, p. 88).

Mullin et al. (2000) outlined seven specific elements that constitute the sport product: (a) the game form itself; (b) the event and its stars; (c) the ticket; (d) the organization; (e) the facility; (f) equipment, clothing, and novelties; and (g) personnel and processes. The *game form* is explained as the generation of winners and losers, which accounts primarily for the popularity of sport. The *event and its stars* represents the idea that human drama is central to any sporting event. The *ticket element* recognizes the promotional opportunities that can be provided via the ticket stub. Of particular importance to the community is the reputation of another element of the sport product—the *organization*. The *facility* is a tangible aspect of sport that can be controlled by managers. Onsite vendors generate the *element of equipment, clothing, and novelties*, or in other words, all merchandise that is offered at the event related to the sport. *Personnel and processes* refers to the level of service that sport customers receive while attending or participating in sport.

The Sport Atmosphere

Many of these elements pertain to several aspects of the total sport experience, whereas some may be related to just one or two. It is important to further classify these elements of the sport product so that situations can be developed that simultaneously address both the unique aspects of sport and the elements of the sport product. We suggest that there are five categories that encompass all classifications of the sport product and define the total sport atmosphere. Figure 14.2 illustrates the unique aspects of sport and their relationship to the sport atmosphere categories.

Three aspects of sport contribute toward the makeup of all five of the sport atmosphere constructs: (a) sport is intangible and subjective, (b) sport enables social facilitation, and (c) prices are determined by the marketer's sense of what the consumer wants. Sport is interpreted in myriad ways by a variety of people. Consequently, the intangible and subjective aspect of sport relates to every component of the sport experience. Because sport is most often enjoyed in groups, the concept of social facilitation also applies to each construct. Additionally, sport marketers cannot always pinpoint what

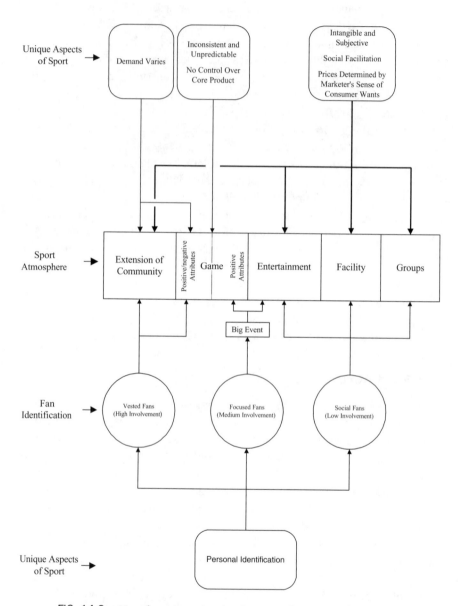

FIG. 14.2. How the unique, situational aspects of sport contribute to the sport atmosphere.

their customers want, and these wants are embedded in all five of the sport atmosphere constructs.

Extension of Community. This construct contains both the tangible aspects of the organization and the intangible, emotional, elements, such as pride, that are gained vicariously through the team or athletes as representatives of a locale. "Although the success of the team reflects personally upon individual fans, it also reflects upon the collective identity of the community" (Sutton, et al., 1997, p. 17).

The other unique aspects of sport that are a part of this component of the sport atmosphere include (a) personal identification, and (b) demand varies. According to Sutton et al. (1997), personal identification can be broken into distinct levels of fan identification. Vested or high involvement fans use sport as an extension of their community. Also, how the community feels about the sport product often determines the ebbs and flows of its demand.

Game. The game combines the game form itself, the participants, teams, and any emotions of the experience tied directly to the outcome of the game. Situations that deal with the status of the team, both before an event and during an event, can be developed from this construct.

Demand also varies depending on the attractiveness of the sport, which is determined by the performance of its athletes. The vested fan also takes an extreme interest in the game and has a strong team identification regardless of how well the athletes are performing. Additionally, the focused or medium involvement fan (Sutton et al., 1997) is attracted to the game itself, but only when it is popular. "Behavior is directly correlated to team performance" (Sutton et al., 1997, p. 17). Additionally, the inconsistent and unpredictable nature of sport is an inherent aspect of the game itself, as is the reality that sport marketers cannot control the core product.

Entertainment. People who are less concerned with the outcome of the sporting event than they are with the overall quality of the entertainment experience characterize this category (Sutton et al., 1997). Relevant situations for this category would include any attempts by the sport producer to enliven the sport atmosphere through manipulation of off-field conditions at the facility.

The focused fan also attends for entertainment reasons other than having an interest in the game itself (Sutton et al., 1997). The *big event syndrome* is when focused fans "may also be attracted to the 'event,' that being the big game" (Sutton et al., 1997, p. 17). Social or low involvement fans (Sutton et al., 1997) attend primarily for the entertainment value of the sport atmosphere.

Facility.   The facility where the sport product occurs, as well as the quality of service that consumers receive, comprise the parts of this category. Physical situations related to the condition of the facility and the professionalism of its staff are applied here. As part of their overall sport experience, social fans will engender more satisfaction or dissatisfaction based on their evaluation and enjoyment of the sport facility.

Groups.   This final category refers directly to the socially facilitating nature of sport, wherein individuals consume the sport product in groups. With the understanding that the enjoyment of sport is often heightened through group interaction, specific situations in sport can be developed through this construct. Although most sport is consumed in groups, it is the social fans (Sutton et al., 1997) who are more attracted to sport through its "opportunities for social interaction within the community" (Sutton et al., 1997, p. 17).

SPECTATOR SPORT ATMOSPHERE SITUATIONS

The seven unique aspects of sport that are situational in nature are related to at least one of the five constructs of the spectator sport atmosphere. Situations can be developed that align themselves with each of these five components (Fig. 14.3). For operational purposes, the sport marketer must first differentiate the time when the situation will occur in accordance with each of the atmosphere constructs. We suggest sport situations are based on three periods: (a) pre-game, (b) anticipated, and (c) in-game.

Pre-game situations refer to situations surrounding the event that are present before its start. Sport marketers can use information they have collected about these situations in the past to more effectively market their product when these situations occur again.

Anticipated situations represent predicted situations that spectators will experience once they arrive at the event. Knowing what combinations of anticipated situations are most likely to have the biggest impact on the spectator's enjoyment of the event can determine what services should be offered to specific segments to heighten their satisfaction.

In-game situations are the aspects of the game being played and on which the marketer can capitalize if strategic moves are made quickly. These situations are more closely related to niche marketing, where "the emphasis . . . is on

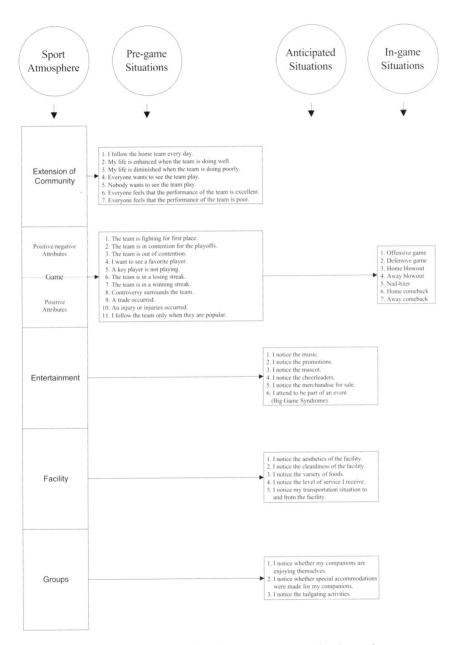

FIG. 14.3. Pre-game, anticipated, and in-game situations related to each construct of the sport atmosphere.

similar unique needs and consumption patterns of a small group of customers" (Shani, 1997, p. 10). For instance, if sport marketers know from previous research that families are more apt to purchase merchandise if the home team is winning by 10 points or more at halftime, then a certain number of the circulating vendors can be switched from selling food to selling merchandise in the designated family sections at intermission.

Based on these three periods, the following situations were developed for each of the five constructs of the sport atmosphere:

1. Extension of community
2. Game
3. Entertainment
4. Facility
5. Groups

Although these situations were developed based on a review of literature and our experience, they should not be considered an exhaustive list. They are provided as examples of logical and probable situations.

Extension of Community (Pre-Game Situations)

1. *I follow the home team every day.* This situation is based on research conducted by Pooley (1978), who indicated that fans with high identification levels devote a large part of their day to following their team.
2. *My life is enhanced when the team is doing well.*
3. *My life is diminished when the team is doing poorly.* Through the principle of association, fans are emotionally tied to their teams (Cialdini, 1976).
4. *Everyone wants to see the team play.*
5. *Nobody wants to see the team play.* The situations presented in 3. and 4. address the principle of social proof (Cialdini, 2000), where "we view a behavior as correct in a given situation to the degree that we see others performing it" (Cialdini, 2000, p. 100).
6. *Everyone states that the performance of the team is excellent.* This situation is an example of a community basking-in-reflected-glory of their team by publicly announcing their desire to be associated with the team (Cialdini, 1993).
7. *Everyone says that the performance of the team is poor.* This situation is an example of a community distancing itself from their team if the team is not performing well (Cialdini, 1976).

Game (Pre-Game Situations)

1. *The team is fighting for first place.* A situation in which the team is vying for a division, conference, or league title.
2. *The team is in contention for the playoffs.* A situation in which the team is not battling for first place but is still in the playoff fight.
3. *The team is out of contention.* A situation in which the team has no hope of making the playoffs.
4. *I want to see a favorite player.* A situation in which a spectator is attending solely to see an athlete.
5. *A key player is not playing.* A situation in which an integral member of the team or a fan favorite is not playing.
6. *The team is in a losing streak.* A situation in which the team has lost three or more games in a row.
7. *The team is in a winning streak.* A situation in which the team has won three or more games in a row.
8. *Controversy surrounds the team.* A situation involving the team that has drawn considerable media attention.
9. *A trade occurred.* A situation in which a player has recently been traded.
10. *An injury or injuries occurred.* A situation in which a key injury or a rash of injuries have occurred.
11. *I follow the team only when they are popular.* This situation applies to bandwagon fans who follow the team only when it is fashionable to do so (Sutton et al., 1997).

In-Game Situations

1. *Offensive game.* A situation in which the game is high scoring.
2. *Defensive game.* A situation in which the game is low scoring.
3. *Home blowout.* A situation in which the home team is winning by a comfortable margin. Point differentials that would be considered blowouts are specific to each sport.
4. *Away blowout.* A situation in which the away team is winning by a comfortable margin. Point differentials that would be considered blowouts are specific to each sport.
5. *Nail-biter.* A situation in which the game is closely contested.
6. *Home comeback.* A situation in which the home team came back from a blowout margin to at least turn the game into a nail-biter. Point differentials that would be considered blowouts are specific to each sport.

7. *Away comeback.* A situation in which the away team came back from a blowout margin to at least turn the game into a nail-biter. Point differentials that would be considered blowouts are specific to each sport.

Entertainment (Anticipated Situations)

1. I notice the music.
2. I notice the promotions.
3. I notice the mascot.
4. I notice the cheerleaders.
5. I notice the merchandise for sale.
6. I attend to be part of an upcoming event.

Facility (Anticipated Situations)

1. I notice the aesthetics of the facility.
2. I notice the cleanliness of the facility.
3. I notice the variety of foods.
4. I notice the level of service I receive.
5. I notice the parking situation.
6. I notice my transportation situation to and from the facility.

Groups (Anticipated Situations)

1. I notice whether my companions are enjoying themselves.
2. I notice whether special accommodations were made for my companions.
3. I notice the tailgating activities.

OPERATIONALIZING PERSON–SITUATION SEGMENTATION

In 1982, Dickson developed the practical procedures for situation–person segmentation. One of his first recommendations was the need for management to understand which situations are most pertinent to their organization. "It is not suggested that every possible usage situation should be described. Managerial judgment is required to identify the determinant characteristics of usage situations to be used in the major market research undertaken in . . . the process" (Dickson, 1982, p.62).

Adapted from Dickson's (1982) procedure, the following eight steps provide a guideline that sport marketers can follow to successfully employ person–situation segmentation.

Step 1. Undertake a benefit, product perception and reported market behavior segmentation survey of consumers. Measure benefits and perceptions by usage situation, as well as by their level of fan identification. Assess situation usage frequency by recall estimates or usage situation diaries (Belk, 1979). Research indicates it is easier for consumers to recall their behavior when it is connected to a particular situation than behavior not connected to a situation (McDonald & Goldman, 1980). This step identifies which situations are most salient to specific groups of fans.

Step 2. Construct a person–situation segmentation matrix. The rows are the major usage situations or fan identification levels and the columns are groups of users identified by a single characteristic or combination of characteristics, such as consumption communities, values, attitudes, and so forth.

Step 3. Construct a second matrix that groups the most important person–situations with geodemographic or demographic groups. Rank the cells in the matrix in terms of aggregate customer preferences. The person–situation combinations that result in the greatest preference for each designated geodemographic or demographic group would be ranked first.

Step 4. State the major benefits sought and unique market behavior for each non-empty cell of the matrix. Some person types will never consume the sport product in certain usage situations.

Step 5. Position your competitors' sport product within the matrix. The product feature they promote and other marketing strategies can determine the person–situation segments they currently serve.

Step 6. Position your sport product within the matrix using the same criteria as in step 5.

Step 7. Assess how well your current sport marketing strategy meets the needs of the identified person–situation submarkets compared to the competition.

Step 8. Identify market opportunities and strategies based on the submarkets' size, needs, and competitive advantage.

CONCLUSIONS

A nested model of segmentation for sport marketing has been introduced—SportNEST—and the theoretical foundation has been laid with a discussion of procedures for utilizing its innermost nest–person–situation factors—to segment the sport consumer market. The nested approach to segmentation provides sport marketers with a tool that not only can be used in the simple grouping of customers and potential customers using traditional segmentation approaches but also identifies more sophisticated segments through the grouping of customers by purchase situation, events, and personal characteristics. Although this analysis provides a reasoned first step for the use of person–situation segmentation in sport, empirical studies using the prescribed techniques must be conducted in the future to validate this viewpoint.

Factor analyses of the situations for each of the five sport atmospheres are recommended to validate, condense, as well as add breadth to the situations relevant for specific sports. After this, data collection from actual sport organizations should be conducted to test the basic theory and assess its applicability to actual practice.

REFERENCES

Aaker, D. A. (1998). *Strategic Market Management* (5th ed.). New York: John Wiley & Sons.

Adams, A. J. (1982, May 16). Lifestyle research: A lot of hype, very little performance. *Marketing News, 5.*

Assael, H. (1987). *Consumer Behavior and Marketing Action* (3rd ed.). Boston: Kent.

Backman, S. J. (1994). Using a person–situation approach to market segmentation. *Journal of Park and Recreation Administration, 12*(1), 1–16.

Belk, R. W. (1974, May). An explanatory assessment of situation effects in buyer behavior. *Journal of Marketing Research, 11,* 156–163.

Belk, R. W. (1975, Fall). Situation variables and consumer behavior. *Journal of Consumer Research, 2,* 157–164.

Belk, R. W. (1979).

Bonoma, T. V., & Shapiro, B. P. (1991). How to segment industrial markets. In R. J. Dolan (Ed.), *Strategic Marketing Management* (pp. 156–167). Boston: Harvard Business School.

Bonoma, T. V., & Shapiro, B. P. (1983). *Segmenting the Industrial Market.* Lexington, MA: Lexington Books.

Brooks, C. M. (1994). *Sports Marketing: Competitive Business Strategies for Sports.* Englewood Cliffs, NJ: Prentice-Hall.

Cialdini, R. B. (2000). *Influence: Science and Practice* (4th ed.). New York: HarperCollins.

Cialdini, R. B., Borden, R. J., Thorne, R. J., Walker, M. R., Freeman, S., & Sloan, L. R. (1976). Basking in reflected glory: Three field studies. *Journal of Personality and Social Psychology, 34,* 366–375.

Croft, M. J. (1994). *Market segmentation*. New York: Routledge.

Dickson, P. R. (1982, Fall). Person–situation: Segmentation's missing link. *Journal of Marketing, 46*, 56–64.

Dubow, J. S. (1992). Occasion-based vs User-based benefit segmentation: A case study. *Journal of Advertising Research, 32*(2), 11–18.

Engel, J. F., Blackwell, R. D., & Miniard, P. W. (1995). *Consumer Behavior* (8th ed.). Chicago: Dryden Press.

Grunig, J. E., & Hunt, T. (1984). *Managing Public Relations*. Fort Worth, TX: Harcourt Brace Jovanovich.

Grunig, J. E., & Repper, F. C. (1992). Strategic management, publics, and issues. In J. E. Grunig (Ed.), *Excellence in Public Relations and Communication Management* (pp. 117–157). Hillsdale, NJ: Lawrence Erlbaum Associates.

Haley, E. I. (1968). Benefit segmentation, a decision-oriented research tool. *Journal of Marketing, 32*(3), 30–35.

Kotler, P. (2001). *Marketing Management*. Englewood Cliffs, NJ: Prentice-Hall.

Kotler, P. (1997). *Marketing Management: Analysis, Planning and Control* (9th ed.). Englewood Cliffs, NJ: Prentice-Hall.

Kotler, P., & Andreasen, A. (1987). *Strategic Marketing for Nonprofit Organizations* (3rd ed.). Englewood Cliffs, NJ: Prentice-Hall.

Magnusson, D. (1981). Wanted: A psychology of situations. In D. Magnusson (Ed.), *Toward a Psychology of Situations*. Hillsdale, NJ: Lawrence Erlbaum Associates.

McDonald, S. S., & Goldman, A. E. (1980). Strategies of segmentation research. In G. B. Hafer (Ed.), *A Look Back, a Look Ahead* (pp. 30–42). Chicago: American Marketing Association. [Reprinted in Person–situation: Segmentation's missing link. *Journal of Marketing, 46*, 56–64 (1982, Fall)].

Michman, R. (1983). *Marketing to Changing Consumer Markets*. Westport, CT: Praeger Publishers.

Mullin, B., Hardy, S., & Sutton, W. A. (2000). *Sport Marketing*. Champaign, IL: Human Kinetics.

Pitts, B. G., & Stotlar, D. K. (2002). *Fundamentals of Sport Marketing*. Morgantown, WV: Fitness Information Technology.

Pooley, J. C. (1978). *The sports fan: A psychology of misbehavior.* (CAPHER Sociology of Sports Monograph Series). Calgary, Alberta [Reprinted in Creating and Fostering Fan Identification in Professional Sports. *Sport Marketing Quarterly, 6*(1), 15–22 (1997)].

Plummer, J. T. (1974). The concept and application of life style segmentation. *Journal of Marketing, 38*(1), 33–37.

Radder, J. M. (1982, January 22). Marketing diagnostics analyzes situations, reveals how consumers select products. *Marketing News, 15*, 11.

Shani, D. (1997). A framework for implementing relationship marketing in the sport industry. *Sport Marketing Quarterly, 6*(2), 9–15.

Shoham, A., & Kahle, L. R. (1996). Spectators, viewers, readers: Communication and consumption communities in sport marketing. *Sport Marketing Quarterly, 5*(1), 11–19.

Smith, W. R. (1956). Product differentiation and market segmentation as alternative marketing strategies. *Journal of Marketing, 21*(2), 3–8. [Reprinted in J. Engel, H. Fiorillo, & M. Cayley, (Eds.), (1972). *Market Segmentation: Concepts and Applications* (pp. 29–35). New York: Holt, Rinehart & Winston].

Sutton, W. A., McDonald, M. A., Milne, G. R., & Cimperman, J. (1997). Creating and fostering fan identification in professional sports. *Sport Marketing Quarterly, 6*(1), 15–22.

Taylor, J. W. (1986). *Competitive Marketing Strategies*. Radnor, PA: Chilton.

Weinstein, A. (1987). *Market Segmentation: Using Demographics, Psychographics and Other Segmentation Techniques to Uncover and Exploit New Markets*. Chicago: Probus.

Ziff, R. (1977). Psychographics for market segmentation. *Journal of Advertising Research, 11*(2), 3–10.

Understanding Ambush Marketing: Implications of Information Processing

Vassilis Dalakas
Berry College

Robert Madrigal
University of Oregon

Rick Burton
University of Oregon

Defined as "a cash and/or in-kind fee paid to a property (typically in sports, arts, entertainment or causes) in return for access to the exploitable commercial potential associated with the property" (Ukman, 1996, p. 1), *sponsorship* is increasingly becoming a popular way for companies to pursue their target consumers. In 1999 alone, companies spent more than $22 billion worldwide; approximately 31% was spent in the United States, 36% in Europe, and 33% in other countries (Meenaghan & O'Sullivan, 2001). Nowadays, most sporting events rely heavily on sponsorship funding. For example, the Atlanta Olympic Games raised $540 million in sponsorship from companies (Speed & Thompson, 2000), and the 2000 Olympic Games in Sydney generated $550 million from the International Olympic Committee's (IOC) 11 worldwide sponsors as well as an additional $315 million from local sponsors (Landler, 2000).

The increased popularity of sponsorship has been accompanied by a marketing tactic referred to as *ambush marketing*. Ambush marketers attempt to associate their brand to a property (an event or organization), without paying the rights fee required for an official sponsorship, in the hopes of tapping into the goodwill or equity associated with that property. Ambushers anticipate that this goodwill will then be transferred to or "rub off" on their brand. At the very least, ambush marketers hope to create confusion regarding the official sponsorship, expecting that consumers will not give credit to those companies, usually competitors, who are in fact official sponsors of the property. Several marketers use ambush marketing to diminish the likely impact of their competitors who are sponsors.

Ambush marketing may take place in a variety of forms. A great deal of controversy surrounds the issue of what exactly constitutes ambushing and how appropriate or ethical such techniques are (Meenaghan, 1994; O'Sullivan & Murphy, 1998). For example, critics of ambush marketing denounce it as an unethical tactic that violates fair business practices and jeopardizes various events by discouraging sponsors from investing in them (Coker, 1996; Payne, 1998). Because ambushing undermines the effectiveness of a sponsorship, potential sponsors tend to view official sponsorship in more skeptical terms. Darby Coker (1996), the director of Marketing Communications of the Atlanta Committee of the Olympic Games (ACOG), labeled ambush marketing as *parasite marketing*, whose net effect is "diluting the value of sponsorship, jeopardizing athlete training and the ability to hold the Olympic Games without government support" (personal interview).

Despite ethical concerns, ambush marketing appears to be a technique commonly used by many companies (Retsky, 1996). The proponents of ambush marketing stress the competitive nature of business as the principal reason for trying to minimize the gains that a competitor is likely to make. Jerry Welsh (Brewer, 1993) clearly communicated the ambushers' point of view when he stated that "this isn't religion or virginity here, it's business. Marketing is a form of warfare, and the ambush is a helluva weapon" (p. 70).

Given that ambush marketing has only recently begun to be investigated in the academic literature (Sandler & Shani, 1989; Shani & Sandler, 1998), there has been relatively little theorizing on how the process may work. Moreover, emphasis has been primarily given to the ethical and legal aspects of the topic (Doust, 1998; O'Sullivan & Murphy, 1998; Payne, 1998; Townley, Harrington, & Couchman, 1998) rather than on theory about consumer processing of ambush marketing attempts. Meenaghan (1994) has stressed the need to establish a research agenda to develop a better understanding of how consumers perceive ambushers and, more importantly, the conditions that determine the effectiveness of sponsorship in general and ambush marketing in particular.

This chapter views sponsorship as a communication vehicle used by companies to enhance or influence brand image. Companies associate their brands with certain properties in the hope that positive attitudes held by their target customers toward the property will be transferred to their brands and, ultimately, influence purchase behavior (Javalgi, Taylor, Gross, & Lampman,

1994). Ambush marketers seek to obtain the same benefits of association without incurring the cost required to legally obtain official sponsorship status. Thus, both official sponsors and ambushers hope to favorably influence consumers' attitudes toward their brand as a result of a perceived association. An underlying assumption, of course, is that consumers do in fact make an association between the brand and the property. Accordingly, for both official sponsors and ambushers, the explicit persuasion attempt being made is to convince customers that an association does in fact exist between their brands and the property.

We view information processing relative to the association between a company and a property in terms of the elaboration likelihood model of persuasion (ELM; Petty & Cacioppo, 1986). We assume that the strength of an attitude toward a company (accrued as a result of a sponsorship or ambushing) depends on the consumer's motivation and ability to process the perceived association between the company and that particular property. Hence, stronger positive attitudes toward the company will result when the consumer actually credits or recognizes that the company is responsible for making a preferred event possible and a logical fit exists between the brand name and the property. In the absence of extended processing, the consumer may only be generally aware of an association between the two and have a favorable attitude toward the company, but this attitude should be relatively weak. Within this theoretical paradigm, the consumer's persuasion knowledge (Friestad & Wright, 1994) relative to the tactic of ambush marketing is proposed as an ability factor that is likely to moderate the consumer's attitude toward an ambush marketer. The chapter concludes with a discussion of managerial implications and suggestions for future research.

THEORETICAL FRAMEWORK

The ELM (Petty & Cacioppo, 1986) suggests that people must have both the motivation and the ability to process a persuasive communication in order for message elaboration to occur. Specifically, the model suggests that a continuum of elaboration exists that is anchored by central route processing at one end and peripheral processing at the other. Motivated individuals with the ability to process a message are more likely to engage in central route processing. Central route processing is characterized by greater levels of information processing. Attitudes formed via the central route tend to be more resistant and persistent in the face of counter-arguments (Haugtvedt & Wegener, 1994). In contrast, peripheral route processing is characterized by

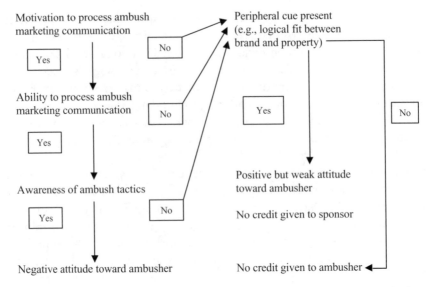

FIG. 15.1.   A modified representation of the Elaboration Likelihood Model to ambush marketing persuasion attempts.

low involvement learning that is dependent on cues in the environment to persuade. As such, attitudes formed as a result of peripheral route processing tend to be weaker and less resistant to change. Along these lines, Figure 15.1 outlines our theoretical framework to better understand the effectiveness of ambush marketing.

Motivation to Process

Motivation's role in information processing has been recognized as important in a number of attitude models (Chaiken, 1987; Fazio, 1990; MacInnis, Moorman, & Jaworski, 1991; Petty & Cacioppo, 1986). Conscious processing tends to predominately influence the cognitive component of attitudes. When processing motivation is low, consumers allocate few cognitive resources to process the message, whereas high processing motivation leads consumers to engage in more effortful message processing (Petty, Cacioppo, & Schumann, 1983). Previous research indicated that consumers often lack the motivation to process information to which they are exposed in a thoughtful or deliberate manner (Kardes, 1994; Wyer & Srull, 1986). Consistent with this premise, studies have indicated that most consumer information processing and learning occurs under conditions of low-involvement (Hawkins & Hoch, 1992). This suggests that, in most cases, consumers will lack the motivation to recognize official sponsorship, let alone differentiate ambushers from official sponsors, which facilitates ambushing efforts. In a study of 1,500 consumers following the conclusion of the 1996 Atlanta Olympic Games, Shani and Sandler (1998) found that consumers exhibited confusion and lack of knowledge about the rights of official sponsors, the different levels of sponsorship, and the commitment to the event that was associated with each sponsorship level.

When consumers lack the motivation to process, they will often rely on peripheral cues to make sense of a communication. The ELM suggests that when motivation or ability to process is low, information processing is likely to follow a peripheral route to persuasion. Attitudes in this case are formed on the basis of simple cues such as the logical match that exists between an endorser and a brand (Kahle & Homer, 1985). Simply put, if the fit between a company and a property appears to be a reasonable match (e.g., lifestyle or attribute congruity), consumers may accept the association at face value (e.g., consumers perception of Nike, an ambusher, as an official sponsor of the 1996 Olympics). Speed and Thompson (2000) found that perceived fit between a sponsor and a sponsored property elicits positive consumer responses to the sponsorship association. Consumers, in this case, engage in a form of processing that reflects an affective rather than a cognitive response, similar to the process of classical conditioning (Janiszewski & Warlop, 1993; Shimp, Stuart, & Engle, 1991). Under this view, in the case of sponsorship, the property is viewed as an unconditioned stimulus that elicits the unconditioned response of positive affect. The brand represents a conditioned stimulus that is paired with the property in the hope of also eliciting a positive affect. Under this mechanism, consumers' reaction to a particular brand would be similar to their reaction to the property itself.

In addition to the unconditioned response that "rubs off" on companies associating with a particular property, ambushers may also benefit from a perceived effort factor (Kirmani, 1990; Kirmani & Wright, 1989). That is, consumers are likely to develop positive attitudes toward a company when they perceive that the company is making a major effort to promote itself. Given that sponsorship of a property can be seen as such an effort, consumers will tend to think more favorably of companies they *perceive* as sponsors of major properties. For example, an IOC tracking study confirmed this. It is revealing that there are extremely positive consumer feelings toward companies that are identified as Olympic sponsors. More than 80% of the consumers surveyed viewed Olympic sponsors as "industry leaders, successful, vital/energetic, dedicated to excellence, and deserving 'my' business" (Coker, 1996, personal interview). Such positive attitudes create a desirable appeal for marketers to construct ambush efforts in order to be associated with the Olympic games.

Ability to Process

In addition to an individual's motivation to process an association between a company and a sponsored property, the ELM recognizes the individual's ability to process the message as another critical factor. Ability entails individual characteristics such as prior experience, knowledge, and familiarity with an issue, but it is also influenced by the message context. Three ability variables are considered here: situation ambiguity, consumer level of arousal, and consumer knowledge of ambushing as a communication tactic.

When processing effort is relatively low, ambiguity in a message context may increase the consumer' vulnerability to misleading claims (Kardes, 1994). Ambiguity describes a situation that has "the potential for multiple interpretations" (Ha & Hoch, 1989). Popular events, such as the Olympic Games, can be quite susceptible to such ambiguity due to the large number of companies competing for consumers' attention. For example, at the Atlanta Olympic Games, there were more than 40 official sponsors and suppliers, a situation that increased the likelihood that consumers wound not be able to recognize the official sponsors. Ambush marketers often use specific strategies to reinforce this ambiguity. For example, a company can sponsor the broadcast of an event without sponsoring the actual event. This is likely to create confusion in regard to who the actual event sponsors are. Similar strategies include sponsoring athletes who participate in the event to the extent that when consumers attend the event, they assume the same company also sponsors the event. Campbell's Soup, a non-sponsor of the 1998 Winter Olympics, used American Olympic skaters Tara Lipinski, Nicole Bobek, and Michelle Kwan in its ads during the 1998 Winter Olympics, leading consumers to perceive Campbell's as an Olympics sponsor (Horovitz, 1998). Nike's case with the 1996 Atlanta Olympics is an illustration of how successful such an approach can be because, according to the press, a large part of the American public perceived (inaccurately) that Nike was an official Olympic sponsor (Coker, 1996, personal interview).

Ambiguity and confusion can also frustrate consumers, and, consequently, they can reduce the likelihood that consumers take the time required to differentiate between official sponsors and ambushers. Therefore, consumers end up developing a sense of apathy toward ambush marketing practices (Shani & Sandler, 1998). In this case, ambiguity does not necessarily help the ambusher directly, but it does nullify the effectiveness of official sponsorship. This means that the ambusher can still benefit by hurting a competitor who is an official sponsor.

A second ability variable that has been found to influence ability to process persuasion attempts is a consumer's level of arousal (Pham, 1996). Given that many consumers are exposed to sponsorship or ambush marketing stimuli *during* sporting events, which may increase their level of arousal, we would expect high arousal to lead to lower elaboration of such information. Very high arousal may impair processing capacity and prevent consumers from processing messages extensively. Consistent with this premise, Pham (1992) found that high arousal among viewers of a sporting event led to lower recognition of the sponsorship stimuli that were projected at the event. In certain cases, ambush marketing can increase the arousal associated with a specific event simply by contributing to the overall excitement. For example, Nike's banners in the Atlanta Olympics may have added to the festive and exciting atmosphere and raised the consumers' arousal level, making it harder for consumers to differentiate between official sponsors and ambushers.

A third ability variable, prior knowledge, also influences a consumer's ability to process a persuasive communication. We propose that consumer reaction to sponsorship and ambush marketing is moderated by the consumers' persuasion knowledge in regard to the tactic of ambush marketing. The Persuasion Knowledge Model (Friestad & Wright, 1994) suggests that people develop and use persuasion knowledge to cope with persuasion attempts. Such knowledge includes what consumers "believe about how to persuade others and what they believe is generally known by others about how to persuade" (Friestad & Wright, 1994, p. 3). Of direct relevance to our discussion regarding awareness of ambush marketing attempts are the following specific components of persuasion knowledge: (a) consumers' beliefs about marketers' tactics, (b) consumers' beliefs about the effectiveness and appropriateness of marketers' tactics, and (c) consumers' beliefs about marketers' persuasion goals and their own coping goals. Hence, a consumer's awareness of ambush marketing as a communication tactic is likely to sensitize him or her to occasions when such a tactic is being used. Moreover, once a consumer is aware of an ambush marketing attempt, his or her beliefs about how appropriate or ethical such a technique is will influence his or her reactions toward the ambusher. However, because of the massive sponsorship efforts during the past few years, there is high clutter, minimizing consumer ability to recognize official sponsors or ambushers and, maybe more importantly, making consumers care less about official sponsorships or the level of sponsorships, such as worldwide sponsor, partner, and so on (Shani & Sandler, 1998).

It has been suggested that consumers have an unfavorable opinion of companies that "do not play fair." For example, senior researcher at Yankelovich Partners, Caplan (1993), noted: "There is a sense that integrity, credibility, and competence are lacking. Consumers are wary of misrepresentation, exaggeration, and hype and are determined to stamp deception out" (p. 1). This is confirmed by the IOC tracking study that showed consumers did not approve of companies getting a free ride. Eighty-four percent of the consumers who were surveyed said their opinion of a company is lowered if they see it as pretending to be an Olympic sponsor (Coker, 1996, personal interview). Other studies, however, indicate less of a consumer concern about ambush marketing and more of a sense of apathy instead (Shani & Sandler, 1998). Believing that someone is intentionally trying to deceive them should lead consumers to have a more negative reaction to the ambusher. Ambush marketing may be seen as an attempt to cheat the sponsored property, the competitors who are official sponsors, or the consumers themselves (which may be of more personal relevance to the consumer). Consumers may have a positive initial reaction toward a company; however, if they find out that the company used a heavy-handed manipulative technique to create that positive reaction, consumers are very likely to change their original position (Cohen & Areni, 1991). This would suggest that knowledge of ambushing as a persuasion tactic moderates consumers' attitudes toward ambush marketers. Specifically, such companies would be viewed negatively if consumers are aware that such a tactic was used.

IMPLICATIONS FOR FUTURE RESEARCH

Ambush marketing is a unique and controversial method of marketing communications that involves four distinct audiences: properties organizations that sell sponsorships, official sponsors, ambushers, and consumers. Properties (e.g., the IOC or the NFL) view the ambushers' actions as opportunities lost. Had the ambusher paid for an official alignment, the property organization would have realized significant revenues. Moreover, by over-saturating the property's market, the presence of an ambusher diminishes the effect of official sponsorships, making it more difficult for the property to service the official sponsors and attract sponsors in the future.

Official sponsors are concerned that their investment becomes less valuable. Because sponsorship is used as a tool for differentiating from competitors and gaining market share, ambushing is very bothersome to official sponsors, especially in competitive industries such as athletic footwear, soft drinks, or affinity credit cards, where a single market share point may be worth tens of millions. For the same reason, investing in ambushing may be both affordable and strategic for an ambusher. Essentially, an ambusher may be less concerned about winning (i.e., eliciting positive consumer attitudes or winning market share) and more concerned about not losing (i.e., preventing competitors from building brand equity and increasing their market share).

We investigated how and why ambush marketing may be effective in regard to consumer processing of ambushing attempts. The conditions that facilitate an ambusher's attempt to form an association with a liked property are low consumer motivation to process, low ability to process, and lack of knowledge of ambush marketing tactics.

Increasing consumer's awareness of ambush marketing as a communication tactic should reduce the possibility that ambush marketing attempts will go undetected. As discussed earlier, consumers have little motivation to process messages and to acquire knowledge about ambushing practices on their own. Thus, in order to minimize ambushing, sponsored parties and official sponsors should take the initiative to educate consumers. The Summer Olympic Games in Atlanta provided an example of how important it was to educate consumers about the official sponsors well before the event took place. The ACOG ran an extensive advertising campaign trying to create awareness about who the official sponsors were in order to increase consumer knowledge about the issue and to enable consumers to recognize any company that would try to gain by an association with the event without being a sponsor (Coker, 1996, personal interview). Potential sponsors should require similar methods of sponsor protection from a property so that the consumers are clearly aware of who the official sponsors are without being confused by ambushers. Moreover, sponsors themselves should communicate their association with the properties, in order to minimize the possibility of ambushing. For example, Coca Cola advertised aggressively its official sponsorship of the 1996 Olympics by spending $300 million on advertising, which may explain why Pepsi, its main competitor, did not try to ambush (Olympic sponsors struggle with clutter, 1996). It may not be unusual for sponsors to spend substantial amounts of money to acquire the rights to sponsor a property but not to spend any additional money on advertising such an association to the consumers, openly inviting their competitors to ambush. In the words of a sponsorship director: "it is like people spend all this money to buy an expensive toy but then they don't want to spend any money to buy the batteries to make the toy run" (Henderson, 2001, personal interview).

Although it is important to inform consumers about ambushing, it is also important for official sponsors to communicate why this particular property is seen as being important. Otherwise, just as ambushing may be seen as a marketing tactic aimed at persuading consumers, so too will official sponsorship be seen as just another marketing tactic engaged to try to convince consumers to buy their products. Moreover, companies should pursue properties that appear to be a good fit for their brands (e.g., a shoe company sponsoring a track event). Consumers are more likely to develop strong positive attitudes toward a sponsor when such a fit exists, whereas they may discard an association, albeit true, where there is no logical fit between the sponsor and the property (Kahle & Homer, 1985; Speed & Thompson, 2000). Along these lines companies should also pursue properties with highly identified fans. Strong identification with the property elicits positive responses to the property's sponsor (Dalakas, Rose, & Aiken, 2001; Madrigal, 2000, 2001). More importantly, fans who deeply care about a property will be more likely to have the motivation to process information regarding who sponsors their beloved property; the high awareness of NASCAR sponsors among NASCAR fans exemplifies this tendency.

Although the awareness of official sponsors may have increased, many consumers may be increasingly less concerned with who is an official sponsor and who is not, due to increased commercialization of numerous properties and aggressive spending by all companies involved. Future research should look further into how ambush marketing may be potentially causing consumer burnout in regard to sponsorships and other marketing communication methods. It is possible that the additional clutter created by ambushers is making consumers less willing to care about sponsor status.

Another issue that needs further investigation relates to the attitude–behavior link. Attitudes formed through central routes are considered to be more predictive of behavior. Under this premise, ambushing may be a high-risk strategy; when consumers have the motivation and ability to process an ambush marketing attempt and are aware of ambush practices, their negative attitude toward the ambusher may have a more noticeable effect on their behavior. Along these lines, future research should examine the extent to which attitudes toward ambushers make consumers intentionally avoid purchasing from these companies. Finally, a topic of interest would be to investigate how individual differences among consumers influence perception of ambushing and reactions toward ambushers. Examining consumers' individual perceptions about cheating and tracing these perceptions to their personal value systems can provide interesting and useful findings.

REFERENCES

Brewer, G. (1993, September). Be like Nike? *Sales and Marketing Management, 145*, 67–74.

Caplan, B. (1993, July). The consumer speaks—Who's listening? *Arthur Andersen Retailing Issues Letter, 5*, 1–5.

Chaiken, S. (1987). The heuristic model of persuasion. In M. P. Zanna, J. M. Olson & C. P. Herman (Eds.), *Social Influence: The Ontario Symposium* (vol. 5, 3–39). Hillsdale, NJ: Lawrence Erlbaum Associates.

Cohen, J. B., & Areni, C. S. (1991). Affect and consumer behavior. In T. S. Robertson & H. H. Kassarjian (Eds.), *Handbook of Consumer Behavior* (pp. 188–240). Englewood Cliffs, NJ: Prentice Hall.

Coker, D. (1996, September 4). Director of marketing communications of the Atlanta Committee of the Olympic Games, personal interview.

Dalakas, V., Rose, G., & Aiken, K. D. (2001). Soft drinks, auto repair, and baseball: Sports fans' perceptions of sponsors and fans' intentions toward the sponsors. In B. Ponsford (Ed.), *Proceedings of the Association of Marketing Theory and Practice Conference* (pp. 114–118).

Doust, D. (1998, July). The ethics of ambush marketing. *The Cyber-Journal of Sport Marketing, 1*, 1–9.

Fazio, R. H. (1990). Multiple processes by which attitudes guide behavior: The MODE model as an integrative framework. In M. P. Zanna (Ed.), *Advances in Experimental Social Psychology* (vol. 23, pp. 75–109). San Diego: Academic Press.

Friestad, M., & Wright, P. (1994, December). The persuasion knowledge model: How people cope with persuasion attempts. *Journal of Consumer Research, 16*, 354–360.

Ha, Y-W., & Hoch, S. J. (1989, June). Ambiguity, processing strategy, and advertising-evidence interactions. *Journal of Consumer Research, 21*, 205–218.

Haugtvedt, C. P., & Wegener, D. T. (1994, June). Message order effects in persuasion: An attitude strength perspective. *Journal of Consumer Research, 21*, 205–218.

Hawkins, S. A., & Hoch, S. J. (1992, September). Low involvement learning: Memory without evaluations. *Journal of Consumer Research, 19*, 212–225.

Henderson, J. (2001, December 2). Sponsorships and event marketing manager, Chick-fil-A, personal interview.

Horovitz, B. (1998, February 1). USA Today, Campbell's skates by; Ads on thin ice with olympics officials p. 3B.

Janiszewski, C., & Warlop, L. (1993, September). The influence of classical conditioning procedures on subsequent attention to the conditional brand. *Journal of Consumer Research, 20*, 171–189.

Javalgi, R. G., Taylor, M. B., Gross, A. C., & Lampman, E. (1994, December). Awareness of sponsorship and corporate image: An empirical investigation. *Journal of Advertising, 23*, 47–58.

Kahle, L. R., & Homer, P. M. (1985, March). Physical attractiveness of the celebrity endorser: A social adaptation perspective. *Journal of Consumer Research, 11*, 954–961.

Kardes, F. R. (1994). Consumer judgment and decision processes. In R. S. Wyer, Jr., & T. K. Srull (Eds.), *Handbook of Social Cognition* (vol. 2, Applications, pp. 399–465). Hillsdale, NJ: Lawrence Erlbaum, Associates.

Kirmani, A. (1990, September). The effect of perceived advertising costs on brand perceptions. *Journal of Consumer Research, 17*, 160–171.

Kirmani, A., & Wright, P. (1989, December). Money talks: Perceived advertising expense and expected product quality. *Journal of Consumer Research, 16*, 344–353.

Landler, M. (2000, September 29). Fighting marketing pirates: Olympics sponsors guard their investments. *The New York Times*. p. C1.

MacInnis, D. J., Moorman, C., & Jaworski, B. J. (1991, October). Enhancing and measuring consumers' motivation, opportunity, and ability to process brand information from ads. *Journal of Marketing, 55*, 32–53.

Madrigal, R. (2000). The influence of social alliances with sports teams on intentions to purchase corporate sponsors' products. *Journal of Advertising, 29*(4), 13–24.

Madrigal, R. (2001). Social identity effects in a belief-attitude-intentions hierarchy: Implications for corporate sponsorship. *Psychology and Marketing, 18*(2), 145–165.

Meenaghan, T. (1994, September/October). Ambush marketing: Immoral or imaginative practice? [point of view]. *Journal of Advertising Research, 34*, 77–88.

Meenaghan, T., & O'Sullivan, P. (2001). The passionate embrace—Consumer response to sponsorship [editorial]. *Psychology and Marketing, 18*(2), 87–94.

O'Sullivan, P., & Murphy, P. (1998, July). Ambush marketing: The ethical issues. *Psychology and Marketing, 15*, 349–366.

Olympic sponsors struggle with clutter; some prevail. (1996, July 22). *IEG Sponsorship Report, 15*, 1, 4–5.

Payne, M. (1998, July). Ambush marketing: The undeserved advantage. *Psychology and Marketing, 15*, 323–331.

Petty, R. E., & Cacioppo, J. T. (1986). The elaboration likelihood model of persuasion. In L. Berkowitz (Ed.), *Advances of Experimental Social Psychology* (vol. 19, pp. 123–205). New York: Academic Press.

Petty, R. E., Cacioppo, J. T., & Schumann, D. (1983, September). Central and peripheral routes to advertising effectiveness: The moderating role of involvement. *Journal of Consumer Research, 10*, 135–146.

Pham, M. T. (1996, March). Cue representation and selection effects of arousal on persuasion. *Journal of Consumer Research, 22*, 373–387.

Pham, M. T. (1992). Effects of involvement, arousal, and pleasure on the recognition of sponsorship stimuli. In J. F. Sherry Jr. & B. Sternthal (Eds.), *Advances in Consumer Research* (vol. 19, pp. 85–93). Provo, UT: Association for Consumer Research.

Retsky, M. L. (1996, July 1). One person's ambush is another's free speech. *Marketing News, 30*, 14.

Sandler, D. M., & Shani, D. (1989, August/September). Olympic sponsorship vs. "ambush marketing": Who gets the gold? *Journal of Advertising Research, 29*, 9–14.

Shani, D., & Sandler, D. M. (1998, July). Ambush marketing: Is confusion to blame for the flickering of the flame? *Psychology and Marketing, 15*, 367–383.

Shimp, T. A., Stuart, E. W., & Engle, R. W. (1991, June). A program of classical conditioning experiments testing variations in the conditioned stimulus and context. *Journal of Consumer Research, 18*, 1–12.

Speed, R., & Thompson, P. (2000). Determinants of sports sponsorship response. *Journal of the Academy of Marketing Science, 28*(2), 226–238.

Townley, S., Harrington, D., & Couchman, N. (1998, July). The legal and practical prevention of ambush marketing in sports. *Psychology and Marketing, 15*, 333–348.

Ukman, L. (1996). *IEG's Complete Guide to Sponsorship: Everything You Need to Know About Sports, Arts, Event, Entertainment and Cause Marketing.* Chicago: IEG, Inc.

Wyer, R. S., Jr., & Srull, T. K. (1986, July). Human cognition in its social context. *Psychological Review, 93*, 322–359.

V

Social Issues and Sports Marketing

Any topic as all-encompassing as sports marketing will inevitably touch on a variety of important societal topics. Sports marketing has been implicated in a vast array of both positive and negative social consequences. This section presents four chapters that deal with aspects of this perspective. Chapter 16 looks at sports and violence in advertising. Chapter 17 considers tobacco-related issues, especially from a Canadian perspective. Chapter 18 considers social marketing and sport. It develops a seven-step program to enhance the effectiveness of social marketing. Chapter 19 looks at the influences of advertising and price versus social factors in shoe and clothing purchase decisions.

16

Aggressive Marketing: Interrogating the Use of Violence in Sport-Related Advertising

Steven J. Jackson
University of Otago

David L. Andrews
University of Maryland

Arguably, few of us would have predicted that marketing and selling sport shoes would become one of the most controversial human rights issues of our times. However, sport shoes now figure prominently within contemporary debates about the advent and attendant effects of global capitalism. Indeed, the politics of transnational production and consumption of sport commodities has resulted in an increasing number of both scholarly critiques and human rights campaigns (Ballinger & Olsson, 1997; Enloe, 1995; Jackson, 1998; Sage, 1999; Shaw, 1999). As a result, we are now in a situation in which global sport companies are engaging in increasingly aggressive marketing and public relations campaigns while a smaller, less powerful, group of critics attempts to challenge and expose the conflict, exploitation, and abuse that serves as the very basis of the success of these transnational corporations (TNCs).

Nike, for example, the world's most successful sport shoe company, now ranks amongst the top 1,000 corporations internationally with gross earnings of about $8.9 billion (www.nike.com, 2003). Employing high profile, international sporting celebrities along with innovative and often controversial advertising campaigns, Nike has developed what could almost be described as a cult following among its consumers and has become the standard by which all other corporate models are compared (Goldman & Papson, 1998). Yet, Nike has also been the subject of criticism on many fronts including, first and foremost, its unashamed and unapolegetic exploitation of developing nation labor in Korea, Taiwan, Thailand, Vietnam, Indonesia, and China (Brubaker, 1991; Enloe, 1995; Sage, 1999); the corruption and monopolization of youth and high school sport in America, and the use of advertising that reinforces sexist (Cole & Hribar, 1995) and racist (Cole, 1996; McKay, 1995) stereotypes. It is the advertising campaigns of Nike and several other sport companies that have been the subject of intense global scrutiny by scholars, policymakers, and others concerned with human rights. One of the most recent concerns about the nature of sport advertising focuses on the issue of *violence* (Jackson, 1998).

This chapter examines two increasingly interrelated realms of popular culture, namely sport and advertising, with a focus on the problem of violence which is, or is becoming, naturalized within both. The study of advertising in general is important because as Leiss, Kline, and Jhally (1990) note, "ads are not only about selling, for they operate in a social context and have social effects" (p. 387). Thus, we must try to sift out those aspects of advertising practice that have potentially negative social effects, including conflict and violence, and seek to address them as precisely as possible.

Here, we provide a preliminary analysis of the intersection of sport, media, advertising, and violence/aggression in order to explore the implications of a capitalist consumer culture that appropriates violence in order to sell commodities. Specifically, we do the following:

1. Briefly describe the contemporary context of media violence and the significance of sport as a site of analysis.
2. Discuss the social significance of advertising.
3. Highlight the significance of the sport violence–advertising link.
4. Provide examples of the different ways in which sport violence is used in advertisements.
5. Illustrate how certain global sporting ads are being challenged and resisted within a specific local context.
6. Conclude with a few questions that we hope will stimulate future research.

Throughout the analysis we attempt to examine the parallel rhetoric and discourses of violence/aggression within both sports' and capitalisms' armatures of marketing and advertising.

CONTEXT OF VIOLENCE IN THE MEDIA

Over the past 30 years, there has been increasing concern directed at the media's role in producing and representing violence (Barker & Petley, 2001; Carter & Weaver, 2003; Dyson, 2000; Hamilton, 1998). Judging by its near-global focus with respect to both popular deliberations and state policy debates, violence is arguably the media industry's primary public relations problem. Indeed, the international growth and formal organization of anti-media violence watchdogs could justifiably be called a social movement. Critics of media violence, citing predominantly behaviorist-centerd research that they have been fairly successful in lobbying into scientific proof in support of their agenda, charge that there are strong direct, or at least indirect, effects of televisual violence (Eron, 1993, 1995; Huesmann & Eron, 1986). The result, they argue, are declining morals, desensitized audiences, and ultimately escalating levels of conflict and violence in society.

For the most part, concerns about violence have been directed at the potential effects that the largely, but not exclusively, American-produced cartoons (e.g., *Power Rangers*), movies (e.g., *Natural Born Killers, Pulp Fiction*), dramas, and real life programs (e.g., *Cops*) have on audiences, especially children. Strikingly, few studies have directly focused on the potential impact that mediated sport violence has on audiences (Goldstein, 1983). This is surprising given the dramatic influence that sport has been suggested to have on the development of important cultural values. Moreover, the lack of research in the area of sport when compared to other forms of televisual violence appears conspicuous given that it is the *degree of reality* that appears to be a key feature of whether or not violence is likely to be modeled or copied (Young & Smith, 1989). Several factors that enhance the degree of reality with respect to reproducing aggression have been identified, including the novelty or uniqueness of the act, how realistically the act is presented, whether it appears justified, if the model is prestigious, whether or not the model is rewarded (or goes unpunished), whether observers perceive they will be rewarded for the same behavior, and when the physical and social environments portrayed are similar to those later encountered (Baron, 1977). Arguably, sport and its value system, along with the media-manufactured heroes who serve as its exemplars, embody many of these features. Thus, there may be a legitimate basis for concern given that in a relative sense, the pain and injury inflicted on victims of sports violence have tangible moral, legal, and physical consequences. Within the context of advertising, the symbolic representation of violence by athletes in TV commercials may be more powerful than other mediated expressions of violence because audiences are aware that these role models have, in some instances, demonstrated *real* violence on the field, on the court, or in the rink with corresponding real consequences (real blood, real injury, real suffering, and so on). In fact, one could argue that it is the real violence on the playing field that, to some extent, gives athletes (e.g., National Basketball Association [NBA] star Denis Rodman or boxing's Mike Tyson) their capital currency as symbolic violent perpetrators in the first place.

The *degree of reality* may be the most important factor but there are certainly others that justify sport as a site for the analysis of violence. For example, it is important for us to recognize its historically legitimated context for the expression of a dominant physical masculinity (Kaufman, 1987; Messner, 1990, 1992a, 1992b), the halo effect surrounding sport as an arena entrusted for the transmission of positive social values, the prominent but misguided theories concerning sports' cathartic function for the channelling of undesirable aggressive tendencies, and the perennial reproduction of the war-sport-aggression trilogy.

Thus, sport in and of itself is an important site for the study of violence. However, it is equally important to acknowledge that sport, at least elite media-produced sport, has become an entertainment commodity. As such, it is subject to the same market and capitalist accumulation forces facing other *products*, including the need to attract and continually expand the size of its audience or consumer base. In order to attract and maintain their audience, the sport industry, in conjunction with its many corporate alliances, has developed innovative marketing and advertising campaigns. As a result, sporting contests have become multidimensional entertainment and merchandising events, where the specific commodity being sold is increasingly difficult to identify. One particular feature that not only is highlighted but also has become a naturalized feature of some sporting events is conflict and violence. The very rules of sporting codes such as boxing, ice hockey, football, and rugby legitimize the idea that conflict is resolved through the demonstration of physical superiority, often expressed through violence and aggression. Moreover, what is startling are the similarities between the dominant themes associated with certain sports and the discourses of aggression and violence employed within capitalism's armatures of advertising and marketing. Consider the following newspaper headlines that effectively illustrate how the very competition between rival athletic footwear companies is defined by the media through discourses of conflict, war, and aggression (emphasis added).

Campaign for British Knights to Escalate Sneaker Wars (Foltz, 1991)
Shoe Businesses' Star-Studded Sneaker War (Yorks, 1990)
Reebok Fights to Be No. 1 Again (Foltz, 1992)

Rivals' Ads Hammer Nike (Magiera & Sloan, 1991)
Nike's Olympian Trademark Fight (1992).

Seemingly, discourses of conflict, war, sport, and masculinity have become
the language of postmodern capitalism. This is evident in the perspective of
powerful individuals such as Nike's CEO, Phil Knight, who readily admits
that he views competition with Reebok as *war without bullets*. This point is
reinforced in Nike's Principles, better known as The 10 Commandments,
which, among other things, informs its employees that "We're on *offense*.
All the time, Perfect Results Count—Not a perfect process. Break the rules;
fight the law; This is as much about *battle* as about business" (Branded; Nike
documentary, BBC, 1996).

In light of these examples, perhaps we should not be too surprised that
aggressive and violent themes and imagery are translated into sport advertising campaigns. Maybe this is why Nike and other companies are able
to employ particular athletes known for their aggressive styles (e.g., Eric
Cantona, Nike; Denis Rodman, Converse; Shawn "Kamikaze" Kemp, Reebok)
without much public concern. In effect, they are utilizing (exploiting) the socially acceptable space of sport as an arena within which to engage in what
Goldman and Papson (1996) referred to as *sign wars* with their corporate
opponents, simultaneously reproducing the link between sport and violence,
violence and masculinity, and, finally, sport and capitalism.

Before turning to a discussion about the social significance of advertising,
we would like to make one brief point about the popular use of the term
aggression. Increasingly, the word *aggression* has become a taken-for-granted
feature in many areas of life, including war (e.g., military aggression), interpersonal conflict (e.g., individuals are often said to have aggressive tendencies),
medicine (e.g., treating an injury or disease aggressively), and the economy
(e.g., aggressive marketing). Arguably, given that the concept is interpreted
in both positive and negative ways, it "may already be lost in terms of any
ideological struggle over meaning" (Jackson, 1993, p. 10). This is one reason
why we have refrained from attempting to provide precise, distinguishing
definitions of the concepts aggression and violence.

THE SOCIAL SIGNIFICANCE OF ADVERTISING

Advertising has become the cornerstone of postindustrial, postmodern, promotional culture (Leiss, Kline, & Jhally, 1990). From the economic standpoint
of production, it is estimated that advertising and associated sales activities

now constitute about 60% of some corporate budgets. In the United States, for example, total advertising is estimated to be about $125 billion per year, which translates into about 4% of the total gross national product (Harms & Kellner, 1991). In addition, demonstrating the overall economic significance of, and the need to examine production and consumption in tandem rather than in isolation, the cost of advertising is, in most cases, passed on to consumers. This occurs both directly through higher prices and indirectly through the tax deductions that corporations receive. Despite these economic implications, it is important to understand some of the broader social changes that have occurred in advertising, particularly with respect to the relationship between consumers and the commodities they buy (Best, 1989; Jhally, 1987).

Historically, as our relationship with objects or commodities has shifted from use value to exchange value to surplus value and now sign or symbolic value, the role of advertising has also changed. Once serving to simply create consumer awareness about product availability and function, advertising, as part of our mediated, image-based culture, now plays a symbolic role where "individuals depend on it for meaning—a source of social information embedded in commodities that mediate interpersonal relations and personal identity" (Harms & Kellner, 1991, p. 45). Evidence of the cultural significance of advertising is demonstrated by the fact that some advertisements cost more to produce than the TV programs they sponsor. Further evidence of this significance is manifest through the rising number of TV programs whose sole focus is advertisements such as *Jaspar Carrot on Commercials*, *World's Funniest Commercials*, and *World's Naughtiest Commercials*. Such is the pervasiveness and transparency of advertising within contemporary popular culture that it is taken for granted and often indistinguishable from other media consumption. As Robert Goldman in his book Reading Ads Socially (1992) noted, "Advertisements saturate our everyday lives. . . . Yet, because ads are so pervasive and our reading of them so routine, we tend to take for granted the deep social assumptions embedded in advertisements. We do not ordinarily recognize advertising as a sphere of ideology" (p. 1).

Conceptualizing advertising as a sphere of ideology provides us with a more powerful framework for analyzing the links between particular social problems and the discourses that represent, reproduce, and resist them. Indeed, we can think about ads as ideological discourses that do the following (Goldman & Papson, 1996):

1. Socially and culturally construct our world
2. Disguise and suppress inequalities, injustices, irrationalities, and contradictions

3. Promote a normative vision of our world and our relationships
4. Reflect the logic of capitalism

All of these ideological discourses can be directly or indirectly linked to con-flict and violence. Moreover, shifts in the philosophy and strategies of the contemporary advertising industry are making formerly taboo aspects of cul-ture, such as violence, more acceptable (Beckett, 1991). As Goldman and Papson (1996, pp. v–vi) noted:

> At every turn, the pressure is on to find fresher, more desirable, and more spectacular images to enhance the value of products. . . . As sign value compe-titions intensify, advertisers invent new strategies and push into fresh cultural territory, looking for uncut and untouched signs. Under such circumstances no meaning system is sacred, because the realm of culture has been turned into a giant mine.

Arguably, one of the new strategies is the appropriation and exploitation of violence. In the sneaker wars, where it was once the bigger the sport celebrity the greater the sign value, the times have changed. Whereas sport companies once tended to focus on a few dominant individuals such as Michael Jordan, Joe Montana, and Wayne Gretzky who epitomized the image of the healthy, wholesome celebrity athlete, shifts in demographics and market trends have forced advertisers to find new avenues to reach their target audience. Enter Denis Rodman, Eric Cantona, Charles Barkley, and others who offer a point of difference that challenges dominant notions of the ideal athlete. Sometimes this is achieved through physical appearance, such as Denis Rodman's revolv-ing rainbow of hair colors, body piercings, tattoos, and clothing, including one public appearance in a wedding gown. Another example is NBA star Charles Barkley's campaign in which he proclaimed, "I am not a role model," which not only inverts the popular link between sporting heroes and youth but also indirectly opens up potential spaces for less than desirable behavior on the part of star athletes. Finally, it appears as if advertisers are making deliberate use of athletes, including those just named, who are often at the center of controversy and conflict and who tend to exhibit an aggressive, sometimes violent image.

At this point we provide a few specific examples in order to demonstrate the various ways in which violence is used in advertising. To date, several cate-gories have been identified that provide a very basic framework through which to classify and understand the diverse ways in which violence is being used in contemporary sport advertising. Among these categories are the following:

1. Use of violence in the promotion of specific sports and/or sporting events (e.g., Australian Rugby League's State of Origin, State of Conflict, State of War or Super League's When Two Tribes Go to War campaign)
2. Commercial videos that provide edited and commodified violence (e.g., former National Hockey League coach Don Cherry's Rock 'em Sock 'em series, which now boasts 15 volumes)
3. Humour
4. Morality plays: good vs. evil
5. Appropriation of culturally sensitive themes
6. Social construction of masculinity (e.g., Budweiser beer's *The Enforcer* and Russell Athletic Wear's *Dressed to Kill*)

To be clear from the outset, this is a preliminary outline and although specific categories are named, there is considerable overlap. For purposes of illustration, we provide a more detailed description of two of these categories: humour and morality plays. In turn, we describe and discuss the politics and contradictions of national broadcast policy with respect to the censorship of violence in advertisements. The intention is to demonstrate how *global* advertisements face *local* resistance. Specifically, we refer to a Reebok shoe commercial that was censored and banned from New Zealand TV due to excessive violence. A brief description and critical analysis of each example follows.

CASE 1: WILSON SPORTING GOODS ADVERTISEMENT

In actual fact, this advertisement is a combination of both humor and a moral message. The commercial is for Wilson Sporting Goods, although it does not identify any specific product. The setting is somewhat ambiguous but appears to be during the era of Genghis Khan. The scene opens with the images and sounds of soldier's shields being beaten in rhythm as men, women, and children scatter in confusion and fear. As the camera pans back we can see the battle lines being drawn between a large military force, displaying swords, axes, spears, and shields on one side and what appears to be a band of poorly armed villagers on the other. Standing in front of the fierce military unit is a gigantic, bearded and fierce-looking man (presumably the leader) who is wearing a helmet and types of ancient body armour. As he walks toward the intimidated villagers he bellows out:

"Art thou cowering dogs?"
"Is there not one among thee who is a man?"

After a brief silence a young boy pushes his way forward from the back of the crowd of villagers. Upon seeing the would-be challenger, the titan of a leader begins to laugh uncontrollably. However, during the laugher the young boy pulls out a sling-shot and eventually hurls an object that enters the titan's mouth and chokes him to death. The stunned crowd then watches as the boy approaches his victim to retrieve his lethal weapon. As he opens his hand we see a rock with a large "W" representing the Wilson trademark. As the former picture fades, text and a voice-over emerge: "Wilson: The right equipment makes the difference."

In many respects, this ad is constructed around the classic David versus Goliath story. The audience is positioned to immediately despise the oversized, aggressive giant who represents evil while finding sympathy for the young challenger who represents good. In this case, violence is justified because it is used for altruistic purposes, namely, to combat evil. Moreover, humour is invoked by inserting a contemporary marketing logo, an imprinted "W" on an ancient lethal projectile, the stone that kills the giant. One way of interpreting this advertisement is that violence is permissible if it is justified and it can be justified if it is directed at those we consider to be the enemy.

CASE STUDY 2: NIKE'S *GOOD AND EVIL* AD

This ad features a team consisting of some of the world's most famous soccer players including Ronaldo, Maldini, Campos, Wright, Brolin, Kluivert, Costa, and Cantona. The setting is an ancient coliseum or amphitheater that suddenly turns dark as the moon eclipses the sun. Simultaneously, a voice-over begins: "And on that day a dark warrior rose to earth ... to destroy the beautiful game." This is followed by the stamping of a hoof, which sets off a fire as the audience gets a glimpse of an angry, horned, devil-looking character. At this point, what appears to be a piece of raw flesh is thrown onto the dirt playing field and the game begins. It is quickly evident that the team of famous soccer stars represents the *good* team that faces a squad of masked satanic apostles who represent the *evil* team seemingly led by Satan himself. The initial part of the game sees the evil team completely dominating the good team by using illegal and punishing forms of violence such as charging and kicking. However, just as it appears as if evil will triumph, the good team rebounds to take control. Various camera shots ensue, featuring a vast array of superior ball handling skills. Finally, the ball is trapped by Eric Cantona, the Nike swoosh clearly displayed on his boots. As he looks at the Satan-like figure, who is now playing goalkeeper, he says "au revoir." Then, with a powerful kick, he drives the ball through the evil figure causing it to explode. Suddenly the eclipse begins to clear and Nike's trademark "Just do it" slogan appears on the screen.

Without going into too much detail, there is considerable religious symbolism displayed in this ad in order to establish the fact that good must triumph over evil. Not unlike the previous Wilson Sporting Goods ad, it would appear that Nike is using forms of conflict, aggression, and violence as a means to promote its brand. Likewise, similar to the Wilson commercial, there is an implied message that violence is an integral part of sport and given that all of the characters featured appear to be male, the link to a dominant form of masculinity is reinforced. However, just as important is the fact that violence is sanctioned as long as it is justified. In this case, it is justified through both retaliation and in the struggle of good over evil. Because many sporting contests are constructed and promoted within the context of conflict, war, and animosity, the rationalization for the use of violence is facilitated.

There are several seemingly inherent contradictions within the ad itself. For example, France's Eric Cantona who, at the time, played for Manchester United, is represented as the saviour for the good team. However, it seems somewhat hypocritical to cast Cantona as the champion of evil given that he has been reprimanded and even banned for his violent sporting outbreaks, the most famous incident being the game at Selhurst Park during which he leapt into the stands to kick a spectator. No doubt Nike and its advertising agency were using Cantona intentionally, but what kind of message does this send to a young audience? According to the ad's creative director David Helm, "We set it up as fantasy . . . I don't think kids are going to be out there kicking each other in the stomach because of it (Whittle, 1996). Helm may be right. On other hand he may be wrong. Should the media err on the side of conservatism or expand and endorse the range of cultural themes and artefacts available for appropriation in the name of capitalism?

The Wilson Sporting Goods and Nike good versus evil commercials are only two examples from a growing list of ads that are using violent and aggressive themes, images, and narratives as part of their campaign. It would seem that there are no barriers or boundaries concerning the exploitation of our cultural terrain. However, this does not mean that the viewing public have no means to challenge or resist. Most nations have established some form of public policy to address the issue of violence on TV. Unfortunately, advancing global televisual technology, for example, the use of satellite and digital transmission, makes it increasingly difficult to monitor the ever-expanding availability of potentially harmful material. Likewise, the specific area of advertising is often left to some form of industry self-regulation, thus providing for less scrutiny and control.

At this point, we focus on the problems we have presented and how they are being dealt with in one particular context, namely, New Zealand. Specifically, we focus on how a national advisory body in New Zealand challenged and eventually banned one sporting advertisement for Reebok shoes because of excessive violence.

To begin, it may be useful to provide a brief overview of the context within which advertising regulation occurs within New Zealand. There are two basic phases to the review process. The first phase requires that before being aired, all TV ads must initially be screened and rated by the Television Commercials Approvals Board (TVCAB). The TVCAB auditions and accepts approximately 11,000 commercials annually, which are in turn classified for specific viewing times. However, despite this safeguard, there is a second phase that allows any member of the public to lodge a complaint if he or she feels that an advertisement breaches the *Advertising Codes of Practice* (1995).

With respect to violence, there are two relevant codes: number 4, Decency and number 5, Honesty.

The code for decency states: "Advertisements shall not contain statements or visual presentations which clearly offend against prevailing standards of decency or cause undue offence to the community or to a significant section of the community" (p. 14).

The code for honesty states: "Advertisements must be framed so as not to abuse the trust of the consumer or exploit his/her lack of experience or knowledge" and, more specifically, "Advertisements must not contain anything which lends support to acts of violence" (p. 14). As a matter of interest, in the past 5 years, at least five sport-related advertisements have been banned due to public complaints, including companies such as Nike, Reebok, and Lynx (Grainger & Jackson, 1999, 2000). What follows is an overview of how one particular Reebok advertisement was challenged, in this case by the TVCAB.

CASE STUDY 3: REEBOK SHAWN KEMP KAMIKAZE AD

In 1995, Reebok submitted an advertisement to the TVCAB, an agency established to review all advertisements before public screening. The commercial was rejected by the TVCAB before it ever went to air, hence, there was no official complaint made, nor the need for an Advertising Standards Complaints Board (ASCB) hearing. Nevertheless, the commercial gained considerable publicity, including a focused discussion led by TV3's Bill Ralston during his dedicated segment of the evening news.

In brief, the ad features a one-on-one game of basketball between the NBA's Shawn Kemp and an animated, high-tech, grim-reaper figure who challenges opponents by warning: "Only those with superhuman ability may enter my court." Kemp takes up the challenge, stating: "I've got next," which results in the hooded skeleton-figure transforming into a warrior. A physical contest ensues and Kemp, with the aid of his Reebok Kamikaze basketball shoes, drives hard to the basket emitting what has been described as a primal scream, causing the warrior to explode.

The TVCAB ruled that the ad contained excessive and gratuitous violence. The official TVCAB transcript was not available for this case. However, the basis of the decision-making process can be surmised by piecing together various publicly recorded media reports and discussions on the subject. For example, in an official memorandum to Reebok (NZ) Ltd.'s advertising agency MOJO, TVCAB's executive director, Winston Richards, explained:

> Our view, consistent with our previous decisions and with relevant determinations of the Advertising Standards and Complaints Board, is that the level of aggression and violence are totally unacceptable in an advertisement for sports shoes.... the basic concept of a shoe advertisement which turns basketball into a battle is likely to be unduly offensive to a significant section of the community.... and therefore amendments to this advertisement are unlikely to make it acceptable. (Reebok commercial banned in New Zealand, 1995, p. 1)

According to Reebok's marketing manager, Jeremy O'Rourke, the ad simply combines two popular teenage activities, basketball and video games, and translates these through Shawn Kemp's *kamikaze* style of play in order to reach their intended target market. But, this argument did not sway the TVCAB. For example, during his appearance on *TV3's Ralston* program, Winston Richards countered Reebok's O'Rourke:

> Basketball is theoretically a non-contact sport... it doesn't really matter that the character is computer generated... the key is the violence... it does carry the standard techniques for enhancing violence in cinematic-type terms... it has all the elements of enhanced violence through sound effects and the obscured activity where you're not quite sure what happens. (Ralston, TV3 News, 1995)

According to Richards, the fact that the violence in the advertisement is part of a fantasy competition between a sport hero and an animated video character is largely irrelevant. The banning of the ad, or more accurately the refusal to approve it for airing, was clearly a shock to Reebok. In the words of Reebok (NZ) Ltd. general manager Ian Fulton, he was "staggered" (Reebok commercial banned in New Zealand, 1995). Reebok had invested a lot of time and energy into the Kamikaze campaign, and posters, based on the TV commercial, were already in circulation in sport stores and on the streets. In Fulton's words: "It is painful to see this work go to waste because of the television ban" (Reebok commercial banned in New Zealand, 1995, p. 2).

There are several interesting features surrounding the banning of this ad. First, although it is not stated in the official memorandum sent to Reebok, statements by the TVCAB's executive director, Winston Richards, in newspaper and TV interviews, allude to the American source of the violence in advertising production. For example, he stated: "There seems to be a trend over the past couple of years, originating in America, to have increasingly violent and aggressive sport-shoe commercials and in our view they are inappropriate" (Sport shoe advert ban stuns Reebok, 1995, p. 7). Later, when challenged with the fact that the same advertisement was playing successfully in almost every other Reebok market, Richards replied:

> It is an American commercial that is certainly played in America and Australia. But we are more conservative when it comes to violence than America, and quite properly so in my view, and more conservative than Australia, and that is quite clearly spelled out in Complaints Board decisions (TV3's *Ralston*, 1995).

Richards not only targeted America as the source of the violence within advertising but also made it clear that New Zealand is different from both the United States and Australia with respect to local policy on the problem. Here, Richards employed the term *conservative* to connote a national censorship policy.

A second notable feature of the Reebok Kamikaze ban is that it received considerable attention within both local and international media. In fact, there were a number of local newspaper articles referring to how the case was being reported overseas. The local concern for the global media coverage of the Reebok case can be interpreted in at least two ways. On the one hand, it is an indication of New Zealand's "Davey versus Goliath" attitude toward challenging American and other multinationals and asserting its local culture and identity (perhaps reminiscent of its anti-nuclear stance against the United States in the 1970s and 1980s). On the other hand, these media reports could be interpreted as subtle critiques of New Zealand conservatism, which could potentially impede international trade links and the advancement of the local economy. In short, there was an apparent fear within some sectors that New Zealand would gain a reputation for being overly resistant, indeed, bordering on paranoid, to global economic development (Goll, 1995). The basis of this fear was confirmed by the fact that the Reebok case was linked to other recent bans of non–sport-related advertisements in New Zealand. For example, Goll (1995:1) in an *Asian Wall Street Journal* article titled "New Zealand bans Reebok, other ads it deems politically incorrect for TV," discussed the recent banning of Coca-Cola Co., Bayerische Motoren Werke AG (BMW), and Chanel SA ads.

Third and finally, it would be neglectful to completely ignore the issue of race, given that Shawn Kemp is black. In brief, we simply posit the question of whether or not there is any possibility of a global/local disjuncture within the context of racialized sporting others in New Zealand. At this point, it seems premature to make any conclusive statements. Indeed, there is some evidence to suggest that black athletes, as well as musicians and other popular culture icons, are fixtures of fascination among New Zealand youth (Allison, 1991; Lealand, 1994). A couple of studies, for example, have examined the popular presence of American sporting culture in general and Michael Jordan in particular in New Zealand (Andrews, Jackson, Carrington, & Mazur, 1996; Jackson & Andrews, 1996, 1999). These authors have suggested that in addition to being attracted to their extraordinary athletic talent, New Zealand youth are fascinated with the excitement and *difference* offered by American culture. Moreover, the identification of Maori and Polynesian youth in New Zealand may have another dimension. As Wilcox (1996: 123) noted:

> Maori and Polynesian youth . . . tend to identify with the music, dress, and styles of their African-American counterparts [where] they find . . . a focal point of re-sistance, a means of challenging the hegemony of New Zealand's overwhelm-ingly white power structure through membership in a transnational tribe.

Thus, identification with what they perceive to be their oppressed, trans-Pacific brothers and sisters may be exhibited through consumption of American popular culture, but it may also reflect a more serious agenda of racial politics. Perhaps it is this "black sporting Pacific" that is contribut-ing to unfounded and irrational fears among particular factions within the New Zealand community. For example, it may be that concerns about Amer-ican televisual violence may be exacerbated by local articulations of street gang culture and perceived rising levels of violence in general. That is, local censorship could be interpreted as a form of resistance against threatening im-ages of America, constructed through the intersection of sport, technology, and commodified images of violence and racial otherness. Obviously, further research is necessary in order to more fully understand the potential link between local media censorship and the perceived threat of racialized others within sport and other advertising campaigns. The Reebok Kamikaze case study is complex, particularly in light of the fact that it received so much publicity and was linked to much wider issues about cultural and racial politics in New Zealand.

DISCUSSION: VIOLENCE IN ADVERTISING

No doubt advertising agencies and those whom they represent give careful thought to the use of violence especially given the potential backlash and public relations nightmare that could result. As previously noted, the current climate appears to propel and condone an accelerated use of controversial ad campaigns including those appropriating violence. This is in addition to the already overwhelming number of ads that use violence indirectly through the construction and confirmation of dominant forms of masculinity. By drawing on dominant masculine images and hegemonies, advertisers can easily appropriate and articulate a wide range of themes that confirm male identity, physicality, and aggression. Moreover, these ads contribute to the naturalization of sport as a site of conflict and violence/aggression as acceptable means of conflict resolution.

The debate about the effects of televisual violence will no doubt continue. Hopefully, future debates will be informed by research, which accounts for the complexity of violence in terms of both how it is defined and expressed. Likewise, as this analysis has tried to suggest, it is important that future research interrogate the diverse ways in which violence is being represented and reproduced in all areas of social life, including the popular cultural realm of advertising. As Joseph Turkow argued: "With budgets that add up to hundreds of billions of dollars, the industry exceeds the church and the school in its ability to promote images about our place in society—where we belong, why, and how we should act towards others" (1997, p. 2). If Turkow is even partially correct, advertising's role in contributing to conflict and violence certainly bears scrutiny.

CONCLUSION

Advertising as a privileged form of discourse provides a cultural kaleidoscope through which we can examine social relations, the construction and confirmation of identities, and the appropriation of increasingly shocking and controversial themes, through which the logic and power relations of capitalism are negotiated and reproduced.

The use of violence in advertising may be a phase that the industry is going through, but given that advertising draws on cultural themes and artefacts constitutive of everyday life, it should not be trivialized or ignored. Nor should we overlook the contradictory framework within which violence is reproduced through mediated sport, including advertising. On the one hand the media may use violence in sport as a means of attracting audiences who are then sold to advertisers. On the other hand, particular institutional segments of the media may criticize violence that, in fact, they themselves are producing.

To further highlight the complexity and incestuous nature of the sport–media–advertising relationship, it is important to recognize that the media are supported by advertisers who have an increasingly central role in owning the sporting events, stadiums, players, and networks through which their products are represented and circulated. As such, advertising reveals that violence can be "contained within a strategic, yet contradictory framework" (Jackson, 1993, p. 11). In light of the fact that this is a preliminary analysis, we conclude by offering a set of questions that will hopefully stimulate future research.

1. Historically, at what point, and as a consequence of what social forces, did contemporary advertising begin to appropriate violence as a means of selling commodities?

2. To what extent does the need to use violence to sell commodities impact on (a) its consumers, and, (b) cultural values both within and outside of sport.

3. To what extent is the culture of violence articulated to the ideology of postmodern capitalism in order to legitimize its strategy for efficiency, productivity, and profit.

4. How is the culture of commodified violence articulated to various identities: national, gender, racial or ethnic? Consider, for example, the 1996 Michael Johnson Nike ad whose narrative stated: "there are two sides to every sprinter, the side that leaves his opponent blue and lifeless by the side of the track, and the other, *darker* side."

5. What is the global/local nexus of violent advertisements: (a) how are American companies able to use their exaggerated portrayals of authentic American culture and identity (e.g., through violent images of black athletes) to appeal to foreign markets, and, alternatively, (b) how do local broadcasting codes censor global (American) violent products, such as cases of disjuncture?

6. What is the basis of advertisers' decisions to use controversial and potentially alienating campaigns featuring themes of violence.

REFERENCES

Advertising Codes of Practice. Advertising Standards Authority: Wellington, New Zealand.

Allison, P. (1991). Big Macs and baseball caps.: The Americanisation of Auckland. *Metro, 124,* 124–130.

Andrews, D. L., Jackson, S. J., Carrington, B., & Mazur, Z. (1996). Global Jordanscapes: The place of American sport culture within national populist imaginaries. *Sociology of Sport Journal, 13,* 428–457.

Ballinger, J., & Olsson, C. (1997). *Behind the Swoosh: The Struggle of Indonesians Making Nike Shoes.* Uppsula: Sweden. Global Publications Foundation.

Barker, M., & Petley, J. (2001). *Ill Effects: The Media Violence Debate.* London, U.K.: Routledge.

Baron, R. A. (1977). *Human Aggression.* New York: Plenum.

Beckett, J. (1991, October 14). Controversial ads are sometimes most effective. *San Francisco Chronicle,* p. B3.

Best, S. (1989). The commodification of reality and the reality of commodifications. *Current Perspectives in Social Theory, 9,* 23–51.

'Branded' (1996). Nike Documentary, BBC Television, Producer: Peter Swain.

Brubaker, B. (1991, March 10). The sneaker phenomenon, part 1 of 2: Athletic shoes: Beyond big business; industry has a foothold on defining social values. *Washington Post,* p. A1.

Carter, C., & Weaver, K. (2003). *Violence and the Media.* Milton Keynes, U.K.: Open University Press.

Cole, C. (1996, April). P.L.A.Y., Nike and Michael Jordan: National fantasy and the racialization of crime and punishment. *Working Papers in Sport and Leisure Commerce.* Memphis: University of Memphis.

Cole, C., & Hribar, A. (1995). Celebrity feminism: Nike style post-Fordism, transcendence and consumer power. *Sociology of Sport Journal, 12,* 347–369.

Dyson, R. (2000). *Mind Abuse: Media Violence in an Information Age.* New York: Black Rose Books.

Enloe, C. (1995, March/April). The globetrotting sneaker. *Ms.* 10–15.

Eron, L. (1995). Media violence. *Pediatric Annals, 24*(2), 1–3.

Eron, L. (1993, summer). No doubt about it, media violence affects behavior. *Media and Values, 64,* 14.

Foltz, K. (1991, February 20). Campaign for British Knights to escalate sneaker wars. *New York Times,* p. D17.

Foltz, K. (1992, March 12). Reebok fights to be No. 1 again. *New York Times,* pp. C1, C3.

Goldman, R. (1992). *Reading Ads Socially.* London: Routledge.

Goldman, R., & Papson, S. (1998). *Nike Culture.* London: Sage.

Goldman, R., & Papson, S. (1996). *Sign Wars.* New York: Guilford Press.

Goldstein, J. (Ed.). (1983). *Sports Violence.* New York: Springer-Verlag.

Goll, S. D. (1995, July 24). New Zealand bans Reebok, other ads it deems politically incorrect for TV, *Asian Wall Street Journal,* p. 1.

Grainger, A., & Jackson, S. (1999). Resisting the swoosh in the land of the long white cloud. *Peace Review, 11*(4), 511–516.

Grainger, A., & Jackson, S. (2000). Sports marketing and the challenges of globalization: A case study of cultural resistance in New Zealand. *International Journal of Sports Marketing and Sponsorship, 2*(2), 111–125.

Hamilton, J. (1998). *Channeling Violence: The Economic Market for Violent Television Programming.* Princeton: Princeton University Press.

Harms, J., & Kellner, D. (1991) Critical theory and advertising. *Current Perspectives in Social Theory, 11,* 41–67.

Huesmann, R., & Eron, L. (1986). *Television and the Aggressive Child: A Cross-National Comparison.* Hillsdale, NJ: Lawrence Erlbaum Associates.

Jackson, S. J. (1993). Beauty and the beast: A critical look at sports violence. *Journal of Physical Education New Zealand, 26*(4), 9–13.

Jackson, S. J. (1998). Doing a little sole searching: Critical reflections on Nike and globalisation. *Journal of Physical Education New Zealand, 31*(1), 14–17.

Jackson, S. J., & Andrews, D. L. (1996). Excavating the (Trans) National Basketball Association: Locating the global/local nexus of America's world and the world's America. *Australasian Journal of American Studies, 15,* 57–64.

Jackson, S. J., & Andrews, D. L. (1999). Between and beyond the global and the local: American popular sporting culture in New Zealand. *International Review for the Sociology of Sport, 34*(1), 31–42.

Jhally, S. (1987). *Codes of Advertising: Fetishism and the Political Economy of Meaning in the Consumer Society.* New York: St. Martin's.

Kaufman, M. (1987). The construction of masculinity and the triad of men's violence. In M. Kaufman (Ed.), *Beyond Patriarchy: Essays by Men on Pleasure, Power and Change* (pp. 1–29). Toronto: Oxford University Press.

Lealand, G. (1994). American popular culture and emerging nationalism in New Zealand, *National Forum: The Phi Kappa Phi Journal, 74*(4): 34–37.

Leiss, W., Kline, S., & Jhally, S. (1990). *Social Communication in Advertising* (2nd ed.). London: Routledge.

Magiera, M., & Sloan, P. (1991, February 25). Rivals' ads hammer Nike. *Advertising Age,* pp. 3, 54.

McKay, J. (1995). "Just Do It": Corporate sports slogans and the political economy of "enlightened racism." *Discourse: Studies in the Cultural Politics of Education. 16*(2), 191–201.

Messner, M. (1990). When bodies are weapons: Masculinity and violence in sport. *International Review for the Sociology of Sport, 25,* 203–219.

Messner, M. (1992a). Sport, men and gender. *Power at Play: Sports and the Problem of Masculinity* (pp. 7–23). Boston: Beacon Press.

Messner, M. (1992b). Sport and gender relations: Continuity, contradiction and change. *Power at Play: Sports and the Problem of Masculinity* (pp. 149–172), Boston: Beacon Press.

Nike's Olympian trademark fight. (1992, July 11). *New York Times,* p. 17.

Ralston, B. (1995). TV3 News, New Zealand.

"Reebok Commercial Banned in New Zealand," (1995, June 19). *Reebok New Zealand Inc. Press Release.* Auckland: New Zealand, p. 1.

Sage, G. (1999). Justice do it! The Nike transnational advocacy network: Organization, collective actions and outcomes. *Sociology of Sport Journal, 16*(3), 206–235.

Shaw, R. (1999). *Reclaiming America: Nike, Clean Air, and the New National Activism.* Berkeley: University of California Press.

Sport shoe ban stuns reebok. (1995, June 20). *The Dominion,* p. 7.

Turkow, J. (1997). *Breaking up America: Advertisers and the New Media World*. Chicago: University of Chicago Press.

Weaver, K. (1996). The television and violence debate in New Zealand: Some problems of context. *Continuum: The Australian Journal of Media and Culture, 10*, 64–75.

Wernick, A. (1991). *Promotional Culture: Advertising, Ideology and Symbolic Expression*. London: Sage.

Whittle, I. (1996, June). Judgement day. *Goal*. London: IPC Magazines.

Wilcox, L. (1996). Saatchi rap: The worlding of America and racist ideology in New Zealand, *Continuum: The Australian Journal of Media and Culture, 10*, 121–135.

www.nike.com

Yorks, C. L. (1990, June 13). Shoe businesses' star-studded sneaker war. *Los Angeles Times*, p. E1.

Young, K., & Smith, M. (1988–89). Mass media treatment of violence in sports and its effects. *Current Psychology: Research and Reviews, 7*(4), 298–311.

Smoke and Ashes: Tobacco Sponsorship of Sports and Regulatory Issues in Canada

Timothy Dewhirst

University of Saskatchewan

Sponsorship of sports and cultural events has been a part of the promotional mix for Canadian tobacco manufacturers throughout the 20th century. In 1903, for example, the Red Cross tobacco brand was a prominent sponsor of a high wire act, in which a person crossed the Montmorency waterfalls that are located in the province of Quebec. A 1932 promotional campaign for Turret—a tobacco brand oriented toward the blue-collar class according to Imperial Tobacco documentation—offered cash prizes to those correctly estimating the number of goals that would be scored by National Hockey League (NHL) teams. Sweet Caporal, another brand offered by Imperial Tobacco, sponsored the first Canadian football radio broadcasts during the 1930s (Cunningham, 1996).

Despite these examples from the earlier part of the 20th century, there have been two later defining periods for when sports and cultural sponsorship became an increasingly important component of the promotional mix for Canadian tobacco manufacturers. First, tobacco sponsorship became more prominent during the late 1960s and early 1970s, when cigarette advertising was voluntarily withdrawn from TV and radio. Second, expenditures substantially increased during the late 1980s and early 1990s with the implementation of the Tobacco Products Control Act (TPCA), which severely limited conventional forms of advertising. In the current political–legal context, key issues being debated are whether youth remain an important target of tobacco promotional activities and whether tobacco sponsorship promotions are most aptly classified as lifestyle or informational advertising. This chapter focuses on these issues by reviewing academic literature, trade press, annual reports, and policies, as well as by examining internal industry documents publicly accessible as a result of Canadian court proceedings. The main source of evidence of Canadian industry practices is tobacco industry documents that have been made public through two court proceedings: (a) the 1989 Canadian trial to decide the constitutionality of the TPCA, and (b) the 2002 Quebec Superior Court trial in which Canada's three major tobacco manufacturers challenged the constitutionality of the Tobacco Act.

A SHIFT TO SPONSORSHIP ONCE BROADCAST ADVERTISING WAS WITHDRAWN (1972)

It was not until the late 1960s and early 1970s that the sponsorship of sports and cultural events became an increasingly significant part of the promotional mix for Canadian tobacco manufacturers. The shift toward sponsorship reflected the reality that many other important means of promotion were no longer viable options. Starting in 1964, Canadian tobacco companies voluntarily agreed to confine cigarette advertising on TV to hours after 9 P.M. (Canadian Tobacco Manufacturers' Council [CTMC], 1964). In 1970, incentive programs were a marketing practice discontinued in response to government pressure. *Incentive brands*—those offering redeemable coupons, prizes, or gifts—had become an important marketing strategy considering that they accounted for greater than 50% of the total Canadian cigarette market in 1969 (Imasco Ltd., 1970; Imasco Ltd., 1971). Effective January 1, 1972, cigarette advertising was voluntarily withdrawn from the broadcast media altogether (CTMC, 1971). This industry initiative could be seen as a public relations move aimed at warding off impending government regulation, considering that the federal Health Minister at the time, John Munro, had introduced Bill C-248—an Act that included stipulations to ban cigarette advertising—on June 10, 1971 (Cunningham, 1996; Imasco Ltd., 1972).

Tobacco companies turned toward sponsoring broadcast sports and cultural events as a means to compensate for lost broadcast advertising exposure. Imperial Tobacco, Canada's largest tobacco manufacturer, recognized in its marketing plans that "as a result of current and possible future TV restrictions, the opposition [competitors] has become increasingly active in the sponsorship of major events across Canada. Therefore we can as a company foresee the possibility of sponsoring most of these events with one of our own brands" (1970, p. 566628113). In a review of its competitors' promotional activities as of July 1970, Imperial Tobacco claimed, "we can certainly see a big swing towards sponsorship of national or regional events" (1970, p. 566628132). Within this corporate document, Rothmans was used as an example of a competitor with prominence because it was the sponsor of special events caravans, Canadian Open Tennis Tournaments, and the Canadian Equestrian Team. Roughly 4 years later in an annual report, the parent company of Imperial Tobacco stated that, "marketing activities, particularly for cigarettes, have changed significantly since the industry's withdrawal from broadcast advertising. More advertising is now associated with spectator events, although total advertising expenditures are down" (Imasco Ltd., 1974, p. 8).

There were several examples of new or expanded sponsorship properties during the early 1970s. Anticipating the withdrawal from broadcast advertising, Imperial Tobacco signed a 5-year contract with the Royal Canadian Golf Association during November 1970 in order to link its Peter Jackson cigarette brand with the Canadian Open Golf Championships, and the agreement also included the sponsorship of provincial tournaments. Another Imperial Tobacco cigarette brand, Player's, began sponsoring auto racing in Canada in 1961, yet announced that this support would be extended toward regional events in 1971 (Imasco Ltd., 1971). Also in 1971, the tobacco manufacturer formed the du Maurier Council for the Performing Arts to provide grants toward music, ballet, and theater-related performing groups on behalf of their du Maurier brand (Imasco Ltd., 1972).

Similar trends were being observed elsewhere. In fact, it has been noted that the tobacco industry's involvement in sports and cultural sponsorships during the 1970s and 1980s was a significant factor in the general development of sponsorship as a marketing discipline (Cornwell, 1995; Meenaghan, 1991; Otker & Hayes, 1987). Cigarette advertising was banned from the broadcast media in the United Kingdom in 1965, for example, and the resulting shift in tobacco industry promotional spending largely contributed toward the overall growth of sponsorship expenditures that was observed during the 1970s (Marshall & Cook, 1992; Taylor, 1984). In the United States, federal legislation—the Public Health Cigarette Smoking Act—stipulated that broadcast advertising for cigarettes was banned, commencing January 2, 1971. Although the primary response of American tobacco manufacturers was to forward their advertising spending toward the print media, there was also a notable shift toward sponsorship (Feinberg, 1971; Stoner, 1992; Teel, Teel, & Bearden, 1979; Warner,

1985). Notably, Virginia Slims began sponsoring women's professional tennis in 1970, and Winston Cup auto racing and Marlboro Cup horse racing debuted in 1971 and 1973, respectively (Crompton, 1993; O'Keefe & Pollay, 1996; Wichmann & Martin, 1991).

THE TOBACCO PRODUCTS CONTROL ACT
TAKES EFFECT (1989)

The late 1980s and early 1990s marked a second defining period in which tobacco sponsorship of Canadian sports and cultural events grew substantially. The dramatic increase in sponsorship expenditures was primarily driven by the TPCA, which was enacted in 1988 and took effect on January 1, 1989. Up until this time, the tobacco industry self-regulated by establishing a voluntary advertising code in 1964, with amendments being made to the code in 1971, 1976, and 1984. Although the TPCA stipulated that tobacco product advertising was banned, sponsorship remained permissible if the full name of the manufacturers (rather than the brand names) were placed on promotional materials. In response to the imposed advertising regulations, the Canadian tobacco industry invested heavily in the sponsorship of various events, and advertising and promotional support remained a significant component of this investment. Documentation from the CTMC (1987, 1997) indicates that sponsorship contributions grew more than six-fold from 1987 to 1995. Sponsorship became an attractive promotional tool once conventional advertising was no longer permitted.

"Shell" Companies Were Formed
for Sponsorship Purposes

The TPCA stipulated that tobacco products offered for sale in Canada were not to be advertised. The Act did go on to note, however, that this statement did not apply to foreign media or to the sponsorship of sports and cultural events. Sponsorship was still allowable if the name of a company was used on promotional materials. Thus, as the TPCA took effect, Canadian tobacco companies hastily registered their various brands or trademarks as separate corporate entities for sponsorship purposes. RJR-Macdonald formed Vantage Arts Ltd. and Export 'A' Inc. as subsidiary companies. Vantage and Export 'A' are cigarette brands offered by RJR-Macdonald.[1] Rothmans, Benson & Hedges

---

[1] RJR-Macdonald Inc. was re-named JTI-Macdonald Corp. after Japan Tobacco Inc. purchased R.J. Reynolds International in 1999.

formed Craven "A" Ltd., Belvedere Ltd., Rothmans Ltd., and Benson & Hedges Inc. as subsidiary companies for sponsorship purposes. Imperial Tobacco created four new companies for the purpose of advertising and promoting the sponsorship of sports and cultural events: Player's Ltd., du Maurier Ltd., Matinée Ltd., and du Maurier Council for the Arts Ltd. (Descoteaux, 1989). Player's, du Maurier, and Matinée are cigarette brands manufactured by Imperial Tobacco.

In its 1988 annual report, Imperial Tobacco acknowledged that the TPCA was being challenged on constitutional grounds, but while awaiting the outcome they were "prepared to make the best of the few communication opportunities that are still available. We have, for example, incorporated a number of associated entities that will serve as vehicles for the sponsorship of a variety of sports and cultural events" (Imasco Ltd., 1989, p. 8). During the same year, an internal document for Imperial Tobacco stated that "in a very real sense the company's expectations are that [the TPCA] C-51 will not end tobacco marketing, but will bring about very major changes in how that exercise is conducted. . . . Imperial's extensive sponsorship portfolio is being restaged under new corporate names that will allow them to continue exploiting the huge equity in their investments in this area" (cited in Pollay, 2002, p. 11).

In a press release, Imperial Tobacco's Chairman and CEO, Jean-Louis Mercier, claimed that the entities were formed to eliminate an unfair disadvantage imposed on the company by the TPCA. It was argued that RJR-Macdonald and Rothmans, Benson & Hedges had already formed corporate names that were directly related to one or more of its major trademarks, thus Imperial Tobacco publicly justified the newly formed "shell" corporations as a means to remain competitive with the other two major tobacco manufacturers (Descoteaux, 1989). Despite their public position, internal documentation revealed that Imperial Tobacco was in fact the forerunner in this strategic move: "ITL led the way with brand corporations under which to conduct sponsorship activities" (Imperial Tobacco, 1994, p. 38). This statement reaffirmed British American Tobacco's (1991) claim that RJR-Macdonald followed Imperial Tobacco's lead with respect to forming shell companies.

It should be evident that sponsorship companies, such as Player's Ltd. and du Maurier Ltd., were easily identifiable as cigarette brand names. The omission of Ltd. or Inc. was often apparent in the news coverage of the events that were sponsored by tobacco companies. For example, newspaper articles (Canadians suffer, 1994; Davidson, 1994) routinely referred to the Matinée Ltd. International women's tennis tournament as the Matinée International. Such an omission might not seem significant, but by not including *Ltd.*, this tournament appeared to be sponsored by a tobacco brand name product.

This was not permitted according to the TPCA. Tobacco companies could obviously avoid responsibility for such omissions by stating that they were not responsible for journalists who were ignorant of the regulations.

The corporate entities that were formed by tobacco manufacturers for sponsorship purposes had logos, trademarks, typography, and coloring that closely resembled those on the brand name packages. Thus, the colors and designs used on particular tobacco brand packages became the key mechanisms of promotion under the restrictions of the TPCA. Unlike conventional tobacco product advertising, health warnings were not necessary for ads promoting the sponsorship arrangements of tobacco shell companies.

Brand Exposure Was Maintained on Television and Radio

Sponsoring sports and cultural events provided tobacco companies with several opportunities to circumvent the existing advertising regulations. Sponsorships allowed tobacco companies to gain access to various media that, according to the TPCA, would otherwise not have been permitted. Sponsorship programs were considered critically important because they were a means of providing "broadcast brand i.d." (RJR-Macdonald, 1996a, p. 80150 3496). Export 'A' Inc., for example, sponsored The Skins Game that included premiere male professional golfers (such as Jack Nicklaus, Fred Couples, Greg Norman, Ernie Els, Nick Faldo, John Daly, Mike Weir, and David Duval) and was televised nationally by the Canadian Broadcasting Corporation (CBC). According to RJR-Macdonald (1996b), "The Skins Game has become one of the top televised golf events in Canada over its three year existence. . . . The event gives Export 'A' Inc. an unparalleled opportunity to 'own' five hours of weekend television and represents a leveragable [sic] advertising opportunity in the two to three month window leading up to the event" (p. 80151 3320). Imperial Tobacco (1993a) observed, "a solution to the quality of viewership [sic] is available through the hour or more broadcast of our major events. With appropriate on-site signage, they become one hour commercials" (p. 014723).

Player's, a leading Canadian cigarette trademark, has been a long-time and prominent Championship Auto Racing Teams (CART) sponsor for Canadian Champ car racers such as Jacques Villeneuve, Greg Moore, Alex Tagliani, Patrick Carpentier, and Paul Tracy. Villeneuve won the Indianapolis 500 and the 1995 CART championship while sponsored by the corporate entity, Player's Ltd. In recognition of Villeneuve's achievements in 1995, he was awarded the Lou Marsh Trophy for being voted Canadian athlete of the year.

Exposure for Player's Ltd. was obviously not limited to TV coverage of the auto racing events because photographs of the winning driver often appear in magazines, newspapers, and television newscasts. Competing tobacco manufacturer, Rothmans, Benson & Hedges, observed that, "over the past 23 weeks and with three quarters of the Player's season completed, Imperial [Tobacco] has amassed an average of 4 broadcast hours a week that does not include Player's advertising and news coverage" (cited in Pollay, 2002, p. 47).

Imperial Tobacco monitored the minimum exposure that would be attained for Player's during CART races according to the placing of its drivers and whether they controlled the television coverage:

Controlling Television: There is no magic to controlling television, the concept is quite simple and based on being in control of what the audience sees. As an outline let me review what a team sponsor might expect of a car running in 6th place. IndyCar will make all efforts to cover each team twice, once when they announce the race and once when the race is on. Clearly if you are not part of the lead group your coverage is limited. However, with control of television one can guarantee oneself the following:

Promotional Bumpers by Network prior to race	4 minutes
Show Opening Segment	1 minute
Commercial Bumpers	1 minute
Leader Boards	1 minute
In show segments	2 minutes
Pit Action with dedicated cameraman	2 minutes
Post Race Interviews with driver	2 minutes
	13 minutes

This then will quadruple your coverage on the air. (cited in Pollay, 2002, p. 47, 48)

Clearly, brand exposure is maximized in auto racing sponsorship if the sponsored driver is a front-runner or successful. And as a primary sponsor of the Molson Indy CART races that are held annually in Toronto and Vancouver, Player's is able to exercise control of the TV coverage for events located in Canada.

Canadian tobacco companies continued to place their promotional efforts on radio as well. In 1993, Craven "A" Ltd. began sponsoring country music on 59 radio stations as a means of circumventing the ban on broadcast cigarette advertising. According to Rothmans, Benson & Hedges, "Craven 'A' Ltd. Today's Country was launched June 5th, 1993. Radio broadcast grid has 59 affiliates for a 90% placement rate, ahead of our 60% estimate for this point in time" (cited in Pollay, 2002, p. 46). Within a few years, Craven "A" Ltd.-sponsored country music concerts were being taped for rebroadcast on 74 radio stations across Canada (Rothmans Inc., 1995). Meanwhile, Belvedere Ltd. and Export 'A' Inc. were sponsoring various rock concerts. Rothmans, Benson & Hedges proceeded with a music-based promotion of Belvedere by developing "a media program for Quebec and the Maritimes to deliver on-going image and awareness to 18–24 target consumers through the use of mediums such as Musique Plus and Radiomutuel" (cited in Pollay, 2002, p. 40). RJR-Macdonald, through its Export 'A' "Smooth" line extension, sought to "reinforce brand imagery by utilizing New Music Series . . . Innovative tour sponsorship which has supported 175 bands performing over 1000 shows across Canada utilizing the Smooth Plugged New Music tour bus . . . Media Support: Radio, Urban newspapers, Posters, Retail Pamphlets, Internet, Street Banners, Club advertising" (cited in Pollay, 2002, p. 40, 41).

There are several reasons why it is desirable for tobacco manufacturers to have the broadcast media (most notably, TV) persist as a part of the communications mix. Rothmans, Benson & Hedges explained the relevance of TV coverage for its Belvedere Rock program: "Television was chosen to form part of the total communication mix for this program. Its role was to provide the perception of mass, total reach and credibility" (cited in Pollay, 2002, p. 47). This is consistent with the commonly cited advantages of selecting TV as a media choice for promotion. TV allows for extensive market coverage considering that 98% of American households have at least one TV and an average viewing time of 8.5 hours per day (Arens, 1999). The reach of TV is also impressive, which is illustrated nicely by the fact that the attendance for the 2002 Formula One race held in Montreal was 117,000, yet the number of TV viewers for each Formula One race is estimated to be 300 million (Hawaleshka, 2001; Race report, 2002). TV is perceived to be the most authoritative and influential medium, thus it offers advertisers a prestigious image. Although the production and airtime costs of TV advertising are potentially quite high, promoting on TV communicates to viewers that the brand is a major player. Sight, sound, and movement may also be combined on TV, which allows product use or brand imagery to be demonstrated with impact (Arens, 1999).

Additional Loopholes Exploited Within Existing Advertising Regulations

Canadian tobacco manufacturers exploited several other loopholes among the stipulations of the TPCA. The TPCA did not permit tobacco companies to promote tobacco products on billboards, but sponsoring sports and cultural events allowed billboards to be constructed that supposedly advertised the tobacco company's association with the event. In some cases, however, sponsorship billboards continued running long after the events being promoted were finished. Imperial Tobacco was scrutinized in a newspaper article by Mellor (1992) for a du Maurier Ltd. billboard that promoted an equestrian event taking place in October yet remained standing the following January.

The TPCA also did not allow the purchasers of tobacco products to be offered the right to participate in a related contest, lottery, or game. By sponsoring sports and cultural events, however, tobacco companies were able to stage contests. Export 'A' Inc., through its sponsorship of a salmon fishing showdown in 1992, held a contest offering Canadian $50,000 cash as first prize. Benson & Hedges Inc. serves as another example because its *Symphony of Fire* contest (reflecting the shell company's sponsorship of fireworks) gave contestants an opportunity to win a 1-week cruise vacation.

The TPCA prohibited the use of tobacco brand names on non-tobacco items, yet logos of the shell companies were placed on items such as T-shirts, hats, and towels. From 1994 to 1996, the Player's Ltd. Racing Team issued catalogues through direct mailings, magazines, bars, and various race events that enabled consumers to purchase branded items such as rugby and polo shirts, jackets, key chains, knapsacks, and cargo bags. The Canadian tobacco industry's voluntary advertising codes (CTMC, 1964, 1971, 1976, 1984) stipulated that all models used in cigarette ads were to be at least 25 years old, yet tobacco sponsorship promotions often depicted athletes, celebrities, or other event participants who were younger.

THE TOBACCO ACT: ANOTHER POLICY FACING A CONSTITUTIONAL CHALLENGE

The Tobacco Act (Bill C-71) was implemented in 1997 and established as a replacement of the TPCA and the Tobacco Sales to Young Persons Act. The TPCA needed to be replaced because in September 1995, in a five-to-four decision, the Supreme Court of Canada ruled that it was unconstitutional. Imperial Tobacco and RJR-Macdonald had legally challenged the TPCA, claiming that it was an infringement of commercial expression as stated by Section 2(b) of the Canadian Charter of Rights and Freedoms. Following the Supreme Court ruling, the Canadian tobacco industry adopted a new voluntary advertising code and resumed conventional advertising in February 1996. Thus, conventional cigarette advertising continued for roughly 1 year before Canadian tobacco companies had to adhere to the stipulations of the Tobacco Act.

The Tobacco Act places a ban on lifestyle advertising, while informational advertising remains permissible assuming that it is placed in adult establishments, in publications with a minimum adult readership of 85%, or in mailings addressed to adults by name. This legislation has been adopted to protect a specific marketing segment (i.e., youth) that is deemed to be particularly vulnerable to manipulative advertising. With respect to tobacco sponsorship activities, amendments were made to the Tobacco Act (i.e., Bill C-42) in December 1998, which stipulated a 5-year transition period before a total tobacco sponsorship ban is imposed. Imperial Tobacco, JTI-Macdonald, and Rothmans, Benson & Hedges challenged the constitutionality of the Tobacco Act, but a Quebec Superior Court decision in December 2002 upheld the legislation (Denis, 2002). Canada's three largest tobacco manufacturers have appealed the Quebec court ruling, and it is expected that the Quebec Court of Appeal and the Supreme Court of Canada will eventually hear the case.

According to the tobacco industry, the Tobacco Act places unreasonable limits on commercial expression. Under the broader title of "Fundamental Freedoms," Section 2(b) of the Canadian Charter of Rights and Freedoms guarantees everyone the "freedom of thought, belief, opinion and expression, including freedom of the press and other media of communication" (Laskin, Greenspan, Rosenberg, Penny, & Henein, 1994, p. CA-1). Section 1 of the Charter, however, does allow reasonable limits or restrictions on expression assuming that the policy objectives are pressing and substantive. With tobacco use representing the single most important cause of preventable illness and premature death in Canada—it is linked with a greater number of deaths among Canadians than the total caused by car accidents, suicides, murders, AIDS, and illicit drug use combined—smoking is clearly a national health problem and a pressing and substantive concern (Cunningham, 1996). Establishing what are *reasonable* limitations on commercial expression proves more contentious. Key issues before the court include (a) justification that youth currently remain a target of tobacco promotional activities and thus represent a specific segment worthy of protection; and (b) distinguishing between lifestyle advertising and informational advertising, as well as establishing which classification best describes sponsorship promotions (Sparks, 1997).

Youth: A Key Target of Tobacco Promotional Activities

The promotion of tobacco products has long been a hotly contested issue, stimulating questions about whether youth are targeted by specific marketing campaigns. The Tobacco Act states that one of its purposes is "to protect young persons and others from inducements to use tobacco products and the consequent dependence on them" (p. 3). Thus, in a legal context whereby it is being justified as appropriate and necessary to severely restrict tobacco promotions, attention is often drawn toward establishing whether many promotional activities are in fact directed toward youth.

The rationale for why tobacco companies would direct their promotions toward youth is that the pivotal period for smoking initiation in Canada is 13 to 14 years of age, with very few smokers beginning beyond adolescence (Health Canada, 1996). According to industry research, "Recall of cigarette adoption among respondents suggests that peer pressure and image are/were the key motivational factors. . . . Most indicated that they had their first cigarette between the ages of 10–15" (Rothmans, Benson & Hedges, 1991, p. 27365). Smokers are also known to be extremely brand loyal, so the brand choice of consumers during the early stages of their smoking "careers" becomes crucial. Market research prepared for RJR-Macdonald recognized that "smokers exhibit extremely high levels of brand loyalty," and "loyalty to cigarette brands remains very strong . . . Only 3% of all smokers are considered 'convertable' [sic]" (Harrod & Mirlin, 1995, p. 80154 2410). In the United States, brand switching among smokers is less than 10% annually, with less than 8% switching companies (Cummings, Hyland, Lewit, & Shopland, 1997). Comparable estimates for Canada could likely be lower considering that merely three manufacturers account for more than a 99% share of the domestic cigarette market, and Imperial Tobacco alone commands a 70% market share.

Tobacco industry representatives have publicly denied that they market their products to youth, yet internal corporate documents indicate otherwise. Pollay and Lavack (1993), Cunningham (1996), Pollay (2000), and Dewhirst and Sparks (2003) reviewed Canadian tobacco industry documents that were manifest in proceedings assessing the constitutionality of the TPCA and found that youth are a target of tobacco marketing activities. Internal documents from the British tobacco industry and its leading advertising agencies also revealed that youth are a key group for marketing purposes (Hastings & MacFadyen, 2000). Glantz, Slade, Bero, Hanauer, and Barnes (1996); Perry (1999); and Cummings, Morley, Horan, Steger, and Leavell (2002) have examined U.S. tobacco industry documents and reached similar conclusions.

To cite some specific examples, two Imperial Tobacco planning documents from the early 1980s, *Fiscal '80 Media Plans* and *Fiscal '81 National Media Plans*, included the age segment 12 to 17 years old among the identified target groups for several of the company's brands and trademarks. Another Imperial Tobacco (1987) document, *Overall Market Conditions—F88*, stated:

If the last ten years have taught us anything, it is that <u>the industry is dominated by the companies who respond most effectively to the needs of younger smokers</u>. Our efforts on these brands will remain on <u>maintaining their relevance to smokers in these younger groups</u> in spite of the share performance they may develop among older smokers. (p. 6)

A few years later, another internal document for the company revealed, "I.T.L. has always focused its efforts on new smokers believing that early perceptions tend to stay with them throughout their lives. I.T.L. clearly dominates the young adult market today and stands to prosper as these smokers age and as it maintains its highly favourable youthful preference" (cited in Pollay, 2002, p.19).

RJR-Macdonald, the third largest tobacco manufacturer in Canada, recognized that "new smokers are critical to continued growth in the market" (1989a, p. 80108 9826) and "in order to make further inroads into the younger segment, we must continue to project an image that is consistent with the needs and values of today's younger smokers" (1989b, p. 80118 3934). The company claimed, "the younger segment represents the most critical source of business to maintain volume and grow share in a declining market. They're recent smokers and show a greater propensity to switch than the older segment. Export [the best-selling cigarette brand manufactured by RJR-Macdonald] has shown an ability to attract this younger group since 1987 to present" (RJR-Macdonald, 1989b, p. 80118 3930). Another internal document entitled, *Export "A" Brand Long-Term Strategy*, included "new users" under the subtitle, "Whose 'behaviour' are we trying to affect?" (RJR-Macdonald, 1987, p. 800230290).

Acting as an indicator that the marketing practices of Canadian tobacco manufacturers have not changed during more recent times, a Rothmans, Benson & Hedges document from the mid-1990s stated, "a strong regular length business is key to attracting younger users and ensuring a healthy future franchise" (cited in Pollay, 2002, p. 19). Another mid-1990s document for the firm recognized the need to "identify products and activities which will strengthen RBH's position among the key 19–24 age group to gain a much larger share of starters," and "although the key 15–19 age group is a must for RBH there are other bigger volume groups that we cannot ignore" (Rothmans, Benson & Hedges, 1996, p. 002756, 002757). According to Imperial Tobacco documentation, "marketing activities have historically been and continue to be targeted at younger smokers due to their greater propensity to change brands" (1995, p. 018110). When reviewing the corporate documents, it is important to recognize that references to "younger smokers," "younger users," "starters," "potential starters" and "new smokers" indicates that adolescents are likely the age segment being discussed.

Despite an obvious interest in recruiting new smokers, the tobacco industry maintains that their promotions do not influence overall consumption levels but rather affect the market share of each brand. The basis for sponsorship expenditures, it is argued, is to defend existing share and to increase it at the expense of the competition. The CTMC (1997) stated, "a 1% market share of the cigarette market is worth approximately $22 million in annual net sales revenue to a manufacturer, not including any federal or provincial tobacco or sales taxes" (p. 8). A British American Tobacco (1984) document, however, contradicts the argument that merely market share is influenced by stating the company's objective is to *expand industry volume* by maximizing instances of starting through relevant products and attitude change. Attitude change can be facilitated through promotional activities, and academic research has shown that youth disproportionately smoke heavily advertised brands (Pollay et al., 1996). Even if one was to accept the argument used by the tobacco industry that its promotions are only aimed at existing smokers—encouraging them to either remain loyal to the brand they smoke or to switch brands if they are smoking a competitor's brand—it seems dubious that the promotions would reassure smokers about choosing a particular brand, yet not reassure them about continuing to smoke more generally. Overall consumption levels would be affected if promotions encourage smokers to continue smoking rather than quit.

The aforementioned documents reflect the marketing practices of the respective tobacco companies generally. It seems reasonable that numerous sponsorship campaigns would be directed toward similar targets as part of an integrated marketing plan. Interoffice correspondence at RJR-Macdonald (1996b) indicated, "generally younger smokers tend to be more aware of sponsorship events than older smokers" (p. 80151 3337). Tobacco-sponsored events that include young spectators, volunteers, and participants have been the source of criticism. Dewhirst (1999) demonstrated that a mascot representative of the Craven A cigarette brand was interacting with young children at the Craven A–sponsored *Just for Laughs* comedy festival in Montreal. When Imperial Tobacco sponsored the Canadian Open Tennis Championships in Toronto and Montreal, teenage volunteers (including the ball-boys and ball-girls) wore uniforms bearing the trademarks, logos, and coloring of cigarette brands (Physicians for a Smoke-Free Canada, 1996). Tobacco control groups and many health practitioners have also expressed concern about the age of the participants for events that are promoted by tobacco companies. In women's professional tennis, for example, many of the world's top players are teenagers. Jennifer Capriati was the champion of the 1991 Matinée Ltd. International tennis championships when she was 15 years old, and as a result she was featured in several ensuing promotional materials. Interestingly, when Martina Hingis won the 1999 du Maurier Open in Toronto at 18 years of age, she was still not of legal smoking age in the province of Ontario.

RJR-Macdonald (1996a, p. 80150 3496) has described sponsorship as being equivalent to advertising, thus it is perhaps not surprising that studies indicate youth recognize advertising of tobacco-company sponsored events as advertising for tobacco products (Health Canada, 1996; Rootman & Flay, 1995). A study by Charlton, While, and Kelly (1997) has found that English boys, aged 12 to 14, who enjoy watching Formula One auto racing, are nearly twice as likely to smoke compared to those who do not follow Formula One. Sparks (1999), after assessing the relative contribution of sponsorship to brand awareness among 14-year-old boys and girls in New Zealand and reviewing previous research on tobacco sponsorship and youth, concluded, "selectively targeted cigarette sponsorships can help to build positive brand associations and awareness in the youth (starter) market and thereby contribute to the customer-based equity of the sponsoring brand" (p. 256).

Tobacco Sponsorship Promotions: A Form of "Lifestyle" Advertising

A second key issue during recent court proceedings has been to make a distinction between lifestyle advertising and informational advertising. Making such a distinction was suggested by the decision of the Supreme Court of Canada during the TPCA trial. The majority judgment identified that by not distinguishing between *brand preference* and *lifestyle* advertising, it was not clear whether the objectives of the TPCA could have been met with less intrusive measures (Manfredi, 2002; Wyckham, 1997).

The Tobacco Act defines *lifestyle advertising* as "advertising that associates a product with, or evokes a positive or negative emotion about or image of, a way of life such as one that includes glamour, recreation, excitement, vitality, risk or daring" (p. 8). *Informational advertising*, meanwhile, is described as a promotion that provides factual information to a consumer about the product's characteristics, price, or availability.

Looking to leading marketing and advertising textbooks, lifestyle is considered to establish the ways in which one's time and money is spent and reflect which activities are most valued. *Lifestyle* is defined as a person's pattern of living that becomes manifest in his or her activities, interests, and opinions (Kotler, Armstrong, & Cunningham, 1999; Lamb, Hair, & McDaniel, 2000;

Wells, Burnett, & Moriarty, 1989). *Lifestyle advertising*, then, involves the association of products and brands with particular activities, interests, and opinions, appealing to a specified segment of consumers. The activities, interests, and opinions that are depicted in an ad may reflect the actual or desirable lifestyles of either current or prospective consumers. According to Tuckwell (1988), in an attempt to match the lifestyle of the product user, one may appeal to "their looking-glass self." Lifestyle advertising can be accomplished through the portrayals of people, settings, and objects (or combinations thereof). Some leading textbooks on marketing and advertising do not make extensive use of the phrase *lifestyle advertising*, however, and prefer to use terminology such as *image advertising* and *transformation advertising*. *Transformation advertising* has an objective of building a product or brand personality or image and making the experience of consumption seem richer, warmer, and more enjoyable (Wells, Burnett, & Moriarty, 1989). Consumers often use the same terminology to describe brands and people, such that particular brands are perceived as expressing excitement, success, sophistication, ruggedness, and so on (Aaker, 1996).

Brand imagery or personality has traditionally been seen by the tobacco industry as very important to communicate. According to an Imperial Tobacco document, *1971 Matinée Marketing Plans*, "without price differentials and without easily perceptible product differentiation (except for extremes, e.g. Matinée versus Player's) consumer choice is influenced almost entirely by imagery factors" (1970, p. 566628090). Roughly 25 years later, Rothmans, Benson & Hedges claimed, "in the cigarette category brand image is everything. The brand of cigarettes a person smokes is their identity. Cigarettes tell others who they are as a person. There is a strong emotional connection to the brand, the image it projects about the smoker, not only to themselves but to others" (cited in Pollay, 2002, p. 13). Another internal document indicates that the taste qualities of cigarettes are developed only after an appropriate brand personality has been selected: "Must think imagery/brand personality first and then develop the products with taste qualities/product and package attributes that reinforce image" (cited in Pollay, 2002, p. 14). The role of lifestyle, meanwhile, is to "promote and reinforce the social acceptability among the peer group to smoking as a relaxing, enjoyable self-indulgence" (Imperial Tobacco, 1979b, p. 13).

Contemporary Canadian industry documents indicate that the function of many tobacco sponsorship promotions is consistent with the objectives of lifestyle advertising. Canadian firms recognize that lifestyle and imagery is conveyed by sponsorship communications. According to Imperial Tobacco, "opportunities to utilize image advertising in Sponsorship communication should be exploited" (1992, p. 013870). Rothmans, Benson & Hedges (1993) considered sponsorship to be "one of the few image-enhancing marketing tools available" and looked to "use sponsorships as a means to establish and build upon lifestyle image associations through targeted selection, strong promotional programmes and professional execution, all of which reflect the desired character and image" (p. 005381). RJR-Macdonald recognized, "our sponsorship approach must be consistent with our brand position to enhance image reinforcement" (1996b, p. 80151 3317).

With conventional cigarette advertising severely restricted in Canada, tobacco manufacturers have directed their promotional dollars toward sponsorship and attempted to have the content of the sponsorship promotions resemble their previous conventional ads as much as possible. In 1992, Imperial Tobacco acknowledged, "we have already begun the transition from event advertising to more image based advertising. We still need to fully exploit the communications value inherent in our sponsorship involvement. Until further regulatory change, this is the means by which we will replace traditional brand/trademark image advertising" (cited in Pollay, 2002, p. 11). According to RJR-Macdonald:

> Associative marketing allows us to associate the brand with images which we are prevented from using in brand advertising. In other words, the actual sponsorship is simply the price we pay in order to feature a particular image in our advertising. Although there are many additional benefits to traditional sponsorship programmes such as promotional extensions, our primary concern is with the image advertising potential around the sponsorship. We are attempting to alter a brand's image and, in our view, this is best achieved through advertising which we control. (1996c, p. 80154 2472)

To exploit a brand's link with a particular image, several tobacco sponsorship promotions communicate that the cigarette brand is a *general* supporter of an activity (i.e., Export 'A' sponsors an extreme sports series, Player's sponsors auto racing, Matinée sponsors fashion, and du Maurier claims to sponsor music, photography, and nightlife), without specifying any details about the particular events being sponsored.

Tobacco companies have found that a challenge with event sponsorship advertising is the duration that the accompanying promotional campaign can effectively run. In other words, if a 1-day event is being sponsored, it proves difficult to justify promoting the event throughout the year. RJR-Macdonald specified that sponsorship vehicles should be selected that "spread throughout the year to provide continuity" and "support the brand sell message that is the same in non-event periods" (cited in Pollay, 2002, p. 9). Similarly, another document from the company included "duration" and "timing seasonality" as important criteria for judging sponsorship opportunities (cited in Pollay, 2002, p. 9). According to Imperial Tobacco, "in terms of understanding, it is very clear that while the event itself is a communications vehicle, the true value is the amount of targeted imagery communications which surround the event. It gives us the legitimate excuse to promote. In analyzing event operation costs, the goal will be to identify expenditures which will not effect our image, and re-channel to communications" (1992, p. 013835).

The objectives and budgets sections of tobacco industry documents, pertaining to sport and cultural sponsorship, are dominated by the importance of enhancing or reinforcing brand imagery. Reflecting on the implementation of the TPCA, Rothmans, Benson & Hedges claimed, "today (1988-) sponsorship is the only means whereby company trademarks can be exposed to the public. The image of the activity and the broadcast exposure received in large part determine trademark awareness. ITCO event inventories are being streamlined and investment is being made in broadcast programming and broad scale image communication" (1995, p. 008593). One Imperial Tobacco (1993b) document bluntly stated that the primary objective of sponsorship advertising is to communicate image, and selling tickets to the sponsored event is only a secondary objective. "Specific Objective: To communicate relevant sponsorship imagery to its target group—national versus local. To maintain year-round presence of this imagery on a national basis.... A secondary objective is to promote ticket sales for the events" (p. 014435). Canadian tobacco sponsorship promotions, in many cases, link a cigarette brand with a particular image at the expense of providing important information about the actual event being sponsored (i.e., neglecting to indicate which athletes or teams are participating, the cost of attending, where tickets may be purchased, or where the event is being held).

Tobacco companies select to sponsor sports and cultural events possessing symbolic imagery or personalities that are desirable to link with their respective brands. The objective is to have the image of a sports or cultural event transferred to the sponsoring brand: "Borrowed Imagery: Association with sporting events creates a situation where, because of the perceived 'personality' of the sport, sponsoring corporations can 'borrow' imagery from that personality in order to strengthen their own public perception" (cited in Pollay, 2002, p. 13). According to Imperial Tobacco:

> With regard to the brand or corporate image, the sponsor gives the impression of seeking to associate itself with the image of the event or of those

who participate in the event. When a company sponsors a tennis or golf tournament, a regatta or the classical arts, this is interpreted by the public as a kind of expression (by the sponsor) of the temperament of the company. Depending on the event sponsored, the company appears young, self-assured, master of itself, classical, adventurous, etc. (cited in Pollay, 2002, p. 13)

Don Brown, Chairman, President and CEO of Imperial Tobacco, claimed, "sponsorship is still limited in the degree to which it delivers a specific product attribute message. The value lies in matching imagery of the event to that of the product or service" (cited in Gross, 1994, p. 67).

To illustrate the matching of a cigarette brand and a sponsored sports event along imagery dimensions, du Maurier—the best selling cigarette brand family in Canada and described by an industry insider as "a high quality, upscale, young brand in Canada with a solid image" (Bingham, 1992, p. 500028180)—has sponsored prestigious tennis, equestrian, and golf events. Du Maurier was the title sponsor for the professional men's and women's Canadian Open Tennis Championships that alternated annually each summer between Toronto and Montreal (both of these tournaments were categorized as top-tier tournaments, and only the four Grand Slam tournaments were considered to be of greater importance), as well as the Ladies Professional Golf Association (LPGA) tournament held in Canada. The du Maurier Ltd. Classic represented one of the four major championships on the LPGA tour. The apparent objective with these sponsorship properties was for the upscale, aspiring, high quality, and classy dimensions associated with the events (and sports) to be transferred toward the du Maurier brand. The notion of a sporting event's image being transferred to a brand through event sponsorship promotional activities is consistent with the academic research findings of Ferrand and Pagès (1996), Milne and McDonald (1999), and Gwinner and Eaton (1999).

For the title sponsor, the process of image matching and transfer is also applicable to the event's participants (i.e., celebrities) and the co-sponsors (Dewhirst & Hunter, 2002; Kahle & Homer, 1985; Kamins & Gupta, 1994; Lynch & Schuler, 1994; McCracken, 1989; Misra & Beatty, 1990). Popular auto racer Jacques Villeneuve, for example, has been characterized as a wild child, rebel, and daredevil (who engages in a very high risk sport), which makes him a desirable person to link with cigarette brands that are marketed with such imagery (Dewhirst & Sparks, 2003). When du Maurier sponsored the Canadian Open Tennis Championships, BMW was a co-sponsor, which exemplifies co-branding and image matching opportunities being exploited with sponsorship partners. Du Maurier and BMW complement one another with respect to how the brands are positioned in their respective product category. Such brand matching is consistent with McCracken's (1988) concept of "Diderot unities," which emphasizes that the meaning of goods is largely determined by their relationship to other goods.

Player's, du Maurier, Matinée, Benson & Hedges, and Export 'A' currently represent the Canadian cigarette brands most prominently depicted in sponsorship promotions. Player's continues to sponsor CART auto racing, whereas du Maurier supported 271 art groups during 2002. By promoting grants that are provided to Canadian fashion designers, Matinée is linked with images of relaxation, youthfulness, self-expression, and indulgence (Imperial Tobacco, 1993a). Benson & Hedges sponsors the Gold Club Series, which features leading DJs performing in club settings. Export 'A', which is positioned according to dimensions of adventure, masculinity, and independence, sponsors an extreme sports series (Dewhirst, in press; Pollay, 2001). It has been observed that the extreme sports series consists of activities involving competitors who succeed because of their willingness to take extreme risks, and the promotions for these events appeal to the viewer's desire for independence because the selected activities are all individual sports.

It should be apparent that Canadian tobacco companies sponsor a diversity of events, yet the majority of sponsorship expenditures are toward sports events (the budgets for arts and cultural sponsorship are considerably lower). This weighting reflects sponsorship spending generally, as it is estimated that sports events account for at least two thirds of sponsorship expenditures (Copeland, Frisby, & McCarville, 1996; Linstead & Turner, 1986; Shanklin & Kuzma, 1992). During the mid-1990s, the annual contributions by Player's toward auto racing accounted for roughly one sixth of the total sponsorship expenditures by all Canadian tobacco companies (CTMC, 1997; Gross, 1994).

CONCLUSION

It has been demonstrated here that tobacco sponsorship largely evolved once other elements of the promotional or communications mix were no longer permissible. Put simply, sponsorship became one of the best available promotional options for Canadian tobacco companies. The industry quickly found that despite cigarette advertising being withdrawn from the broadcast media in 1972, cigarette brand exposure could persist on TV and radio if broadcast sporting and cultural events were sponsored. The Canadian trend toward sponsorship was consistent with the U.S. experience. Despite cigarette advertising becoming prohibited on U.S. TV in 1971, Blum (1991) and Siegel (2001) have illustrated that by sponsoring sports such as auto racing, U.S. tobacco companies continue to receive millions of dollars worth of low-cost national TV exposure.

In 1988, the TPCA was legislated, which was significant due to the restrictions it upheld. Under the stipulations of this Act, tobacco product advertising was not permitted. Advertising that promoted the sponsorship arrangements of tobacco companies could not reveal tobacco products. The capacity of the TPCA to ban tobacco advertising in Canada was limited, however. This relative powerlessness was largely due to the Act's numerous loopholes, the most notable of which allowed the formation of corporate entities by tobacco companies. Used for sponsorship purposes, these corporate entities employed logos and trademarks that closely resembled those found on the tobacco products (i.e., packages) of their parent companies. Obviously, such a strategy allowed the ostensibly prohibited dissemination of these logos and trademarks in the mass media.

After reviewing internal tobacco industry documents from Canada's three principal firms, it is revealed that the primary objectives for sponsoring sports and cultural events are to increase brand awareness (through continued brand exposure) and to enhance or reinforce brand image. Tobacco brands continue to gain widespread exposure on TV through the sponsorship of sports and cultural events and in effect circumvent supposed bans on broadcast advertising. In an attempt to enhance or reinforce brand imagery, tobacco companies identify sports and cultural events possessing complementary symbolic properties, with a common goal of having the image that is linked to the event transferable to the sponsoring brand.

The Tobacco Act has replaced the TPCA, but like its predecessor, it faces a constitutional challenge. The Supreme Court of Canada is expected to eventually hear the case. The Tobacco Act appears to place reasonable limits on expression considering that its objectives are pressing and substantive, while internal corporate documents reveal that youth remain a key target of tobacco promotional activities and many tobacco sponsorship promotions are a form of lifestyle advertising. If the Tobacco Act and its amendments (i.e., Bill C-42) are upheld, tobacco sponsorship will become banned in Canada, effective October 2003.

ACKNOWLEDGMENTS

The author would like to thank Richard Pollay for his helpful comments and financial assistance toward this project. While writing this chapter, Timothy Dewhirst was the recipient of a National Health Ph.D. Fellowship from Health Canada / Canadian Institutes of Health Research.

REFERENCES

Aaker, D. A. (1996). *Building Strong Brands*. New York: The Free Press.

Arens, W. F. (1999). *Contemporary Advertising* (7th ed.). Boston: Irwin / McGraw-Hill.

Bingham, P. M. (1992, July 27). *Canada: Du Maurier* [letter addressed to J. Rembiszewski, D. Brown, & R. Cooper]. British-American Tobacco Company Limited. Bates No. 500028180.

Blum, A. (1991). The Marlboro Grand Prix: Circumvention of the television ban on tobacco advertising. *New England Journal of Medicine, 324,* 913–917.

British American Tobacco Co. (1984, October 1). *Potential areas of investigation activity*. Bates No. 102694881.

British American Tobacco Co. (circa 1991). *Canada*. Bates No. 500118797.

Canada. (1998). *An Act to Amend the Tobacco Act*. Ottawa: Queen's Printer for Canada.

Canada. (1997). *Tobacco Act*. Ottawa: Public Works and Government Services Canada.

Canada. (1988). *Tobacco Products Control Act*. Ottawa: Department of National Health and Welfare.

Canadians suffer fall at windy Matinee. (1994, August 16). *The Globe and Mail*, p. C7.

Canadian Tobacco Manufacturers' Council. (1997). *Brief on Bill C-71 to the Standing Senate Committee on Legal and Constitutional Affairs*. Ottawa.

Canadian Tobacco Manufacturers' Council. (1987). *A Brief to the Legislative Committee of the House of Commons on Bill C-51*. Ottawa.

Canadian Tobacco Manufacturers' Council. (1984). *Cigarette and Cigarette Tobacco Advertising and Promotion Code of the Canadian Tobacco Manufacturers' Council*. Ottawa.

Canadian Tobacco Manufacturers' Council. (1976). *Cigarette and Cigarette Tobacco Advertising and Promotion Code of the Canadian Tobacco Manufacturers' Council*. Ottawa.

Canadian Tobacco Manufacturers' Council. (1971, September 15). *Cigarette Advertising Code of the Canadian Tobacco Manufacturers' Council*. Ottawa.

Canadian Tobacco Manufacturers' Council. (1964). *Cigarette Advertising Code of Canadian Tobacco Manufacturers*. Ottawa.

Charlton, A., While, D., & Kelly, S. (1997, November 15). Boys' smoking and cigarette-brand–sponsored motor racing. *Lancet, 350,* 1474.

Copeland, R., Frisby, W., & McCarville, R. (1996). Understanding the sport sponsorship process from a corporate perspective. *Journal of Sport Management, 10,* 32–48.

Cornwell, T. B. (1995). Sponsorship-linked marketing development. *Sport Marketing Quarterly, 4,* 13–24.

Crompton, J. L. (1993). Sponsorship of sport by tobacco and alcohol companies: A review of the issues. *Journal of Sport and Social Issues, 17,* 148–167.

Cummings, K. M., Hyland, A., Lewit, E., & Shopland, D. (1997). Discrepancies in cigarette brand sales and adult market share: Are new teen smokers filling the gap? *Tobacco Control, 6,* S38–S43.

Cummings, K. M., Morley, C. P., Horan, J. K., Steger, C., & Leavell, N-R. (2002). Marketing to America's youth: Evidence from corporate documents. *Tobacco Control, 11,* i5–i17.

Cunningham, R. (1996). *Smoke and Mirrors: The Canadian Tobacco War.* Ottawa: International Development Research Centre.

Davidson, J. (1994, August 17). Graf humbles American, contemplates life without tennis. *The Globe and Mail,* p. C5.

Denis, A. (2002, December 13). Quebec Superior Court decision rendered by Judge André Denis. *JTI-Macdonald Corp., Imperial Tobacco Canada Ltd., and Rothmans, Benson & Hedges Inc. v. The Attorney General of Canada.*

Descoteaux, M. (1989, February 16). *Imperial Tobacco Incorporates Four New Corporate Entities* [press release]. Montreal: Imperial Tobacco Limited.

Dewhirst, T. (in press). Male youth, extreme sports, and the gendering of smoking: A case study of Export 'A' brand marketing in Canada. In L. Fuller (Ed.), *Sexual Sports Rhetoric Globally.* Binghamton, NY: Haworth Press.

Dewhirst, T. (1999). Tobacco sponsorship is no laughing matter. *Tobacco Control, 8,* 82–84.

Dewhirst, T., & Hunter, A. (2002). Tobacco sponsorship of Formula One and CART auto racing: Tobacco brand exposure and enhanced symbolic imagery through co-sponsors' third party advertising. *Tobacco Control, 11,* 146–150.

Dewhirst, T., & Sparks, R. (2003). Intertextuality, tobacco sponsorship of sports, and adolescent male smoking culture: A selective review of tobacco industry documents. *Journal of Sport and Social Issues, 27,* 372–398.

Feinberg, B. M. (1971). Content analysis shows cigarette advertising up twofold in 14 magazines. *Journalism Quarterly, 48,* 539–542.

Ferrand, A., & Pagès, M. (1996). Image sponsoring: A methodology to match event and sponsor. *Journal of Sport Management, 10,* 278–291.

Glantz, S. A., Slade, J., Bero, L. A., Hanauer, P., & Barnes D. E. (1996). *The Cigarette Papers.* Berkeley: University of California Press.

Gross, G. (1994). The feeling's mutual. *Racquet Sports Magazine, 9,* 66–71.

Gwinner, K. P., & Eaton, J. (1999). Building brand image through event sponsorship: The role of image transfer. *Journal of Advertising, 28,* 47–57.

Harrod & Mirlin Ltd. (1995, December 12). Export "A" franchise: Advertising strategy recommendations. Prepared for RJR-Macdonald Inc. Exhibit D-178, *JTI-Macdonald Corp., Imperial Tobacco Canada Ltd., and Rothmans, Benson & Hedges Inc. v. The Attorney General of Canada.* Quebec Superior Court.

Hastings, G., & MacFadyen, L. (2000). A day in the life of an advertising man: Review of internal documents from the UK tobacco industry's principal advertising agencies. *British Medical Journal, 321,* 366–371.

Hawaleshka, D. (2001, June 25). Grand prix wizardry. *Maclean's, 114,* 40–41.

Health Canada. (1996). *Youth Smoking Survey, 1994: A Technical Report.* Ottawa: Minister of Supply and Services Canada.

Imasco Ltd. (1989). *Annual Report 1988.*

Imasco Ltd. (1974). *Annual Report 1973.*

Imasco Ltd. (1972). *Annual Report 1971.*

Imasco Ltd. (1971). *Annual Report 1970.*

Imasco Ltd. (1970). *Annual Report 1969.*

Imperial Tobacco Ltd. (1995, January). Trademark strategies and projects—1995—market strategy and development. Exhibit D-176, *JTI-Macdonald Corp., Imperial Tobacco Canada Ltd., and Rothmans, Benson & Hedges Inc. v. The Attorney General of Canada*. Quebec Superior Court.

Imperial Tobacco Ltd. (1994, March 4). Imperial Tobacco Ltd. competitor analysis. Exhibit D-173, *JTI-Macdonald Corp., Imperial Tobacco Canada Ltd., and Rothmans, Benson & Hedges Inc. v. The Attorney General of Canada*. Quebec Superior Court.

Imperial Tobacco Ltd. (circa 1993a). 1993 communications plans. Exhibit D-197, *JTI-Macdonald Corp., Imperial Tobacco Canada Ltd., and Rothmans, Benson & Hedges Inc. v. The Attorney General of Canada*. Quebec Superior Court.

Imperial Tobacco Ltd. (1993b, July 12). 1994 communications plan. Exhibit D-198, *JTI-Macdonald Corp., Imperial Tobacco Canada Ltd., and Rothmans, Benson & Hedges Inc. v. The Attorney General of Canada*. Quebec Superior Court.

Imperial Tobacco Ltd. (1992). Sponsorships–communications plans 1992. Exhibit D-196, *JTI-Macdonald Corp., Imperial Tobacco Canada Ltd., and Rothmans, Benson & Hedges Inc. v. The Attorney General of Canada*. Quebec Superior Court.

Imperial Tobacco Ltd. (circa 1987). Overall market conditions—F88. Exhibit AG-214, *RJR-Macdonald Inc. v. Canada (Attorney General)*.

Imperial Tobacco Ltd. (circa 1980). Fiscal '81 national media plans. Exhibit AG-223, *RJR-Macdonald Inc. v. Canada (Attorney General)*.

Imperial Tobacco Ltd. (circa 1979a). Fiscal '80 media plans. Exhibit ITL-13, *RJR-Macdonald Inc. v. Canada (Attorney General)*.

Imperial Tobacco Ltd. (circa 1979b). Creative guidelines. Exhibit AG-29, *RJR-Macdonald Inc. v. Canada (Attorney General)*.

Imperial Tobacco Ltd. (circa 1970). 1971 Matinée marketing plans. Exhibit AG-204, *RJR-Macdonald Inc. v. Canada (Attorney General)*.

Kahle, L. R., & Homer, P. M. (1985). Physical attractiveness of the celebrity endorser: A social adaptation perspective. *Journal of Consumer Research, 11*, 954–961.

Kamins, M. A., & Gupta, K. (1994). Congruence between spokesperson and product type: A matchup hypothesis perspective. *Psychology and Marketing, 11*, 569–586.

Kotler, P., Armstrong, G., & Cunningham, P. H. (1999). *Principles of Marketing* (4th ed.). Scarborough, ON: Prentice Hall Canada.

Lamb, Jr., C. W., Hair, Jr., J. F., & McDaniel, C. (2000). *Marketing* (5th ed.). Cincinnati: South-Western College Publishing.

Laskin, J., Greenspan, E., Rosenberg, M., Penny, M., & Henein, M. (1994). *The Canadian Charter of Rights, annotated*. Aurora, ON: Canadian Law Book.

Linstead, S., & Turner, K. (1986). Business sponsorship of the arts: Corporate image and business policy. *Management Research News, 9*, 11–13.

Lynch, J., & Schuler, D. (1994). The matchup effect of spokesperson and product congruency: A schema theory interpretation. *Psychology and Marketing, 11*, 417–445.

Manfredi, C. P. (2002). Expressive freedom and tobacco advertising: A Canadian perspective. *American Journal of Public Health, 92*, 360–362.

Marshall, D. W. & Cook, G. (1992). The corporate (sports) sponsor. *International Journal of Advertising, 11*, 307–324.

McCracken, G. (1989). Who is the celebrity endorser? Cultural foundations of the endorsement process. *Journal of Consumer Research, 16*, 310–321.

McCracken, G. (1988). *Culture and Consumption: New Approaches to the Symbolic Character of Consumer Goods and Activities*. Bloomington, IN: Indiana University Press.

Meenaghan, T. (1991). The role of sponsorship in the marketing communications mix. *International Journal of Advertising, 10*, 35–47.

Mellor, C. (1992, January 10). Outdated Du Maurier billboard burns up anti-smoking group. *The Chronicle-Herald*, p. A6.

Milne, G. R., & McDonald, M. A. (1999). *Sport Marketing: Managing the Exchange Process*. Sudbury, MA: Jones and Bartlett.

Misra, S., & Beatty, S. E. (1990). Celebrity spokesperson and brand congruence: An assessment of recall and affect. *Journal of Business Research, 21*, 159–173.

O'Keefe, A. M., & Pollay, R. W. (1996). Deadly targeting of women in promoting cigarettes. *Journal of the American Medical Women Association, 51*, 67–69.

Otker, T., & Hayes, P. (1987). Judging the efficiency of sponsorship: Experience from the 1986 soccer World Cup. *ESOMAR Congress, 15*, 3–8.

Perry, C. L. (1999). The tobacco industry and underage youth smoking. *Archives of Pediatrics and Adolescent Medicine, 153*, 935–941.

Physicians for a Smoke-Free Canada. (1996, March). *Tobacco Advertising and Sponsorship Increase Children's Smoking*. Ottawa.

Pollay, R. W. (2002). How cigarette advertising works: Rich imagery and poor information [Expert report prepared for *JTI-Macdonald Corp., Imperial Tobacco Canada Ltd., and Rothmans, Benson & Hedges Inc. v. The Attorney General of Canada*; Quebec Superior Court]. Toronto: Ontario Tobacco Research Unit.

Pollay, R. W. (2001). Export "A" ads are extremely expert, eh? *Tobacco Control, 10*, 71–74.

Pollay, R. W. (2000). Targeting youth and concerned smokers: Evidence from Canadian tobacco industry documents. *Tobacco Control, 9*, 136–147.

Pollay, R. W., & Lavack, A. M. (1993). The targeting of youths by cigarette marketers: Archival evidence on trial. *Advances in Consumer Research, 20*, 266–271.

Pollay, R. W., Siddarth, S., Siegel, M., Haddix, A., Merritt, R. K., Giovino, G. A., & Eriksen, M. P. (1996). The last straw? Cigarette advertising and realized market shares among youths and adults, 1979–1993. *Journal of Marketing, 60*, 1–16.

Race report [Report: Canada]. (2002, July). *F1 Racing*, p. 146.

RJR-Macdonald Inc. (1996a, September 12). Export "A" Inc.—How do we build a success story, 1997 and beyond. Exhibit D-192, *JTI-Macdonald Corp., Imperial Tobacco Canada Ltd., and Rothmans, Benson & Hedges Inc. v. The Attorney General of Canada*. Quebec Superior Court.

RJR-Macdonald Inc. (1996b, March 25). Sponsorship objectives and strategies [inter-office correspondence from Nancy Marcus to Patrick Mispolet]. Exhibit D-200, *JTI-Macdonald Corp., Imperial Tobacco Canada Ltd., and Rothmans, Benson & Hedges Inc. v. The Attorney General of Canada*. Quebec Superior Court.

RJR-Macdonald Inc. (1996c, September 16). Re: Export 'A' brand—1997 communications in Québec [letter to Daphne Bykerk, Vice President Marketing, RJR-Macdonald Inc. from Eric Blais, Vice President, Director of Strategic Planning, Harrod & Mirlin Ltd.]. Exhibit D-193, *JTI-Macdonald Corp., Imperial Tobacco Canada Ltd., and Rothmans, Benson & Hedges Inc. v. The Attorney General of Canada*. Quebec Superior Court.

RJR-Macdonald Inc. (1989a, February 1). Competitive business development strategies for the 1990s. Exhibit D-226, *JTI-Macdonald Corp., Imperial Tobacco Canada Ltd., and Rothmans, Benson & Hedges Inc. v. The Attorney General of Canada*. Quebec Superior Court.

RJR-Macdonald Inc. (1989b, October 5). Export A family brand positioning statement. Prepared by J. Walter Thompson Ad Agency. Exhibit D-175, *JTI-Macdonald Corp., Imperial Tobacco*

Canada Ltd., and Rothmans, Benson & Hedges Inc. v. The Attorney General of Canada. Quebec Superior Court.

RJR-Macdonald Inc. (1987, October 21). Export "A" brand long-term strategy. Exhibit AG-15, *RJR-Macdonald Inc. v. Canada (Attorney General).*

Rootman, I., & Flay, B. R. (1995). *A Study on Youth Smoking: Plain Packaging, Health Warnings, Event Marketing and Price Reductions.* Toronto: Ontario Tobacco Research Unit.

Rothmans, Benson & Hedges Inc. (1996). Strategic plan—1997/98: Sales and marketing. Exhibit D-170, *JTI-Macdonald Corp., Imperial Tobacco Canada Ltd., and Rothmans, Benson & Hedges Inc. v. The Attorney General of Canada.* Quebec Superior Court.

Rothmans, Benson & Hedges Inc. (1995, August). Craven "A" Ltd. 1995 review. Exhibit D-194, *JTI-Macdonald Corp., Imperial Tobacco Canada Ltd., and Rothmans, Benson & Hedges Inc. v. The Attorney General of Canada.* Quebec Superior Court.

Rothmans, Benson & Hedges Inc. (1993, October). Strategic plan—1994/95: Sales and marketing. Exhibit D-195, *JTI-Macdonald Corp., Imperial Tobacco Canada Ltd., and Rothmans, Benson & Hedges Inc. v. The Attorney General of Canada.* Quebec Superior Court.

Rothmans, Benson & Hedges Inc. (1991, February). Segmentation—Phase 1: Focus group research Ontario/Quebec. Prepared by Johnston & Associates. Exhibit D-201, *JTI-Macdonald Corp., Imperial Tobacco Canada Ltd., and Rothmans, Benson & Hedges Inc. v. The Attorney General of Canada.* Quebec Superior Court.

Rothmans Inc. (1995). *Annual Report 1995.*

Shanklin, W. L., & Kuzma, J. R. (1992). Buying that sporting image: What senior executives need to know about corporate sports sponsorship. *Marketing Management, 1,* 58–67.

Siegel, M. (2001). Counteracting tobacco motor sports sponsorship as a promotional tool: Is the tobacco settlement enough? *American Journal of Public Health, 91,* 1100–1106.

Sparks, R. (1999). Youth awareness of tobacco sponsorship as a dimension of brand equity. *International Journal of Sport Marketing and Sponsorship, 1,* 236–260.

Sparks, R. E. C. (1997). Bill C-71 and tobacco sponsorship of sports. *Policy Options, 18,* 22–25.

Stoner, R. H. (1992). 200 mph cigarette ads: A comparison of international restrictions on tobacco sports sponsorship. *Hastings International and Comparative Law Review, 15,* 639–670.

Taylor, P. (1984). *Smoke Ring: The Politics of Tobacco.* London: The Bodley Head.

Teel, S. J., Teel, J. E., & Bearden, W. O. (1979). Lessons learned from the broadcast cigarette advertising ban. *Journal of Marketing, 43,* 45–50.

Tuckwell, K. J. (1988). *Canadian advertising in action.* Scarborough, ON: Prentice-Hall Canada Inc.

Warner, K. E. (1985). Tobacco industry response to public health concern: A content analysis of cigarette ads. *Health Education Quarterly, 12,* 115–127.

Wells, W., Burnett, J., & Moriarty, S. (1989). *Advertising: Principles and Practice.* Englewood Cliffs, NJ: Prentice-Hall.

Wichmann, S. A., & Martin, D. R. (1991). Sports and tobacco: The smoke has yet to clear. *The Physician and Sportsmedicine, 19,* 125–131.

Wyckham, R. G. (1997). Regulating the marketing of tobacco products and controlling smoking in Canada. *Canadian Journal of Administrative Sciences, 14,* 141–165.

18

Social Marketing of Sport

John J. Jackson
University of Victoria

This chapter illustrates some of the major consequences of social marketing programs that have been used to promote sport participation in many parts of the world during the past 30 years. Upon considering the results of some such campaigns, it is evident that strategical mistakes have been made by the proponents. A strategy is suggested that is likely to lead to more successful outcomes.

Marketing has a pejorative ring in some academic circles because it seems to suggest manipulation (Rogers & Leonard-Barton, 1978). *Social marketing* (Kotler & Zaltman, 1971), on the other hand, began about 40 years ago with the rhetorical question, "Why can't you sell brotherhood like you sell soap?" (Wiebe, 1952). Well, it seems to be more complex because, often, social marketing campaigns seek to convince people to do something that they may perceive to be unpleasant or not pleasurable. Campaigns have dealt with such issues as anti-smoking, drug abuse, nutrition, and energy conservation. But in a survey of U.S. smokers, although 9 out of 10 wanted to quit, 57% expected they would still be smoking in 5 years' time. Similarly, many people would like to lose weight and floss their teeth but they do not—they seem to be impeded by inertia (Rogers, 1983). For this chapter's purposes, social marketing is the design, implementation, and control of programs calculated to influence the acceptability of social ideas, that is, to diffuse socially beneficial ideas that do not entail the sale of commercial products (Rogers, 1983).

In the next section I examine social marketing consequences in the realm of sport.

SPORT FOR ALL

In 1949, 10 European countries founded the Council of Europe with this broad aim: "To achieve greater unity between its members for the purpose of safeguarding and realizing the ideals and principles which are their common heritage and facilitating their economic and social progress" (Council for Cultural Co-operation, 1964:1).

By 1964, the Council of Europe had 17 member countries, and it had established the Council for Cultural Co-operation (CCC) in 1962 with both the Committee for Out-of-School Education and Cultural Development (CCC, 1964). It was the latter body that adopted the slogan "Sport for All" as the appropriate expression to cover a long-term European aim. At the 10th session of the CCC (June 6–10, 1966) a "Declaration of Principle" was made, which asserted that it was the responsibility of the institutions concerned with sport to help "all citizens, irrespective of age, sex, occupation or means, to understand the value of sport and to engage in it throughout their lives" (Council of Europe, 1971). The Council of Europe defined *sport* as "free, spontaneous physical activity engaged in during leisure time: its functions being recreation, amusement and development" (Council of Europe, 1971:5–6).

By 1970, six countries—Norway, Sweden, The Netherlands, Iceland, West Germany, and Denmark—had established national campaigns intended to increase mass participation in sport, as a result of Council of Europe prompting. Credit must go to Norway for introducing a novel campaign under the slogan "Trim," for trim has a similar meaning in most European languages and evokes the idea of fitness, neatness, well-being, and smartness. The Council of Europe expressed the hope that the word *trim* might become synonymous with fitness campaigns throughout and beyond member countries, and countries adopting such campaigns should, through the Council of Europe, co-operate with each other by exchanging views and knowledge gained from experience (Barry, 1970).

In March 1975, a conference of European Ministers Responsible for Sports was held in Brussels, and draft recommendations for a European Sport for All Charter were drawn up (Council of Europe, 1975; CMS (74) 10, and CMS (75) 15). This Charter was officially adopted by the Council of Europe committee of ministers on September 24, 1976 under the heading "On the Principles for a Policy of Sport for All."

Sport Participation Canada (PARTICIPaction) was incorporated in 1971 as a private, nonprofit company with the stated intention "to promote more physical activity among all Canadians" (Kisby, 1972). It was hoped that national promotion would be matched or surpassed by an equally powerful force at the grassroots level, which would involve the broad base of physical education and recreation leadership in the country. Toward those ends, Saskatoon, Saskatchewan was selected by PARTICIPaction in February 1972 as a demonstration community. Thus, what PARTICIPaction was trying to market at Saskatoon by means of mass communication was very similar to what had been earlier initiated within the Council of Europe's "Sport for All" movement.

Conferences (Trim and Fitness International) to enable inter-country exchange of ideas began on a biennial basis in Norway in 1969. By the time of the 1973 Frankfurt-on-Main conference, 19 countries (Austria, Belgium, Canada, Denmark, Federal Republic of Germany, Finland, France, Iceland, Ireland, Japan, Mexico, The Netherlands, Norway, Poland, Sweden, Switzerland, United Kingdom, United States, Yugoslavia) were showing active interest in co-operating to achieve the objective "Sport for All." This co-operation took the form of each country's delegate explaining what his or her country had done and was doing regarding administration, personnel, finance, and communication methods. However, no country represented at Frankfurt-on-Main had been able to measure the effectiveness *of* its program (Jackson, 1978).

Mass Communication Consequences

It was with this background that the initial research was undertaken at the site of the world's most intense social marketing campaign. It was reasoned that outcomes of campaigns would very likely be less successful elsewhere. There were several research purposes but principal among them were efforts to find out (a) how successful such mass media communication campaigns were as far as creating awareness was concerned, and (b) how successful they were in effecting behaviour change. From the outset, it was recognized that consequences are always difficult to measure and that they occur over time. Further, pretesting was not possible nor was using a Canadian control group. Thus, when consequence studies are carried out, they are only able to measure the consequences at a cross-section in time. This chapter, then, first mainly reports on two cross-sectional studies of PARTICIPaction's campaign in Saskatoon as measured after the initial major thrust of the campaign in 1973 and again 15 years later in 1988. Further, it presents findings from a similar inquiry conducted in Vancouver in 1989 where the national (but not the inter-personal) communication efforts had been in effect since PARTICIPaction's founding.

Briefly, PARTICIPaction's purpose was summarized by Kisby (1972:10–14) when he said, "Our goal in simple terms is to change the lackadaisical attitude of Canadians toward physical activity. To coax them out of their easy chairs into the fresh air or to the nearest gym, skating rink, swimming pool, tennis court, hiking trail . . . anywhere they can walk, run, skip, jump and enjoy themselves . . . COME ALIVE! is the real message."

To market this message nationally, the mass media was used. For exam-ple, TV commercials said the average 30-year-old Canadian was only as fit as the average 60-year-old Swede. Short amusing messages were broadcast on radio and were accompanied by catchy tunes. More discursive messages designed to promote PARTICIPaction's aims were displayed on milk cartons. In Saskatoon, all the national media messages were used on TV, in the local newspapers, and on local radio stations. However, a much more concentrated effort was made at Saskatoon where, additionally, more interpersonal com-munication was used that involved local opinion leaders. Overall, the mass media communication effort was probably the most intense one of its type that had ever been used.

Detailed reports of the findings have previously appeared in Jackson (1975:51–53, 1976:25–31, 1979:89–100, 1991:33–38, 1992:369–375, 1994:29–33). It is sufficient to state here that all the studies used scientific research methods involving representative samples of the cities' populations. Each sample included 400 subjects who were interviewed using structured ques-tionnaires in the earlier studies and then by telephone surveys in the later Saskatoon and Vancouver studies.

Summary and Conclusions

Based on the Saskatoon studies, the following specific conclusions concerning awareness and behaviour change appear to be justified. For comparison pur-poses, the first numbers are the 1988 percentages, indicating 15 years' mass media communication campaigning; the 1973 to 1974 percentages appear in parentheses immediately following these numbers.

1. Awareness. Approximately 87% (90%) of the total population can be expected to be made aware of a PARTICIPaction Saskatoon-type cam-paign.

TABLE 18.1
Mass Communication Consequences in Various Locations.

Locations	Awareness (%)	Behavior Change (%)
Saskatoon 1974 (Jackson, 1975, 1976)	90	15
Saskatoon (Bailey & Nixon, 1983)	94	N/A
Saskatoon 1988 (Jackson, 1991)	87	16
Edmonton 1974 (Jackson, 1979)	72	10
Victoria 1978 (Jackson, 1979)	72	10
Windsor (Jolicoeur, 1979)	"almost all"	10
National (Bailey, 1983)	71	N/A
Vancouver 1989 (Jackson, 1992)	68	10

2. Behavior change. After a PARTICIPaction Saskatoon-type campaign, approximately 30% (24%) of an adult population can be expected to adopt physical activity but, later, about 14% (9%) will reject it, leaving 16% (15%) as continuing new adopters.

In the 1989 Vancouver study, the findings were similar to those in other locations where the population had been subjected to the national campaign only, as opposed to the more intense local campaign in Saskatoon: 67.9% of the population was aware of PARTICIPaction and 10.3% of the subjects positively changed their exercising behavior as a result of the campaign. The other similar national-only findings are listed in Table 18.1 and relate to Edmonton (1974), Victoria (1978), Windsor (1979), and national (Bailey, 1983). Broadly, the awareness was 72% and behavior change was 10%.

The data in Table 18.1 illustrate that awareness of PARTICIPaction in Saskatoon is high and that it declined 3% between 1974 and 1988. This almost negligible decline is probably accounted for by the fact that the intensity of the campaign lessened slightly during this period, and new residents are constantly moving into the city. All the reported Saskatoon data show that such intense mass media communication campaigns do create a very high degree of awareness. It is important to note that mass communication in Saskatoon was very intense and was supplemented by interpersonal communication. Thus, the more intense Saskatoon campaign accounts for the difference between the Saskatoon data and the other awareness figures reported in

Table 18.1. The non-Saskatoon findings result mainly from national mass media communication and are remarkably consistent.

The data in Table 18.1 indicate that exercising behavior change, as a result of intense mass media communication campaigns, is at about 15% and that it has remained constant over a 15-year period. Where the campaign was less intense, the behavior change was 10%. It should be remembered that these behavior changes, although perhaps slight, are consequences of PARTICI-Paction mass communication campaigns. Generally, then, such campaigns do not greatly effect behavior change. In looking at these data, it should be kept in mind that the adoption standard may be very low. Thus, the overall exercising level may be worse than it appears.

Activity Levels

It is progressively more difficult to isolate the effects of PARTICIPaction–Saskatoon-type campaigns because of increasing attention being given in the media to cholesterol, smoking, aerobics, jogging, better recreational facilities, and so on. However, to cross-check these findings with other measures of exercising behavior, the following data are presented. They help to provide a fuller information base before developing a new social marketing strategy for increasing participation in sport.

Policymakers should pay some attention to studies that have attempted to determine what percentages of mass populations engage in strenuous enough activity to produce a cardiovascular training effect. As a parallel enquiry to the one conducted by Jackson (1991) in Saskatoon, it was found that 20.6% of the population participated in strenuous exercise at least three times per week. To substantiate this finding further, two other studies are cited. First, Stephens, Jacobs, & White (1985) estimated that approximately 20% of the U.S. and Canadian population exercised with an intensity and frequency generally recommended for cardiovascular benefit. The second relevant study was done in the United States by White, Powell, Hogelin, Gentry, & Forman (1987) using telephone interview data aggregated from 30 surveys and 22,236 respondents. They showed that 21% of the U.S. adult population did exercise of sufficient severity and regularity as is "commonly recommended to maximally reduce the incidence of coronary heart disease." (p. 307)

Different but interesting macro-data were found in *The Wall Street Journal* (Cohen, 1993:C1). It was reported that American Sports Data, a Hartsdale, New York, research firm found that "one American in five who exercises regularly is still outnumbered by three couch potatoes." Moreover, the survey found that the number of frequent participants in the United States peaked in 1990 then declined by 4.8% in 1991 and again by 2.7% in 1992. In the United Kingdom, 14% of men and 4% of women did vigorous activities of 20 minutes duration three times per week (Allied Dunbar, 1992). The U.K. Sports Councils had adopted the slogan "Sport for All" but had not used mass communication means to spread the word. It seems reasonable, however, to assume that activity levels in continental Europe would not be markedly different from those reported in North American and the United Kingdom.

Based on all these findings, it seems that at least three perspectives initially could be taken by policymakers. One point of view is that governments should stop spending money on these types of mass communication marketing campaigns because their effect has remained constant over 15 years and no further progress seems to be being made. Also, those who will exercise do so anyway. Alternatively, it could be argued, that it is necessary to keep reminding people, by mass communication means, of the need for regular strenuous exercise so that the 20% level of participation can be maintained. Proponents of such mass communication programes need to seek other sound evidence of their programs' utility if they are to justify being allowed to continue (for other than political reasons). Or, they should consider developing a social marketing program similar to the one presented next.

SOCIO-PSYCHOLOGICAL MECHANISM

What is the socio-psychological mechanism, or process, necessary to effect behavior change in "Sport for All," physical activity, smoking, diet, and other areas of social marketing? Two sources provide most useful guidelines: the Cartwright (1949) model and the "diffusion of innovations" literature.

Cartwright Model

Being aware of the lack of success of mass media campaigns, an interdisciplinary group of researchers at Stanford University, which was concerned with decreasing cardiac risk factors, turned to the Cartwright (1949) model when designing their three communities' behavior modification study. The Cartwright (1949) model was concerned with the sale of U.S. war bonds and it stated that three kinds of changes must be achieved to modify behavior: (a) changes in cognitive structures, that is, what people know or understand; (b) changes in affective structures, that is, what people want to do; and (c) changes in action structures, that is, what people actually do. Cartwright

(1949) noted that mass media campaigns are usually ineffective in that although they might be reasonably successful in influencing information and attitudes (a and b) they typically do an inadequate job of promoting and guiding specific actions or the behaviors advocated in the campaign. In other words, (c) is missing and this leads to considering the diffusion of innovations literature.

Diffusion Research Findings

Diffusion of innovations refers to the way new ideas spread within social systems. The "innovation" does not have to be objectively new but only perceived as new by the would-be receivers. "Sport for All" can be viewed as an innovation by those who are suddenly put in the position of deciding whether to adopt it or reject it. Rogers (1983) described diffusion of innovations as, "essentially a social process in which subjectively perceived information about a new idea is communicated." He has been collecting and analyzing diffusion of innovation studies (3,083 by the time of his 1983 book) since the very early 1960s. Based on the studies, he formulated generalizations about the processes. Of particular relevance in this chapter are the following:

1. Mass media channels of communication are relatively more important at the knowledge function and interpersonal channels are relatively more important at the persuasion function in the innovation-decision process.
2. Cosmopolite channels are relatively more important at the knowledge function and localite channels are relatively more important at the persuasion function.
3. Interpersonal communication is likely to be more effective than mass communication in the behavior change function. In particular, communication intended to change behavior needs to be between homophilious dyads.

Homophily is the degree to which pairs of individuals (dyads) who interact are similar in certain attributes such as beliefs, values, education, social status, and the like. Heterophily is the mirror opposite of homophily (Rogers & Shoemaker, 1971). A successful example of such interaction is found with the "barefoot" doctors in China. They are paraprofessionals who are socially closer to the lower status members of the user system that they serve. Recruited in their villages, they receive some medical training, then they continue to do some farm work and provide some medical services. Being socially close, they are regarded as peers by the villagers (Rogers, 1983).

Suggested Social Marketing Mechanism

Building on Cartwright (1949) and Rogers and Shoemakers' (1971) general-izations, an adaptation of Lovelock and Weinberg's (1989) market targeting model is added to present the following seven-step mechanism to enhance the social marketing of "Sport for All."

Step 1. Define the country's (or institutions) "Sport for All" objectives and set priorities.

Step 2. Identify which groups (markets) within the overall population are key to achievement of objectives. For example, the groups may be by age, sex, occupational class, geography, and so on. This is market definition.

Step 3. Examine key groups (markets) to determine needs, personal characteristics, and current behavior patterns. This is analysis of target markets and should include assessing the socio-psychological characteristics of the inactive/moderately active population subgroups and the conditions that might be affecting the activity levels.

Step 4. Based on this analysis, further divide key groups (markets) into target segments that are sufficiently different to merit tailored strategies. For example, use particular strategies for the old, the young, ethnic groups, or lower occupational classes.

Step 5. Develop efficient marketing strategies targeted at each segment. This is the key persuasion function and it is in this step where something like a network of homophilious dyads needs to be established. The "network" should consist of a variety of forms from the simple dyad, through local opinion leaders of groups or through individuals generally who have the social closeness found in the barefoot doctors of China. To illustrate by way of a sport example, if an occupational class 1 person (e.g., a judge) says to an occupational class 7 person (e.g., an unskilled laborer), "You ought to try playing squash," not much is likely to happen. Alternatively, if an unskilled worker (who believes in squash) says to another unskilled worker, "Come and have a game of squash at the public court," the invitee is more likely to accept and, therefore, more likely to take up squash or some other sport.

It is at this point in the process that the social marketer should take account of the fact that individuals' cognitive and affective structures are open for influence. The concept of exchange applies, "What's in it for me?" And the rate of adoption will be influenced by the would-be adopter's perceptions of (a) the relative advantage of adopting "Sport for All" (the innovation) (i.e., is it better than the present state of inaction?); (b) the compatibility of the innovation so far as existing values and past experiences are concerned; (c) the complexity of the innovation (i.e., is it difficult to understand and use?); (d) the trialability of the innovation (i.e., could it be tried and rejected or is it all or nothing?); and (e) the observability of the innovation (i.e., are the claimed benefits obvious or not?) (Rogers & Shoemaker, 1971).

Facilities for "Sport for All" and programming need to be reconsidered by promoting countries and institutions. In the developed countries, there are many excellent sports facilities and trained staff, but officials and staff need to work through these suggested strategies if they really want to achieve "Sport for All."

Step 6. Monitor the results for each target segment and evaluate the relative success of the social marketing strategies in efficiently achieving the desired objectives.

Step 7. Based on the evaluation, make any needed modifications to the segmentation approach employed and to the marketing strategies directed at each target segment. Thus, ongoing improved social marketing tactics can be worked out to improve the execution of strategy described in steps 1 through 6.

CONCLUSION

Evidence illustrates that "Sport for All" has not been achieved. In developed countries, excellent sports facilities and trained sport professionals exist. Policymakers need to require their professionals to work through the social marketing strategies described here. It is complex but, given this guidance, intelligent professionals ought to be able to use these social marketing strategies to make much more progress toward achieving "Sport for All." An important aside is that success would lead to considerably greater opportunities to market commercial sports goods and services.

REFERENCES

Allied Dunbar (1992). *Allied Dunbar National Fitness Survey Summary.* London: The Sports Council and the Health Education Authority.

Bailey, D. A., & Nixon, H. R. (1983). *A study of fitness importance, physical activity patterns, and awareness of Saskatoon citizens compared to baseline Canadian data.* Mimeographed Report, University of Saskatchewan, College of Physical Education.

Barry, J. (1970). *Sport for all: national campaigns.* Paper read at CCPR Annual Conference, Lilleshall, England, Dec. 3, (mimeographed).

Cartwright, D. (1949). Some principles of mass persuasion: Research on the sale of U.S. war bonds. *Human Relations, 2,* 253–267.

Cohen, L. P. (1993, July 15). Exercise decline takes pep out of some stocks. *The Wall Street Journal,* p. C1–2.

Council for Cultural Co-operation. (1964). *Training the Trainer.* Strasbourg, France: CCC, Sec. III, Out-of-School Education, No. 3.

Council of Europe. (1971). *Planning the Future (VIII).* Strasbourg, France: CCC/EES (71) 22.

Council of Europe. (1975). CMS (75) 15. *Draft recommendation on the European Sport for All Charter.* Conference of European Ministers Responsible for Sport, Brussels, March 20–21.

Jackson, J. J. (1994). Communication and "sport for all" in historical perspective, *International Journal of Physical Education, 31*(2), 29–33.

Jackson, J. J. (1992). Research-based strategies for diffusing leisure in the New Europe (pp. 369–375). In *Leisure and New Citizenship.* Bilbao, Spain: ELRA Congress.

Jackson, J. J. (1991). Mass participation in physical recreation. A 15-year study in Saskatoon. *Recreation Canada, 49, 3,* 33–38.

Jackson, J. J. (1990). An assessment of exercising Behavior in Saskatoon. *British Journal of Physical Education Res. Supp., 8, 21, 4,* 19–24.

Jackson, J. J. (1979). Some consequences of PARTICIPaction's campaign in Victoria. *Review of Sport and Leisure, 4, 2,* 89–100.

Jackson, J. J. (1978). Sport for all (pp. 486–504). In Lowe, B., Kanin, D. B., & Strenk, A. (eds.) *Sport and International Relations.* Champaign, IL: Stipes.

Jackson, J. J. (1976). Some consequences of PARTICIPaction's campaign at Saskatoon. *Canadian Association for Health, Physical Education and Recreation Journal, 42,* 25–31.

Jackson, J. J. (1975). Getting people involved in activity. *Recreation Canada, 33, 5,* 51–53.

Jolicoeur, C. M. (June 1979). *The marketing of fitness in Canada and the United States.* Paper read at the CAHPER Conference, Winnipeg, Manitoba.

Kisby, R. (1972). PARTICIPaction. *Canadian Association for Health, Physical Education, and Recreation Journal, 38,* 10–14.

Kotler, P., & Zaltman, G. (1971). Social marketing: An approach to planned social changes, *Journal of Marketing, 35,* 3–12.

Lovelock, C. H., & Weinberg, C. B. (1989). *Public and Nonprofit Marketing.* Redwood City, CA: The Scientific Press.

Rogers, E. M. (1983). *Diffusion of Innovations* (3rd ed.). New York: The Free Press.

Rogers, E. M., & Leonard-Barton, D. (1978). Testing social theories in marketing settings. *American Behavioral Scientist, 21,* 479–500.

Rogers, E. M., & Shoemaker, F. (1971). *Communication of Innovations: A Cross-Cultural Approach* (2nd ed.). New York: The Free Press.

Stephens, T., Jacobs, D. R., & White, C. C. (1985). A descriptive epidemiology of leisure-time physical activity. *Public Health Reports, 100,* 147–157.

Wiebe, G. D. (1952). Merchandising commodities and citizenship on television. *Public Opinion Quarterly, 15,* 679–691.

White, C. C., Powell, K. E., Hogelin, G. C., Gentry, E. M., & Forman, M. R. (1987). The behavioral risk factor surveys: IV. The descriptive epidemiology of exercise. *American Journal of Preventive Medicine, 3,* 304–310.

19

Teenagers' Perceptions of the Influence of Advertising and Price Versus Interpersonal, Social Factors on Their Purchases of Brand Name Athletic Shoes and Clothing

Timothy P. Meyer
University of Wisconsin-Green Bay

Katheryn Gettelman
MarketProbe, Milwaukee, WI

Thomas R. Donohue
Virginia Commonwealth University

Consumer decision-making and consumer behavior are complex processes, influenced by a combination of factors, many of which are interrelated (Blackwell, Miniard, & Engel, 2001; Burnett, Moriarity, & Wells, 2002; O'Guinn, Semenik, & Allen, 2002; Solomon, 1994). Although some consumer decisions are simpler than others, and which factors are more or less important vary from consumer to consumer and from one purchasing context to another, it is reasonable to conclude that combinations of factors are an integral and inherent attribute of consumer decision-making and the consumer behavior processes.

Of the many factors involved in influencing consumer behavior, some are more controlled by marketers (e.g., price, packaging, advertising, and so on), whereas others are generally beyond their direct control because they involve situated individuals affected by social, interpersonal factors (e.g., social status, peer group norms, ethnicity, and so on). Marketers have become highly skilled at studying these social, interpersonal factors and capitalizing on them in areas where they can establish themselves in a new product category or position their brands to generate business in that category. For certain consumers in specific product categories, the mix of influential factors can be identified and controlled to successfully position one brand versus competitors' brands. By having the right product at the right price, positioned to capture the attention and imagination of the target audience, a company can come to dominate market share and maintain that dominance, provided of course that the company delivers a consistent quality brand for initial purchase and for repeat purchases. The history of marketing, however, clearly demonstrates the enormous difficulty of being successful in this regard. Sports marketing provides a history of successes and failures. There is no magic formula that guarantees success. Some brands have succeeded despite major missteps along the way, managing to learn from mistakes and correct them promptly and satisfactorily. Others have failed, despite a promising start or some early, long-term success followed by failure, due in part to more aggressive and effective competitors.

This chapter identifies teenagers' perceptions of the influence of advertising and price factors in comparison to social, interpersonal major factors affecting their consumer behavior, including peers, parents, and personal choice. We looked at two related product lines: brand name athletic shoes and brand name athletic clothing. Purchase decisions and brand preferences were measured for first-time purchases and current purchases. The athletic footwear / apparel industry represents a major economic force in the United States and around the world with equally enormous economic consequences. U.S. revenues alone are near the $50 billion mark (Cassidy, 2002).

BACKGROUND AND PREVIOUS RESEARCH

Peer influence on teenagers' behavior is routinely acknowledged in the academic research literature and in the popular media. As Bochner (1994) pointed out, "One of the more robust findings in social psychology is the power of the peer group to influence adolescent behaviour and attitudes (p. 70)." One obvious area of peer influence is in the consumer behavior of teens.

The research literature in social psychology has long documented the role played by social, interpersonal factors such as peers (e.g., friends), parents, older siblings, as well as intrapersonal variables such as self-esteem, rebelliousness, resistance to authority, and so on as factors that influence a wide range of teen behaviors. Among the most studied are preteens' and teens' use of tobacco, alcohol, and other controlled substances (Fisher & Bauman, 1988; Michell & West, 1996; Wang, Fitzhugh, Eddy, Fu, & Turner, 1997)

Not all teen behaviors are alike; when it comes to the influence of peers, several general categories exist: a best friend or best friends; those who are part of a friendship group; others who are seen quite regularly in common locations and who are the same age; others who are older, respected, and admired; others who are older and ignored or disliked or not respected. Depending on the specific behavior in question and role or roles played by other potentially influential factors, different peers can have different effects on the behavior of teenagers. For smoking or drinking, friends or the friendship group may be extremely influential for some teens in their decision to start and to continue smoking or to not start smoking or to stop smoking. For others, the influence of older, very popular peers (e.g., a popular high school senior to a freshman) can have a huge impact on smoking decisions, both smoking and non-smoking.

It is also clear that some behaviors are more important than others and seem to matter more to most teens. Most, if not all, of these behaviors are strongly influenced by their peers to one degree or another at various stages in their development. For example, the decision to become a regular smoker or an underage drinker seems more important than which brand of soft drink or fast food place is selected. One or more brands may be acceptable without appearing to deviate from accepted behavioral norms that dominate much of teens' behavior. Most importantly, picking the accepted brands of soft drinks or fast food places represents an easily implemented choice. More important categories than soft drinks or fast food choices would be items such as clothing or hairstyles. How one looks and what one wears are often perceived by most teens to have potentially enormous social consequences. This holds true for teens who value the display of conformity with visible, established group norms and for those teens who seek membership in a certain group and are quick to adopt that group's standards. Clothing and shoes are two excellent examples of instantly visible behaviors (*American Demographics*, 2003). Everyone else at school can see what each person is wearing. This means that both style of clothing and shoes and specific brands are crucial to being accepted by peers generally or by specific peer groups. For example, a Nike beret may be the hat choice for certain groups whereas a baseball cap with a professional sports team's logo might be the choice for another group. Members dress alike in some if not all respects, and those who wish to affiliate find that wearing similar apparel is an overt indication of the desire to become a member.

Social, interpersonal factors such as peers, parents, older siblings, and intrapersonal variables have been routinely identified in previous studies of young consumers in many different product categories (Bearden & Etzel, 1982; Zollo, 1999). In the area of teenagers' clothing preferences, several studies have documented the role played by peers, including what teens, even pre-teens, choose to wear as part of a group of which they are already a member or for a group to which they aspire to be a member (Forsythe, 1991; Haynes, 1993; Hilfiger, 1997; Wilson & Sparks, 1996; Zollo, 1999). Other research has looked specifically at athletic shoes or athletic clothing (Costley & Brucks, 1992; Evans, 1991; Lee & Browne, 1995; Meyer, Gettelman, & Donohue, 2001; Peter, 1988).

While some previous research has studied how different types of advertising messages produce different effects on teenagers' attitudes toward brands or purchase intentions, only two studies to date have provided data on perceptions of advertising's influence on the brand preferences for athletic shoes (Lee & Browne, 1995; Meyer, Gettelman, & Donohue, 2001). The Lee and Browne study examined only current brand preferences for athletic shoes and not for athletic clothes and was limited to black American teens; it was further limited by not presenting a broad range of factors that could influence purchase decisions that would allow for a comparison of the relative influence of one factor versus others. Although the acknowledgment of advertising's influence with certain athlete celebrities endorsing specific brands of athletic shoes is important, how advertising compares to other influences cannot be determined.

The study reported in this chapter was based on the earlier pilot study reported by Meyer, Gettelman, and Donohue (2001). They presented older teenagers with a range of factors that could influence purchase decisions of athletic shoes and athletic clothing and asked them to indicate the degree of influence for each of these factors at two key purchase points: first-time purchase and current purchases. The addition of first-time and current purchases allowed them to compare how the various influence factors had changed over time, which ones had changed and in which direction (more or less perceived influence), and which ones had stayed pretty much the same. This pilot study was limited by small sample size and by the homogeneity of the sample (nearly all respondents were white and from smaller cities). Moreover, this study incorporated only responses to the numerically coded scales and did not include open-ended items to provide examples of how various factors influenced respondents' purchase decisions.

RESEARCH HYPOTHESES

Based on results of the pilot study, we hypothesized the following:

1. For the initial purchases of athletic shoes and athletic clothing, advertising and price would be rated significantly less influential than same-sex friends, perceived quality, and personal choice.
2. For current purchases, perceived quality, price, and personal choice would be significantly more influential than all other factors.
3. For current purchases, price would be significantly more influential than it was for initial purchases; advertising and peer influence (friends and non-friends) would be significantly less influential.
4. For both initial and current purchases, females would be significantly more likely than males to be influenced by their peers (opposite- and same-sex friends).
5. Given the presence of some substantial ethnic diversity in the sample of respondents we studied, we predicted that same sex peer influence would be significantly greater for black males than white males or females in the brand name athletic shoes category. Wearing brand name athletic shoes remains a very important consideration among black adolescent males to a greater degree than among whites and in comparison to females, black or white (Lee & Browne, 1995).

METHODOLOGY

The Sample

We surveyed 248 undergraduates who were enrolled in a basic, introductory communications course at a large urban university in the mid-Atlantic region of the United States. Most of the students enrolled were not communication majors and were taking the course to satisfy general university requirements. The sample was skewed toward females (60%). Approximately three fourths of the sample consisted of 17- to 19-year-olds, with more than 90% ages 17 to 22. Of the total sample, 32% were black, 65% were white, and 3% ethnicities other than black or white.

Procedures

Participants were guaranteed anonymity by using a cover sheet that contained only a space for the student's name. When the student turned in the completed questionnaire, the cover sheet was removed by the research assistant and placed in a separate pile for recording participation for the extra credit. In this way, students were free to answer all questions openly and honestly without fear that their responses would be matched to their names. Students were also informed that their answers would in no way affect their standing in the university, with the professor teaching the course, or in the course itself. Students participated voluntarily to earn extra credit toward their final course grade. More than 99% of the class participated, ruling out any volunteer bias in the results.

The Questionnaire

Participants filled out a questionnaire that elicited personal, demographic information: age, gender, year in school, ethnicity, type of household (campus or off-campus). For the category of athletic shoes, two situations were posed for respondents. The first asked them to think about the first time they purchased a pair of brand name athletic shoes. The second asked them about current purchases of brand name athletic shoes. For the category of athletic clothes (again brand name athletic clothes), the same two situations were used: first-time purchase and current purchase. For each area, participants rated nine influence factors on a 1–7 scale with a "1" representing "no influence" and a "7" indicating "very influential." The factors were advertising, price, the athlete who wears them, personal choice, perceived quality, same-sex friend, opposite-sex friend, other peers (not friends), and parents. We also asked open-ended questions that elicited written responses from each person regarding the circumstances surrounding their first purchase of brand name athletic shoes and clothes and their most recent purchases of each. These responses provided descriptions in each respondent's own words of what went on at the time of first and most recent purchases.

We focused on athletic shoes and athletic clothing because these areas represented a market characterized by rapid growth over the last 15 to 20 years. Women's brand name athletic clothes currently generate more than $15 billion in annual sales, $3 billion more than men's brand name athletic apparel (Warner, 2002). We also focused on these items because brand name athletic shoes and clothing as a market have been driven by the youth segment, accounting for a majority of sales and maintaining teens as customers as they move to adulthood (Warner, 2002).

Statistical Analysis

The appropriate statistical model for analysis of results was a within-groups multivariate analysis of variance (MANOVA) design. The .05 level of statistical significance was used for the overall Wilk's test and for follow-up comparisons of individual means via Scheffe's test. MANOVA tests across factors in each of the four areas (shoes and clothing, first-time and current purchase) revealed Wilk's with a level of statistical significance beyond the .0001 level.

RESULTS

The first research hypothesis tested dealt with the perceived influence of marketer-controlled factors (i.e., advertising, price) as compared to non–marketer-controlled factors (peers, parents, perceived quality, personal choice). The results for athletic shoes are presented in Table 19.1. For first-time purchases of shoes, price was rated as somewhat influential, but significantly less influential, than personal choice, perceived quality, and same-sex friends. Moreover, advertising was significantly more influential than price and statistically equal to perceived quality and same-sex friend. This was a departure from the results of the pilot study where results showed both price and advertising significantly lower than personal choice, perceived quality, and same-sex friends. For current shoe purchases, however, advertising is

TABLE 19.1
Athletic Shoes*

Influence	First-Time Purchase	Current Purchase
Advertising	4.88b	3.58c[†]
Price	3.66c	5.64b[†]
Personal choice	6.25a	6.61a
Perceived quality	5.03b	6.34a[†]
Same sex friend	5.23b	2.59d[†]
Opposite-sex friend	4.27c	2.77d[†]
Other peers	4.42b	3.39c[†]
Parents	3.06d	1.93cd[†]
Athlete wearing	2.83d	1.65d*

*The higher the mean, the *greater* the perceived influence.
[†]Means marked with an asterisk indicate a significant difference for the means in that *row*. *Column* means marked with common subscripts are *not* statistically significantly different from one another at the .05 level or less.

TABLE 19.2
Athletic Clothing*

Influence	First-Time Purchase	Current Purchase
Advertising	4.56bc	3.49c
Price	4.18c	5.70ab[†]
Personal choice	5.86a	6.29a
Perceived quality	4.57bc	5.79ab[†]
Same-sex friend	5.02b	3.28c[†]
Opposite-sex friend	4.67bc	3.66c[†]
Other peers	4.60bc	2.98d[†]
Parents	3.56cd	2.16e[†]
Athlete wearing	3.44cd	2.09e[†]

*The higher the mean, the *greater* the perceived influence.
[†]Means marked with an asterisk indicate a significant difference for the means in that *row*. Column means marked with common subscripts are *not* statistically significantly different from one another at the .05 level or less.

significantly less influential compared to advertising in the first-purchase condition, whereas price was significantly more influential compared to first-time purchase. Again, personal choice and perceived quality were most influential. Peer influence (friends and non-friends) was also significantly less influential when compared to first-time purchases.

Although the pattern that emerged with athletic clothing purchases had some expected similarities to the shoes category, there were some notable differences. For initial purchases, personal choice and same-sex friend emerged as the most influential factors, followed by perceived quality, advertising, opposite-sex friends, and other peers. These results are displayed in Table 19.2. For current purchases, personal choice, perceived quality, and price were significantly more influential than advertising, same-sex friend, and opposite-sex friend; these factors in turn were significantly higher than other peers and parents. Like shoes, advertising significantly decreased while price increased from initial to current purchase of clothes. Statistically significant decreases in influence for initial to current purchases were noted for same-sex friend, opposite-sex friend, other peers, and parents.

Of particular importance was the lack of perceived influence of the specific athlete wearing a particular brand of athletic shoes or clothes. This factor was the lowest rated of all for initi.l and current purchases. Moreover, there were significant drops from initial to current purchases for both shoes and clothes. At first glance, these findings would appear to suggest that competitors who use celebrity athletes to promote their brands are not getting much in the way of results for this hefty investment. This is not the case. Specific athlete endorsers help sell individual brands of shoes and clothing to those customers who are already committed to the product categories. While in the earliest stages of brand name athletic shoes and clothes, some of these same athletes might have helped sell prospective consumers on the general category, their role has clearly evolved to creating and maintaining specific brand identity and brand loyalty. For example, Michael Jordan undoubtedly helped sell a great many young consumers on the idea of buying and wearing Nike shoes in the early days of such campaigns, and in so doing, he helped a new category to emerge and become a huge, distinct market that transcended the use of athletic shoes only for participation in sports to general usage in many different life activities.

Other results dealt with the factors of gender and ethnicity of respondents. For the gender variable, some important male–female differences emerged. For initial purchase of shoes, males were significantly more influenced than females in the area of perceived quality. Here, there seems to be a clear connection between marketing and advertising of specific brands that have focused on the important of how the shoe is made and level of performance that it helps deliver. These messages were apparently more influential for males than females.

Other male–female differences centered on the influence of friends. For both initial and current purchases of shoes, females perceived significantly more influence than males for opposite-sex friends. For current purchases of shoes, same-sex friends were significantly more influential for females than males. In the clothing category, females perceived significantly more influence than males for both same- and opposite-sex friends. These differences held for both initial and current purchases. Thus, for both shoes and clothes, females reported significantly more reliance on their friends as sources of influence affecting their purchase decisions in comparison to males.

For the ethnicity variable, two key differences emerged. For initial purchases of both shoes and clothes, black males reported significantly more influence of same-sex friends than black females or white males or females. Responses to open-ended questions asking respondents to describe the circumstances surrounding their initial purchase of brand name athletic shoes provided some clear evidence of how crucial it was to be wearing athletic shoes (as opposed to regular shoes) and the "right" brand (Nike as opposed to Converse) to be accepted by their close friends and their friendship group. Some described the pressure as enormous. "You better not show up wearing anything but Air Jordans, and not just when we were playing ball" and similar types of comments punctuated the importance of style and brand. The importance of same-sex friends remained for current purchases among black males for both shoes and clothes, but as a factor, same-sex friends significantly declined as reported influences. As one respondent described the difference from initial to current purchases, "I still care what my friends think about what I wear, but it doesn't seem to matter all that much. You don't have to worry so much about wearing something different."

DISCUSSION AND IMPLICATIONS

Discussion

The results of this study clearly suggest that social, interpersonal factors, those that are not under the direct control of marketers, are perceived by teenagers as significantly more important than advertising and price, factors that are controlled by marketers of brand name athletic shoes and clothes. Advertising, however, was a very important factor, especially in initial purchases of shoes. For the initial purchases of brand name athletic clothes, advertising was still an important influence factor, although not as important as it is for shoes. Over time, advertising's perceived influence diminishes, just like the perceived influence of friends and peers.

On the other hand, price increases in importance and influence from the initial purchase to current buying behavior in both the shoe and clothing categories. Price has a dimension where it relates to perceived quality (shoes that cost $175 are judged to be better quality than shoes that sell for $65). In this regard, advertising and marketing have an indirect role. The aura created around the release of the next generation of Air Jordans, for example, would be fundamentally changed if the price dropped to $75. Even if the shoe's quality was not compromised in any way, consumer perception would undoubtedly be that the new version was cut-rate or somehow cheapened, making it far less desirable. In this manner, price can help drive perceptions of quality, but the product itself must deliver consistent quality and performance (e.g., durability, style, and so on) to maintain brand loyalty. Deficiencies in the quality of the shoe would lead to the brand falling out of favor, generating negative word of mouth and declining sales. This would hold true regardless of how compelling and mesmerizing the advertising and marketing campaigns were in getting the target market's attention.

Another dimension of price emerges when the issue of "who has to pay for the shoes or clothes" comes into play. In the initial purchase situation, most respondents mentioned that their parents paid for them entirely or most of the purchase price. Later on, demands for the high priced brands were met with parental comments like "No way I'm spending that kind of money for a pair of shoes. You want those, you pay for them." This meant that either a lower cost brand would be purchased or the preferred, higher priced brand would be purchased, but less frequently. The latter choice was the one referred to most often. Better to have a worn out pair of Nikes than a brand new pair of a cheaper brand.

Related to this discussion of price, perceived quality was another factor that became significantly more important over time. Again, advertising and marketing have important roles to play in influencing these quality perceptions. But the shoes and clothes must be well made and wear well over time to validate claims of brand quality. If the quality of workmanship is not apparent in the actual use of the brand, customers will switch to a better brand that delivers on quality in the product itself, not just in the advertising or marketing claims.

These findings point to the importance of peer influence in the purchase decisions made for athletic shoes and athletic clothing. It should be emphasized that peer influence is not confined to best friends (same-sex or opposite-sex); the perceived influence of peers who are not friends was also very important, especially for first-time purchases. The findings reported here were consistent with the pilot study. This process suggests a common process for first-time purchases of athletic shoes and clothing that a lot of attention needs to be paid to what "everyone else is wearing" (Hilfiger, 1997). Friends are important, but so are other peers—what they are wearing—probably including other kids at school who are in the same grade or higher grades. What is important here is to pick the right brand to fit in and to avoid the embarrassment of picking a brand that is not cool. Zollo (1999) reported results from a national teen survey that showed the importance of brands rated as "cool" to influence how their peers perceive them and to avoid being a nerd or uncool. Mangleburg, Grewal, and Bristol (1997) also found that wearing the right brand label was very important in peer relations among adolescents, females more than males.

It is also clear that females are more reliant on peers than males as sources of influence in their purchases of athletic shoes and that the gender difference remains even for current purchases. It may be that female teens are in fact more influenced by their peers compared to males or that males are less inclined to admit to being influenced by peers. Nonetheless, females appear to care more about what their peers are wearing than males.

The results of this study also show that peer influence wanes in importance as teens age. This finding was confirmed in the significant shifts from first-time purchase to current purchases for both brand name athletic shoes and athletic clothing. Peer influence may still be there, but the importance of wearing only those brands that seem acceptable to peers has been substantially reduced. It could also be that a pattern is established for certain brand preferences over time, to the point where peers' preferences are no longer noticed unless there is a dramatic change in styles or preferred brands. In this sample, as in the pilot study, Nike was the overwhelming choice for first purchases of athletic shoes and clothing and remained the dominant brand for current purchases. Until or unless another brand comes along that catches on with teens, what ranks as a cool or acceptable brand will remain exactly that. And, unlike some brands that seem to be only appropriate for certain age groups, brand name athletic shoes and clothing stay with people from teen first purchase into adulthood.

Implications

The results of this study have some important implications for sports marketers of brand name athletic shoes and athletic clothing. The most obvious implication is that positioning a given brand as cool among the target market is essential; the brand must strike a responsive chord, the younger the better and the sooner the better. Brand loyalty in the athletic shoes and clothing categories persists from pre-teen through young adulthood (and probably beyond).

Marketers need to maintain a substantial promotion and advertising push to keep the brand cool and acceptable. Nike's success in this regard is clear evidence of how to establish a brand and brand image and how to maintain them. Notably, when Nike's brand share was threatened after initial success, the company revitalized its marketing, advertising, and promotional efforts to propel the brand back to dominance. As Nike experienced more problems with declining sales in the late 1990s, the continued use of a distinctive Nike image helped to maintain market leadership and dominance, although not at the same high level the company once enjoyed. Even Nike could not control the shift of a considerable segment of the youth market as they switched from athletic shoes to boots and more rugged footwear (Kaufman, 2000).

It also seems wise for sports marketers to continue to think in terms of promoting not just a brand of shoes or clothing but also a lifestyle where a specific brand is identified or associated with people who do certain things or do them in a certain way. Nike, Reebok, and Adidas have all done this and have enjoyed varying degrees of success. No other competitor has employed a different strategy to successfully challenge this approach. In this regard, it is important to note the reliance by teens on being part of an acceptable group. A useful strategy for advertisers to follow would include an emphasis on how a particular brand of shoes or clothing reflects a certain image and that the image is one shared by others who also present admirable traits or attributes. In this regard, Nike's recent attempts to expand the women's market for clothing and shoes is another excellent example of positioning to be the cool brand among the competition (Warner, 2002).

There are also implications for social psychology and the influence of peers. Regarding consumer behavior, peer influence seems most effective in first-time purchase situations and remains in force for some time before showing some evidence of reported decreases in influence. It was also surprising that non-friend peer influence was nearly as important as same-sex or opposite-sex friends. This stands in contrast to other teen behaviors where friends are far more important than non-friend peers in exerting influence (Bochner, 1994). Evidently, sometimes it makes a difference if your peers are friends or non-friends, and sometimes it does not, as in the case of brand preferences for athletic shoes or clothing.

It also seems clear that research needs to acknowledge that the process through which peers have influence over other teens is very complex. One important distinction seems to be how peers have influence (Michell & West, 1996), another is who the peer is. In the first case, there is a difference between a friend who engages in a certain behavior but does not overtly try to persuade a friend to do likewise and a friend who actively encourages or demands that a friend to conform as a required dimension of friendship. For example, a teen might say something to this effect to his or her friend: "I smoke marijuana. You're my friend, so you should smoke too. This is something that we should do together as friends." Or, there may be no pressure to smoke or not to smoke, depending on group dynamics.

Who the peer is also makes a difference. Research (Michell, 1994; Michell & West, 1996) indicated that one such distinction was among friends, a friend, or a best friend. Teens often refer to those they see regularly and appear to get along with as *friends*. Someone closer to the individual who shares much in common might be labeled *a friend*. An even closer person would be labeled *a best friend* or *my best friend*. Moving from *friends* to *a friend* to *a best friend* suggests the degree of influence or pressure to conform increases in many key behavioral categories. How these differences manifest themselves in the area of clothing or footwear choices presents an interesting and formidable challenge for future research.

FUTURE RESEARCH

More research is needed to accomplish several key objectives:

1. Studies that include more product types
2. Studies that incorporate different ways of measuring the comparative impact of the marketer-controlled and non–marketer-controlled factors; in this regard, developing different items or protocols to make respondents think about how advertising may be (or may have been) influencing them; for example, for consumers who always buy Nike, does the advertising for Nike matter?
3. Studies that incorporate a panel of adolescents studied from age 10 to 25 years, including those who drop out of school, do not attend college, and so on.
4. Studies that use different research methodologies to try and assess some of the same variables; for example, is it possible to combine self-report procedures with other forms of data collection (e.g., hidden observation, depth, individual or ethnographic-type interviews)?

LIMITATIONS

This study is limited in a number of ways. First, it uses only a sample of older teens attending a university. Still, the products studied here are both very appropriate for college teens. Second, the use of recall by students of their past purchases may pose some accuracy problems. What about those who cannot remember much, if anything, about their initial purchases? Perhaps surprisingly, only four respondents said they could not remember anything about their initial purchases. The use of open-ended questions that asked students to describe the circumstance surrounding their initial purchases revealed that such purchases were indeed memorable. These results speak to the significance of the occasion and to their entry into the product category as a first-time consumer.

SUMMARY

This study has looked at how teenagers' perceptions of various influence factors have affected their purchase decisions for brand name athletic shoes and athletic clothing. The study's primary emphasis was on differences between the marketer-controlled factors of advertising and price in comparison to the social, interpersonal factors not controlled by marketers. Respondents rated both major types of factors as they perceived them to have influence on their first-time and current purchases of brand name athletic shoes and clothing. Results showed that various forms of peer influence were more important than price and advertising (marketer-controlled factors) for first-time purchases of shoes and clothing, especially for young females, and that peer influence was significantly less important for current purchases. Brand loyalty, however, remained high, suggesting that sports marketers need to place a great deal of emphasis on creating a positive image that reaches young people well in advance of their teenage years. Moreover, the image for a brand of athletic shoes or clothes needs to be driven by lifestyle attributes of which the brand itself is a key ingredient. Advertising plays a fairly steady role in influencing consumers over time, although other non–marketer-controlled factors are perceived by teens to be more influential in their decisions of which name brands of athletic shoes and clothing they purchase.

REFERENCES

American Demographics. (2003, May). Peer pressure. p. 22.

Bearden, W., & Etzel, M. (1982). Reference group influences on product and brand purchase decisions. *Journal of Consumer Research, 9,* 183–194.

Blackwell, R., Miniard, P., & Engel, J. (2001). *Consumer Behavior* (9th ed.). Orlando, FL: Harcourt.

Bochner, S. (1994). The effectiveness of same-sex versus opposite-sex role models in advertisements to reduce alcohol consumption in teenagers. *Addictive Behaviors, 19,* 69–82.

Burnett, J., Moriarity, S., & Wells, W. (2002). *Advertising: Principles and Practices* (6th ed.). Upper Saddle River, NJ: Prentice-Hall.

Cassidy, H. (2002, January 28). Reebok taps hip-hop for young men, Nike returns; industry eyes rebound. *Brandweek,* p. 8.

Costley, C., & Brucks, M. (1992). Selective recall and information use in consumer preferences. *Journal of Consumer Research, 18,* 464–474.

Evans, R. (1991). Incorporating normative social influence into a diffusion model. *Psychology Reports, 68,* 1185–1186.

Fisher, L., & Bauman, K. (1988). Influence and selection in the friend-adolescent relationship: Findings from studies of adolescent smoking and drinking. *Journal of Applied Social Psychology, 18,* 289–314.

Forsythe, S. (1991). Effect of private, designer, and national brand names on shoppers' perception of apparel quality and price. *Clothing and Textiles Research Journal, 9,* 1–6.

Haynes, J. (1993). Consumer socialization of preschoolers and kindergartners as related to clothing consumption. *Psychology and Marketing, 10,* 151–166.

Hilfiger, H. (1997). Parents, teens to spend big bucks on back-to-school shopping. *Fairfield County Business Journal, 36,* 15.

Kaufman, L. (2000, February 9). Cooling consumer demand for athletics shoes shrinks Nike's profit. *New York Times*, p. C1.

Lee, E., & Browne, L. (1995). Effects of television advertising on African American teenagers. *Journal of Black Studies, 25*, 523–536.

Mangleburg, T., Grewal, D., & Bristol, T. (1997). Socialization, gender, and adolescent's self-reports of their generalized use of product labels. *Journal of Consumer Affairs, 31*, 255–279.

Meyer, T., Gettelman, K., & Donohue, T. (2001). College students' perceptions of the influence of advertising and price versus non–marketer-controlled factors on their purchases of brand-name athletic shoes and clothing. In M. Moore & R. Moore (Eds.), *Developments in Marketing Science, 24* (pp. 17–24). San Diego: Academy of Marketing Science.

Michell, L. (1994). *Smoking Prevention Programmes for Adolescents: A Literature Review.* Oxford, United Kingdom: Directorate of Health Policy and Public Health; Anglia and Oxford Regional Health Authority with The National Adolescent and Student Health Unit.

Michell, L., & West, P. (1996). Peer pressure to smoke: The meaning depends on the method. *Health Education Research, Theory and Practice, 11*, 39–49.

O'Guinn, T., Semenik, R., & Allen, C. (2002). *Advertising and Integrated Brand Promotion* (3rd ed.). Belmont, CA: South-West.

Peter, J. (1988). Gender, youth possessions, college costs, and parental assistance. *Youth and Society, 20*, 148–158.

Solomon, M. (1994). *Consumer Behavior.* Boston: Allyn and Bacon.

Wang, M., Fitzhugh, E., Eddy, J., Fu, Q., & Turner, L. (1997). Social influences on adolescents' smoking progress: A longitudinal analysis. *American Journal of Health Behavior, 21*, 111–117.

Warner, F. (2002). Nike's women's movement. *Fast Company, 61*, 70–75.

Wilson, B., & Sparks, R. (1996). 'It's gotta be the shoes': Youth, race, and sneaker commercials. *Sociology of Sport Journal, 13*, 398–427.

Zollo, P. (1999). *Wise Up to Teens: Insights Into Marketing and Advertising to Teenagers.* Ithaca, NY: New Strategist Publications.

Author Index

Olson, J. C., *156*
Olsson, C., 307, *323*
Oneal, M., 108, *131*
O'Neil, 163, *171*
Ortony, A., 69, 70, *79*
O'Sullivan, P., 293, 294, *304*
Otker, T., 329, *350*

P

Pagès, M., 344, *348*
Palmeri, C., 116, *131*
Pang, S., 120, *131*
Papson, S., 308, 311, 312, 313, *323*
Parker, K., 180, 182, 183, *188*
Paulus, P. B., 163, *171*, 241, *255*
Payne, M., 294, *304*
Pearton, R., 4, *25*
Pechmann, C., *157*
Penner, L. A., 163, *170*
Penny, M., 336, *349*
Perry, B., 163, *169*
Perry, C. L., 337, *350*
Pertschuk, M., 214, *222*
Peter, J., 368, *380*
Petley, J., 309, *323*
Petrecca, L., 213, *221*, 223, *238*
Pettigrew, T. F., 246, *254*
Petty, R., 120, *131*
Petty, R. E., 133, 138, 139, *157*, 185, *188*, 295, 296, *304*
Pham, M. T., 298, 299, *304*
Phelps, M., xviii, *xix*
Pitt, L., 193, *210*
Pitts, B. G., 273, *291*
Platow, M. J., 75, *79*
Plummer, J. T., 275, *291*
Pollay, R. W., 214, *221*, 330, 331, 333, 334, 337, 338, 339, 341, 342, 343, 344, 345, *350*
Pollio, H. R., 32, *65*
Pollock, P. H., III, 163, *170*
Pooley, J. C., 286, *291*
Pope, N., 193, 209, *210*
Powell, K. E., 358, *363*
Pracejus, J. W., 176, *189*
Prensky, D., 5, *25*

Price, L., 84, *104*
Price, L. L., 81, 85, 91, 92, 93, 94, 95, 102, *103*
Pruitt, S. W., 226, 227, 237, *238*

R

Radder, J. M., 274, *291*
Rajaretnam, J., 183, *189*
Ralston, B., 318, 319, *324*
Ramirez, G. G., 226, *237*
Rangan, N., 226, *238*
Rangaswamy, A., 179, *189*
Rao, A. A., 181, *189*
Rao, H., 182, *187*, 248, *252*
Ray, C., 84, *103*
Ray, M., 163, *169*
Real, M. R., 212, *221*
Reddy, S. K., 181, *189*
Reicher, S. D., 242, *254*
Reinke, S., *155*
Reis, H. T., 187, *189*
Repper, F. C., 272, 275, 276, 278, *291*
Retsky, M. L., 294, *304*
Reynolds, B., 195, *210*
Reynolds, F. D., 13, *26*
Richardson, K. D., 73, *78*
Riessman, C., 30, *65*
Rogers, E. M., 353, 354, 360, 362, *363*
Rokeach, M., 85, 89, *103*
Roll, R., 225, *238*
Rooney, J. F., 260, *269*
Rootman, I., 340, *351*
Rose, G., xvii, *xix*, 20, *25*, 73, 76, 77, *78*, 79, 82, 86, 87, 88, 89, 90, 91, 92, 93, 94, 95, 96, 98, 99, 100, 101, *103*, *104*, 260, 268, 302, *303*
Rose, R. L., 81, 82, 85, 86, 87, 91, 92, 93, 94, 95, 96, *102*
Rosenberg, M., 336, *349*
Roslow, A. F., 220, *221*, 224, *238*
Roslow, S., 177, *189*
Rossman, G. B., 197, *210*
Roy, A., 182, *188*
Roy, D. P., 237, *238*
Rubin, A. M., 162, *170*

Subject Index

Boxing, 310
Brand awareness, sponsorship and, 193, 212, 223–224, 237, 346
Brand equity, 175
Brand image
  college athletic program sponsorship and, 209
  event sponsorship and, 223–224, 237
  licensing and, 268
  sports image and enhancing, 193
  sport sponsorship and, 180, 212
  tobacco sponsorship and, 341–345, 346
Brand loyalty
  cigarette smokers and, 337
  in market segmentation, 274
  teens and, 376, 379
Brand preference, 340
Brand promotion, sports sponsorship and, 193
Brand recall/recognition, celebrity endorsers and, 133, 135, 142
Brands
  college athletic program sponsorship and authentication of, 206
  combined, 181
  extensions of, 179, 181
  global, 268
  positioning, 175
  repositioning, 180
Brigham Young University, 196
British American Tobacco, 331, 339
Brunswick Tournament, 185
Bryant, Kobe, 195
Budweiser, 266, 314
Business Week, 111, 268

C

Cadbury, 183
Camaraderie
  attending sporting events and, 20, 73
  high-risk sports and need for, 93–94, 96, 100
Campbell's Soup, 298
Camping, 7, 8

Campus bookstore, as retailer for athletic clothing, 204
Canada
  incidence of exercise in, 358
  Sport Participation Canada, 355–359
  tobacco sponsorship in. *See* Tobacco sponsorship
Canadian Broadcasting Corporation (CBC), 332
Canadian Charter of Rights and Freedoms, 335, 336
Canadian Equestrian Team, 329
Canadian Open Tennis Championships, 339, 344, 345
Canadian Open Tennis Tournaments, 329
Cantona, Eric, 311, 313, 316
Capriati, Jennifer, 340
CAR. *See* Cumulative abnormal return
Cartwright model, 359–360
Case study method, 196
The Cats' Paws, 37
CBC. *See* Canadian Broadcasting Corporation
CCC. *See* Council for Cultural Co-operation
Celebrity athlete endorsers
  affect transfer and, 179
  effect on stock price, 226, 230–231
  influence on teen buying behavior, 371, 372–373
  See also Endorsement
Center for Research in Security Prices database, 230
Central route information processing, 295, 302
Champion brand, 203, 204
Championship Auto Racing Teams (CART), 332, 345
Champs Sports, 264
Chanel SA, 320
Characterization-correction model, 138
Charity donations, basking in reflected glory and, 75–76
Cheating, 89–90
Chicago Bears, 73, 261
Chicago Bulls, 194
Chicago Cubs, 28, 72
Chicago Gospel Festival, 186